KINDLING THE FLAME

150 Years of the Irish National Teachers' Organisation

NIAMH PUIRSÉIL

Gill Books

Gill Books
Hume Avenue
Park West
Dublin 12
www.gillbooks.ie

Gill Books is an imprint of M.H. Gill & Co.

© Niamh Puirséil 2017

978 07171 7977 0

Indexed by Eileen O'Neill
Print origination by Carole Lynch
Printed by CPI Group (UK) Ltd, Croydon, CRO 4YY

This book is typeset in Linotype Minion and
Neue Helvetica.

The paper used in this book comes from the
wood pulp of managed forests. For every tree
felled, at least one tree is planted, thereby
renewing natural resources.

A CIP catalogue record for this book is available
from the British Library.

5 4 3 2 1

FOREWORD

'Remember: the past won't fit into memory without
something left over; it must have a future.'

(JOSEPH BRODSKY)

The regard in which the Irish National Teachers' Organisation is held among the education partners and in communities the length and breadth of Ireland is first and foremost a tribute to the work of its members in schools. For a century and a half teachers' school work has been supported by the work of the INTO to unite and organise, improve salaries and conditions of employment and raise education standards.

It is fitting therefore that the 150-year anniversary of the INTO is marked by the publication of this history of the organisation. Its pages trace the growth and development of the INTO from a scattering of loosely connected local associations into the strong, united and cohesive organisation of today.

The INTO is Ireland's largest and longest-established teachers' union, and the only one organised across the entire island. This book records the struggles and successes, and details key events over 150 years. It also puts current challenges into perspective. The years leading to 'INTO 150' have seen a programme of austerity imposed which has included cuts to teachers' pay, employment and funding for schools, north and south. While these have been extremely challenging for the current generation of INTO members, they did not pose an existential threat to the organisation like that experienced at the end of the nineteenth and in the early twentieth century.

Some one hundred years ago, the INTO was less than 9,000 strong; today membership numbers approach 45,000. Without a full-time official or dedicated office for almost its first 50 years, now the INTO has offices in Dublin and Belfast and a professional staff working to pursue its objectives. The challenges faced today have a familiar resonance with the past – organising and representing members on issues such as salaries, conditions of employment and the advancement of education.

In the past 20 years we have seen several pieces of education legislation. These set a context for school provision and regulation of the teaching profession as the INTO moves beyond this significant anniversary.

We record particular thanks to Dr Niamh Puirséil for her dedicated work in researching and writing this book. Professor John Coolahan and Noel Ward have acted as an advisory support throughout and their contribution is also acknowledged.

We hope that this book will help enhance an appreciation of the INTO's and of teachers' contribution to education and society, and that members will draw inspiration and energy from this history to continue that positive work over coming years.

Sheila Nunan, General Secretary
John Boyle, President
October 2017

PREFACE AND ACKNOWLEDGEMENTS

Speaking to the centenary congress of the Irish National Teachers' Organisation in Easter 1968, the president, Jerry Allman, recalled how, in January 1871, a western bishop addressed a letter to one of his parish priests instructing him to dismiss a teacher unless this teacher ceased his activities in the INTO. The bishop apparently went further and sent a copy of the letter for publication to the *Irish Times*. Here is an extract from it:

> The teachers should not be made into fine gentlemen, or raised to an eminence so high as to dissipate all affinity between them and the parents of their pupils. The teachership should remain prizes for the poor and not for the rich, and if the scale of salaries should cause our future teachers to spring from the ranks that now produce clerks, doctors, or the like, I should sincerely deplore this very grave calamity. (*An Múinteoir Náisiúnta*, May 1968)

This tells us a great deal about Irish society; the poor were expected to know their place, and their teachers likewise. The role of the INTO was to undermine this view, not only of the position of teachers but the idea that the children they taught deserved no better than they had. It was often an unpopular view among the elites of Ireland. National teachers' efforts to organise faced fierce resistance and their attempts to secure a status that reflected their responsibilities were fought tooth and nail, but they proved largely successful.

In a 1955 essay called 'Problems in Research on Teachers' Organizations', George A. Male, an American education scholar, argued that teachers and researchers needed to:

> … understand more fully how and why teachers changed from a motley, unorganised, hardly distinct group in society to a more solidified, united, highly organised, highly self-conscious pressure group and the effect of all this on the status of teachers, the power wielded by teachers as a group, the quality of education offered in our schools and the relationship of the organised teaching profession with other organised groups in our society.

This history aims to do that for one of the world's oldest nationwide teachers' unions, the Irish National Teachers' Organisation. The INTO is a significant force in Irish public life and in Irish education, and has been for so long that it would be easy to take for granted the organisation's status and that of its members. No more than any union, its strength did not fall from the sky but was forged over decades, and against considerable odds, by the men and women who made up its membership and activists. From its first meeting in August 1868, it built itself up from its grassroots against official opposition, surviving official censure, splits, divisions and bans. After partition, it continued to operate on the whole island of Ireland, expanding its membership in the North to include teachers at all levels, while in the South it remained the only union for primary school teachers. In many other countries, multiple unions operate in the same area, but in Ireland, in the South at least, the INTO managed to resist factions and remains a united union for all teachers at primary level, while in the North it works alongside other unions at primary and post-primary levels.

This book is about the organisation itself and its role in education and in professionalising teaching, fighting for the status of teachers and helping develop an esprit de corps among them, but it is about much more than that. As well as teaching and education, and the many fights over pay and conditions, it tells a story of multiple struggles over 150 years. After decades of fighting campaigns against the British administration for recognition, for better salaries, for pensions and for decent conditions, it had to fight them all over again against governments in Dublin and Belfast.

Teachers battled not only temporal powers but religious ones. The influence of the Churches on education in Ireland cannot be understated. Paid by the state but employed by the Churches, teachers were often at the mercy of their local priests or rectors, which meant that the teachers often found themselves fighting on two fronts, between Church and state. The power of the Catholic Church, in particular, is one that looms large over this study.

Equally significant in this study is the issue of gender. In a profession that was predominantly feminised, women had to fight hard against the multiple discriminations they faced over the years, demanding equal pay for equal work as well as facing marriage bars both north and south of the border. Though they represented a majority of teachers, this was not reflected in the officerships of the organisation and it was a long struggle before the INTO at an organisational level came to reflect its members.

The themes of politics, class, gender and power are interwoven through the story of the INTO, along with how an organisation that was non-political (i.e. neither nationalist nor unionist) and non-sectarian had to negotiate the inevitable challenges thrown up in a country that was often split along national and religious lines. There were many struggles along the way, but the INTO's ability to remain united is one of its greatest successes.

This is the first full scholarly history of the organisation. A book, *100 Years of Progress: The Story of the INTO*, was published to mark its centenary. Written by T.J. O'Connell, general secretary from 1916 to 1947, it is a valuable account of the organisation, but it is, perhaps inevitably, closer to a memoir than a history. It also features very little on the organisation in the North after 1922. O'Connell noted that someone else was engaged in that project at the time; alas, if it had been started, it never saw the light of day. O'Connell expressed the hope that his work might serve as a source book for others in the future, and that is certainly the case. The INTO has had other historians from within its ranks since. Among these, Síle Chuinneagáin has done especially great service with her terrific work on Catherine Mahon, the INTO's first woman president, and the organisation in her times. Eugene McCormick's study of the 1946 teachers' strike has been valuable. Former deputy secretary the late Michael Moroney's study on teachers' salaries and pensions has been a great resource.

Noel Ward, the deputy general secretary, has published a number of important studies on the organisation and I have been very lucky to have had the benefit of these as well as several interviews he conducted with activists and officials over the years, which have been invaluable. Noel was a driving force behind bringing this book to life, and I am very grateful for his help and support throughout this project. The project was supervised by Professor John Coolahan. John has a deep knowledge of the history of Irish education not only as a scholar but also as an actor, from when he started out as a young national teacher to his work advising on education policy. He was always helpful, encouraging and unflappably good-humoured, and I am most grateful to him for his help. Any errors, omissions or points of view, however, are my own. This book was commissioned by the INTO and I was given every assistance by it, but the work is entirely my own, arrived at without interference, gentle or otherwise. It is worth mentioning, however, that I am not a stranger to the organisation. As a small child, I often found myself packing envelopes destined for the members of District XV, where my father, Séamus, was branch secretary. He was vice-president and president during the arbitration dispute in the mid-1980s when I most often saw him on TV; and I occasionally had to act as an administrative assistant at home, in contravention of all child labour regulations and trade union best practice. He has always been a terrific support and font of INTO lore, not always fit to print. Thanks also to my tremendous mother who, though not a teacher herself, accidentally married into the INTO and, for a time, lost a daughter to it.

Members and former members, officials and former officials have been so generous with their time and I am grateful to everyone who spoke to me, formally or informally, on or off the record, or who rooted around in boxes and attics for material, most of whom are listed at the back of the book. The staff in the INTO have all been such a great help, and particular thanks are due to Ann McConnell, Georgina Glackin, Selina Campbell, Lori Kealy and David Cooke in Parnell Square and to Christine McDonnell, Nuala O'Donnell and Seamus Hanna in College Gardens. Thanks also to the CEC and to the northern secretary, Gerry Murphy, and the general secretary, Sheila Nunan, for their support. Many thanks to everyone in Gill Books, especially Conor Nagle, Catherine Gough, Jason O'Neill and Teresa Daly. Thanks also to Jane Rogers. Thanks are due to all the staff in the archives and libraries I consulted in the course of the research. I have used a variety of private papers, including those of politicians and churchmen, as well as public records and publications. As is so often the case in trade unions, spring cleaning or moving – or, in the case of the Northern office, a raid by the Luftwaffe – have meant that not all the records have survived through the years, but most of the INTO's printed material has done, as has a great deal of its private material since the 1940s.

Perhaps to echo T.J. O'Connell's foreword 50 years ago, this is a history of the INTO but there is more to be done. To cover 150 years in one volume that might be easily read is not an easy task and not everything can be given its due. Events of recent years are not covered in depth. This study is an effort to take a historical long view. There were too many policy matters ongoing and too little distance to treat of more recent times as they deserve but I hope that others will find aspects of interest and take up the baton from here.

Niamh Puirséil
Dublin, October 2017

ABBREVIATIONS

AMN	*An Múinteoir Náisiúnta*
ASTI	Association of Secondary Teachers in Ireland
BNS	boys' national school
CCMS	Council for Catholic Maintained Schools
CEC	Central Executive Council, elected by members to govern the INTO
CEU	Council of Education Unions
CHA	Catholic Headmasters' Association
CIU	Congress of Irish Unions
CORI	Conference of Religious of Ireland
CPC	Central Propaganda Committee
CPSMA	Catholic Primary School Managers' Association
CTU	Council of Teachers' Unions
DATI	Department of Agriculture and Technical Instruction
DD	Dáil debates
DDA	Dublin Diocesan Archives
DENI	Department of Education, Northern Ireland
DES	Department of Education and Science (1997–2010) or Department of Education and Skills (2010 to date)
DIB	*Dictionary of Irish Biography*
EIS	Educational Institute of Scotland
ELB	education and library board
GNS	girls' national school
FWUI	Federated Workers' Union of Ireland
HC	House of Commons debates
HL	House of Lords debates
ICTU	Irish Congress of Trade Unions, the name of the umbrella congress for Irish unions from 1958 following the merger of the ITUC and the CIU
IFUT	Irish Federation of University Teachers
ILO	International Labour Organisation
ILP&TUC	Irish Labour Party and Trade Union Congress
INTO	Irish National Teachers' Organisation
IPNTU	Irish Protestant National Teachers' Union, a ginger group of teachers in the INTO who taught in schools under Protestant management, established 1899

IPP	Irish Parliamentary Party
IRA	Irish Republican Army
ISW	*Irish School Weekly*
ITGWU	Irish Transport and General Workers' Union
ITJ	*Irish Teachers' Journal*
ITUC	Irish Trade Union Congress, the umbrella group for Irish unions founded in 1894. When it established its political wing in 1914, it became the ITUC&LP and between 1918 and 1930 was the ILP&TUC. A group of unions split from it in 1943 to form the CIU, but the two groups reunited in the 1950s and became the ICTU in 1958
ITUC&LP	Irish Trade Union Congress and Labour Party
JAM	junior assistant mistress
LEA	Local Education Authority
NAI	National Archives of Ireland
NAS	National Association of Schoolmasters, later amalgamated with the Union of Women Teachers to form the NAS/UWT (NASUWT)
NAS/UWT	National Association of Schoolmasters/Union of Women Teachers
NATFHE	National Association of Teachers in Further and Higher Education
NC	Northern Committee of the INTO
NCCA	National Council for Curriculum and Assessment
NCSE	National Council for Special Education
NILP	Northern Ireland Labour Party
NIO	Northern Ireland Office
NLI	National Library of Ireland
NPC	National Parents' Council
NS	national school
NT	National Teacher, the qualification awarded on completion of teacher training until the Bachelor of Education (BEd) degree was established in 1974
NUI	National University of Ireland
NUT	National Union of Teachers, first established for English teachers in 1870 as the National Union of Elementary Teachers
OECD	Organisation for Economic Co-operation and Development
P2000	Partnership 2000 (1997–2000)
PCW	Programme for Competitiveness and Work (1994–1996)
PDs	Progressive Democrats
PEBR	Primary Education Review Body
PESP	Programme for Economic and Social Progress (1991–1994)
PNR	Programme for National Recovery (1987–1990)

POWU	Post Office Workers' Union
PPF	Programme for Prosperity and Fairness (2000–2003)
PRONI	Public Record Office of Northern Ireland
PTU	Principal Teachers' Union
SAC	Strike Administrative Committee
SD	Seanad debates
SIPTU	Services, Industrial, Professional and Technical Union
STSG	Separated Teachers' Support Group
TUI	Teachers' Union of Ireland, previously the VTA
USI	Union of Students in Ireland
UTU	Ulster Teachers' Union
VC	Vigilance Committee, early name for the Northern Committee of INTO
VTA	Vocational Teachers' Association, subsequently the TUI
WCOTP	World Confederation of Organisations of the Teaching Profession (merged with IFFTU in 1993 to form Education International). A US-based non-political (neither communist nor anti-communist) international teachers' umbrella group established in 1952, of which the INTO was a founder member
WTU	Women Teachers' Union
WUI	Workers' Union of Ireland
YTAC	Young Teachers' Action Council

CONTENTS

CONTENTS

BEGINNINGS, 1868–1900

Poverty is ever a dangerous element in society:
it is especially dangerous when it coexists with
intelligence.[1]

ducation is political. It is about more than learning to read and to write; it is about shaping generations and who chooses the image in which they are shaped. Over centuries, it has been fundamental to identity and loyalty – whether in maintaining religious observance or helping to form a national sense of self. The power that derives to anyone who controls education makes it hotly contested and this was particularly the case in nineteenth-century Ireland, which was administered by London through Dublin Castle. A state-controlled elementary school system was set up in Ireland 30 years after the Act of Union, at a time when few European countries had universal primary education. Prior to 1831, elementary schooling in Ireland was unco-ordinated and sometimes controversial. An estimated 200,000 to 300,000 children, mostly Catholic, still attended the hedge schools, which had their origins in the era of the Penal Laws, where children were taught reading and writing outdoors or in barns by untrained school masters. In the early nineteenth century there were also a number of educational societies which were run in a more organised way, most notably the Kildare Place Society, founded in 1811. Ostensibly non-sectarian, this Protestant educational society funded by the British exchequer was accused by the Catholic Church of proselytism, which gravely limited its appeal. In 1831, the then Chief Secretary, Lord Stanley, wrote what became known as the 'Stanley Letter', which envisaged a state-appointed Board of Education which would oversee a system of schools that would be part-funded from the central exchequer. One of the main objects had been to establish schools that were not run by different denominations but would rather 'unite in one system children of different creeds', and the idea was for the schools to be run jointly by different denominations, with religion of any kind to be excluded from the classroom. Coming at the time of Catholic emancipation and an increasingly robust Catholic Church on the one hand and of increasing fundamentalism and proselytism within Protestantism on the other, this idea was idealistic and doomed.

The Whig government's attempt to bring uniformity to Irish schooling and attempt a radical piece of religious and social engineering[2] required popular support, and none was forthcoming. The idea of non-denominational education was anathema to both Catholic and Protestant churches alike. The opposition that arose, however, was less about the desire to teach dogma or bible studies in school hours and more about the idea of the state interfering outside its rightful sphere. Writing in 1838, John McHale, the Catholic archbishop of Tuam, warned that it was a slippery slope, and that 'From the extraordinary power now claimed by the state over a [religiously] mixed education, it would soon claim a similar despotic control over mixed marriages, and strive to stretch its net over all ecclesiastical concerns.'[3] It was a view that became more prevalent in the Catholic Church by the middle of the century, when the spectre of communism was haunting Europe and, in Ireland, Cardinal Cullen led the fight for denominational education, battling against the 'Godless Colleges'. It was not merely that an education was of no value unless it was a Catholic education, but a secular or mixed education was actively detrimental.

Opposition from Catholic and Protestant Churches made the scheme envisaged by Stanley unworkable, and by 1851 the national school system was effectively denominational in practice.[4] Schools were run by clerical managers, usually the local parish priest or rector, who hired and fired teachers as they saw fit. But these were not the national teachers' only employers, since they also laboured under the Commissioners of National Education, who set out the rules for national schools, and represented the interest of the state, which paid most of the teachers' salaries, which were poor. During the mid-nineteenth century, only one in three teachers were trained, and their salaries reflected this. They were paid considerably less than many office workers at the time. Teachers would later demand that their position should be at least equal to that of excise officers, clerks in the post office or customs, but they earned a fraction of those rates: while the salary of an excise officer began at £60, the highest salary of a third class teacher was £24.[5] Part of the reason for the high rate of untrained teachers at this time was that there were no denominational training colleges and Catholic managers refused to employ any teacher who had been trained in the non-denominational state training colleges, preferring untrained teachers who were untainted by secularism to those who might have consorted with Protestants.

The structure of the education system is well described by John Coolahan in *Irish Education: History and Structure*:

The control structure of the national school system reflected an interesting division of power between the central and local bodies. At the top of the pyramid was parliament which retained final authority and voted annual grants. The Lord Lieutenant, assisted by the Chief Secretary, appointed Commissioners, approved rules and liaised with the government. The Commissioners of National Education held the important powers of distributing funds and approving schemes, of setting out rules and regulations, of controlling the curriculum, of publishing and sanctioning textbooks, of suspending teachers and removing managers. The inspectors acted as agents of the Commissioners to ensure that regulations were carried out.

Describing the position of the national school teacher at the bottom of the pyramid, the historian of Irish education D.H. Akenson noted that:

[A]lthough the system could not run without them, one would never have surmised this fact from observing the way [national teachers] were treated. Teachers were hired and fired at the manager's whim. They had, until late in the century, no appeal rights in case of dismissal. They were not civil servants and were treated as day labourers rather than as educated men. Although under the thumb of the local manager, their salary came mostly from the central establishment. Until the last quarter of the nineteenth century they remained unrepresented, unappreciated cogs in the system.[6]

The regulations under which the teachers worked were far-reaching, extending to their lives outside the classroom as well as inside. Among the Rules for National Schools was an instruction that teachers were 'to avoid fairs, market and meetings – but, above all, *political* meetings of every kind; to abstain from controversy'. Intended largely to quarantine teachers so as to avoid infecting their schools with politics, the notion of 'controversy' could be broadly interpreted to include expressing an opinion about their working conditions, with the publication of a letter to a newspaper on a matter of education regarded as a potentially seditious act. Not surprisingly, these rules were not always adhered to. In March 1848, in the middle of the Famine and when the Young Ireland movement was at its height, the Commissioners warned teachers that to engage in any political action except voting rendered them liable to dismissal; they also warned them not to use school houses for political meetings or allow petitions to be signed there.[7] These rules were policed by inspectors, who could be found chasing teachers out of schools where they had gathered for meetings.[8]

In 1849, the Irish Teachers' Redress Committee, made up of local branches, was launched. Its main demands were security of tenure, inspectoral reform and improved pay, but it was censured by the Commissioners, who issued a circular which set out their disapproval of teachers writing to journals on any subject, but especially about education. Teachers were warned against making 'National Education, the proceedings of the commissioners, or their officers or managers, a matter of comment in any publication, WITHOUT THE CONSENT OF THE COMMISSIONERS' on pain of losing their salary.[9] The teachers had the support of the nationalist press. *The Nation,* the paper of Young Ireland, was particularly sympathetic to the teachers, whom it described as 'the hardest worked, worst paid, and most useful class in their country', and the *Freeman's Journal* was critical of the attempt to gag the 'poor school slaves'.[10] The circular of November 1849 having failed to deter the organisers of the Redress Committee, the Commissioners felt the need to issue a further threat in September of the following year. Not only would the Commissioners not enter into any correspondence with the committee or any similar organisation, or meet with any of its representatives, but any teacher ignoring their warning would be liable to immediate dismissal.[11] Despite the Commissioners' assertion that there was nothing to redress, the appearance of the Redress Committee coincided not only with pay increases but also changes in payment, with salaries being paid quarterly instead of twice yearly from July 1850.[12] While the Redress Committee enjoyed active support for a time, with a number of local associations around the country, by the summer of 1851 it had effectively disappeared. In the absence of a central organisation to enable united action, the local associations perished.[13]

There was another attempt to organise towards the end of the 1850s, which resulted in a deputation of teachers travelling to London in June 1861, before the Education Estimates were passed in Westminster.[14] Along with around eight Irish MPs, John J. Smythe of Clontarf and Cork man Patrick O'Callaghan met the prime minister, Lord Palmerston, and secured a promise of up to £60,000 extra funding, if the Board of Education would apply for it.[15] The board, however, did not apply for the money. As one INTO writer would later put it, 'keep the teachers down; keep them poor; this was the alpha and omega of the Board's policy'.[16] After 1861, there were no nationwide efforts to organise, but a small number of local associations continued to meet. Sometimes these were subject to unwanted attention from the authorities in Dublin, although intervention was not always fruitful.[17] These local groups occasionally organised petitions, or memorials, to the Commissioners and the government in an effort to publicise the teachers' grievances, but they could have no real strength and real influence without a united national movement. The question was how such a movement could come into being without being put down by the Commissioners, and, crucially, how it might be sustained.

Organising the teachers had become a matter of urgency when, in 1867, the government announced it was going to appoint a committee of inquiry into national education in Ireland. Chaired by the Earl of Powis, from whom it took

its name, the commission sat between February 1868 and May 1870 and investigated five main areas: denominational teacher training; the instruction
afforded in national schools; the salaries and mode of payment of teachers; the
efficacy of the Board of National Education; and religious teaching in schools.
The paltry levels of pay had been the teachers' greatest grievances, but they
feared that the commission might recommend the system of 'payment by
results' that had been introduced in England in 1862. Powis might afford the
teachers the opportunity to put their case forward for increased basic salaries
without payment by results where failure to do so could prove very damaging
indeed, so in 1867 work towards founding a new organisation began.

The first moves were made by the Dublin Association, which had been
founded in 1863, and which was home to teachers from the surrounding
counties of Kildare, Meath and Wicklow.[18] Since the Commissioners refused to
have any dealings with the teachers themselves, the solution was to go outside
the teaching body for an advocate who would be free to speak on the teachers'
behalf without fear of sanction.

To this end, the Dublin Association approached Vere Foster, a noted philan-
thropist with a particular interest in education. Born in Copenhagen in 1819,
Foster's father was a diplomat and a non-resident Irish landowner. The young
Foster had been somewhat directionless, but following his father's death in 1847,
he found his course in life, using his family wealth for the benefit of the Irish
poor, an especially large constituency in post-Famine Ireland. His first project
was assisted emigration, and towards the end of the 1850s Foster turned his
attention to education. Using an inheritance from his late brother, he began to
fund repairs of dilapidated schoolhouses, putting in wooden floors where there
had been clay, buying seats and desks for the pupils and teachers where there
had been none, and buying requisites like maps and blackboards for the
classrooms.[19] During the 1860s, he had come up with a headline copy book
designed to help pupils with their handwriting. Printed in Belfast, where he
lived after 1867, the copy books sold millions throughout the English-speaking
world. They were hugely profitable, and Foster could have made his own fortune
from them, but instead he ploughed the proceeds into funding his school
building work. As a public figure with a proven commitment to national
education, and already well known to the Dublin teachers, Vere Foster would be
an ideal teachers' champion. Originally, the Dublin Teachers' Association
thought that Foster might write a pamphlet on their behalf and dispatched one
of their members, Jeremiah Henly, a teacher in Roundwood, to seek him out. He
tried to contact him through the publishing company run by Robert Chamney,
which had published some of Foster's earlier pamphlets.[20] Foster proved eager
to help, and after discussion he and Henly hatched a plan that was rather more
ambitious than initially envisaged. Instead of a pamphlet, there would be a

monthly journal, published by Chamney's and supported by Foster. Chamney was the publisher and ostensibly the editor, teachers being prohibited from commenting on educational matters or engaging in controversy, but in fact the role of editor was fulfilled by a number of teachers, with Henly the chief leader writer, although it was several years before the genesis of the journal, and Vere Foster's role in it, was ever publicly explained.[21]

The first issue of the *Irish Teachers' Journal* (*ITJ*) was published in January 1868 and featured a letter from Foster outlining the teachers' grievances, wishing the journal well and, most important, encouraging the teachers to organise. This – 'uniting our scattered forces by means of Teachers' Associations in connection with a central controlling body' – was the journal's primary objective.[22] The journal was 'strictly non-political [neither unionist nor nationalist] and non-sectarian and devoted solely to the subject of education'. The number of local associations grew steadily, their meetings reported in the pages of the *Journal*. By the summer of 1868, the *ITJ* had a circulation of around 4,000.[23]

Though generally well received, one of the early complaints about the journal highlights an issue that would prove a challenge in the future – that the journal's non-political stance made it 'un-Irish' and 'un-national'. Critics pointed to the unadorned masthead, and protested that 'all symbolical tokens of poor Ireland, such as the Harp, Shamrock and Round Tower are absent [and] that the ancient language, literature and history of Ireland are never alluded to',[24] but the editor, while wondering why anyone would think that everything Irish should be covered in shamrocks, felt that few would attach any importance to the matter. No doubt he was correct, but political sensitivities were high at the time and only became more acute in the following years, and while it was easy enough to keep the journal free of shamrocks, avoiding politics would prove challenging in the tumultuous years ahead. The first issue of the *Teachers' Journal* was published about a month after the Manchester Martyrs had been executed, electrifying nationalist Ireland; the following year, in November 1868, W.E. Gladstone would lead the Liberals to an election victory, ushering in a new era in British policy towards Ireland; but a reader might search in vain for any suggestion of events not directly related to education, and the only time politics was mentioned was when there was a general election on the horizon, with teachers encouraged to lobby their local candidates on matters of education.

By the summer, efforts to establish a national organisation were advancing well. On 20 June 1868, Dublin-based teachers met to discuss forming a Central Teachers' Association to bring the teachers of Ireland together in one body, their aim being to use 'every legitimate means to raise the social position of the teacher and give him the status in society which is freely accorded to him in other countries'. Out of this came another meeting, on 15 August, when a couple of dozen men – and they were all men – gathered in a small room on 33 Denmark

Street for 'decidedly the largest meeting of teachers ever in Ireland'.[25] Although women joined the organisation as full members from the beginning, they played little active role in the organisation in its first decades. The men at the first meeting came from around Ireland as representatives of local associations of teachers which had been forming over previous months; their purpose, as the secretary of the meeting James Kavanagh put it, was to consolidate these local groups into a 'solid phalanx in order to obtain their just rights'. The proceedings were rather shambolic and devoted largely to recitations of the teachers' grievances, to the detriment of practical matters of organisation. Almost immediately work began to organise another national congress, one that might prove more businesslike. It was this second December congress that really launched the new organisation. In August, teachers representing not more than 30 local associations had met to discuss joining forces. Now, only four months later, there were nearly three times that, even if only 42 of these had contributed funds to the central organisation, giving it a paid-up membership of 683. The smallest association had six members, the largest 52.[26] It had made significant progress in its first few months, but with some 13,611 recognised teachers working in the country,[27] growing the organisation would be a mammoth task. With John Harte, a teacher in Ringsend, acting as secretary, and presided over by Vere Foster, the teachers spent two days laying the foundations of the new organisation.

The first congress had decided that the teachers' campaign ought to focus on salaries and pensions. The new organisation's methods were to petition the heads of the government in Dublin and in London, and local associations were encouraged to meet their local MPs to secure their support. By March of 1868, 36 out of 101 MPs had pledged to support the teachers' claims in parliament, and by June the support of 62 MPs had been secured.[28] Although the Education Commissioners in Ireland refused to deal with the national teachers, the British regime proved more open. In the INTO's first year, representative members travelled with Vere Foster to London to present a memorial signed by thousands of national teachers to the lord lieutenant and another, six months later, to the chief secretary.[29] These trips were time-consuming and costly for an organisation without any resources, but the teachers' presence was felt during the debate on the Education Estimates at the end of July, when the their grievances were raised by several Irish MPs.

The INTO was partly successful in securing an audience with the Powis Commission, which was still sitting. It submitted a memorial of grievances and secured a hearing for four teachers, one from each province. While the Powis Commission insisted it would only hear from teachers individually, not as INTO representatives, INTO activists met with the individuals beforehand to guide them and brief them on statistics. As well as those four teachers, Vere Foster was invited to give evidence. Before doing so, he sent a questionnaire to each local association and in September 1869 published the responses in a 74-page pamphlet.[30] This was in addition to an INTO pamphlet which had been produced for MPs to outline the teachers' case. 'The Duties and Obligations of Every System of Primary Education in Ireland: or, The Irish Teachers' Grievances'[31] was written by the association's secretary, John Harte.

THE ORGANISATION IN THE EARLY YEARS: AN UNHOLY TRINITY?

By the end of its first full year in existence, the association was already a serious force. Although the Commissioners continued to ignore it, it had met with the lord lieutenant and the chief secretary, secured the support of more than half of the Irish MPs, published a manifesto of concerns and had them debated in parliament; and membership was steadily growing, with 2,565 individual members, compared with fewer than 700 a year earlier.[32] Having operated on an ad hoc basis until now, the association adopted a new set of rules at its congress in Dublin after Christmas 1869 and listed its objectives:

1. The objects of the National Teachers organisation are, and shall be, the promotion of education in Ireland and the social and intellectual elevation of the Irish National Teachers
2. That no political or religious topic shall be introduced at meetings.

The Central Committee's role was to be purely executive and now, rather than comprising members of the Dublin Association, as had been the case, it would be composed of eight teachers, four from Dublin and four from surrounding counties.[33] These eight members of the Central Committee would be put before delegates *in globo* so that, in effect, the committee was drawn from a small pool of teachers and to begin with was simply nominated as a whole without a genuine election. During the early years, the numbers at congress, which was held in Dublin each year in the days after Christmas, were small. In 1871, for instance, there were 47 present, but despite (or perhaps because of) this, they were nearly always fractious gatherings.[34] Congress, as chaotic as it often was, was the governing body of the association and all matters of policy were to be decided on by its delegates at its annual meeting; these directives were then to be put into action by the Central Committee and the central secretary.

Behind its straightforward structure, with the politicking and rivalries that arise in any organisation, there was an unusual tension at work. For one thing, there was the rather complicated relationship between the association and the *Irish Teachers' Journal*. Strictly speaking, the two were completely separate entities. The association had no financial stake in the journal, and no editorial control over it, although much of it was written by a small number of activists. This was born out of expedience; the writ of the Commissioners being as it was, it was impossible for the teachers to have an official publication of their own, and the lack of any evident ties between the two allowed the teachers an element of plausible deniability in the event of any controversy. Without editorial oversight or control, however, the journal could take positions contrary to those of the organisation or detrimental to its interests. Similarly, the relationship between the association and Vere Foster was complex. Foster was the teachers' benefactor – he had lent his name and his time to the association – and was recognised for this by being elected president of the association at congress, over which he presided from December 1868. Foster, however, was not a teacher, was not a member of the association and was in no way answerable to it. He had strong views on a number of controversial educational issues, notably his vocal support for mixed (i.e. non-denominational) education and for using local taxation to fund teachers' pay, which were highly contentious within the INTO. In a sense, then, the teachers' movement in its early years was not so much a united organisation with an accountable decision-making structure but a trinity of three quite separate, but dependent, parts. This worked well enough as long as they all agreed, but it created problems when they did not.

THE VEXED QUESTION OF TENURE

During the early days nothing could cause a row more quickly than the mention of tenure and the issue of who ran schools. Teachers were paid by the state but worked under a local manager, usually the local parish priest or rector whose power to hire or fire was effectively unlimited. Teachers laboured under their managers' whims and stories of their unreasonable demands and arbitrary behaviour were the stuff of legend, such as the teacher who was obliged to act as a butler to his manager on particular occasions.[35] While the problem was almost universally acknowledged, there was disagreement over the wisdom of pursuing a solution since it was inevitable that it would lead to a clash with the ecclesiastical bodies. Delegates rejected an attempt to discuss the question at the INTO's first congress in December 1868 as 'inexpedient', but before the following year's congress, the *ITJ* raised the subject again in a series of editorials, resulting in a heavy mailbag of deeply mixed responses.[36] One member of the Wexford NTA complained about the tone used by critics of the managers, which 'expressed in a very discourteous, if not insulting language which exhibits a want of taste as well as deficiency of judgement'. As well as the allusion to Russian serfdom, this included epithets such as 'Egyptian bondage', 'Turkish slavery', 'petty tyrants' and 'uncontrolled despotism'.[37]

At the INTO's second annual congress in December 1869, delegates had before them a motion on managerial power. Immediately, one Belfast teacher sounded a warning note and proposed an amendment calling for the motion to be expunged, since 'if carried it might have the effect of breaking up the organisation but would have no beneficial consequences', while making it likely that the Roman Catholic clergy would use their veto against the organisation.[38] The amendment was defeated by a 'large majority', however, and the original resolution passed to applause. Later 14 delegates submitted a letter to formally record their opposition to the managerial question being discussed in the first place.[39] They also asked for the letter to be published in the journal, which became a forum for a battle between the 'managerialists' and 'anti-managerialists' that raged on for months.[40] Vere Foster was vocal in his criticism of the 14 dissenters and the *ITJ* took a similar editorial line, which, along with the particularly sharp correspondence, did nothing to advance fraternal spirit among the members. Feelings ran high throughout 1870, and the controversy escalated following the December congress, when a motion on the managerial situation was passed at a public session, prompting a walk-out by Dublin delegates in protest.[41] One Monaghan teacher received a severe admonishment from his bishop for having been in attendance when this happened, and given a warning that he would be fired if it happened again.

The Dublin Association did its best to get the INTO to abandon any discussion of school management,[42] although it seems to have been in the minority. But there was an appreciation for the depth of division on the matter and the danger it posed for an organisation barely three years old, so when delegates met for the 1871 congress in December, following a very stormy debate, they voted by 22 votes to 18 to defer any further discussion of the issue.[43] While the question was set aside for the INTO, the *Teachers' Journal* was not bound by congress, and continued to publish editorials and correspondence on the subject for months.

POWIS AND PAYMENT BY RESULTS

In May 1870, a little over two years after its appointment, the Powis Commission published its report. In all, it made 129 recommendations, but central to them was its finding that the standard of learning among school children was 'very much less than it ought to be'. To address this, the report recommended that all teachers should be trained and that there should be better salaries and conditions to improve the calibre of the profession.[44] The report recommended the introduction of two of the INTO's key demands – that each school should have a residence for the principal teacher to live in free of rent, and that teachers be assisted with paying into a deferred annuity scheme for pensions[45] – but its recommendation on salaries and their make-up was less positive. As teachers had feared when the commission had been established, Powis recommended payment by results on top of a fixed salary.

The revised salary structure, introduced across the country with effect from September 1872, saw teachers classified into three grades, on which their basic salary was based. This continued to be paid quarterly, via their managers, whom teachers had to visit in person to collect their pay. Fees based on pupils' examination results were then paid annually on top of basic pay, which meant that teachers went from year to year not knowing their income, on top of which there were habitual delays in the payment of the results fees. Another reason the INTO opposed the scheme was that, it argued, it was untenable in a country without compulsory education where, consequently, attendance rates were low. How was it fair to base teachers' pay on the results of pupils who were not obliged to attend school in the first place? The INTO's policy was for payment by results to be abolished entirely, but in the meantime, its salary campaigns focused on ensuring that any pay increases were awarded through the basic salary rather than being allocated by the results fees.

Payment by results did have one good outcome for teachers, though, when it was used as a bargaining tool to push through another Powis recommendation, namely that managers would be obliged to enter into a contract with the teacher. Powis had recommended that this contract would specify the teachers' duties and pay, and oblige either side to give three months' notice of termination. Any manager dismissing a teacher would have to have their decision ratified by a board, and if the dismissal was not so ratified, the teacher would be entitled to three months' salary.[46] In December 1872, the Board of National Education offered managers two forms of agreement, providing for compensation of three months' salary to teachers dismissed without 'sufficient cause' or where there was no 'serious misconduct'.[47] The Catholic clerical managers vehemently opposed this, arguing that secularist statesmen were interfering in the Church's managerial rights,[48] but by February 1873 the parties had reached a compromise and managers agreed on the principle of the contract of employment. Hailed at the time as the 'Teachers' Magna Carta', it meant that arbitrary dismissals, though still possible, would at least have to be compensated by three months' pay.[49] Though far from ideal, it was an important advance that allowed the 'vexed question' to be set aside, for the time being at least.[50]

PENSIONS AND FUNDING

In 1874, the teachers turned their attention to salaries and pensions and adopted a new approach for its campaign, holding large public meetings in Dublin and in provincial towns in an effort to gain popular support. These were well attended by local dignitaries, including local and national politicians of every political hue, and now that the management question was off the agenda, clergy from all denominations were happy to give their backing, echoed in many letters of support from bishops around the country. The organisation began to take a more strategic approach to politics around this time. Representative politics in Ireland had been undergoing its most significant change since Catholic emancipation, with the Home Rule League established in November 1873, and

60 Home Rulers were elected to Westminster at the February 1874 general election. That election also saw the defeat of the Gladstone-led Liberal government, replaced by a Conservative government with a large majority under Benjamin Disraeli. A Dublin-based Queen's Counsel, Charles Henry Meldon, was among the new Home Rule MPs, and he quickly became associated with the Teachers' Organisation. His first public association was in April 1874, when he chaired a public meeting of the national teachers of Dublin at the Antient Concert Rooms in Dublin and, around the same time, tabled a Commons motion calling for an increase in teachers' salaries.[51] In no time, he had effectively established himself as the national teachers' parliamentary secretary, although he was seldom, if ever, referred to as such. The teachers' relationship was very much with Meldon, as an individual, rather than with his party, and this allowed the organisation to maintain a good relationship with Irish MPs across the Home Rule–Unionist divide.

The first result of the teachers' and Meldon's lobbying was the National School Teachers (Ireland) Act 1875, described as 'An Act to provide Additional Payments to Teachers of National Schools in Ireland'. Essentially an attempt by the Conservative government to extricate itself from some of the burden of results fees, demanding that a greater proportion of them should come from local sources, it proved problematic since local authorities were not obliged to charge an education rate and, it turned out, most did not. It was around this time that the INTO and Vere Foster fell out for good. Foster had been complaining in the press about the INTO's opposition to payment by results,[52] on which teachers were unanimously opposed, and when he did so on the eve of a Commons debate on the matter,[53] he had finally overstepped the mark. Branded a 'meddling busybody'[54] by opponents, the fact was that the organisation to which he had played midwife was now ten years old and growing in strength and confidence, and was not prepared to tolerate the interference of outsiders, regardless of how helpful they had been in the past. No comment would be made on the subject, and this all but marked the end of Foster's connection with the teachers' movement. He did not attend another congress or meeting for another ten years, when he attended the first annual congress to be held in Belfast in Easter 1896.[55]

The teachers' other campaigns at this time were on residences and pensions. From 1870, teachers had been entitled to a retiring gratuity equal to one year's salary for every ten years of service, but this came nowhere close to the teachers' demand for a full pension.[56] Meldon raised the issue with the chief secretary in the Commons in March 1875, and discussions followed on the nature of such a scheme, but it never materialised. The government put a proposal to the INTO in 1877, but it was August 1879 when the National School Teachers (Ireland) Act 1879 finally passed through parliament. It established a statutory pension scheme

effective from 1 January 1880 with a 'pension fund' using £1.3 million appropri-
ated from the Irish Church Temporalities Fund, set up after the Church of
Ireland had been disestablished. Teachers would be obliged to pay a contribution
to the fund, and in 1880 a new basic salary scale was introduced, with across-the-
board increases as compensation for the pension contributions. As Michael
Moroney noted, 'while the provision made by the act was a big advance, the
actual amounts paid as pensions were very small' and depended on the teacher's
age, number of years' completed service and the teacher's 'class' for salary
purposes. This meant that a man's pension could be as high as £71 or as low as
£15, while a woman's could be £58 at most or as little as £12.[57] The greatest cause
of complaint about the scheme at the time, however, rested on the age of
retirement, which was 65 for men and 60 for women, both regarded as being too
old.[58] Nevertheless, the pension scheme was a crucial victory for the teachers'
movement, and its greatest achievement yet. A little more than a decade after the
National Teachers' Organisation had been established, it had made significant
advances on three of its four key grievances: teachers now had a pension scheme
where before there had been none; they had a contract of employment where
they did not before; and the provision of residences had been greatly improved.
Only on salaries did they remain distinctly empty-handed.

Meldon was hailed as the hero of the hour, 'the teachers' great and vigilant
champion'. The *ITJ* commissioned a portrait of him and advertised it in the
journal, for sale to teachers who might display it as a mark of their gratitude.
The *Journal* pronounced 'that the name of Meldon will be cherished and
respected so long as there is a teacher to conduct a primary school in this
country',[59] although for his part, Meldon acknowledged the role played by the
three INTO presidents, Boal, Traynor and Ferguson, with whom he had worked
over the previous five years. But if Meldon got the lion's share of the credit for
this success at the time, his glory was relatively short-lived. Far from being
cherished and respected, he fell out of favour with the INTO soon after, and his
name does not appear once in later accounts of the INTO's history.

The other significant victory in 1875 was the passing of the Residences Act.
The Act made provision for the purchase or erection of residences for national
teachers. This provided for a grant of half the estimated cost for the erection,
improvement or purchase of a house for the teacher (up to £100), as well as
making loans of up to £250 available. The loans were to be paid back, half by the
Commissioners of Education and half by the managers. In practice, the
managers' liability was often paid by the teacher, but it made affordable housing
available to teachers, usually attached to their schools, and represented one of the
greatest successes of the organisation in its early years. The provision of loans for
residences was discontinued shortly after the outbreak of the Great War in 1914.[60]

THE 'NEW DEPARTURE' AND THE NORTH'S DEPARTURE

The introduction of pensions through the 1879 Act was a high point, after which a rather fallow period followed. There were important incremental reforms, such as a simplification of the teachers' examinations for promotion, and some modifications to the Residences Act, but there were no landmark reforms.[61] A period of crisis had begun in Ireland. In the same month as the Act was passed, the National Land League had been established at a meeting in Castlebar, County Mayo, and compared with the problems arising out of the land agitation, the teachers' grievances were of little interest to the British government (with Gladstone leading his second government from June 1880). The land war raised the temperature of everything, and for the teachers, whose campaign had been pursued with such deliberate propriety, this was not an entirely comfortable state of affairs. Towards the end of 1881, a special meeting of the CEC unanimously resolved to recommend to the associations that they desist for a time from holding public meetings because this left them at the mercy of the speakers on the platform. This concern arose when a parish priest who was chairing a meeting in Ballaghaderreen made a comparison between the salaries of teachers and the police, the latter having nothing to do 'but shoot down innocent people'.[62]

Charles Meldon had continued to speak for the teachers in the Commons, but the lack of notable gains in the early 1880s caused some to reconsider their tactics and allies. This was never made public but a clue to the direction that the INTO was taking was to be found among the invited guests to the congress banquet in December 1883. They included two MPs for the Irish Parliamentary Party (IPP), the successor to the Home Rule Party from 1882. One was T.M. Healy, then a young Parnellite, first elected in 1880, who had come to prominence during debates on the 1881 land bill and who was prosecuted, alongside Michael Davitt, for a speech he had given in Carlow, for which he was imprisoned in February 1883.[63] The other was Thomas Sexton. One of Parnell's 'principal lieutenants', he had entered the Commons in the same election as Healy. He had been imprisoned with Parnell in Kilmainham in October 1881 and had signed the 'No Rent Manifesto' issued that month.[64] The presence of these two MPs, both recently jailed for their anti-government activities, was provocative. Privately, the two had agreed to attend the congress banquet – the highlight of the proceedings – only if, among the endless succession of toasts to Queen Victoria and to the lord lieutenant, all the honoured guests and so on, the loyal toast to the lord lieutenant was omitted. The omission of the toast to the lord lieutenant was noted and a number of delegates tried unsuccessfully to raise the matter at congress the next day, while a letter of protest signed by 14 delegates (nine of whom were from Ulster) was also rejected, prompting them to exit the hall as a body 'amidst derisive cheering'.[65] The delegates objecting to the omission of the viceregal toast complained that it was a deliberate and underhand attempt to introduce politics into proceedings, but they were alone in this. Although the incident was much remarked on in the press, even the unionist publications concluded that it was a regrettable but certainly not treacherous act.[66] T.M. Healy's remarks at the banquet had been somewhat controversial, however. Alluding to recent pay increases for 'the lordly Irish constable' conceded after a strike during August and September, he noted, to laughter, that 'pressure is the mother of reform'.[67] 'If the government learned by means of the velvety phrases of Mr Meldon or the more rugged language of men like myself,' Healy remarked, concluding to cheers, 'the fact that the teachers are a force, and being a force are capable of being a danger they would soon, to use a vulgar phrase, "knuckle under".' If mild by modern standards, it was more militant than the teachers had ever been before. The *Belfast Weekly Post* accused the assembly of treason, while the Commissioners of Education took exception to the tone; following an inquiry into proceedings, they issued a circular to national school managers in April.[68] This began by reiterating its guidance to national teachers from 1849, which had effectively prohibited the Teachers' Redress Committee. Stating that the character of recent meetings of the teachers had caused it to revise its view of the Teachers' Association, the Commissioners reminded teachers of the rule prohibiting their attendance at meetings, and above all political meetings. It also pointed to the rule stating that national teachers should be 'persons of Christian sentiment, of calm temper and discretion [who] should be imbued with the spirit of peace, of obedience to the law and loyalty to their sovereign ... Of all the public servants in the country the most studious to render an example of dutiful submission to authority and of avoidance of politics ought to be the National Teachers', and if they wished to discuss their own 'rights, privileges and claims at meetings', they would have to do so 'temperately'. If they were present at a meeting where anything was said or done of an 'objectionable character – namely, anything bordering upon political controversy, or criticism of the administration of the board, or the conduct of its officers or the action or policy of the Government', the teacher was expected to make a public disavowal, followed by an open withdrawal of the teacher from the meeting.[69]

This attempt to put the INTO on notice did not amount to much. The *Teachers' Journal* was bullish about the circular, and the circular did nothing to influence the political company that the Teachers' Organisation was keeping. On the contrary, during 1884, the Teachers' Organisation abandoned Meldon and his velvety phrases and threw in its lot with the IPP almost entirely. It was not an uncontroversial move, as was clear from the president's address to the 1884 congress. Observing the role played by the IPP in the last session of parliament, to cries of 'hear, hear' and 'no, no', John Nealon observed:

Some members of our organisation have condemned, in no measured terms what they have been pleased to call the new departure in our policy. (Interruption). If by this new departure is means an abandonment of the fundamental principles on which our organisation was founded, I can honestly and truly say that such is not the fact. (applause) The Irish National Teachers' movement exists today as free from the elements of sectarianism and politics as it was in the first hour of its inception (applause).

But if by the phrase a new departure is meant the abandonment of that policy of incapacity and inaction which made our cause and claims the laughing stock of every intelligent man in the community, if it means that a spirit of earnestness, vigour and determination to win our rights has been infused into the organisation, then I cordially agree with those who charge us with having made a new departure. The cant about 'old lines', 'constitutional methods' and so forth will not, I am confident, induce an intelligent body like ours to put aside any legitimate means of winning for the members of the teaching profession in this country that social position for which they have so long struggled and to which their honourable labours so well entitles them.

John Nealon, who took full credit for the 'new departure', concluded his speech by saying 'only the few who are utterly blinded by prejudice' would venture to condemn his action,[70] but while delegates from Derry and Lisburn protested, the latter complaining that he had gone too far, those who took issue with the new departure were very much in the minority, and Nealon was re-elected president by a landslide.[71] It was a divisive tactic, however, on which there was no middle ground. A number of northern associations dropped away from the INTO and eventually, in April 1886, a separate organisation, the Northern Union of Irish National Teachers, was founded at a special congress in Belfast.[72] The new northern union only lasted about two years, however. The chief secretary, Arthur Balfour, was disinclined to spend his time having meetings with two groups with precisely the same grievances, and refused to meet the Northern Union.[73] The northern teachers indicated a desire to return to the fold by the end of 1887, and on 12 May 1888 the two sides met in Dundalk to discuss reuniting. The Northern Union submitted 13 conditions for 'amalgamation',[74] the first that 'no teacher in connection with the organisation shall seek or accept office under any political party, attend political meetings or in any way show himself to be a political partisan', and the next four ran on very similar lines, looking for the INTO to reaffirm that it had no special relationship with any political party, and if any political party was to be dealt with, *all* would have to be dealt with. The other eight conditions outlined the procedures by which the two groups would reunite. The amalgamation became official at the 1888 congress, to great relief all round. Delegates voted that the custom of the previous five years of not holding banquets at congress be continued, just to be sure.[75]

A NEW DECADE, NEW ALLIANCES AND THE EDUCATION BILL 1892

In its report of the December 1888 congress, at which the Ulster teachers had rejoined the INTO, the *Cork Examiner* complained that the proceedings had been 'just a little too goody goody'. It felt that there had been 'just a trifle too much appreciation and affection displayed towards Mr Balfour [the chief secretary] and the government', and remarked that 'the hunting after unity with the Ulster teachers who seceded without just cause a few years ago is not a wholesome sign'.[76] The suggestion that the INTO was pandering to northern loyalists' demands was well short of the mark. In fact, the teachers were about to find a new ally of a considerably different hue. William J. Walsh was appointed the new Catholic archbishop of Dublin in February 1885. His nationalist sympathies were well known, and the appointment was made despite strong opposition from the British government. It was a popular choice, though, and, as his biographer notes, 'within a short time he became the leading figure in the hierarchy, and its chief spokesman on the key issues of land reform, home rule and educational equality for Catholics'.[77] Walsh had an active interest in education at every level. He had been president of St Patrick's College, Maynooth, and had served on the senate of the Royal University of Ireland for a brief period (1883–84). He had been responsible for forming the Catholic Headmasters' Association in 1878, and for many years was one of the most vocal proponents of primary education in Ireland. The INTO had its first meeting with him in October 1885, to discuss teacher training, and had found him very attentive and sympathetic, but it was during 1889 that the organisation and the archbishop became close.

In 1888, local INTO representatives met with Catholic archbishops or bishops of Dublin, Cork, Armagh and Galway to put forward their case for a right to appeal dismissals. The organisation also made representations to the bishop of Waterford in an individual case. A 'most respectable' husband and wife, Mr and Mrs Healy of Clonmel, had been arbitrarily dismissed after 26 years' service. The bishop said he did not have the power to reinstate the two, but would make sure that in future no manager in his diocese would dismiss a teacher out of hand, and that no teacher would be served three months' notice until he had been appealed to. If this was no consolation to the Healy family, who emigrated as a result, the bishop's pledge to establish an appeals process for all dismissals was seen as an important victory, and a process that might be adopted elsewhere.[78] When the issue was discussed at the December 1888 congress, the debate was very measured, with speakers keen to emphasise that they were not casting all managers as dictators, but the fact that a motion on tenure had been tabled at all was enough for a parish priest from

Blessington to send a lengthy screed to the *Freeman's Journal* against the teachers' temerity to raise the matter, which began an ongoing controversy in the *Freeman's* letters page.[79] In fact, the Catholic hierarchy was divided over what should be done and the INTO enjoyed the support of influential advocates on the issue, most notably Archbishop Walsh of Dublin, who recognised the justice in the teachers' limited proposals. Others, however, were firmly opposed to anything that might diminish the managers' right to rule. The managerial question was discussed at the hierarchy's annual meeting in June 1889 and, having failed to agree, again in September; but unanimity on this issue proved impossible. Instead they agreed to continue with things as they stood, where each bishop decided on whether teachers would have a right to appeal dismissal within their own diocese. In Dublin, Archbishop Walsh's position was that any case referred to him would be 'investigated and dealt with', and he asked the INTO to make teachers aware of this.[80] When Walsh agreed to chair the public meeting of the congress a few weeks later, he was left in no doubt as to his popularity in the organisation.[81] Many Catholic bishops were quite unwilling to establish an appeals mechanism in their own diocese, however, and there was no progress whatever for teachers working under Church of Ireland or Presbyterian management, which meant that the managerial question remained far from answered, even if much of the temperature was taken out of it for a while, at least.

Archbishop Walsh's support for the national teachers was especially valuable after relations with the IPP had soured badly around this time. They would become more strained as nationalist politics in the 1890s was riven by the Parnell split, and the political terrain became more treacherous and the atmosphere more toxic. Nationalist Ireland was so deeply divided on the matter, however, that it was difficult to avoid becoming embroiled in the politics of the split, even in relation to matters that, on the face of it, had nothing at all to do with it. At a time when individuals or organisations were expected to pick a side, becoming collateral damage was too easy, particularly given the role of the Catholic hierarchy in toppling Parnell and their continued support for anti-Parnellite politicians thereafter. The 1890s saw a war being fought by the two sides at general elections (1892, after which the anti-Parnellites kept a minority Liberal government in office; and 1895, which saw the Liberals routed), by-elections and local elections, and on a daily basis in the factions' newspapers, in particular the Parnellite *Daily Irish Independent* and the anti-Parnellite *Freeman's Journal* and the *Irish Catholic*, formerly *The Nation*.

The political and religious climate during the Parnellite split would become a particularly thorny issue for the teachers as the decade wore on. In the early 1890s, however, the INTO managed to steer clear of the controversy as it tried to clear a path for the Irish Education Bill 1892, the most significant piece of legislation for primary education for many years. There were two parts to this bill. One part changed how primary education was financed, removing any responsibility for the funding of national schools from local government and placing it all with the imperial government in London. It also introduced a grant for the schools of some £210,000, which in effect increased teachers' salaries by 20 per cent. Naturally the INTO welcomed this, and there was no opposition to this part of the bill from anywhere else, but the other part of the legislation, which dealt with compulsory education, proved problematic. The INTO had long supported compulsory education, not least because the payment by results system could not function fairly without it. The Catholic Church, however, was staunchly opposed to what it portrayed as an infringement of parental rights, and Archbishop Walsh of Dublin, who had advised the INTO on matters relating to the first part of the bill, was one of its most vocal opponents.

The government ignored Walsh's calls to split the bill in two so that the pay section could pass unhindered, but by the time the bill passed through the Commons (opposed by the anti-Parnellite Irish MPs, while the Parnellite MPs and the unionists gave it their support[82]) the sections on compulsory education were so limited that they were effectively meaningless. The pay increase was seen as such a major victory at the time that some teachers thought it could change the whole nature of the INTO, because now they had resolved all their greatest material grievances, 'the meetings of the associations must gradually assume a more professional character', with matters of training and pedagogy replacing the more mundane areas of pounds, shillings and pence.[83] It was naive perhaps, but testament to how much the teachers had achieved together.

At the Easter 1893 congress, the president, D.A. Simmons, reviewed the state of the organisation at 25 years, and observed how far they had come since the INTO began. Where before, the teachers' meetings had had to be held in secret, and 'it was not unusual for the inspector to go about on Saturday on the look-out for the place of meeting in order to scatter it with threats of pains and penalties', now the INTO confidently voiced the opinion of 11,000 men and women (albeit only half of those members) and it was recognised and received by the highest officers of the government and the state. It had accomplished a very great deal in those 25 years, in residences, in establishing a pension scheme and now, finally, in improving teachers' salaries.[84] More than that, the INTO had been largely responsible for popularising education matters. Where once a teachers' congress barely warranted a few paragraphs, there were now weekly education columns in the metropolitan press. Primary education was accepted as an important issue in political and public spheres in a way that was unimaginable when the INTO had started out. A quarter of a century on, teachers could see real progress in their professional lives and know that this had been achieved by their campaigns. Grievances remained though, and first and foremost among them was the managerial question, the 'vexed question' that had divided opinion among members of the organisation from the very beginning and that would pose the greatest challenge to the INTO's existence.

In July 1892, a general election saw the outgoing Conservative government return with the most seats but without an overall majority, leaving the Liberals to form a minority government under Gladstone, with the support of Irish nationalist MPs. The Liberals' return to power after six years caused particular concern to the archbishop of Armagh, soon to be Cardinal Michael Logue, who feared these English secularists would try to dismantle the system of denominational education in Ireland. Crucially, Logue also saw danger closer to home. One of his biographers observed that his 'fear of a rebellion against clerical control of education led him to believe that Parnellite tactics lay behind the genuine grievances of the teachers', and that he was 'convinced that the Parnellites were trying to rouse the teachers against the clergy'.[85] If there was any anticlericalism among the teachers, its roots were in the behaviour of the clergy themselves, but Logue misread the teachers' intentions as entirely political rather than self-interested. To acknowledge that the clergy were themselves the cause of the trouble was to him unthinkable, and instead he took an unnecessarily hostile position towards the teachers.

In the autumn of 1892, the CEC announced it would deal with the managerial question once again. The Catholic hierarchy did not take kindly to this news.[86] At their annual meeting in October, the bishops fired a warning shot. They noted that 'efforts are being made by *a section* of the Teachers' Organisation to effect important changes in the rules of the National Board respecting the existing powers of the managers of schools', and they warned that 'the bishops will have no part in any movement whose object or effect would be to destroy, or even weaken, the authority of the clerical managers over the moral and religious training of the youth of our country'.[87] This was a vast overreaction, when all the INTO wanted was a court of appeal, similar to that established by the archbishop of Dublin, which would apply to all teachers, but if the bishops' aim was to frighten the teachers into abandoning the issue, it did not work.[88] At the following congress, at Easter 1893, the president, D.A. Simmons, promised that 'this distressful grievance will henceforth become the main object of our agitation, and we are determined to be neither cajoled into silence, nor forced to desist in our demands for justice'. Significantly, Simmons was a Protestant who had been trained in the Model School. Taught in Armagh, he had been president of the Northern Union during the split ten years earlier, and was inclined to take a more robust stance on the matter than some of his colleagues. For even though the managers of Protestant schools did not support tenure for teachers, they did not share the suspicion that it was part of a secularist conspiracy. Notably, though, when congress came to discuss the matter, the debate lacked focus, partly because delegates had very different experiences of the system, depending on the diocese in which they taught.[89] There were a number of dismissals in the public domain at the time, but it was the extraordinary case of a teacher in Carlow that was the catalyst for change.

MRS CAREY'S DISMISSAL AND THE MAYNOOTH RESOLUTION

The events around the dismissal case of Bridget Carey are scarcely believable and read more like a melodrama than real life, but the case gives an insight into the powers enjoyed by managers. In August 1892, Mrs Bridget Carey, a teacher in Leighlinbridge, County Carlow, with an excellent record during more than 20 years' service, was served three months' dismissal notice by her manager, Fr J. Connolly, PP. Connolly gave her no reason for his action, and when she wrote to him asking him for an explanation and to reconsider, he declared it such an impertinence that he ordered her to accept three months' pay in lieu of working her notice, and told her he would dismiss her husband, Patrick, the principal of the local boys' school, if she did not accept.[90] Mrs Carey accepted the severance cheque but the following day she met with the bishop, Rev. Dr Lynch, to appeal her case. Following investigations, on 16 October the bishop ordered that she be reinstated immediately. That same night, parents across the school district received anonymous notes warning them to 'send no children of [theirs] to Carey's', and Fr Connolly set up a rival school, the teacher's salary funded from church collections. It collapsed by Christmas, and another effort after the holidays was similarly unsuccessful, notwithstanding efforts to intimidate children attending the two Careys' schools on their way in.

His efforts to vanquish Mrs Carey thwarted, Fr Connolly changed tack and wrote to the Commissioners of National Education in January, accusing Carey of having committed fraud regarding examinations two years earlier. The Commissioners were rightly sceptical but were obliged to investigate, and in early May, the *Carlow Nationalist* reported that the Commissioners had found there was no case to answer.[91] Undeterred, Fr Connolly continued to find petty means to persecute Mrs Carey, and eventually, the stress having become intolerable, she had a breakdown, which resulted in her admission to Carlow asylum in the summer of 1893. It was a deeply distressing turn of events for Bridget Carey and her family, and an extreme example of the consequences of living with a vexatious manager. The story, which had been reported locally and had been referred to in the *National Teacher*, finally made the national newspapers in September after its editor, John Morrin (INTO central secretary 1871–76), wrote to the *Daily Independent* outlining the facts of the case.[92] As news of the story spread, and it finally made the pages of the *Irish Teachers' Journal* for the first time, the INTO's Central Executive was, rather belatedly, compelled to act, establishing an ad hoc sub-committee which was sent to Leighlinbridge to investigate the matter. This prompted Fr Connolly to complain to the Commissioners of National Education that the teachers were investigating him, but while the Commissioners resolved in April that the teachers had been 'inexpedient' in entering into an investigation on a subject of controversy and that their publication of events had been a 'grave breach of duty', no sanctions were issued against the teachers involved.[93] By then the case had effectively been resolved. Mrs Carey was released from hospital and returned to school in February. The following month, Fr Connolly, from whom all the trouble had derived, had tendered his resignation as manager of both the girls' and boys' national schools in Leighlinbridge, although not before he had exacted some final acts of malevolence against the Careys.[94] This included submitting a report form declaring Mr Carey's character 'unsatisfactory', which led to further investigations in the schools. Worse still, he reported 'recently lunatic' Mrs Carey to the Commissioners for having returned to school in February without authority, and wrote to the press describing her as dangerous. The Commissioners, no doubt at the end of their tether with this petty, vexatious priest, were satisfied that she had been certified 'fit and able to resume her duties' by a doctor and took no action.[95]

At the congress after this episode, at Easter 1894, D.A. Simmons in his presidential address robustly asserted the justice of the teachers' demands and the need to persist in their campaign for tenure. He told delegates that 'they must no longer tacitly submit to be trampled but assert their manhood by prudent and courageous resistance to every species of oppression and intolerance', concluding that 'there is no hope of freedom for those who willingly consent to slavery, their own exertions to deserve and win liberty must be precursor of their emancipation … Who would be free, themselves must strike the blow!'[96] The delegates were less incautious, holding the debate on management in private, but the outcome was significant; they voted to make security of tenure the organisation's priority for the year to come.[97] They raised it at a deputation with the chief secretary, John Morley, in July. More provocatively, as far as the Church was concerned, the CEC wrote asking the Board of National Education to ask the Commissioners to take action to secure protection against dismissal during good conduct and efficient service, but the Commissioners declined; they did 'not think it expedient to initiate the discussion of an important change in the rules affecting the relations between Managers and Teachers under the National system'.[98]

The INTO's efforts were trenchantly criticised in the more clerically minded press, with the *Freeman's Journal* arguing that the CEC did not represent Catholic teachers in its attempts 'to secure for Tyrone House further scope for the exercise of the malignant influence of the Castle bureaucrats over the education of the Irish people'.[99] (Tyrone House on Marlborough Street had been home to the Commissioner and Boards of Education since 1835.) The *Freeman* merely took its view from the anti-teacher section of the hierarchy, which had been scandalised by events at congress. Writing to Archbishop Walsh at Easter, Cardinal Logue had observed that 'the Teachers' Congress [was] going full tilt against the managers', and, already resistant to any diminution in the powers of individual managers, noted that he was more determined still because he saw the hand of anti-clericalists in the teachers' campaign.[100] This thinking had been evident in the resolutions adopted at the annual diocesan synod in Armagh on 23 July (over which Cardinal Logue had presided), which included a unanimous protest 'against the dangerous and mischievous agitation of a section of the National teachers of Ireland in reference to the authority of managers over their schools'. They alleged that the teachers' object had been to 'subvert the relations at present subsisting between teachers and managers in favour of direct appointment and dismissal by the state' and, ominously, exhorted Catholic teachers in the archdiocese to 'at once disassociate themselves from a movement fraught with grave peril'.[101] Six weeks later, clergy in the neighbouring diocese of Clogher adopted similar resolutions condemning the teachers' 'dangerous and mischievous agitation'.[102] If the hostility towards the teachers had not subsided by the time the hierarchy came together for its annual meeting on 10 October 1894, however, a degree of pragmatism had become apparent. The bishops released a statement regretting the efforts by some prominent members of the INTO to bring about changes which were 'subversive of the legitimate authority of the managers of schools', but the good news for Catholic teachers was that the arrangement operating in certain dioceses, where no teacher could be dismissed or served with a notice of dismissal until the manager had informed the bishop, and received the bishop's assent, would now be the procedure in every diocese. This procedure became known as the first Maynooth Resolution.

It was an improvement for Catholic teachers, although it had been conceded grudgingly. In 1895, the INTO held a dinner for the Careys in Dublin, where it presented its testimonial to the couple, who were told that 'the defence which you both made in the cause of reasonable security of tenure must ever stand out prominently in the annals of the teachers' organisation and the position of freedom from arbitrary dismissal, which almost every Catholic teacher now enjoys, is largely due to an exposition of the abuse of managerial authority, which, with your aid, the executive of the organisation was enabled to present to the enlightened and sympathetic consideration of the Irish hierarchy'.[103] But if the Maynooth Resolution would have prevented the hardship inflicted on Bridget Carey, it was yet another compromise that fell far short of genuine security of tenure for Catholic teachers. Moreover, Protestant teachers continued to have no security and no right to appeal. The October 1894 resolution de-escalated the situation that was developing between the INTO and the hierarchy, or at least with Cardinal Logue, but the relationship between the two sides remained frosty and any respite in hostilities was only temporary, not least because the issue refused to go away. Protestant teachers continued to call for their position to be secured, with a Protestant teachers' memorial to the

Commissioners of Education organised at the beginning of 1895,[104] and the INTO continued to be led by D.A. Simmons, a Protestant teacher, who was sympathetic to their cause.

THE SECOND MAYNOOTH RESOLUTION 1898

During 1898 two dismissal cases came to light, one in Sligo and the other in Leixlip.[105] In the latter case, Mrs O'Sullivan, the principal of Leixlip Girls School for some 32 years, was summarily dismissed by her manager, Canon Hunt, on 30 October 1897.[106] She immediately wrote to her bishop, Archbishop Walsh of Dublin, but was informed by him that he could not interfere in the matter since she had received an immediate termination notice, rather than being given three months' notice or three months' salary, so she was not subject to the Maynooth Resolution. Mrs O'Sullivan took a case against Canon Hunt for wrongful dismissal and for slander, which went before the court in May 1898. A jury took an hour and 20 minutes to find that Mrs O'Sullivan had been unlawfully dismissed, and slandered by the curate, awarding her the equivalent of three months' salary and £200 damages for slander, as well as costs. After it considered the verdict at its meeting in June, the CEC prepared a memorial to the Commissioners on the managerial question which would bring the organisation into direct and open conflict with the Catholic ecclesiastical authorities. Referring to 'irresponsible managers', and teachers who were 'in a position of practical slavery, not knowing the moment the death sentence may fall upon them from the tongue-slander, unreasoning tyranny, or the dislike arising from mere sentiment', it concluded that the current situation could 'hardly be tolerated much longer' and called for legislation to finally fix the management question.[107] Any demand for a legal intervention into school management would have provoked a hostile enough reaction from the hierarchy on its own, but the indelicate language would add fuel to the fire, with the *Nation* appealing to Catholic teachers to dissociate themselves from the 'anti-clerical' members of the committee.

The O'Sullivan case had illustrated the loophole in the original Maynooth Resolution, and when the hierarchy held its summer meeting in Maynooth at the end of June, they revised the regulations to close it. They did so, however, in the most malign pastoral ever directed towards the teachers, declaring that it was their 'duty to issue this solemn admonition, and to warn our flocks against the dangerous errors advocated by those misguided men, amongst whom, we regret to say, are some few who call themselves Catholics'. The pastoral also warned that teachers were being misled by 'a few designing men who are unable to conceal the anti-Catholic and irreligious spirit which is the mainspring of the campaign against the Managerial System'.[108] Such a volley would have proved a challenge had the INTO been united against the bishops' attack, but the executive was divided. The majority supported the memorial, backed by the

National Teacher and to a lesser extent by the *Daily Independent,* which maintained that the teachers merely wanted adequate job security. The minority, which supported the hierarchy, was led by the INTO vice-president, Patrick Owens, and the *Irish Teachers' Journal,* whose editor was a 'protestant of a most uncompromising type' and was accused of taking that side to boost circulation.[109] This faction was supported on the outside by the *Daily Nation,* which accused the INTO of having been taken over by 'secularists', and the *Freeman's Journal.*[110] Owens, the vice-president, flooded the newspapers with letters criticising his colleagues, among them the 'renegade' Catholics on the executive (the CEC having comprised eight Catholics, four Protestants and two Presbyterians[111]) and produced a stream of leaked reports, or alleged reports, from CEC meetings, including lists of who voted how.[112]

By the end of 1898, relations between the hierarchy and the INTO, never good to begin with, had entirely broken down. The INTO had, through misunderstandings and pride and poor judgement, managed to fall out with Archbishop Walsh during 1896. At the time he scolded them that they had not 'very many friends whom they can afford to alienate', and felt obliged out of friendliness to inform them that the INTO had become 'a synonym for ingratitude'.[113] Now they had alienated their most important ally among the hierarchy and the bishops turned their faces from the teachers entirely. They refused to receive any correspondence from the INTO, let alone meet them, 'in the present circumstances',[114] while Cardinal Logue had warned the Drogheda association that he would not adhere to the new Maynooth regulations if he was to be overruled by the 'clique in Dublin'.[115] Eventually, pragmatism won over principle, and on 7 January 1899 the CEC passed a motion by six votes to four to 'unreservedly withdraw' the memorial, while seeking protection for those not covered (i.e. teachers in Protestant schools);[116] however when congress met at Easter a couple of months later, the president, Robert Brown, was defiant, warning that if the managers did not let go of some of their power, the teachers, who 'are neither secularist, anti-clerical nor socialistic confiscators, will not cease agitating'.[117] This, along with a resolution calling for a court of appeal for Protestant teachers – watered down from a call for the Board of Education to play a role[118] – saw a chorus of disapproval from the nationalist press. As the *Freeman* disingenuously asserted, in their campaign against the managerial system the teachers 'will accept nothing but State – that is, Castle – protection'.[119]

Events at congress had an immediate and terrible effect. First, with Cardinal Logue's approval, the Catholic managers in the ecclesiastical province of Armagh, consisting of Ulster and parts of Leinster and Connaught, pledged to enforce a boycott of INTO members in their schools. Teachers were expected to sign a declaration that they were not a member of the INTO and would not join 'as at present constituted without first tendering my resignation'.[120] There was one exception to the ban in Armagh, in the diocese of Raphoe, where Bishop O'Donnell stated it would never run. The CEC met the next week and withdrew the memorial,[121] but this fell short of what was demanded of them, and weeks later the clerical managers of the province of Tuam followed Armagh's example, complaining that while the INTO executive had 'withdrawn the futile but obnoxious memorial', 'they had not as yet either retracted or apologised for the terms in which it was drawn up'.[122] This meant that half the country was now under the ban, although the provinces of Cashel and Dublin did not follow. Archbishop Walsh had his differences with the INTO, but he disagreed with Cardinal Logue's claims that the organisation had become a hotbed of secularists. As he noted in December 1900, he regretted that the INTO had done certain things 'that seemed to me capable of being easily misrepresented as hostile – though I knew, of course, that they were not at all hostile – to the idea of the teachers having, as every right-minded man recognises that they should have, an organisation, and a powerful organisation, to safeguard and protect their interests'.[123]

The ban was fully in force for about 18 months. An attempt to repudiate the memorial for Catholic teachers at the 1900 congress in Derry had fallen short of a full retraction and far below the required threshold of remorse, but during the summer, the CEC unreservedly withdrew the memorial, and in October it issued a statement affirming that only a 'correct and becoming attitude towards the bishops and priests of Ireland' would be tolerated in the organisation. It also recommended that INTO members in each diocese arrange a meeting with their respective bishops to remove any misunderstanding over the organisation's aims.[124] Gradually, the ban ceased to be enforced, although it was not officially withdrawn until 1904 and 1905. Soon after, the central council of the Catholic Managers' Association 'rejoiced at the disappearance of friction' between the Catholic national teachers and themselves.[125]

The ban caused serious damage to the INTO. Although membership figures from the time are not entirely reliable, there were some 5,250 members in 1899, which fell to around 3,660 by 1902. As well as the individual membership falling off, which was inevitable, with teachers facing dismissal otherwise, there had been a danger of schism. There was at least one case, in Cork in the summer of 1899, where local associations began work to establish a Catholic National Teachers' Association, with the support of the local bishop.[126] But when the CEC agreed to put teachers' rights of tenure beyond the Pale, they risked another split, since having secured the rights of Catholic teachers with the Maynooth resolutions, the organisation now pledged itself not to campaign for the rights of its Protestant members. Not surprisingly, there were some individuals and associations in the north who felt this meant there was no place for them in the INTO, and that they should leave, but three prominent Protestant members,

David Elliott and John M. Thompson of Belfast and George Ramsay of Cookstown, intervened. With the support of the president, James Hegarty, the three set about forming a separate committee for Protestant teachers,[127] which held its first embryonic meeting at Elliott's home in August, attended by a dozen prominent teachers. Then, at the end of August, after careful consideration, they held a public meeting at Portadown Town Hall, presided over by ex-president Robert Brown.[128] This Protestant Teachers' Committee was established in a spirit of pragmatism, in an effort to preserve the organisation's unity rather than sow division, since in Brown's words, 'the executive had thrown the managerial Jonah overboard to save the organisation in view of the threatened boycott of its members by the clerical authorities'.[129] There were individuals who tried to stoke sectarianism – notably the former vice-president Owens – but accusations of a Protestant cabal in the organisation were dismissed by one of the Protestants on the CEC, J.J. Hazlett, who responded that there was 'no such thing as the sect in congress. In the Teachers Organisation neither religion nor political distinctions are recognised and in this teachers set an example which might, with much benefit, be copied by other sections of the general community.'[130]

In 1900 the Protestant Teachers' Committee became the Irish Protestant National Teachers' Union (IPNTU), organising branches in all parts of the country; it gained 300 members in its first eight months.[131] While it had no official relationship with the INTO, its members were expected to be members of both organisations.[132] The IPNTU's two objects from the beginning were to ensure security of tenure and improve the conditions of work, and to afford help and advice to any (Protestant) teacher who was in trouble with their manager through no fault of their own. It would also have a third object, however, which ran quite contrary to the position of the INTO proper, namely that control of schools would be removed from all Churches. As it observed:

> Every thoughtful man who sees the unsatisfactory state of our Irish schools is fully aware that so long as the present system, which makes the practical control of primary education a mere secondary object of bodies (Churches to wit) which are primarily concerned with far other issues, prevails, so long will the interests, mental and physical of our children, be sacrificed. Every true patriot, therefore, looks forward to the time when the control of education will pass from the clutch of the church, which is only laid on to strangle and destroy, to bodies popularly elected for this sole purpose; to the time when rate-built, rate-equipped, rate-supported schools will receive and educate in comfort and decency the youth of old Ireland. For the coming of that glad millennium we wait, we work, we pray. When it comes our supreme object will have been attained and our union can retire into the unseen.[133]

This was anathema to the Catholic Church, which suspected, incorrectly, that this was the position of the INTO as a whole. The creation of the IPNTU represented a compromise on the part of Protestant teachers in order to secure the unity and security of the organisation. It is possible that had the controversy over tenure continued in the organisation as a whole, it would have done irreparable damage. Between 1899 and 1902, the INTO's membership suffered a 30 per cent drop, which began to recover once the ban was lifted.[134] However, it removed the questions of tenure and the control of schools outside the remit of the INTO at precisely the time when someone with the political will to change this took the reins in Education. A chance for change was on the horizon, but had it come too late?

Chapter 2 ⌒

'YEARS OF CIVIL WAR': THE INTO AND THE STARKIE REGIME, 1900–1921

'Teachers plodding all their lives to teach on behalf of the empire at a wage which a navvy would refuse.'

By 1900, the Parnell split had effectively ended. The newly united Irish Parliamentary Party (IPP) faced political competition from the United Irish League, but the deeply poisonous parliamentary factionalism of the 1890s, which had affected Irish life far beyond Westminster, was no more. The general election of 1900 had seen the Conservatives return with a secure majority and they remained in office until the Liberal landslide of 1906, which was secured on a platform that had expressly ruled out home rule, though with a promise of limited devolution.[1] This meant that home rule was entirely off the agenda for the first ten years of the century. Political and cultural life flourished outside party politics as the movements that had emerged in the late nineteenth century continued to grow. Most notable of these, insofar as the INTO is concerned, was the Gaelic League, which had been established in 1893, and grew rapidly at the turn of the century from 120 branches in 1901 to 593 in 1904.[2] The teaching of the Irish language in schools was an important goal of the Gaelic League and other proponents of the Irish language, and they were careful to develop a good relationship with the INTO at this time. This period also saw the growth of progressive and radical politics, including the political and economic separatism of Arthur Griffith's Sinn Féin, and the first wave of feminism, which saw the emergence of organisations for women graduates and campaigns for women's suffrage. The second decade of the century was tumultuous for Ireland and the world at large. It saw the introduction of the third Home Rule Bill; the formation of the Ulster Volunteers, and later the Irish Volunteers; industrial unrest and the Dublin lockout; the outbreak of the Great War; then the Easter Rising of 1916 and the political events that followed. Naturally, these events profoundly affected the INTO and the circumstances in which it operated, but more than anything, the INTO's energy at this time was defined by its battle with one man, W.J.M. Starkie, the last resident commissioner of national education in Ireland.

Dr W.J.M. Starkie was appointed in February 1899. He succeeded the late Christopher Redington, whose inauspicious period of office had begun after Sir Patrick Keenan died in 1894. For someone who brought in the hated payment by results, Keenan developed an oddly high status in the INTO, and in 1962, a plaque in his honour was erected in Tyrone House.[3] Starkie, on the other hand, would always remain an ogre.

Starkie had not been an obvious choice for the role. A Catholic from Sligo, he was a classical scholar by profession, and had been president of Queen's College Galway in the two years preceding his appointment. Though he had canvassed extensively for the post, by his own admission he had 'not hitherto been concerned with primary education' and knew very little about it.[4] Starkie arrived at Tyrone House at a crucial juncture. He took up his post at a time of imperial economic retrenchment caused by the cost of the Boer War; then there were the major reforms already afoot in education, which Starkie would be responsible for implementing, as well as initiating his own. He had a lot to do, and no money with which to do it. Starkie was intelligent and energetic – perhaps overly so, for the speed with which he brought about the changes, and his lack of delicacy in so doing, did much to make enemies of the INTO, and began what was described by T.J. O'Connell as 'those lean and frustrating years for teachers' and by one INTO president (in 1913) as 'thirteen years of civil war' (although the hostilities would continue for several more years).[5]

There were four main areas of dispute: a revised school programme, introduced in 1900; an entirely new scheme of salary and promotions, which was brought in the same year; changes to the inspectorate and a policy of dismissal for inefficient teachers; and finally, the introduction of a number of new rules, which would have far-reaching consequences.

NEW PROGRAMME AND NEW SALARY SCHEME

A revolution in national education had been widely anticipated, but this 'civil war' was not inevitable. In fact, Starkie's tenure started off quite well. His first major address, at the Albert Model Farm in Glasnevin in February 1900, was sympathetic to the teachers. He spoke of the need for comprehensive reform, and his desire to inspire teachers with a desire for self-development, and of how he intended, to this end, to remove some of the barriers to advancement that existed at the time. He criticised 'the elaborate mosaic of pounds, shillings and pence' that made up the results system, and the speech was warmly welcomed by the INTO.[6] The teachers' hopes grew when, shortly after, Archbishop Walsh made disparaging remarks about payment by results in a newspaper interview. Unfortunately, these raised expectations only led to greater resentment when the hoped-for reforms failed to appear. Starkie's first major task was to oversee the implementation of a major reform of the primary curriculum. This had its origins in the report of the Commission on Manual and Practical Instruction, popularly known as the Belmore Commission, established in 1897 at the behest of Archbishop Walsh. Following a process that included public meetings, evidence from 186 witnesses, visits to 119 schools in England, Scotland, Germany, Holland, Switzerland and Denmark, as well as Ireland, and a wide-ranging review of contemporary educational literature, the Belmore Commission published its report in June 1898.[7] It proposed a scheme which included the introduction of kindergartens (which it acknowledged might be challenging in small schools), and new subjects including hand and eye training, drawing, elementary science, agriculture, cookery, laundry and domestic science and needlework (for girls), as well as singing and drill, or PE. The new programme, published in 1900, was a progressive, radical shift from a narrowly academic programme towards more practical subjects, and a different educational philosophy that moved away from rote learning. But since all the existing subjects were considered essential, the new subjects were merely shoehorned into the old programme, with class time for the older subjects reduced to make space. Moreover, while the commission had researched widely, the inspectorate had had little input in the revised programme and, crucially, the teachers had had none. Starkie believed that since the teachers had given evidence to the Belmore Commission, it was unnecessary to consult them again, which meant that while the teachers broadly supported the new programme, they felt as though it was imposed on them and they had not had the chance to object to its few 'serious faults and shortcomings'.[8] There were complaints from the outset that the curriculum was overloaded and impractical, but the failure to consult teachers was regarded as a snub and was deeply felt. It was around this time, in May 1900, that Starkie refused a request to meet an INTO deputation, and in so doing, as future president Catherine Mahon put it, a 'long-drawn battle began'.[9]

Already unhappy, teachers woke on 14 July to find details of an entirely new system for the classification and payment of teachers in the national newspapers. There had been no warnings beforehand, and nothing had prepared them for the nature of the changes. The classification, or status, of teachers, earned through many years of service and through the challenging summer examinations, was removed overnight, with half the teachers in the country demoted. In fact, it was worse than overnight, since the rules were retrospective from 1 April. Teachers would be categorised into three grades, each with a fixed minimum and maximum salary, and with a quota on the number in each grade.[10] Some grades depended on the number of pupils in the school, so that no teacher in a school with an average attendance of fewer than 70 pupils could be promoted to the First Section of First Grade. If the average attendance fell below 30 for any reason, their salary would be reduced.[11] First-class teachers in remote schools with small numbers of pupils were now demoted to third class through no fault of their own and with no warning, while promotion to the highest grade was impossible for anyone not in a large school.[12] Of the 374 schools in County Tyrone, for instance, only 26 had more than the 70 pupils needed to secure the highest grade.[13] The CEC immediately sought a meeting with Starkie, who refused to meet them, so a deputation travelled to London to raise their concerns with the chief secretary. He gave them a sympathetic hearing, but told them there was nothing he could do, and advised them to seek a meeting with the Board of Education. When they did so on their return, they were informed in the standard fashion that it was 'not the practice of the board to receive deputations'.[14] After one final attempt to secure a meeting with Starkie, the CEC resigned themselves to defeat.[15] The INTO faced another setback at this time, when Archbishop Walsh, frustrated by the mismanagement of teachers' appeals over their reclass-ification and Starkie's failure to support him on the matter, resigned from the Commissioners. It was testament to Starkie's poor political judgement that he managed to lose the board's most committed educationalist so needlessly, and Walsh's better judgement would be missed.

THE BELFAST SPEECH

In September 1902, Starkie travelled to Belfast to give an address on education to the British Association that proved hugely controversial. The speech was an appeal for the restructuring of Irish education. Starkie complained that national school managers were financially and administratively incompetent. He also complained about the situation of lay teachers in Catholic intermediate schools. He had spoken of the 'ruinous effects' of the indifferent managers who ran Irish primary schools, whose neglect demoralised teachers and left schools as mere hovels akin to 'half-ruined tenement houses' with outhouses as 'dangerous sources of disease and death'. To say such things at all was contentious; to do so in Belfast, of all places, was incendiary. The speech was generally considered by commentators to have been 'ill-advised and naïve'.[16] That what he said was correct was beside the point; rather, it was seen as a direct and unprecedented assault on Catholic management. For its part, the Catholic Church was vehement in its opposition to the speech, and more practically, the Catholic Clerical School Managers' Association, later the Catholic Primary School Managers' Association (CPSMA), was established in October 1902 to preserve the system and look after the interests of the managers within it. If Starkie had expected that the teachers would support him in his attack on the managers, he was quite mistaken. It may have been that many in the INTO agreed with Starkie's sentiments, but the organisation was emerging from its ban by Catholic managers in half the country; to side publicly with Starkie would have caused ructions. That the INTO and the resident commissioner's relationship was frosty, to say the least, only copper-fastened the INTO's disinclination to lend its support. Officially, the INTO was appalled by Starkie's speech. Privately, however, one member of the executive, the Dublin-based Protestant J.J. Hazlett, wrote to him to say that when he had seen him earlier that day on a deputation, he had 'quite forgot' to deliver an important message.

> I was very specially requested by the Protestant teachers to say that the views put forward in your Belfast paper, relative to managers and the managerial system, have their entire approval and they are deeply grateful to you for expressing those views in public, and also for the other sympathetic references made in the same paper to the general body of teachers. Indeed I might say that I do not think there is a teacher of any creed in all Ireland who is not thoroughly delighted with your statement about the managers and the managerial system because they know but too well that those statements are absolutely true.
>
> As for the deputation today, I believe it will be productive of much good. It has removed numerous misconceptions. You have been regarded hitherto as being inimical to the teachers' interest [but] the deputationists are now convinced that you are the best friend of the teachers and the best friend of education. This belief will very soon spread and I think you'll find that the attitude of the Journals published in the interests of the teachers will be very different in the future to what it has been in the past.
>
> The deputationists are extremely thankful to you for the exceedingly kind and courteous manner in which you received them and for your sympathetic attitude towards them.[17]

None of this could be said publicly, however. Rebuilding the organisation in numbers and in influence was a challenge. Vilified in the press, without friends in the hierarchy or in politics, the INTO was by now without a single champion. Even when one of its own CEC members, Thomas O'Donnell, was elected as an MP for West Kerry at the 1910 general election, it was problematic, for O'Donnell was a Parnellite, and 'particularly critical of the cautious, clericalist, conservative, middle class wing of the anti-Parnellite known as Healyites', with a reputation of being a radical.[18] Trained in the Model School in Marlborough Street, and a vocal critic of the managerial system, O'Donnell may have been the first teacher to be elected to Westminster, but in the circumstances, his views meant this was not met with great enthusiasm.[19] O'Donnell did provide an important and much-needed voice for the teachers during his early years in Westminster, but his relations with the organisation were not close and soured badly during 1902 over the distribution of a grant, which the INTO anticipated would go towards education but which ended up going towards a railway for Dingle, in O'Donnell's constituency. When, in 1906, it was decided to secure the services of a parliamentary secretary from among the ranks of the Irish MPs, John Murphy, O'Donnell's neighbour in East Kerry, was appointed instead. That arrangement was not successful and ended after a couple of years.[20] At organisational level, the CEC worked hard to increase the membership and influence of the organisation. By the end of 1902, after two years of decline, the association returns had begun to increase, and there were reports of associations reviving,[21] but while things had begun to move in the right direction, they were too slow. There was a more concerted effort to reorganise from 1904, when a list of the 8,000 or so non-associated teachers was drawn up. Each was sent a letter from the central secretary impressing upon them the INTO's role in improving teachers' conditions over the previous 35 years, and the benefits of joining, which now included the services of an eminent barrister as standing counsel, who would provide advice on cases at no cost to the individual member.[22] Association secretaries were encouraged to canvass locally, and members of the CEC travelled around the country for meetings to rally teachers to the organisation. The CEC report for 1904–5 observed that this had been a success, noting that 'in most places the local associations were strengthened in number and roused into greater activity while in others new associations were called into existence or old and inactive ones revived'; but, notwithstanding the work done by members of the CEC during the year, the increase in membership 'primarily rests on local associations'.

'A SPIRIT OF OBEDIENCE AND LOYALTY TO THE SOVEREIGN'

By 1905, the organisation was steadily rebuilding and internal controversy and factional fighting were largely consigned to the past. This was partly as a result of the management question being quarantined in the Irish Protestant National Teachers' Union (IPNTU), and a change to the way the CEC was elected by district, which ensured the election of more Protestant representatives on the executive than had been the case in recent years. Nevertheless, the CEC remained predominantly Catholic, and the religious – and political – balance of the organisation remained delicately poised. But if the organisation was successfully avoiding any sectarian pitfalls, outsiders could not be relied upon to do likewise, and an incident at the 1905 congress in Sligo threatened to overturn the careful work of recent years. With rather too familiar echoes of the controversy some three decades earlier, the incident arose over a toast at the congress banquet, when some 15 or 20 local dignitaries walked out when they saw that the first toast on the menu was to 'The King'.[23] The incident was widely reported in the press, with the Dublin *Daily Express* pointing its finger at the 'pernicious influence' of Gaelic Leaguers on the teachers' 'treasonable and seditious and revolutionary' behaviour and the matter of the 'disloyal Irish teachers' was raised in the House of Lords by Lord Oranmore and Browne, who asked what the Board of National Education was doing in the face of this disloyalty.[24] A letter from INTO president J.J. Hazlett to Starkie was read to the House, in which he explained that the incident had been exaggerated in the press and that no teachers had been involved, but was confident that the executive would 'entirely dissociate themselves from and repudiate the regrettable and unpardonable conduct' of those involved. Speaking for the government, Lord Londonderry said it would make sure the Commissioners were strongly reminded of the 'necessity of working on the rule that teachers were to be imbued with a spirit of obedience and loyalty to the sovereign and would deal effectively with any teacher receiving his pay from the state who displayed disloyalty or inculcated it in the children under his charge'.[25] For his part, Starkie returned to refusing to meet INTO deputations, while the board responded with a new circular which argued that the INTO should have formally repudiated the disloyal action after the event, and it could not pass without rebuke lest it be considered tolerable behaviour. Teachers were also reminded to observe the various prohibitions on politics, meetings, fairs and so on, towards which, the commissioners noted, there had been 'a growing spirit of insubordination on the part of many teachers' and a disregard for the rules, with teachers accused of attending meetings at which 'the board and its officers [were] assailed in a coarse and scurrilous manner'.[26]

As it happened, Hazlett had called on the CEC to dissociate itself from the incident at its first meeting after congress and said he would resign if it did not, and he proved true to his word, although his resignation only emerged through the press in July, and no reason for it was given. Of course rumours abounded, but Hazlett was unforthcoming, although he did write to the *School Weekly* appealing for unity. He assured members that, contrary to some reports, he had not severed relations with the INTO, but noted that had he done so, the majority of the Protestant teachers would probably have followed, which would likely have resulted in the setting up of a 'rival and sectarian' organisation.[27] Notwithstanding Hazlett's appeal for unity, the IPNTU was considering its position relative to the INTO, its general committee deciding to 'hold themselves in readiness to inaugurate a general independent teaching organisation should subsequent events justify such an action'. As O'Connell notes, 'that no development in this direction took place was largely due to the efforts of Messrs Ramsay, Thompson and Elliott, who were responsible for preventing the breakaway in 1899 over the tenure question'.[28]

SMALL SCHOOLS, WOMEN TEACHERS AND RULE 127(b)

The Sligo incident closed down dialogue between the INTO and Starkie at an important time. In 1902, the chief secretary, George Wyndham, commissioned an English inspector, F.H. Dale, to inquire into the Irish national school system, 'as regards premises, equipment, staffing and instruction'.[29] Dale's report was published in 1904 and described an under-resourced system of ill-designed, ill-kept, often insanitary schools, which were often considerably inferior to those in England.[30] Although broadly positive about the revised programme, he noted that the methods of instruction had not changed to meet the needs of the new programme, with the education of infant classes one of the weakest points of the new system.[31] Few of the report's recommendations were enacted, but following belated consultation with the teachers and the inspectorate, and with Dale, a number of changes to the revised programme were made in 1904.[32] Dale's main finding, however, was that the number of elementary schools in Ireland had steadily increased (it had grown by a third between 1867 and 1901) despite a diminishing population, due to increased denominational schooling and the separation of schools by sex and age.[33] Dale argued that this was unnecessary, financially extravagant and detrimental to the students' education. He also felt that boys aged between three and seven years were particularly disadvantaged by this sub-division of schools, which would see infant boys put under the charge of a master, when, in Dale's view, they should be taught by women teachers.[34] The INTO was sceptical, and saw it as merely a money-saving proposal, since women teachers were paid at a lower rate.[35]

The influence of Dale was evident in the new Rules for National Schools published in February 1905. They included a ban on untrained teachers being appointed principals and a new rule that the Commissioners would not allow a new school with an average attendance of fewer than 25 where there was another school of the same denomination within two miles. This was an effort to stop the mushrooming of new schools, coming at least 20 years too late.[36] The most significant new rule was 127(b), which stated that boys under eight years could not enrol in a boys' school without an assistant mistress unless there was no suitable school under a mistress available in the locality. The board argued that this was because women were 'more likely to have the sympathy and patience' needed to look after young children,[37] but it was widely seen as a policy rooted in money-saving, with women costing at least 20 per cent less to employ than men.[38] The *School Weekly* suggested it could mean the 'passing of the male teacher' and one estimate suggested that some 600 male teachers would lose employment as a result of the rule, with many others having their professional grade fall because of lower average attendance.[39] The case of Con MacSweeny, a principal teacher from Aughrim, later a member of the CEC, was raised in the Commons as an example. His salary would be reduced from £130 to £116 per annum if the average attendance fell below 30, but if it fell below 20, his salary would be reduced to only £56; he was merely advised to amalgamate the boys' and girls' schools.[40] This course was unacceptable to the school managers and almost immediately a campaign against it began with the teachers, clergy of all denominations, politicians of every hue, and all newspapers united against it. When the Catholic hierarchy resolved to advise all managers to ignore the rule, it was effectively dead in the water. The teachers and managers were united against a common enemy – the INTO's years in the wilderness had ended at last.

LADY TEACHERS AND CATHERINE MAHON

Looking back, T.J. O'Connell thought it was doubtful if 'any rule introduced by the National Board during the 90 years of its existence caused such a storm of opposition from teachers, managers and the public press as did Rule 127(b)',[41] but, as Síle Chuinneagáin observed, the INTO's efforts to protect the interests of male teachers during the controversy 'was an indication of the status of women within the INTO'. Legitimate as the male teachers' grievances were, women's grievances were not addressed in the same way. By now, women were the majority of national school teachers, although one would never have thought so to look at the INTO's executive, congress or its associated journals. However, as Síle Chuinneagáin notes, the row over Rule 127(b) did lead to a certain reassessment within the INTO about its treatment of women teachers, however. In 1905, women teachers outnumbered men 6,298 to 5,744,[42] and the rule would likely widen the gap further. The creation in 1905 of a new class of assistant teacher, the junior assistant mistress (or JAM), was to increase the numbers of women working in schools further still. In 1905, fewer than one per cent of all teachers were JAMs, but after July 1906, a JAM was to be employed in all schools with an average attendance of between 35 and 50 pupils, so that by 1910 they made up some 15 per cent of all teachers in national schools.[43]

Still trying to recover from the clerical ban, if the INTO wanted to rebuild its organisation and secure the membership of the maximum number of teachers, it had to appeal to the women teachers whom it had so overlooked until now. The introduction of the 'Lady Teachers' Own Page' in the *Irish School Weekly* (*ISW*) in February 1906 was the first attempt to widen its appeal to women. If the editors who had commissioned the page had expected some tips on cookery lessons and sewing, they were rudely disabused in the first column, in which its author, Kathleen Roche, wondered why such a column had not been a feature of the *ISW* from the beginning, though it was 'better late than never'. Noting that the editors had given her a free hand, she continued that they seemed to have 'a lurking suspicion that I am something of a socialist, and an out-and-out advocate of women's rights, for they have modified the freedom which they at first conferred upon me by stipulating that I must not write anything that could be construed by the men teachers as "outrageously insulting".[44] Instead, she offered a call to arms to her sisters in the profession. Pointing to the lack of lady delegates at congress or on the CEC, on which, in almost 40 years, no woman had ever served, and contrasting this with the INTO's sister organisations in England and Scotland, Roche complained that it was 'only in Ireland that [women teachers] are despised, rejected and regarded as noodles'. And why, she wondered, was this? It was because lady teachers had not insisted on having their own grievances attended to. They were in the majority of teachers, and so had it within their power to control the organisation. INTO membership was 6:4 male to female, in a profession which was 6:4 female to male, and the first action women teachers needed to take was to join.[45] Roche, for her part, set her demands high: equal pay for equal work. It was the first time this phrase had appeared in an INTO publication, and it lit a fire immediately, with the *ISW* publishing letters in support from male and female teachers in the weeks afterwards.

Crucially, the matter also made it to the floor of congress a few months later. Inspired by Kathleen Roche's call in the *ISW*, Miss Catherine Mahon, a principal teacher from Birr, and one of just three women delegates that year, tabled a motion on equal pay.[46] In the end the motion – which pointed out that women teachers had to teach every subject that male teachers were obliged to, but also had to teach an extra three hours of needlework; so their salaries ought to be *at the very least* equal to those of men teachers – was not put to a vote, but the matter was referred to the associations for discussion, with Mahon's support.[47] Afterwards, around a quarter of the associations passed resolutions supporting equal pay, although there was a sizeable minority against.[48] Not all support for equal pay from men was borne out of disinterest, since, as Mahon observed, if female teachers cost the same as male teachers to employ, then the chances of them displacing men was significantly diminished.[49]

Any campaign for the rights of women teachers would depend on the women themselves, and would require women's representation on the executive. The ideal outlined by Catherine Mahon was that there would be women representatives in each district, but there ought to be two designated at the very least, just as there had been two places reserved for assistant teachers.[50] There was some opposition to the idea of women's representatives on the CEC and there were some sharp letters back and forth on the matter in the *School Weekly*, but the real work had to happen before the association's quarterly meeting in February 1907 to ensure that women candidates were nominated to run in the CEC elections. Despite their efforts, Catherine Mahon alone secured enough nominations to run for the CEC, not for her own district but for vice-president. She ultimately came last in a field of three, but she performed very respectably for a newcomer. Nevertheless, congress opened the door to a second shot at a seat on the executive when it adopted a motion providing two designated seats for women on the executive – one for a principal and one for an assistant – to be elected by delegates that year. Mahon was elected as the women's principal representative from a field of six, with a Miss Laramour elected for the assistants. The number of women at congress that year was also a record, with 24 lady delegates, a big increase from the five there the previous year. Securing women's representation on the CEC in 1907 might seem a clear-cut victory, especially to a movement in its infancy, but it is questionable whether it benefited women teachers' interests in the long run, since as Síle Chuinneagáin notes, it 'stunted the process started by women teachers in 1906/7 of organising and agitating for their rights within the INTO'.[51] The concession had come too early and too easily, which meant that the women had not steeled themselves for the fight from the outset. The result was that when the designated seats for women were removed in 1918, the women members were ill-placed to fight for their places against their male colleagues. For now, however, it was a good opportunity to take on their own issues. Mahon campaigned against a number of matters including the forced teaching of cookery. She was also especially active on the CEC and was at the forefront of the INTO's ongoing recruitment campaign. During the campaign for women's representation on the CEC, she had argued that it would encourage more women to join the organisation, and now she was determined to prove it.[52] Over the course of 1907, INTO membership increased by 1,000, or 15 per cent, to 7,484 at the end of the year.[53] Having recovered from the losses in membership sustained around 1899–1902, it was now stronger than ever, with well over half of teachers now members.

AUGUSTINE BIRRELL: A 'FRIENDLY AND POWERFUL ALLY'

A general election in January 1906 ended a period of Conservative dominance, and it would prove to be one of the most significant elections in modern British history, the new Liberal government bringing in a series of major social and political reforms. Home Rule for Ireland had been taken off the table – it was seriously divisive among Liberals and they were anxious to prevent splits on the issue – but the party had pledged to introduce a significant level of devolution to Ireland. However, despite the Liberal Party's long association with the Irish nationalist cause, its non-conformism, its opposition to state support for religious schools and support for state control of education made many in the Irish hierarchy uneasy. Among them was Bishop O'Dwyer of Limerick, who had called on Irish voters in Britain not to vote for a party whose policies would 'cause the faith of thousands upon thousands of poor Catholic children' to be 'lost in Protestant and infidel schools'.[54] The Liberal landslide in 1906 threatened the Irish system of denominational control of education and the Catholic hierarchy was determined to resist. Their fear was heightened by the new Education Bill for England being guided through the Commons by the new president of the Board of Education, Augustine Birrell. It was designed to cut funding for denominational schools, and the hierarchy saw it as a statement of the new government's intent, although ultimately, the bill fell in the Lords, which had a Conservative majority.

The bill's failure precipitated its sponsor's move to Ireland. A liberal non-conformist by upbringing, described as 'a charming, intelligent, and tolerant man',[55] Birrell's association with the Education Bill meant that his arrival in Ireland was greeted with suspicion among the Catholic hierarchy, who feared that he might attempt something similar in his new role as chief secretary.[56] Perhaps because of this, Birrell was astute enough to make friends with the teachers early on. Having already met an INTO deputation in London in February, Birrell's first public speech as chief secretary was to the 1907 congress at the Rotunda in Dublin. He gave a brilliant address designed to win over the crowd, flattering the teachers, acknowledging their dissatisfaction with the board, praising the Irish language and averting to salaries, promotions and civil rights – all of which left delegates charmed and excited to find themselves with 'such a friendly and powerful ally'.[57] Thanking the delegates for their warm reception, he concluded by hoping that if he stayed in office long enough, he would come before them again 'not only with sympathetic words, but with full hands',[58] setting the bar rather too high, since the chance of the Treasury filling his hands for the benefit of Irish teachers was remote.

As it happened, it took Birrell almost a year to secure extra finance for teachers' salaries. The amount fell far short of what they had hoped,[59] and there was considerable disagreement about how the sum of £114,000 would be allocated among the teachers. Eventually, during the summer of 1908, the CEC decided by a margin of one vote that the funds should be divided equally among teachers, regardless of status, grade, university degrees or averages, and, significantly, paid to men and women at the same rate.[60] The resolution came after fierce wrangling, though. Afterwards, the CEC acknowledged the level of anxiety and upset, which had made the matter 'an exceptionally difficult crisis … when the very existence of the organisation was seriously imperilled'.[61] The divisions over the distribution of the Birrell grant were deep, and remained evident more than a year later, surfacing during the election for central secretary that followed the untimely death of the very capable and highly regarded incumbent, Terence Clarke, in June 1909.[62]

There had been debate during the election over whether the position of central secretary ought to be held by a serving teacher. There was a growing belief that the post had become too onerous for a single person with full-time teaching responsibilities. This argument was not new, but calls for a change had become louder, particularly with the rapid increase in membership. Between 1903 and 1909, the INTO had doubled in size to just over 8,000 members, with an unprecedented two-thirds of teachers having joined.[63] Welcome as this was, nothing had been done to adapt or expand the structures of the organisation to help it cope. There were still no full-time officials, no secretariat and no permanent office. In 1912, the Kilkenny congress voted in favour of a permanent full-time general secretary, but unforeseen events meant that this did not come into action until 1916 (see below).[64] The membership fees were far too low. At three shillings per annum, the INTO subscription was a quarter of that of the National Union of Teachers in England, whose membership continued to rise despite increases in the subscription,[65] but instead of increasing the subscription to pay to run the organisation, it was reduced to 2s 6d the following year.[66] This was a problem at a time when, as well as membership levels increasing, the INTO's services also began to expand. Grants in the case of illness had been introduced in 1906 at a rate of 10 shillings for 20 weeks. These had been instrumental in attracting new members, but they had also drained the old reserve fund dry, to the point of bankruptcy.[67] Eventually, after unsuccessful attempts over several years to establish a benevolent fund, an All-Ireland Prize Draw was set up to raise the capital for a fund. The first draw took place at the 1907 congress and raised £2,000, but this was a fraction of what was needed to sustain the fund,[68] and eventually the scheme closed.

THE MANSFIELD DISMISSAL AND THE DILL ENQUIRY

Remarking on the plight of the Irish national teachers in 1910, the chancellor of the exchequer, David Lloyd George, had said it was discreditable to the empire to have 'teachers plodding all their lives to teach on behalf of the empire at a wage which a navvy would refuse',[69] but the INTO had better relations with government ministers than they ever had with education officials at home. In the autumn of 1910, a misunderstanding between Catherine Mahon and Dr Starkie led to her being barred from INTO deputations to see the resident commissioner, leading the CEC to vote (narrowly) that it would not meet with Starkie as long as he refused to meet certain INTO members. Opinion was divided on the decision. Some, like Mahon herself, felt it was a matter of honour and a point of principle that the commissioner could not be allowed a veto on who represented the organisation and that failing to challenge the veto would lead the INTO to become 'a sort of back-kitchen to Tyrone House'.[70] Others were more pragmatic, and felt it was unnecessarily forcing a fight with Starkie,[71] although an attempt to overturn the decision at a CEC meeting in January 1911 failed. But while INTO stopped sending deputations to the resident commissioner, it started sending deputations to the National Board instead. This was facilitated by Philip Ward, the principal of St Paul's Roman Catholic School in Belfast, who had recently been appointed the first teacher representative on the Board of National Education.

The fraught relations between the INTO and the education administration turned into a full-blown crisis during 1912. When new pay scales were brought in at the turn of the century, a new system of inspection was introduced alongside it, and it became a major grievance among teachers. Promotion and increments depended on the merit marks decided on by inspectors, and there had to be consistency of quality over a three-year period. A bad report could have a serious impact on a teacher's salary and there was general dissatisfaction with the new regime. In addition, a more robust approach to inefficient teachers, which had begun before Starkie (though teachers very much identified him with it), had seen a sharp increase in the number of dismissals by the board from virtually nil to 51 in 1905,[72] and it had become more commonplace to issue teachers with fines.

Concerns about particular inspectors in two of the circuits brought the question to a head.[73] First, teachers in Belfast had complained of a steady decline in merit marks and believed they were being marked harder than the rest of the country. Not long after that, in July 1909, a new inspector, W.H. Welply, arrived in Tipperary, which saw the number of 'goods' awarded fall from 81 per cent to 61 per cent, while the 'excellents' and 'very goods' fell by almost half, from 137 to 70.[74] However, when the Tipperary teachers' case was considered by the Commissioners in December 1911, the teachers found *themselves* censured for failing to make their complaints in a timely fashion, and the Commissioners announced that they would reject any future appeals submitted after a similar delay, an extraordinary response to a legitimate grievance.[75] Unresolved, it remained an issue into 1912. In July 1912, the INTO vice-president, Edmund Mansfield, attended a meeting of the association in Clonmel town hall, at which he complained about the Commissioners fining and degrading the teachers, called for Welply's removal from the circuit and criticised Starkie generally for failing to 'move hand or foot' in the teachers' interests. The meeting itself was private, but Mansfield's remarks were reported in the *Clonmel Chronicle* some days later. On learning of this, the Commissioners demanded that Mansfield publicly repudiate his statements,[76] but Mansfield had spoken in private, and had not broken any rules, so he refused, although he was prepared to express regret that the remarks had been published and to apologise to Welply. This was not enough for the Board of National Education, which voted to dismiss Mansfield from his post as principal of Cullen Boys' School with immediate effect. Philip Ward, the teacher commissioner, was alone in dissenting.

The summary dismissal of the INTO vice-president met with outrage. Mansfield's own inspection record was impeccable, and he had the full support of his manager, who released a letter describing the dismissal as a 'wanton and a tyrannical exercise of authority to ruin such a teacher, his future prospects and family'.[77] Decrying the 'reign of Terror in Tyrone House. Ottoman Tyranny of the National Board',[78] the CEC issued a manifesto calling on the government to reinstate Mansfield, and sought the support of Irish and public bodies and associations. It also demanded an inquiry into the matter and pledged to sustain Mansfield in his position, supported by his manager, until he was reinstated.[79] The national and regional press was strongly supportive of Mansfield,[80] while trade unions, associations and local government bodies were quick to heed the CEC's call for support. Dublin Corporation condemned the dismissal as 'a gross and indefensible tyranny', while other councils and boards of guardians across the country also came out in Mansfield's support, as did local branches of the GAA, the Ancient Order of Hibernians, the United Irish League, land and labour associations and the Gaelic League.[81]

Crucially, there was no political divide on the issue. When an INTO deputation travelled to London to meet Birrell, who had recently told the House of Commons that he had no intention of holding an investigation into the dismissal,[82] they brought with them MPs from all Irish parties, as well as the Labour MP Frank Goldstone, who was organisation secretary of the National Union of Teachers and was there as its representative. Initially disinclined to hold an inquiry, Birrell was unable to resist the call from such a formidable delegation, represented by a united body of opinion, Catholic and Protestant, from the north to the south of the country.[83] Afterwards, he wrote to Starkie, who, along with the Commissioners, was deeply unhappy that the inquiry had been granted, to explain how it had come about, and to confer with him about the terms of reference and the composition of the inquiry. Birrell was candid about his frustration with the teachers as a class. They were, he said, 'the same in all parts of the country. In one aspect I love them, in others I simply loathe them. But there they are and until the end of time they will wear the scars of their profession – vanity and conceit, and an even stronger dash of unscrupulousness than is usually to be found outside the criminal classes.'[84]

Though opposed to Mansfield's dismissal, the INTO welcomed the opportunity the crisis had created. After several years in the doldrums, the controversy energised and unified the organisation, and was the impetus for a badly needed review of education policy.[85] In November, Birrell appointed Sir Samuel Dill, professor of Greek at Queen's College Belfast and chairman of the Committee of Intermediate Education in Ireland, to chair the vice-regal inquiry, and the committee was given its warrant on 21 January 1913. Birrell had had to deal sensitively with putting together a group that would be agreeable to all sides. Among the members were two former INTO activists: former central secretary John Coffey, at this time local government general inspector; and, controversially among the Commissioners and to Starkie, Jeremiah Henly, who had been professor of method in the Church of Ireland Training College in Kildare Place since 1901.[86] The committee's terms were to inquire whether the rules, regulations and practice of the Commissioners with regard to inspection of schools and the awarding of increments and promotion to teacher, and the inspectors' methods, were conducive to sound education, to efficiency on the part of the teachers and to fairness and uniformity in their treatment and to suggest any changes arising from their conclusions. They were also to consider the Commissioners' rules and regulations with regard to teachers' conduct 'and especially as to whether such rules and regulations unduly [restricted] the liberty of the teachers in any respect'.[87]

Sitting for a year, the committee met 65 times, and heard evidence from 65 individuals. The evidence from all sides was full and very frank, and for the INTO it provided an opportunity to record the history of the organisation's relations with Starkie since his arrival, which it described as 'thirteen years of civil war'.[88] President Catherine Mahon was characteristically blunt in her evidence, calling for Starkie to be removed as resident commissioner and describing any attempts to reform the board while he was in situ as akin to 'putting a plaster on a cancer'.[89]

Notwithstanding the vexatious tone of much of the evidence, the end report proved very measured. If either side wished for extravagant vindication of their position, they were to be disappointed, but the teachers' key grievances were acknowledged. The committee advised the present system of grading and promotion be modified to allow for more rapid promotion of able and promising teachers, and that the present system of merit marks for schools and teachers be abolished. It called for automatic annual increments, unless there was a poor report, and a change to the inspection process. However, as Coolahan and O'Donovan note, it failed 'to shed imaginative light on many of the problems that beset the teachers. While minor changes were suggested, the inquiry did not produce a comprehensive analysis of the inspectorate nor of its linkage with the Office administration', so that 'relations between the INTO and Starkie continued to be rancorous and the inspection system continued to be viewed with suspicion and distrust'.[90]

The final Dill Report was published in January 1914, after Ireland had endured a particularly eventful and difficult 12 months. A Home Rule Bill had been introduced in April 1912, sparking militant loyalist reaction. The year 1913 began with the foundation of the Ulster Volunteer Force, a unionist militia which was pledged to resist home rule in Ulster by force, and ended with the establishment of the nationalist Irish Volunteers in November. Not that the divisions in Irish society were based only on nationalism. The Dublin lockout had begun in August 1913, with members of the Irish Transport and General Workers' Union (ITGWU) locked out of their jobs for being members of the union in a dispute that affected some 20,000 workers and their dependants and lasted until the middle of January 1914. The INTO stayed aloof from the dispute, although the *School Weekly* wondered if it was wise or expedient 'in these days of strikes and socialistic doctrines to have a body of discontented teachers' who might be forced to depart from the path of peaceful agitation,[91] and one teacher in Ennis, presumably not a member, had already warned Starkie that she detected a Larkinite echo in the INTO's recent campaign over Mansfield.[92] The Dill Report may have vindicated the national teachers but they found the Board of Education unwilling to make concessions based on its recommendations, and where the board was open to change – on annual (rather than triennial) increments and more rapid promotions – it dragged its heels. Eventually, when war broke out in Europe at the end of the summer, negotiations on the matter were suspended.[93] There was, however, one notable success at this time, when, after some 18 months of negotiations with the British Exchequer, the INTO secured an entirely new superannuated pension scheme based on the civil service scheme, which was operative from 1 October 1914.[94] On salaries, however, things remained stuck, with the Great War scotching any prospective increase and about to become more of a problem, as wartime price increases ate away at the teachers' purchasing power. In the meantime, the demand for monthly (rather than quarterly) salaries continued to fall on deaf ears.[95]

THE INTO IN THE WAR YEARS

War broke out in Europe at the end of July 1914, with Britain declaring war on Germany on 4 August. The conflict, expected to be over in months, drew on for over four years, and changed the political and social landscape to a degree that was unimaginable when it began. The war's impact in Ireland differed from the rest of the United Kingdom. In 1914 there had been 30,000 Irish men in the British armed forces, and 30,000 reservists, including the volunteers who signed up during the course of the war; some 200,000 Irishmen, Catholics and Protestant, fought with the British forces during the war. While conscription was introduced in Britain in 1916, and was threatened in Ireland in 1918, there was no legal compulsion to sign up. Enlistment in Ireland differed significantly by factors such as geography or occupation, but among teachers it was extra-ordinarily low, and was predominantly among those teaching in Protestant schools.[96] The war led to significant hardship on the home front, with shortages of general goods and the cost of living rising steeply throughout the conflict. With wartime inflation rendering salaries increasingly inadequate, questions of pay dominated the INTO's agenda. The fight for increased pay for teachers, and over how it would be distributed, led to intense friction within the organisation, and at one point threatened the INTO's very existence. Later on, INTO unity was challenged by external factors. The Easter Rising in 1916 and the change in the political climate afterwards would have profound consequences for the INTO, in its membership and its status, and fed its growing militancy. The

INTO was changing. By the end of the decade, the organisation was more than 50 years old, which meant fewer and fewer of its early members were still around. The INTO's sense of itself as a purely professional organisation began to change. Members became increasingly frustrated by the old methods of diplomacy that had failed to reap rewards, with the much-vaunted Dill inquiry being one example of an apparent INTO success that had not borne fruit. Revolutions often take place in the space that exists when raised expectations are unmet, and the general lack of progress after Dill, to which was added the hardship of wartime and the growing sense of militancy on the island generally, created a shift in the INTO that eventually resulted in it becoming a legally recognised trade union, embarking on its first strikes in 1918.

The poor morale of the teachers had interesting consequences. The Board of Education's refusal to reinstate Edmund Mansfield, dismissed in October 1912, was a persistent sore point. One Commissioner confided to Starkie in October 1915 that:

> The discontent of a large section of the teachers is, I hear, having serious effects in directions other than the educational. A friend of mine who has been on a recruiting campaign and visited twenty-three counties tells me that in about every instance where there was active hostility to the recruiting movement, the teacher or teachers in the district were suspected of influencing opinion.[97]

Quite apart from any involvement by teachers in popular anti-recruitment work, the number of national teachers signing up was incredibly low. In response to a parliamentary question from James Craig in August 1918, it emerged that only 59 Irish teachers had enlisted since the outbreak of war four years earlier. In contrast, some 6,000 teachers in England had volunteered in the first year of the war alone.[98] Of those 59, six taught in model schools, 40 were serving in schools under Protestant management and 13 were from schools under Catholic management. There were also around 60 people who were qualified as national teachers but who were not teaching at the time, while there were some 26 students from training colleges, of whom 18 were in Marlborough Street and eight in the Church of Ireland College.[99] The most prominent INTO activist to enlist was Con MacSweeny (Conn Mac Suibhne), a Gaelic League activist from County Cork, who was principal of Aughrim Boys' School in Wicklow and who had been on the executive since 1910. A Redmondite, he was appointed to a war commission in the British army in 1915, and served with the Royal Irish Fusiliers, with subsequent postings in Greece and Egypt, before he returned to teaching in 1920.[100] As a Catholic who had enlisted, MacSweeny was atypical among the teaching body, and if Protestant teachers were vastly under-represented in comparison with their co-religionists in other professions, the attitude towards the war and towards loyalty to the Empire was sharply divided on religious lines, particularly in the last two years of the conflict, as a result of the Easter Rising of 1916 and the conscription crisis in April 1918.

Even if the Mansfield business was not the cause of the disaffection, the time had come, as another Commissioner, the Bishop of Clogher, observed, to settle the matter so as to 'allay the continued smouldering discontent now spreading over all teachers throughout Ireland'.[101] Eventually, as it was approaching its fourth year, the case was resolved, if not quite amicably, in the autumn of 1915. At a meeting between an INTO deputation and the Commissioners, a member of the INTO side put an offer on the table that Mansfield would return to work, if permitted, without back pay. This conceded far less than they had always demanded, namely that Mansfield would return to work only if he was paid the arrears for the period of his dismissal. Mansfield himself was a reluctant part of this bargain, and others were deeply unhappy at events, the most vociferous being Catherine Mahon, who ultimately did not stand again for the CEC at the next election, such was her opposition to the compact.[102]

T.J. O'CONNELL, THE INTO'S FIRST GENERAL SECRETARY

Edmund Mansfield had been elected central secretary unopposed at Easter 1913 following his dismissal but he was clear that he would step down from the position on his reinstatement in school, which he did.[103] The contest for his successor was very significant. A decision by the 1912 congress to appoint a full-time, permanent secretary from the following year had been held over for Mansfield's tenure, but in January 1916, the CEC began to make plans for a contest. Candidates would be selected from among teacher candidates who had 'shown zeal and energy in the interests of the organisation', and their duties would include not only the clerical work of the office but such work as the CEC might direct from time to time.[104] They would work from suitable offices in Dublin (not yet secured), which would also be used for meetings of the CEC and the benevolent fund. Ten men originally put themselves forward as candidates, the nominations being led by T.J. O'Connell of Streamstown, the District 6 representative since 1910.[105]

O'Connell had come to national prominence in the organisation some years earlier, when he was at the forefront of a campaign to abolish Rule 92(j), introduced in April 1911, which compelled pregnant teachers to take three months' leave before and after childbirth, and to pay for a substitute. This rule was unpopular with married women teachers, and O'Connell had direct experience of its consequences when his wife was not allowed to return to work after losing their newborn child in February 1912. When the rule was eventually withdrawn towards the end of the year, O'Connell was given much of the credit.[106] Having put himself forward for the position of central secretary in 1913, only to withdraw in favour of Mansfield, O'Connell immediately led the field when he threw his hat in in 1916. He was followed by James Hegarty, the bottom five candidates securing between one and six associations each.[107] When no candidate secured a majority in the first ballot, the contest went to a second poll, where O'Connell and Hegarty went head to head. Hegarty, the older of the two, positioned himself as 'a tried and proved man' with a 30-year record, having worked tirelessly on the CEC. At 33, O'Connell had less experience but great energy, and had proved himself an effective campaigner during the drive against Rule 92(j), which helped win him support among women teachers. He managed to secure support across other sections too, appealing directly to young teachers, assistant teachers and teachers in rural schools. Hegarty warned that the INTO was in an extremely precarious condition: 'Don't add to its difficulties and dangers by electing untried men to positions where tact, prudence and indeed caution are essential concomitants,'[108] but in the end, O'Connell secured 55 per cent of the vote. Elected the organisation's first full-time permanent secretary, he would remain in situ for the next three decades. Young and energetic, he was well placed to lead the INTO into a new phase, for if Hegarty was correct that tact and prudence would be crucial for the good of the organisation, maybe caution seemed less appealing, while some felt a 'more aggressive policy' was necessary.[109]

Plans to secure a premises for the general secretary (the CEC changed the title of the post from central secretary in September 1916) to work from did not come to fruition – Dublin was not the easiest place to secure property in 1916 – and for his first two years in the post, O'Connell worked from Streamstown, while the CEC continued to hold its meetings in the Gaelic League offices in Parnell Square. It was only in November 1918, after the INTO had purchased 9 Gardiner Place, that O'Connell moved to Dublin, he and his family living in the upstairs flat in the building. A shorthand typist was taken on soon after the new headquarters was set up, and in 1922 they were joined by a full-time treasurer when the long-standing treasurer David Elliott retired and was replaced by Mairead Ashe, a cousin of nationalist icon Thomas Ashe. The difference in having a full-time secretary with a permanent head office can scarcely be exaggerated. Many years later, T.J. O'Connell recalled his first meeting on the CEC in 1910, which took place around a rickety table in the back room of a building on Fleet Street. On that occasion he encountered then-secretary Michael Doyle of Ballymote 'at the foot of the stairs burdened with a particularly heavy suit-case which, he said contained the account books and other official documents as well as correspondence to be placed before the meeting'.[110] Later in 1910, the INTO had been fortunate in securing a commodious meeting room which it rented from the Gaelic League at its headquarters in 25 Parnell Square but its move to Gardiner Place meant that after 50 rather peripatetic years, the INTO had finally made a home for itself.

'THE SCHOOLMASTERS' REBELLION'

O'Connell's election took place just after the Easter congress of 1916, a gathering which was distinctly overshadowed by events in Dublin. Congress was held in Cork, and many delegates found themselves unable to make their way there – one principal from Moygashel had been caught up in the thick of things and spent most of the week sheltering in an Amiens Street restaurant – while those who had managed to get there were inevitably distracted, eager to get news of what had happened.[111] A very small number of national teachers had taken part in the Rising, most notably the principal of Corduff NS, Thomas Ashe of the Dublin Central Association. Ashe was one of around a dozen national teachers arrested in the aftermath of the rebellion (and only one of two ever to be convicted of an offence), one of whom had been in Cork at congress during Easter week and was later detained in error. But if only a very few national teachers had taken part in the Rising, they found the spotlight shone on them nonetheless when afterwards the provost of Trinity College, J.P. Mahaffy, accused the teachers of having inspired the rebels with their seditious teaching in schools, dubbing the Rising 'the Schoolmasters' Rebellion'. His ill-founded claims were rebutted by the INTO president George Ramsay,[112] but were serious enough to prompt an investigation by the Board of Education. Mahaffy refused to come before the board to substantiate his claims and ultimately the board found that from about '5,700 men school teachers' (women, clearly, did not represent a threat to national security) only two or three cases of 'disloyal teaching had been found', and only six teachers had their recognition withdrawn. (One of these, Michael Thornton, or Mícheál Ó Droighneáin, was reinstated, with INTO support, in 1920.)[113]

But if the INTO did not make a statement in support of the Rising, neither did it condemn it, and there was a considerable difference between the organisation as a whole and the IPNTU, which passed a motion at its annual conference in June declaring its 'whole-hearted and unaltered loyalty and devotion to our King and Empire, and our indignant condemnation of a section of our countrymen in trying to raise a rebellion in Ireland at the dictation of, and with the assistance of Germany'.[114] The Rising also put an end to Augustine Birrell's time as chief secretary in Ireland. Perhaps the most sympathetic of the chief secretaries towards Ireland and to teachers, while his period in office began so optimistically, this was a distant memory by the end of his term, when he was tired and distracted. Birrell's departure ended a period of stability in the Dublin Castle regime, as he was followed by a succession of relatively short-lasting occupants. Of course, quite apart from the change in the government personnel, the Rising changed attitudes and the politics of the country over the next few years, and within the INTO, a division of opinion would emerge between the majority of members and some of the Protestant teachers in the north-east of the country.

THE FLANAGAN AND FANORE DISMISSALS

As well as the major issue of securing a war bonus, the new general secretary had to deal with two notable dismissal cases. One, which had just begun, but would be long-running, was that of Mrs Kate Flanagan, an assistant teacher in Kilkeel, County Down. There had been an informal ban on married women teachers in the diocese of Down and Connor during the episcopacy of Dr John Tohill (1878–1914). Around Christmas 1915, some time after his death, the CEC approached Dr MacRory, the new bishop (and future cardinal), with a view to having the marriage ban withdrawn. While MacRory was prepared to withdraw the regulation, he left the implementation of the ban up to individual managers.[115] Mrs Flanagan, then Miss McAlinden, married on 22 January 1916, having had no indication that her manager, Fr McAlister, would not support her continued employment in the school. To her great surprise, on 30 March he served her with three months' notice of dismissal, with no reason. When Mrs Flanagan approached the INTO for help, the organisation was told by MacRory that the matter was one for individual managers, and he could not oblige them to retain a teacher, nor was he prepared to hear an appeal under the Maynooth Resolution. There was a lengthy correspondence between O'Connell and MacRory, printed in a pamphlet prior to congress in 1917, but the bishop was unyielding and the case dragged on into 1919.

The other famous case from the time was that of Michael O'Shea in Fanore, who, similarly, seemed to have been dismissed over the question of a marriage. The Fanore dismissal became notorious locally and in INTO folklore and beyond, recorded in books, ballads and in a television documentary.[116] O'Shea had been the principal of a two-teacher school in Fanore NS, a remote school in north-west Clare.[117] In September 1914, he was dismissed by the parish priest. By O'Shea's account, this was because he had sought permission to marry a local woman, Katie McDonagh, when the priest had wanted him to marry his assistant teacher, Miss Leonard. The priest denied this account and claimed instead that O'Shea had a drink problem. Having fought his case alone at the start, O'Shea then looked to the INTO for help. The case was taken up by the North Clare association (among them P.J. Lenihan, who would become grandfather of two future education ministers) and subsequently by the CEC, but the bishop refused to reinstate O'Shea. The case led to great bitterness locally, with parents sending their children to a 'shed school' run by O'Shea rather than the parish school. In turn, the local bishop refused to confirm any child who went to O'Shea's. The case is too labyrinthine to do it justice here, but it has been forensically examined by Joe Queally and features in Breandán Ó hÉithir's *Begrudger's Guide to Irish Politics*.

What was clear from both cases was that that while the Maynooth Resolution generally prevented arbitrary dismissals, there was still no compulsion to abide by it; and when it did not work, it did not work at all. As a result, the individual cases and the wider question of the Maynooth Resolution took up a great deal of time at the 1916 congress and at congress the following year, when one delegate expressed the hope that 'the war in Fanore is over before the Great War'.[118] It wasn't. Following the 1916 congress, the CEC attempted to secure a revision of the Maynooth Resolution, in effect to make it legally binding, and demanding that in every case the teacher should be entitled to a fair trial in the presence of their accusers before the dismissal notice was issued, after which they should have a final appeal to the bench of bishops.[119] The bishops' response failed to deal with the substantive issue,[120] and congress returned to the matter the following year, passing a very similar resolution to that of the previous year and instructing the CEC to enter into negotiations with the hierarchy with a view to securing acceptance of the National Board's form of agreement, a fair trial in the presence of accusers in dismissal cases, and the right to appeal to the bishop. Significantly, the discussion over the Maynooth Resolution broke a taboo that had been in effect for more than ten years, when two of the ecclesiastical provinces lifted their ban on INTO membership following the controversy over tenure. The renewed discussion was a consequence of the two disputes in particular (and there were others less notable), but also of the rising temperature in the organisation more generally. As one delegate from Clare put it, referring to Fanore, 'our organisation should look to our wounded soldiers. It should be a militant organisation – truly militant and truly powerful – and strong in faith because it has the support of the right of truth and justice.'[121] For their part, the Catholic bishops refused to meet a CEC deputation to discuss the matter and, asserting that the Maynooth Resolution gave ample protection to Catholic national teachers, they declined to take any further steps in the matter.[122] The issue effectively ground to a halt thereafter, as dissatisfaction over salaries and the war bonus became increasingly acute and other matters were put aside.

PAY AND SECTIONALISM

By the summer of 1916, inflation had risen by 65 per cent and, like many people, teachers were finding it difficult to make ends meet. Civil servants had been awarded their first war bonus in July 1915, and teachers were looking for something similar. Eventually, in December 1916, the INTO managed to secure a war bonus, which, unlike the civil servants' bonus, would be paid equally to men and women.[123] The question of equal pay was hard fought by the women teachers. The Treasury's initial offer in October had been to give women teachers half the bonus being offered to men, but, as Catherine Mahon told the CEC at the time, were they 'to act, or act only in a half-hearted, unsuccessful manner' it would be difficult for their sisters in the organisation to see the benefit in continuing their membership, contributing equally to its funds and sharing equal responsibility for its liabilities.[124] This was not an idle threat; at this time in England, there had already been a breakaway of women teachers from the NUT after it had refused to support equal pay as a principle. Women were a majority in the INTO and even if the CEC felt it could do without them in its associations or committees, it could not do without their fees. Throughout October the women teachers campaigned in the national press and the *School Weekly* for their equal bonus, demonstrating, as Síle Chuinneagáin observes, a willingness to fight for the equal bonus themselves rather than rely solely on INTO procedures.[125]

The war bonus was welcomed, but was 'a drop in the ocean of necessity', and the long fight to secure it sucked any goodwill out of the award.[126] It was a greater victory for the women teachers, who had had to fight harder on a point of principle, but there was annoyance in the CEC at least about the women's behaviour, with president George Ramsay remarking that 'the equal rate has been won, not by hysterical appeals in the press advocating one plan of campaign after another … but by reason and arguments placed in black and white before the chancellor of the exchequer', deploring the 'vague threats and hints for marking out a line of future action for the women teachers as separate from the men'.[127] Ramsay argued that the idea of designated CEC seats for women was from 'the old-fashioned days', and the time had come for direct representation. Following lengthy consideration on the best form of representation on the CEC, a scheme was put before the 1917 congress, and a revised version eventually adopted at the 1919 congress. In it, there would be four districts, roughly coinciding with the four provinces, and each would return a principals' representative and an assistants' representative (including JAMs). It would have no designated places for lady teachers.[128] Promoted as a scheme that gave equality to all members, in effect it seriously reduced women's representation on the CEC, and there were a number of lengthy periods up to the 1980s when there was not a single woman representative on the CEC.

Part of the resentment towards women was that they had succeeded in securing an equal bonus. What was to stop any other group who felt neglected doing likewise? Other sectional groups began to emerge. There was an Assistants' Union, soon joined by a Principal Teachers' Union, with branches in Dublin, Belfast and Cork, one for undergraded teachers, the union of diplomees, the transition teachers and the paper-promoted teachers.[129] A rural teachers' union was proposed but never came to fruition and, notably, no women's union had emerged. The Protestant National Teachers' Union might seem to have been a precedent, but that had arisen out of very different circumstances. It was established in an effort to quarantine the question of tenure for Protestant teachers, so as to protect organisation and maintain unity. What existed in 1917 was the opposite: competing sections of teachers prepared to fight the others in the distribution of a sum of £381,000 known as the Duke Grant. Eventually, after two special conferences between the different groups, a compromise was reached which rather crudely removed the source of competition within the organisation, but appeals for unity continued nonetheless. As it turned out, a split was on the horizon, but its origins were political, not material.

THE INTO JOINS THE LABOUR MOVEMENT

Until now, the INTO was not a registered trade union. At the first special conference on the distribution of the Duke Grant, some delegates suggested that the organisation would be stronger as part of the trade union movement and should affiliate with the Irish Trade Union Congress (ITUC), which had been founded in 1894. Following discussion in private, the question was put out for discussion at the associations' October meetings, and was followed by a ballot in November. The CEC produced a circular giving the case for affiliation. It argued that the INTO was a trade union in all but name anyway, and that joining the ITUC would make it stronger while leaving the organisation 'absolutely independent within itself'.[130] As well as looking at practical implications, such as fees, it also looked at the question of social status, advising that affiliation would not require teachers to personally associate with members of any other trade unions, and that affiliation would 'not imply any more than it does now, that the teacher would have to spend his evenings in company with, say, the dock labourer or coal-heaver'. But apart from assuaging concerns about the implications for teachers' professional status – or snobbery, if one is less kind – one of the big issues was the question of 'religion and politics', and here the circular was quite misleading. The claim that the ITUC and all trades councils were 'non-political and non-sectarian' was, as far the first part was concerned, simply untrue. Though first established in 1894 purely as a parliament of labour, ITUC had also been a political party since 1914, when it had renamed itself the Irish Trade Union Congress and Labour Party (ITUC&LP). Although it had not yet contested any national elections by 1917, it was its intention to do so, and this had implications for an organisation whose rules declared it non-political. As for the 'non-sectarian' question, the ITUC&LP was not sectarian or denominational, but while it had long endeavoured to strike a delicate balance between the unionist and nationalist opinions, this was difficult to sustain as the distance between the two sides grew after 1916. The INTO voted to affiliate by 56 per cent, a majority but by no means a large one.[131] On 1 December, following a lengthy discussion on the matter, the CEC meeting resolved to take the steps necessary for affiliation. Only one dissenting vote was cast against the action, that of Isaac McLoughlin from Portadown, who was also the honorary secretary of the IPNTU. This was an indicator of trouble to come. Significantly, the decision to affiliate with the ITUC&LP came only weeks after the October revolution in

Russia, and many of the more conservative members of the INTO became deeply concerned once they realised that the organisation had conjoined with a body that was quite enthusiastic about the Bolsheviks.

During the discussion over whether the INTO ought to become a trade union, the notion of striking had been raised often. Many teachers were reluctant to consider the idea, feeling a duty of care towards the children but also believing that 'their profession was superior to strikes', points of view that arise frequently among teachers over the years, irrespective of place.[132] Others, feeling that traditional methods had proved ineffective, believed that strikes were a necessary weapon in their fight against the treasury. At the end of October 1917, the CEC began to canvass the local associations about holding a strike. This was quite a departure and, as the *Independent* remarked, 'when men of their intelligence and education contemplate such a step their outlook must be dark indeed'.[133] When the majority of responses were positive, the CEC began to privately organise for a strike fund and consider how the strike would operate, with a proposal that, following a ballot, only Dublin teachers, and possibly those in Belfast and Cork, would go on a general strike.[134] Starkie thought they were 'all bluffing',[135] but he was mistaken. After a White Paper containing the details of the Duke Salary Grant Scheme was published in December 1917, the CEC rejected it and called a strike ballot. The ballot was enough for the chief secretary to intervene, and he announced an ad hoc inquiry into education in Ireland similar to one recently held in Scotland, which the INTO had demanded.[136] After a few months' delay the full commission was announced in August 1918, and held its first meeting the next month. Its chair was Lord Killanin, a member of the National Board, who, when he attended the INTO congress earlier in the year, had told delegates (to friendly laughter) that the teachers had the 'entire sympathy of the Board in making a fair and reasonable claim that they should receive proper remuneration for their work'.[137] There were five clergy, one Trinity professor, one Belfast businessman, two government representatives (Bonaparte Wyse from Tyrone House and Maurice Headlam representing the Treasury) and seven teachers (41 per cent, somewhat more than the 25 per cent representation that Starkie had advised).[138]

While the Killanin Commission examined the general question of salaries, the matter of a second war bonus was still outstanding, however, and by September 1918 the teachers' patience was exhausted. The CEC called on members to withdraw from work on Wednesday 2 October 1918 as a sort of pre-strike strike, with teachers expected to attend local branch meetings, where they would sign a pledge to go on general strike from 4 November if the war bonus on civil service terms was not paid before then.[139] The action had the broad support of the trade union movement, politicians, some members of the clergy (including members of the hierarchy) and the popular press, and was lauded excitedly as 'Independence Day' in the organisation. The teachers withdrew their labour on 2 October, but by then the Treasury had already admitted defeat. It waived its objection to the teachers' claim being heard by the Conciliation and Arbitration Board, which ultimately granted the teachers a war bonus, payable from July that year, in November, and a second award in February.[140]

THE CONSCRIPTION CRISIS

'Independence Day' was the INTO's first industrial action, but its first ever strike had taken place the previous April – although this was political rather than industrial. Following Germany's spring offensive on the Western Front in March 1918, the British government decided the time had come to extend conscription to Ireland. The bill to introduce conscription was to go before the Commons on 10 April, and was opposed across nationalist Ireland, from the IPP to Sinn Féin, the Catholic hierarchy and various cultural bodies, with the ITUC&LP one of the foremost organisations in the campaign. As well as an anti-conscription pledge, modelled on the unionists' Ulster Solemn League and Covenant, there was a general strike on Tuesday 23 April. No doubt wary of hostile eyes from the National Board or elsewhere, the CEC encouraged INTO members to put their weight behind the anti-conscription effort in terms which were vague yet unmistakable: 'that at this critical and momentous period in the history of our country, we advise all the members of the organisation to throw in their lot with their fellow countrymen in their various localities, exercise their civil rights to the fullest extent and refuse further to be silent when such issues are at stake'.[141] The IPNTU, however, was vehemently opposed to the INTO's position against conscription, and when its executive met on 27 April, it passed a resolution condemning the CEC for recommending that 'the young men of Ireland shirk their duty to the empire in its time of danger'.[142] This reflected the feeling in the country at large, for while the strike against conscription was broadly observed, in the north-east it was business as usual. The IPNTU's conference in June signalled that it would secede from the organisation if the INTO did not withdraw its support for the anti-conscription campaign and adhere to the organisation's rule that it was non-political and non-sectarian. The anti-conscription campaign succeeded in making it clear that enlistment in Ireland would have to remain voluntary, and the campaign wound down, but the INTO's affiliation to the ITUC&LP remained controversial.

FROM THE GREAT WAR TO THE WAR OF INDEPENDENCE

The armistice was signed on 11 November 1918, but in Ireland this marked a new phase of upheaval. First came the political earthquake that followed the general election on 14 December. This was the first national election to be fought by Sinn Féin, which had won six of nine by-elections in the previous two years, and now took 73 seats; the Irish Party took six and the Unionists 26. This meant there were now only 32 Irish MPs in Westminster, and raised the prospect of a new, independent and illegal parliament – and government – in Ireland. There were now two governments in Ireland: that of Dublin Castle or Whitehall, which was still responsible for paying the teachers' salaries; and the parallel government set up by Dáil Éireann. The existence of Dáil Éireann, and the political movement based on a refusal to recognise the British state's authority in Ireland, made negotiating with Dublin Castle or London problematic. This became sharply apparent when the British government tried to legislate for the Killanin Commission's recommendations.

Some weeks after the 1918 general election, the first Dáil met in the Mansion House in Dublin on 19 January 1919, with many of the newly elected representatives in jail in Britain or on the run. Events in Tipperary that same day marked the beginning of the War of Independence. For more than four years, there would be military and political conflict in Ireland, during which time the island was partitioned, with a parliament established in Northern Ireland and subsequently the Free State set up in the South. Inevitably, this had consequences for the INTO. Some members of the organisation fought in the War of Independence; perhaps 40 of them were interned as a result, and at least one was shot as an informer by one of his colleagues.[143] In common with other unions, the INTO did not pay direct grants or benefits to interned members from union funds, as they had not been imprisoned as a result of their jobs and such payments would have been illegal. However, the 1921 congress established a special voluntary fund to support internee members. The CEC also secured support from The Educational Company, Browne & Nolan's and Fallon Bros, and organised for textbooks, writing materials, blackboards and chalk to be sent to camps where INTO members were held, to enable them to teach lessons, notably in Irish and history, to other internees.[144]

The 1918 election proved the catalyst in the breaking away of significant northern Protestant support for the INTO. Having renamed itself to reflect the importance of its political role, the Irish Labour Party and Trade Union Congress (ILP&TUC) had stood aside at the general election to allow a straight fight between the separatist Sinn Féin Party and the Irish Party. This followed William O'Brien's presidential address at the ILP&TUC congress at Waterford in August 1918 in which he spoke positively of the anti-conscription campaign, praised James Connolly and his fellow rebels, criticised the internment of political prisoners and not only welcomed the Russian Revolution the previous year, but pointed to the influence of the Irish Rising on the Bolsheviks.[145] On 1–2 November, the ILP&TUC held a special congress to discuss Labour's election strategy (that is, would it stand in the election), which also expelled the Sailors' and Firemen's Union because its members in the English docks had refused to transport British Labour delegates to a meeting of the Internationale in Stockholm. The proceedings also saw various statements in support of the Russian Revolution and references to foreign tyranny.[146] This was the last straw for the Lisburn Association, which announced that it was seceding from the INTO on 25 November 1918.[147] Meeting five days later, the CEC spent three hours discussing the situation, now with two northern associations having ceded and others threatening to join them, but by the end the executive had only resolved to talk to the associations about the 'misunderstanding' caused by 'inaccurate and misleading press reports' relating to the ILP&TUC congress in November. Representatives from Banbridge, Tyrone Central and Lisburn then attended the next CEC meeting on 20 December.[148] It was fanciful to imagine that this approach would suffice since it ignored the deep and well-founded concerns about the political leanings of the organisation as a whole, which had seen former IPNTU president Isaac McLoughlin resign from the CEC at the end of October.[149] Indeed, it is difficult not to suggest that the CEC was being rather disingenuous in how it portrayed the dispute, as though some ill-written press reports were at the heart of the problem. Speaking at the Easter congress in 1919, T. Stanage from Banbridge began by highlighting the work he personally had done to resolve the tensions between the two sides, without which the split in the north would be 'a great deal greater'. Spelling it out for the other delegates, he explained:

What we object to was this: we belong to a non-political organisation, and I say that at the meeting of the Trades Congress the very first thing was to send a wire to the Bolshevists congratulating them on the work they are doing. We object to that, and say our delegates had no right to sit at a meeting such as that. Labour stood down entirely at the general election, and we object to that. We want to remain part of an organisation outside politics. We are driving too fast at present.[150]

By now, four associations – Coleraine, Lisburn, Londonderry and Newtownards – had severed their connection with the INTO,[151] but this had not caused undue concern in the organisation as a whole. Perhaps this was partly because sectionalism had become so prevalent in the organisation and the four associations' initial efforts to bring others with them had been unsuccessful, but it also seemed that in the increasingly political climate, unity was no longer a priority. Trouble arose on Thursday morning at Congress when a delegate from Newcastle West moved to suspend standing orders to draw attention to the general strike taking place in the city at that time, known as the Limerick Soviet, which had begun after the city was proclaimed a special military area under the Defence of the Realm Act from 15 April. Many delegates demanded a statement in the strike's support, but the president argued that they should wait until the ILP&TUC executive had released its own, with northern delegates appealing to congress not to make a terrible mistake by forcing a resolution. Amidst cries of 'let them go' and 'cut them out', Mr W. Thornberry from County Tyrone warned that if the resolution was carried there would 'not be four associations, but every association in which there is a majority holding views to the contrary' would leave.[152] The debate was deferred, but when it resumed the next day, there was no meeting of minds. Arguing that supporting the strike in Limerick was not political but 'about the right of labour to earn their bread', Edmund Mansfield was uncompromising:

> Unity was very good but if it came to a question of principle then let them scrap unity (applause). He protested against the bogey of unity being brought forward to cow the majority who were entitled on democratic grounds to rule any organised body. Let them have unity, but let principle, right and justice prevail even if the organisation went 'bang'.[153]

Eventually, an immediate crisis was averted when the motion was referred back to the CEC, but the debate was worrying. Nevertheless, most Protestant teachers remained reluctant to break away. In May 1919, representatives of the four breakaway associations met with the IPNTU, urging the Protestant union to widen its basis 'so as to form an organisation for Protestant teachers and all who object to connection with the Irish Labour council', but when, after lengthy debate, a motion to this effect was put to the IPNTU's annual conference in June, it was defeated by 31 votes to 17.[154] Members of the four seceding associations and other individuals, including the former IPNTU secretary Isaac McLoughlin, met in Belfast on 19 July 1919 to form the Ulster National Teachers' Union, later to become the Ulster Teachers' Union (UTU). As the historian of the UTU has noted, 'but for the political backcloth of Ireland at this period, history would suggest that the union would, like its predecessor the Northern Union of Irish National Teachers, eventually reunite with the INTO as its parent body', and no doubt this was the feeling of the majority of the CEC.[155] In the short term, the INTO's position remained reasonably secure in the north-east, with the UTU thought to have had a membership of around 500 at the beginning of 1921.[156] The INTO, on the other hand, had more than five times that. The situation would only change in the other direction after partition a few years later.

FIGHTING FOR REFORM: THE KILLANIN COMMISSION AND THE MACPHERSON BILL

In February 1919, the Killanin Commission submitted its final report. Dubbed by one newspaper a 'revolutionary scheme', it conceded many of the pay principles sought by the INTO, notably a considerable salary increase, based on a revised scale, for all teachers, along with allowances for qualifications and responsibility and extra increments at the maximum of the scale. It made recommendations on the pension scheme and improved residences, and in other non-pay-related matters made suggestions regarding school attendance and the funding of the primary school system. One area it explicitly avoided was the management question, which would inevitably limit the scope of any reforms.[157] Maurice Headlam, who represented the Treasury on the committee, complained to Starkie:

> All the teachers on the Primary committee agreed with me, privately, that no good would come in Irish education till we have got rid of the autocratic powers of the managers, till we have a unified department, and till we get local interest and local rates. But when it came to backing their opinions by signing my reservations all except one Belfast teacher were frightened to give their name. I must say I never despised a body of men more.[158]

There was a long and frustrating wait for the chief secretary to act on the committee's recommendations, but the delay was because of the scale of the task, with the bill representing the most radical attempt to reform the Irish education system. Finally, on 24 November 1918, the Macpherson Education Bill received its first reading. It provided for something the INTO had campaigned for for decades, namely the dissolution of the hated National Board, along with the Intermediate Board and the Department of Agriculture and Technical Instruction (DATI), which would be replaced by a central Department of Education. The chief secretary would be its president, and there would be two vice-presidents, one representing DATI and another who was not specified. This meant placing Irish education 'entirely under the thumb of a Minister ... who would probably be an Englishman'. Nationalist reaction was predictably negative.[159] Alongside the new department there would also be an advisory council and education committees in each county, which would be responsible for striking a local rate for education, but the management of individual schools remained unchanged. Moreover, in a bid to see off clerical concerns, the bill guaranteed the continuation of denominational teaching in schools.[160] Before the bill was published, Starkie warned Macpherson to prepare himself for furious opposition from the Catholic hierarchy as well as the secretary of DATI, pointing out Bishop Foley's words to a recent meeting of the National Board that 'any bill proposing to make Mr Macpherson responsible to parliament for education would be blown sky high'.[161]

Though publicly circumspect, the INTO was privately delighted with the bill, which was like an INTO shopping list promising proper statutory funding for primary education; improved salaries, pensions and housing for teachers; a scheme for compulsory attendance; a provision for 'the proper heating, cleaning, repairing, lighting and general sanitation of national schools and the provision of school books and requisites (and meals where necessary) for children'; as well as special schools for the education of 'afflicted children'; 'continuation schools for young people whose early education has been neglected'; and a scheme of scholarships for children continuing to intermediate or technical schools.[162] The bill was welcomed by the Protestant Churches and in the unionist press – the *Freeman's Journal* noted the 'Orange delight' over its contents[163] – but among every section of national opinion it was fiercely opposed. The nationalist press, the Irish Party, the Catholic Church and even the ILP&TUC all came out against the bill, which they complained would place Irish education under direct English control, under a department which could be led by any kind of man – whether Orange, Jewish or atheist.[164] The ILP&TUC executive met the day after the Bill's publication and condemned it as 'reactionary and bureaucratic, making a mockery of the Irish people and their demand for a genuinely National and democratic education system',[165] without any consultation with the INTO, its affiliate, which would be directly affected by the bill. The teachers protested, but to no effect. Just as Starkie had predicted, the most significant opposition came from the Catholic hierarchy. Meeting on 9 December, the standing committee of the Irish bishops denounced the bill. Playing the green card, it asserted that the bill had been brought forward 'at the instigation of an intolerant minority', who were attempting to take Irish education away from a board 'composed of Irishmen who know Ireland' and put it in 'foreign fetters'.[166] The bishops' call to arms was followed by the handful of Home Rule MPs left in the Commons, led by Joe Devlin, who managed to filibuster the second reading of the bill on 16 December. This meant it could not be reintroduced that session, although soon after Bonar Law announced that it would be reintroduced as soon as possible in the next session.[167]

Before Christmas, Bishop Hallinan of Limerick had predicted that the teachers as a body would 'rise up in their anger and refuse to touch this unholy thing', but he was mistaken.[168] The CEC issued a statement in the new year which outlined why the INTO supported the bill, arguing that there was little difference between a National Board appointed entirely by the lord lieutenant and a Department nominated entirely by the government.[169] However, while the CEC as a whole fully supported the bill, voices began to emerge against it, beginning with a few anonymous letters to the press, but escalating when Catherine Mahon – who was a staunch separatist – came out in opposition in a letter printed in the *Irish Independent* on 20 January 1920. In it she accused the CEC of having issued an 'apology for the British government in Ireland' and reminded readers of a time when starving people were presented with an ultimatum of 'no reformation, no soup', causing 'two millions of them' to die howling for bread.[170] This emotive and wounding correspondence began a controversy in the letters pages that went on for several weeks, with T.J. O'Connell and Tom Nunan among the CEC on the one side, and Mahon and J.F. O'Farrell, formerly of the CEC, on the other. Mahon had made a number of libellous accusations in the course of her letters, most notably that O'Connell and Nunan had been bribed to support the bill in exchange for jobs in the new department. Mahon having refused to withdraw the accusations, on 20 March the CEC pledged funds to the general secretary and the president for a libel action against their former president.[171] There was considerable discomfort at the idea of INTO funds being used to sue one of its members, still less a former president – when the matter came before congress later that Easter, one delegate described 'the matter of Miss Mahon' as 'the most painful any committee ever brought before them' – but there was also a feeling that Mahon had attacked not only O'Connell and Nunan, but the organisation as a whole. In the end, Mahon, possibly because of her Sinn Féin beliefs, refused to co-operate with the action, held as it was under the British court system, and an interlocutory judgment was recorded against her. No damages were sought and the legal fees were paid by the INTO.[172]

Collectively and individually, the bishops continued to rail against the bill. At the end of January, a meeting of the hierarchy condemned the bill as 'the most denationalising scheme since the Act of Union'.[173] The bill was reintroduced in the Commons on 24 February 1919, to protests from Joe Devlin,[174] and three days later, Cardinal Logue wrote to his brother bishops, in a circular published in the *Independent* the following week. The issue at stake was not merely temporal, he observed, but the 'eternal interests of generations of the children of Ireland', and as such 'this Bill should be resisted by all the legitimate means at our disposal'. This time, rather than appeal to notions of nationalism, Logue put the case against the bill as one of parental rights against the state. 'Though we have not yet, thank God, arrived at the stage dreamt of by the extreme socialists,' he observed, 'when the children of the people shall become the mere chattels of the state, the bill in question seems to tend notably in that direction.' The Sinn Féin MPs' abstentionism made resisting in parliament impossible, so it 'only remains, therefore, for us to fall back on the active and earnest co-operation of our faithful people'.[175] Where Starkie had (ironically) told Macpherson that 'nothing less than the special intervention of the Almighty' would persuade the country to accept his bill, now Cardinal Logue sought divine aid to save the country from 'the threatened calamity'.[176] To this end, he proclaimed a solemn novena in honour of St Patrick and suggested a special appeal to God after the last mass on Passion Sunday. The nationalist papers were full of the bishops' ban on the bill and the proclamation of the novena, but the INTO made no comment. O'Connell later recalled:

> [W]hile the spiritual exercises were generally observed in the city churches there was no evidence of any meetings of parents for the suggested pledge

signing. The parish priest of Berkley Road had the proclamation printed as a leaflet which was handed out at the church entrance. A note in the leaflet asked the congregation to leave it behind them on the church seats; these when collected would show the number opposed to the Bill. Hundreds of these leaflets were afterwards scattered about the church ground and in the adjoining public streets.[177]

In rural areas, however, the protests were more widely observed. Most teachers attended early masses where possible to avoid confrontation, but there were instances of teachers leaving churches when the INTO was attacked from the pulpit, and accounts of teachers having been 'subjected to abuse and humiliation' when they refused to attend the parents' meetings or sign the pledge against the bill. As O'Connell observed, 'if the total number who signed the protest was ever tabulated, which is extremely doubtful, the result was never published'.

This was the backdrop to the 1920 Easter congress, which was supposed to take place in Killarney, but ultimately opened in Dublin after a very last-minute switch. This occurred after the bishop of Kerry barred school children from the convent and monastery schools in Killarney from singing at events during congress week as planned,[178] resulting in an INTO threat to move the congress if the full choir was not reinstated by the Wednesday of Holy Week. Their bluff was called, and when it was clear by Holy Thursday that the bishop was standing firm, the CEC decided unanimously to move congress to Dublin, a vast enterprise, not least in the days of rudimentary communications. The nationalist press had gleefully hoped for a split among the delegates on the INTO's position on the Macpherson Bill, but they were disappointed.[179] It enjoyed broad support and J.F. O'Farrell, one of the few voices against the bill, was roundly defeated when he stood in the election for vice president.[180]

However, whether it was divine intervention or otherwise, by this point the Macpherson Bill had run its course. The strain of being chief secretary for Ireland at this time, living in continual terror of assassination, proved too great for Macpherson, and on 1 April it was announced that he had quit his position.[181] The *School Weekly*'s prophecy that his exit might be the end of the bill proved correct.[182] With Macpherson – and presumably his bill – gone, ex-president Tom Nunan wrote to Cardinal O'Donnell hoping that the two sides might come to co-operate on education matters in the future and warned of the consequences if they did not.

It would in the first place help a great deal to heal up much of the soreness that remains between teachers and managers. Many sharp things were said from the pulpit, teachers in some cases left the churches and the relations remain strained in very many cases. It is not well that this should be. Big changes seem to be pending and in education matters a great and growing power – Labour – is openly out for local control. If the question ever comes to the test it would be well not to have thousands of soured teachers ready to take sides.[183]

Macpherson's successor, Sir Hamar Greenwood, the fifth chief secretary in as many years, ignored the bill for the duration of that parliamentary session, and it was officially withdrawn in mid-December without a second reading.[184] The Macpherson Bill was a progressive, badly needed attempt to reform primary education in the island of Ireland. That it failed was first and foremost due to timing. Had it been introduced ten years earlier, it would undoubtedly have met with resistance from the Church and, more than likely, the nationalist MPs in parliament, but it is questionable whether that would have been sufficient to prevent it. It might have passed through parliament without too much ado, but opposition from the local councils might have made it unworkable. Notably, by the end of 1919, Starkie had come to view them with contempt, writing to Macpherson that while his opinion of the clerical managers remained as poor as ever, 'recent events have led me to prefer a soviet of clerics to blackguard county councillors'.[185] But as Starkie perceptively told Macpherson in that letter, Ireland would not agree to anything from England at that time, and for all its good points, the bill was a dead letter from the start.

The British government had always been adamant that there would be no changes to the pay scales without a new bill, but now, through no fault of the INTO, there was no bill. On 1 June 1920, the INTO made a formal demand to the Treasury for new scales. Eventually at the end of November, after a long process and threatened strike action, they had an offer.[186] It radically changed the teachers' salary structure and abolished the classification of teachers into different grades for salary purposes. It also introduced a common basic scale for all trained teachers, although there were different scales for men and women, and newly appointed teachers in schools with an average of 20 to 29 pupils would be put on the same scale as women. Teachers would begin at the minimum point of the scale and, unless they received poor reports, would enjoy automatic annual increments. There were also supranormal scales for principals rated 'Highly Efficient' at the maximum of the normal scale and for teachers in First Grade after a certain length of service, as well as for principals in Second Grade and assistants in certain circumstances. After so many years of effort and no little friction, Irish primary teachers' pay had been settled at last. Once the new scales had been agreed, however, the British government effectively washed its hands of any future reforms. The INTO lobbied in vain for pension reforms, but as far as London was concerned it was no longer its problem.

GOVERNMENT OF IRELAND BILL

In the autumn of 1919, around the same time as Macpherson's Education Bill was published, another piece of legislation was being drafted of considerably longer-lasting consequence, the Government of Ireland Bill, which would partition Ireland and establish two devolved parliaments, North and South. It was given its second reading in the Commons on 29 March 1920, while the Act came into operation more than a year later, elections for the two parliaments taking place on 24 May 1921. On 25 June, teachers from the six-county area met in Belfast to discuss their future under partition. The meeting was presided over by the president, John Harbison, who began by rejecting the suggestion that the INTO had 'had its day' north of the border, and affirmed its intention to continue operating there, suggesting that it might do so with a small executive for the six counties. Notwithstanding the setting up of the UTU, most Protestant teachers remained INTO members. Harbison spoke to their concerns relating to rumours that INTO funds had been turned over to political organisations and used for the support of teachers who were interned during the War of Independence, explaining that some voluntary subscriptions had been forwarded by teachers for their support but that no INTO funds had been used for this purpose.[187] The meeting was characterised by a determination to keep the INTO working in the six counties, and it unanimously adopted a resolution proclaiming its 'adhesion to the INTO as a distinct educational unit', while recommending that the CEC should sanction the appointment of a 'Vigilance or interim committee to safe-guard the interests of primary education and teachers of the Northern area'.[188]

The CEC consequently appointed a Vigilance Committee comprising four teachers – Harbison, McNelis, Neilly and Caraher – to 'watch, report and make suggestions regarding educational developments affecting the interest in the Northern Area'. In November the Vigilance Committee secured the CEC's permission to expand its membership to include the CEC and finance committee representatives for the Northern area, along with the chairman of each county committee, and an additional member of the Belfast committee, as well as increasing its powers.[189] It made sense to have a specific committee to take care of teachers in the new jurisdiction, but the decision was politically problematic at a time when many nationalists refused to recognise partition. Speaking at the Easter congress in 1922, a delegate from Tyrone Central asked on what authority the decision to establish the committee had been made, and who the Vigilance Committee represented. Harbison, he said, had had 'no right to claim that he represented considerably more than a thousand teachers who don't recognise the Northern government and who don't want to be placed in a false position before the world'.[190] Harbison conceded that they had had no authority to set it up but had merely dealt with the situation as it arose. Their unwillingness to recognise the border, sometimes aligned with support for abstentionism, meant that at the beginning, many Catholics who might have otherwise done so refused to serve on the Vigilance Committee, which represented some 2,800 national teachers of all denominations in the six counties.[191]

Meanwhile, the organisation began to prepare for the new education system in the state that would emerge south of the border. The 1920 congress had directed the CEC to convene a representative conference to 'frame a programme or series of programmes, in accordance with Irish ideals and conditions', in an effort to steer the formation of curricular policy, and particularly the teaching of Irish.[192] The conference eventually took place in 1921, and included representatives from the local councils, the Association of Secondary Teachers of Ireland (ASTI, founded in 1909) and the Gaelic League, with Rev. Timothy Corcoran SJ, professor of education in UCD, attending as an observer.[193] By the time the conference finished its deliberations, the INTO had been outmanoeuvred by the Gaelic League, which had radically advanced the position of Irish in schools, so that Irish had become obligatory in the proposed new curriculum and the only argument was over whether classes should be taught through the medium of Irish.

As 1921 came to a close, the INTO could look back on a period where the organisation had rebuilt itself, and overcome factionalism to the point where, at 12,000 members, it was stronger than ever in numbers and influence, run on a professional basis and a full part of the trade union movement. Instead of fighting a resident commissioner and commission nominated by British politicians, and travelling to London looking for money, the INTO would have to deal with Irish governments and administrations based in Dublin and Belfast. But the future was uncertain, not least on whether partition was merely a temporary measure or something more long-lasting. Either way things would be very different under the new regimes – it was just too early to know how.

Chapter 3 ∽

THE INTO IN INDEPENDENT IRELAND, 1922–1946

'We confidently expect the Ireland of the future will honour the calling of the teacher and appreciate his services, and reward him as he deserves.'

After partition, the education systems in the two parts of the island diverged. In the North, the reforms were largely to the school system and how it was run, whereas in the South, the greatest changes were in the classroom. The system remained largely unchanged at local level but education would no longer be run by a board appointed by the British regime. As T.J. O'Connell noted, there would be no need to send 'deputations across the Irish Sea to pour tales of woe into the ears of British Ministers preoccupied with the multitudinous concerns of a far-flung Empire, and with little time and less sympathy to give'. On the prospects for the teachers of Ireland under the new regime, the *Irish Teachers' Journal* (ITJ) observed that many teachers were asking about this, often in a somewhat anxious tone, but the *Journal* had no misgivings.

> We have boundless faith in the innate reasonableness and sense of justice of the mass of our fellow countrymen and countrywomen … We believe that the love of learning, for which our people were at one time famous, but which has been less conspicuous in our latter-day history, will show forth in strength again in the sunlight, and in the congenial atmosphere of national freedom. Yes, we confidently expect that the Ireland of the future will honour the calling of the teacher and appreciate his services, and reward him as he deserves.[1]

Was this vision of a scholarly utopia where teachers would, at long last, enjoy the status and remuneration long denied them, merely naivety, overexcitement or an effort to soothe the nerves of members who feared what change might bring? Despite significant salary increases in recent years, teachers' conditions of employment remained largely unchanged. One notable reform was that Rule 88(b), prohibiting teachers from playing an active part in public life, had been withdrawn by the board in 1920, and by 1922 a number of national teachers were members of the Oireachtas, but teachers' day-to-day working lives remained the same. The buildings were as decrepit as ever, the managerial system was untouched, the inspection system remained odious and attendance levels were among the worst in western Europe. The room for improvement was vast.

THE NEW REGIME

Things seemed to begin well. Ten days after the new government took office, the Board of National Education was demoted with little ado when it was informed that it would now serve only in an advisory capacity. The new chief executive of national education, Padraig Ó Brolcháin, took the opportunity to note that the teaching profession in the 'economy of the nation can scarcely be over-rated', and how one of the government's first concerns should be to ensure that

> the best types of men and women in the country should be attracted to its ranks and that the conditions under which they give their services to the state should be such as on one hand, to raise the morale of the individual and, on the other, to give him the place in the community to which his talents and high responsibility entitle him.[2]

Weeks later, the two ministers responsible for education attended the Easter congress, and assured delegates that the days of ignoring teachers were over, and that they would have 'a due voice, due weight and due consideration in education plans, schemes and programmes' in future.[3] This was welcome news to delegates, who passed motions calling for the government to establish a commission of inquiry on the future of education in Ireland, which would suggest legislative and administrative changes to place Irish education on 'a proper and progressive basis'.[4]

Not surprisingly, though, with the country teetering on the brink of civil war, education took a back seat. The Free State's first elections were set for 22 June. Having failed to contest the elections in 1918 or 1921, the Labour Party now stood in the 1922 election and asked the INTO, along with other affiliated unions, to nominate candidates. T.J. O'Connell strongly supported doing so, but the CEC did not share his enthusiasm, and decided against nominating anyone directly (although it did pledge £500 to Labour's campaign), and O'Connell called on teachers to give the party their active support in the *ITJ*.[5] Convinced that the INTO's refusal to nominate candidates would diminish its credibility with Labour in the long run, however, O'Connell allowed himself to be selected by local Labour associations in Galway to stand three days before nominations closed.[6] There was no Labour electoral machine in the area, but following an energetic campaign run largely by the local national teachers, aided by members of the Post Office Workers' Union (POWU), and with assistance from the National Union of Railwaymen and members of the ITGWU, O'Connell was elected on the first count. Notwithstanding the initial opposition to his candidature, his election was cause for celebration. With the general secretary now in the Dáil, the INTO had a prominent platform from which to articulate teachers' interests, but there was residual opposition, with some members concerned that his new role would divert his attention away from the organisation. O'Connell was returned at three successive elections before losing his seat in 1932.

Civil war broke out days after the election in June 1922, and teachers were no more immune to the disturbances than anyone else. The INTO head office in Gardiner Place was very close to the centre of the fighting in Dublin: in July it had to close when staff could not reach the building; and CEC meetings were cancelled due to the closure of the railways. Resulting disruption to the postal services, which soon halted entirely after a strike by the POWU, caused problems with communications and with the payment of salaries, particularly in the west and south of the country, and the situation was exacerbated by a government prohibition on the GPO from 'sending cash to any district in which there may be danger of its appropriation by those opposed to the government'.[7] In Kerry, which was hit particularly hard, the county committee dispatched one of its executive, Tom Nunan, to Dublin to pick up the salaries for July and August, a journey which, as T.J. O'Connell noted at the time, was 'not exactly a pleasure trip'.[8] Not that teachers were all detached observers during this time. Teachers fought on both sides, and the sustentation fund established to support members interned by the British government now went to the families of a number of teachers interned by the Free State.[9] More than a year after the conflict had ended in May 1923, the Department of Education withdrew salaries from some 20 teachers for alleged complicity 'in the Irregular revolt' of 1922–23.[10] Between 40 and 50 teachers were held during the civil war and after, with around 20 not recommended for re-instatement,[11] and during the mid-1920s, the CEC spent considerable time trying to reverse this. One person who found it difficult to secure work at this time due to her civil war record was a young Scottish teacher named Margaret Skinnider, who had been gravely injured during Easter week, 1916. Skinnider, who had been a maths teacher in Scotland, was unable to get teaching work after the civil war, and instead worked as a trade union administrator, first in the ITGWU and then the Workers' Union of Ireland (WUI), before securing a position in the King's Inns school around 1926. Some 30 years later, Miss Skinnider would become only the fourth ever INTO woman president.

T.J. O'Connell was not the only INTO activist elected to the Oireachtas in

1922. Former president and one-time central secretary Edmund Mansfield, or Eamonn Mansfield (sometimes Manséal), as he was now known, had won a seat in the Senate, but resigned it only weeks later, in December, in protest against the execution of republican prisoners by the Free State.[12] This was not reported in the *School Weekly*. Mansfield's place was taken by another INTO activist, William Cummins. Overall, however, the INTO worked hard not to become caught up in the conflict. Like the Gaelic League, the *ISW* noted, the organisation 'does well to keep its doors locked against the controversies and contentions that are irrelevant to the work which it has in hand'.[13]

The work at hand for the INTO included strengthening the organisation by increasing membership levels. Compulsory Irish meant that many teachers spent the summer attending one of the six Irish language schools which had been set up to prepare them for teaching the 'New Programme'.[14] Attendance was obligatory for all non-Irish-speaking teachers aged under 45 years.[15] The concentration of so many teachers together provided a unique opportunity for organising; across the country, branches resolved that INTO members would not associate or attend classes with non-members. Monitors were appointed to check membership cards and report names of the 'prodigals' back to vigilance committees, who would keep a record of the 'black sheep'.[16] The boycott was not observed perfectly – there was one complaint that members had been seen talking to 'unassociated' teachers in the yard at Marlborough Street – but it does seem to have made an impact, and by the end of July, *ISW* was reporting that 'the ranks of unassociated … are being thinned out rapidly'.[17] The 'Roll of Honour', a list published in the *ISW* of branches that enjoyed full membership among teachers, grew steadily week by week. On 15 July 1922 it featured five branches; a year later the Report on Organisation could boast that 'already some fifty branches' had claimed the honour.[18] At 12,119, the total number of members for 1922 was the highest in the organisation's history,[19] a remarkable feat considering that the difficulties thrown up during the year had actually caused membership in other unions to fall.[20] In fact, not only had the INTO become the second largest union in Ireland in membership, it also seems to have been the best resourced, having a reserve of almost £36,000.[21] Satisfying as this news was, there were obligatory warnings against complacency and, writing at the end of the civil war, the general secretary observed poor attendance at meetings and a tardiness in paying subs in some quarters.

Another development that added to the sense of community among national teachers at this time was the establishment of the Teachers' Club in 1923. In early 1922, the CEC purchased 36 Parnell Square, then next door to the ITGWU headquarters, as the premises for a new club for teachers, but it was not until 2 November 1923 that members of the Dublin branch managed to open the club.[22] Membership was open to any national teacher who was a member of the INTO, and the club became a vital hub for the INTO in the years to come. Plans were hatched, even political parties formed, and there were times, particularly from the 1940s to the 1970s, when the seat of power in the INTO lay more in the club than in the official headquarters. The club held numerous social activities, including dances, golf and lectures, had a library, and organised outings, all of which helped develop a sense of camaraderie among national teachers working in the city.[23] This esprit de corps was hugely important, helping to establish the Dublin branch as a dynamic and often radical force in the organisation, most notably in the 1946 strike. In the years and decades after, the club became important in passing down the folklore of the organisation to younger generations, so that the great strike of 1946 was still part of the INTO story 40 years later, retold to younger generations by the men and women who were there.

EDUCATION AND THE FREE STATE CONSTITUTION

As teachers returned to school in September 1922, the third Dáil met for the first time. One of the first issues before it was the approval of the Free State Constitution. The main debate on the constitution took place between the government party, Cumann na nGaedheal, and Labour, which was the official opposition, in the absence of the abstentionist anti-Treaty Sinn Féin TDs. As Brian Titley has observed, the debate on what would or would not go into the constitution provided an 'an interesting guide to the educational intentions and attitudes of Cosgrave's administration' as well as its political attitudes more broadly.[24] A committee to draft a constitution for the Free State had been established in January, and had produced its draft early in March,[25] but it was not until the Dáil met in September that its details were made public. Written in the shadow of the Anglo-Irish Treaty, its primary purpose was to set out how the new state would be governed and its status as a British dominion, and though it enunciated citizens' very basic rights, it was not detailed, prescriptive or progressive. It was characteristic of the governing party's view of the state as small and non-interventionist. Article 10 of the new constitution stated only that 'all citizens of the Irish Free State/Saorstát Éireann have the right to free elemental education'. Describing this as 'altogether too meagre', T.J. O'Connell tabled an amendment guaranteeing children the right to food, clothing, shelter and education, and providing for, among other things, free education until an age determined by law, and compulsory attendance.[26] He was backed by his Labour colleagues but no one else, with government ministers bluntly rejecting the amendment. The minister for home affairs, Kevin O'Higgins, argued that the constitution was for setting out 'fundamental rights' and the amendment went too far,[27] but Labour's leader, Tom Johnson, argued that 'the rights of children in the Constitution' ought to be amplified.[28] Johnson pointed to the provisions in the Democratic Programme of the First Dáil, the social and economic framework that he had largely drafted, but government deputies swatted away talk of rights and, with an unassailable majority, the amendment was easily defeated. Kevin O'Higgins' well-worn observation that he and his party colleagues were the 'most conservative revolutionaries' is particularly true here for, as Cathal O'Shannon noted during the debate, the enunciation of explicit rights in education was becoming the norm in post-war Europe.[29]

Though unsuccessful, Labour's amendment attracted attention in ecclesiastical circles and prompted the *Irish Catholic* to denounce it as contrary to the teachings of the Church, declaring, 'to us it is inconceivable that the present or any future Irish parliament should be found ready to acquiesce in principles of education which are essentially repugnant to the Christian doctrine'.[30] The issue the *Irish Catholic* found so abhorrent was the proposal that 'all schools and educational establishments, public and private, shall be controlled by the state within limits to be determined by law', an intolerable encroachment of the state into the Church's sphere of control. In his column in the *School Weekly*, T.J. O'Connell was fairly bullish about the 'prominent clergymen' who were up in arms over Labour's godless amendment. He recalled how only a couple of years earlier the INTO had been accused of trying to 'drive the priests out of the schools' over the Macpherson Bill. 'The INTO survived criticism of that kind and so I daresay will the Labour Party,' he shrugged.[31] At least one local association seemed to take the criticism seriously, with the Granard branch passing a resolution that stated 'that any attempt to place the schools of Ireland under state Control be strongly opposed both upon religious and national grounds'.[32] Elsewhere, the Carrickmacross branch, concerned that the organisation was 'drifting into a political career', sent a number of questions regarding Labour's education policy to the CEC, which wound up in the 'Jottings' column of *ISW*.[33] The branch asked:

(a) what control has the INTO over Mr. O'Connell as TD?
(b) From whom does Mr. O'Connell derive his inspiration in regard to his political educational activities?
(c) Are the CEC definitely committed to the Educational Policy of the Labour Party to the exclusion of every other Party?
(d) By whose authority does Mr. O'Connell suggest fundamental changes in the present Education system?
(e) Are his suggestions to be taken as the considered educational policy of all the teachers in Ireland?[34]

These were not unreasonable questions, and O'Connell was perhaps a little churlish in his response, but he was adamant that he had not advocated anything in the Dáil which had not already been INTO policy for several years.

In effect the INTO's education policy was now Labour's policy, not the other way around. Indeed, O'Connell argued, Labour was unique among Irish parties, including the one in government, in having any education policy at all.

The INTO's influence on Labour was most obvious with the publication in September 1925 of 'Labour's Policy on Education', the report of a special committee of the ILP&TUC executive. Chaired by the Labour leader, Tom Johnson, with T.J. O'Connell acting as vice-chair and M.P. Linehan from INTO head office as secretary,[35] and including the former president, Cormac Breathnach, and ASTI general secretary, Tom Burke, it produced a document which combined the social idealism of the Democratic Programme and the basic demands of the teaching unions, and of the INTO especially. The report was written by Linehan,[36] who had been brought into head office to provide administrative assistance to O'Connell, whose workload had increased since he had entered the Dáil. It was not long before O'Connell's workload became heavier still, when Tom Johnson lost his seat at the general election in September 1927 and O'Connell found himself the new Labour leader, a post he held for five years until he lost his seat in 1932. A Labour activist, Linehan had trained as a teacher before working for some years as an official of the ITGWU.[37] Appointed as a clerk in the INTO, he was promoted to treasurer two years later, when the incumbent Mairead Ashe retired on marriage.

Linehan was very much a conservative trade unionist. He took a keen interest in Catholic social teaching and became a strong proponent of Catholic Action during the 1930s, writing pamphlets and articles on it and keeping a keen eye out for the menace of communism creeping into union or political life.[38] Labour's Policy on Education featured many of the INTO's old reliables, none of which had been tackled by the new government almost four years after independence, among them dilapidated school buildings, reform of inspection and the need for compulsory attendance. The desirability of establishing university training for teachers was also raised, but the method of teaching Irish in national schools – the other issue on which many teachers were becoming increasingly vocal – was fudged. Cormac Breathnach's presence on the committee might explain this. Breathnach was a Gaelic League activist, serving as its president in 1928, and was the INTO's most active supporter of gaelicisation. The key administrative recommendation was a council of education, which would advise the minister.[39] The idea was first floated by the UCC registrar Alfred O'Rahilly in 1922, when he was a member of the committee which was drafting the Free State Constitution, but it was roundly rejected by his colleagues.[40] Convinced of its value, O'Rahilly later expounded on its virtues at the INTO's 1924 congress, where it was adopted as policy. With no support for it in government, some ten years later the INTO took the initiative and tried to organise a council of education itself, as discussed below.

In the absence of the abstentionist Sinn Féin deputies, the government's majority was all but unbreachable. Labour tabled various INTO-inspired reforms in the Dáil, but usually without success. Often, government ministers cited Catholic social teaching for their opposition. The Church's influence on the government was considerable, especially in the area of education. During the debates on the constitution, Minister for Education Eoin MacNeill had rejected calls for any form of compulsory attendance – one of the INTO's main demands at the time – arguing that it was contrary to the principle of parental rights.[41] Some weeks later, however, T.J. O'Connell tabled a far-reaching amendment to the 1892 Compulsory Attendance Act, which passed through the House unanimously.[42] Professor William Magennis, an independent deputy for the NUI constituency and a former member of the National Board, noted this with some surprise. He recalled:

[When he and Deputy O'Connell had] had the audacity to defend compulsory education we were voted down and not only that, but a leading article in one of the leading newspapers was devoted to us to prove what a poor conception of liberty we entertained, how unenlightened we were as to the claims of the individual citizen to be allowed to go his own way uninterfered with by perverse legislators. The Minister for Education, who unfortunately is absent, is absolutely opposed to compulsory education. He claims for the parent the right to do with his child what seems best to himself, and if he has money enough for the purpose, to provide education for his child so that he shall be kept away from the contaminating social influences which the ordinary State school or the Christian Brothers' school might subject him to.[43]

The lack of educational reform was largely ideological. In noting MacNeill's personal attitudes to education, it is worth remembering that he was broadly representative of the usually Catholic, elite middle class, often educated privately before going on to UCD, that made up the government. MacNeill was a sincere and devout Catholic who adhered to Church control of education to the exclusion of the state and had expounded this view in numerous articles over the years,[44] later observing that, 'as Minister of Education during the first year of this government, it appeared evident that the political control of education was State-Socialism in a more radical form than political control of the material means of economic production and distribution'.[45] However, added to his laissez faire attitude towards education, after November 1924 his attention was diverted following his appointment as Irish representative on the Boundary Commission, which rendered him an absentee minister. Whether he would have managed much otherwise is debatable. Eventually, in October 1926, the INTO got its compulsory attendance legislation, although its implementation left a lot to be desired.

One reform MacNeill had been open to but that never came to fruition was changing the qualification for national teaching from the NT (national teacher) award, conferred after two years at one of the training colleges, to a Bachelor of Education (BEd), which would be awarded by a university after three or four years' study.[46] This was the case in Scotland and the INTO felt that teachers' status benefited from it.[47] In the past, national teachers who wished to earn degrees took them externally, but when the NUI was established in 1908, it ended the tradition begun by the Royal University, closing that path to teachers. At the beginning of 1923, the INTO held a conference in Dublin on the university training of teachers, which was attended by representatives from the university colleges of Dublin, Cork and Galway, but nothing came of it.[48] Notably, one of the critics of the idea was Alfred O'Rahilly. A Catholic actionist, O'Rahilly feared the consequences of removing teachers from the training colleges, which were under the control of the bishops, to universities, where they would be mere students working towards a degree. As it was, no progress was made on the issue, and it was another 50 years or so before the INTO got its wish.

There was, however, a significant change to the admission to training colleges at this time. As part of the language revival policy the government wanted to increase the numbers of teachers with fluent Irish, and in an effort to do this it established what were known as preparatory colleges. These were feeder schools, based in the Gaeltacht, where children – 40 per cent from the Fíor-Gaeltacht, 20 per cent from the Breac-Gaeltacht and the remaining 40 per cent from anywhere – would study through Irish before going on to train as national teachers.[49] The INTO was utterly opposed to the preparatory colleges from the beginning and never wavered in its opposition until they were closed in 1959.[50] Its stated reason was that the colleges took in children at 14, which was far too young to make vocational decisions or to be cloistered away, and which ill fitted them educationally or socially thereafter.[51] More accurately, it was opposed because, as one resolution at the 1935 INTO congress put it, 'children from outside the Gaeltacht are practically debarred from entrance to the teaching profession'.[52] This was an exaggeration, but in 1931, for example, over 37 per cent of admissions to teacher training went to preparatory college students, compared with 24 per cent from open competition candidates (the others were pupil teachers at 28.6 per cent and university graduates and untrained assistants at 10 per cent).[53] Calls for recruitment to teacher training to be done through competitive examination became a congress perennial.[54]

'CHANGE THE REGULATIONS'

The condition of national school buildings, and the question of who might pay for their repair, was a cause for concern at this time. The government had no interest in interfering with the position of the Catholic Church in running national schools, and the Church was determined to keep it that way, but while it was happy to enjoy the benefits of controlling the schools, it was less inclined to accept the responsibilities that went with it. National schools were usually vested in local trustees who were responsible for the maintenance and repair of the premises.[55] Government policy was to pay two-thirds of the costs of the upkeep of schools, with local contributions paying the other third,[56] but in practice, the state paid three-quarters, with the local contribution at one-quarter. Speaking on the question in the Dáil in June 1926, T.J. O'Connell argued that the state should pay the full cost of maintenance, and suggested that the funding be raised through local rates, which would be managed by local education committees. Later that year when the Department of Education wrote to the bishop of Galway on the building, reconstruction, maintenance, heating and cleaning of schools, the idea of local committees was mentioned again. The common Church attitude was that such committees might dilute Church control, however, and were out of the question. No action was taken, but the situation deteriorated further, so that between 1926 and 1928, the state found itself bearing four-fifths of the costs. With the national finances in a perilous condition the Department wrote again at the beginning of January 1929, noting that the situation had become quite urgent. The lack of heating and cleaning had begun to attract increasing public attention, and complaints had become more frequent,[57] while a survey conducted of school buildings had put the cost of getting the school building stock to an acceptable standard at an astonishing £1 million, but still the Department's entreaties were blithely ignored.

In August 1933, the Department issued circular 13/33 to managers, reminding them of their obligations and the danger to health posed by the insanitary conditions of many of their schools, and urging them to take 'urgent and effective action' to make sure their schools were in a sanitary condition and 'otherwise made suitable and pleasant places for the children who, by law, are required to attend them'. However, if the Church was often in agreement that the schools were squalid and unsuitable, it did not feel that this was its problem to fix. When it was pointed out in December 1933 that the conditions in the Pro-Cathedral schools, especially the girls' school in Rutland Street, were insufficient under the regulations, one response from Archbishop's House was to 'change the regulations'.[58] By June of 1934, the Department wrote yet again, pointing out that its correspondence on the issue was ongoing for eight years. The bishops and managers met to discuss the matter the following month, and while the managers accepted that there was a problem, they seemed unwilling to take any responsibility, some going so far as to blame the bishops.[59] Eventually, the bishops and managers agreed they would suggest a local contribution of one-sixth of the costs of heating, cleaning and maintenance, and a similar sum for buildings with a small minority, just four of those present, supporting a call for the state to pay the full amount for both. Behind the scenes, the minister for local government and public health, Seán T. O'Kelly (a Knight of Columbanus prone to leaking cabinet information to the Church) had told the bishop of Kildare and Leighlin that the state would be prepared to undertake the entire cost of maintenance,[60] but while Bishop Dignan, for one, supported this, his was a minority view. The suggestion went no further, and the managers' commitment to running clean schools remained as bad as ever; in March 1937 the Department had had to issue a further circular reminding the managers of their responsibilities. The state was fully aware that the condition of schools was unacceptable, but it was unwilling to go beyond periodic attempts to privately prick the Church's conscience, and the Church knew it. Had there been the slightest indication that the state might do something as radical as serve an ultimatum that the Church live up to its responsibilities or leave, there might have been progress, but neither Cumann na nGaedhael nor Fianna Fáil was prepared to take action.

THE CUTS AND THE PENSION FUND CRISIS

The lack of educational or material improvements were frustrating, but they were not the worst problem facing the national teachers. At the end of October 1923, the minister for finance, Ernest Blythe, announced that teachers' wages would be cut by ten per cent from 1 November. His rationale was that teachers' salaries had been increased in 1920 by the old administration when the cost of living was increasing, and now that the cost of living had fallen, teachers' real incomes had increased, so they should be cut again.[61] Old age pensioners were also painted as profiting from falling prices, and similarly faced a ten per cent cut. Blythe's attempt to paint teachers and pensioners as living high on the hog while the country struggled to balance its books failed to convince anyone, not least because it was untrue. As one writer in the *Irish Independent* put it, it was only because teachers were so 'scandalously underpaid' prior to 1920 that they had been given the increase in the first place. Having investigated the matter, 'we are satisfied that teachers, especially male teachers, are not overpaid with any of the branches of the civil service having regard to their great responsibilities and to the fact that their pensions are fixed on a scale not at all commensurate with the civil service scale'.[62] Indeed, higher-paid civil servants were widely identified in the press as being altogether more deserving targets of a cut.[63] The decision to target the teachers rankled all the more because it took no account of the increased workload created by the New Programme, with teachers expected to become fluent in Irish and to teach a whole new course, a task that many teachers had already declared 'impossible'.[64] The whole project of reviving the national language was being put on their shoulders and their reward was that their salaries, and their salaries alone, were to be slashed. Reaction across the local and national press, with the exception of the *Irish Times*, which gave Blythe the benefit of the doubt, regarded this move as arbitrary and unfair.

Special branch meetings were held on the issue, and a well-attended special congress took place in Dublin at the end of November. Delegates were furious that their own government was now treating them worse than its British predecessor, and some delegates complained that the organisation was not fighting the cut with sufficient force. Eventually, the conference passed a resolution condemning the cut and a second authorising the CEC to use 'all the legitimate means at the disposal of the organisation, including all available legal machinery'.[65] This meant that the issue was pursued through the courts via a case taken on an individual member, Martin Leyden, who taught in the Marlborough Street Model School, and so was directly employed by the state, rather than through a patron.[66] The case was heard over two days in July 1924, and the decision, known as the Meredith Judgment, went against Leyden, although he was awarded costs, and the judgment was upheld on appeal in December.

Throughout this time, the organisation continued to lobby all sitting deputies to reverse the cut and also to forestall further cuts that were being threatened. Elements of the membership regarded the threat of more cuts as 'a piece of bluff', while O'Connell, at least, was inclined to take it seriously,[67] and there were sharp words between delegates and the general secretary during the 1924 congress, with complaints that information was being hidden from them.[68] The suspicions among members that they were not being fully informed about negotiations were correct. O'Connell had received confidential information from the education department that officials in Finance were reviewing teachers' salary scales with a view to bringing in further cuts, but the CEC had decided to lobby TDs on the matter without publicity,[69] which may have been good tactics, but it helped fuel the rumour mill. In the end, the ten per cent cut remained, but in March 1926, Blythe announced that he would cut no further, telling the Dáil that while he wanted to cut more, he had decided that attracting people of ability into the profession was more important if education was to be improved, and further cuts would only be a false economy.[70]

The pay cut was only the start of the teachers' money problems. In November 1928, a government-appointed actuary reported that the national teachers' pension fund was in deficit by more than £4.2 million.[71] He suggested two alternatives to make good the deficit: either increase the exchequer contribution to the scheme by £212,000 per annum over a 40-year period; or increase teachers' contributions more than threefold, from four per cent of their salary to 12.5 per cent. Where deficits had arisen before 1922, they had been made good by grants from Westminster,[72] but as the minister for finance bluntly told the CEC, the government was not in a position to offer any further assistance, and the teachers themselves would have to pay, despite the deficit having arisen because the Free State government had failed to pay into the fund as the British government had done. If teachers had paid the difference it would have meant an 8.5 per cent decrease in take-home pay only a few years after the ten per cent pay cut. The organisation was united in agreement that the teachers would not pay, with the 1929 Easter congress instructing the CEC to stand firm against any attempts to make them do so. Blythe softened his position somewhat but there was no mood for compromise among the majority of members, and there followed a lengthy standoff between the two sides. O'Connell was open to negotiations, but the Thomond Committee, a group based in Clare, Limerick and Tipperary and including Eamonn Mansfield, led the resistance. The pension question stalled until the end of 1931, during which time the international economic crisis had made the situation worse. Facing a £900,000 shortfall in anticipated receipts, the minister for finance introduced a supplementary budget on 6 November that proposed raising £450,000 through increased taxation and reducing spending by £450,000 by cutting the salaries of public servants. Three days later, the Minister for Education confirmed to a CEC delegation that teachers would be included in this round of cuts and intimated that this might happen before Christmas. The news spurred the executive into action, and at a special meeting held on 13 November, a proposal was formulated which they hoped would solve the pension issue and keep the pay cut as low as possible. Members would take a five per cent cut in salary and pay a four per cent pension contribution, a combined cut of nine per cent, and the government would take full responsibility for the pension scheme.[73] On 5 December, the minister for finance responded, broadly accepting the offer, but with a six per cent cut and the promise of a review if 'there was a substantial change in the financial position'.[74] Unable to get the cabinet to reconsider their original proposals, the CEC reluctantly agreed to put the offer to members on the understanding that not only teachers would be subject to the cut, and on 19 December a special delegate conference met and decided by 212 votes to 121 to accept the offer.

The dissolution of the Dáil only weeks later, on 29 January, changed the political context. Fianna Fáil made some overtures towards the teachers, including an assurance that they would be included in the promise that public servants paid less than £400 would not be subject to cuts.[75] The election of 1932 was bitterly contested, with Fianna Fáil mounting a significant challenge against the outgoing Cumann na nGaedheal government, and in a battle between the two larger parties, Labour was sidelined. One candidate who found the campaign difficult was T.J. O'Connell.[76] The days of the teachers of Mayo and Galway mobilising en masse for his campaign were long over. As O'Connell reflected in the *ISW* after the poll, a circular to 450 members resulted in about 60 volunteers who gave anything more than perfunctory support, and 'the number of teachers who "took off their coats" and went "all out" to fight the election was under two dozen. I am equally certain that wherever a teacher did work earnestly and energetically the result disclosed itself when the ballot boxes were opened.'[77] O'Connell's first preference vote had fallen by 18 per cent since the last election, and he failed to get in on the last count. Afterwards, he was sanguine: 'I am personally perfectly satisfied with the result. Financially, physically, and mentally, if I may put it so, I shall be better off outside than inside the Dáil.' He would later put his defeat down to the role he had played in the pension dispute,[78] and undoubtedly this was crucial in the failure of teachers to mobilise for his campaign, but at the time he suggested that it was because of his intention to put the Cumman na nGaedhael government out of office and Fianna Fáil in that he had lost his seat.[79]

Aside from O'Connell's loss, the election saw three new INTO members in the Dáil: past president Cormac Breathnach, Eamon Rice and Daniel O'Rourke. All three were elected for Fianna Fáil, the party that had won the most seats at the election, and which, with Labour's external support, took office on 9 March 1932. The three new deputies brought the number of teachers who had served as members of the Oireachtas to seven, the others having been T.J. O'Connell, Mrs Margaret Collins-O'Driscoll (Michael Collins' sister) and T.J. O'Reilly (FF, Kerry) in the Dáil; and INTO activist Maurice Cummins, who had been co-opted to the Senate in 1923, after Eamonn Mansfield resigned his seat.[80] Their presence in the Oireachtas was not without its critics. As early as 1922, the government had considered banning teachers from sitting in the Oireachtas, but at that time Mrs Collins-O'Driscoll was the only teacher deputy, and it was probably too soon to expel Michael Collins' sister from the new parliament of the Free State. The Catholic managers supported a ban on teacher deputies, and around 1925 the Minister for Education Eoin Mac Neill, himself a university professor, returned to the issue. Mac Neill looked to establish a special committee to look into the matter, its terms of reference covering national teachers and secondary teachers, should they at any time in future be paid directly by the exchequer, by which logic university professors were exempt, but other departments sought to widen its parameters to others paid by the public purse, not just national teachers.[81] The committee was unable to complete its work before the term of the Dáil finished, and issued an interim report in May 1927 but it was not reconvened, and there the matter rested until Fianna Fáil came to office in 1932, when Minister for Finance Seán MacEntee picked it up once again. One of his first acts was to consult with the secretary of the Catholic Bishops and the Catholic Managers' Association, but none of the Protestant bishops or managers, since no Protestant teacher had so far become a member of the Dáil.[82] (It would take another 60 years for that to happen, when Trevor Sargent took a seat for the Greens in North County Dublin.) Perhaps predictably, the INTO was not consulted.

MacEntee's reasons for wanting to ban teachers from the Oireachtas were educational and political, among them that 'from the point of view of the

Department of Finance, any arrangement which tends to increase the political power of classes whose livelihood is derived from State funds, is contrary to the interests of the state and the general community'.[83] For its part, the Department of Education was inclined to agree, and put forward the National Board's old argument that teachers standing for election was too divisive. Whatever the benefits of MacEntee's proposal, trying to remove a single profession from the Dáil at a time when that meant disqualifying four members of the government's back benches (and only those four) was bad politics, and nothing came of it. MacEntee tried again some years later, but to no avail. National teachers were already establishing themselves as an important political force in Irish politics generally, and anecdotally tended to support Fianna Fáil, and to vex them over something so relatively inconsequential would be a foolhardy exercise. Over the years, many national teachers were elected to the Dáil, but while they tended to be more sympathetic on education matters, this did not always manifest itself in the type of class consciousness or voting behaviour that MacEntee seemed to suggest.

Fianna Fáil had made promises during the 1932 election and now it was in government with Labour's support. The political context, if not the economic one, had changed greatly, and the INTO voices demanding that the December deal on pay and pension contributions be rescinded grew louder. The CEC elections divided on the matter and opponents of the deal won a landslide, with almost every outgoing member of the CEC from the Free State defeated. A motion which bluntly repudiated the decision of the special congress was passed almost unanimously after a less critical amendment from the CEC had been roundly defeated.[84] As the newly elected CEC member David Kelleher put it, 'they were the greatest Organisation economically and financially in the country and they should not have surrendered like that'.[85] However, in May the new Fianna Fáil government approved its predecessor's cuts with very minor modifications for junior assistants and untrained teachers. MacEntee suggested to a CEC deputation that he was open to some modifications, but substantially the cuts stood.[86] At another meeting a week later, MacEntee was asked about de Valera's assurances about teachers' pay during the election campaign. They 'all knew the value of words', was the minister's reply; it had been an expression of opinion, not a guarantee.

Eventually, in early June, MacEntee offered the teachers a cut of nine, rather than ten, per cent, which was put to members in a referendum at special meetings and was rejected by a massive 13:1 majority.[87] By then, negotiations with MacEntee had come to a halt, and a number of efforts by the Fianna Fáil teachers to secure a meeting with de Valera were rebuffed.[88] He did, however, agree to meet an INTO deputation in January 1933, having just called a snap election. On that occasion, he told the teachers that he would 'abide by the spirit of' the statement he had made prior to the 1932 election, namely that 'he did not propose to reduce the salaries of the lower-paid public servants'.[89] The government's attitude towards teachers' pay over the last year should have taught them to take such assurances with a pinch of salt, but for many teachers, Cumann na nGaedheal seemed to pose a greater threat, and contemporaries observed that teachers were among the most active supporters of Fianna Fáil in that election. As T.J. O'Connell noted of one constituency, 'Mr Blythe was, to put it somewhat vulgarly, run out of public life and the Monaghan Teachers took a hand in running him out',[90] while James Dillon of the Centre Party asked at a public meeting was it not the young teachers who were the most active supporters of President de Valera? 'Every meeting you went to the young teachers were there calling "Up de Valera!"'[91]

Fianna Fáil returned with a majority, but it soon became clear that de Valera's assurances on teachers' pay counted for little. Moreover, while the government wanted to cut the exchequer salary bill generally, Finance believed the teachers were overpaid and was pushing for a straightforward salary cut.[92] This set alarm bells ringing in Education, which countered that the pensions and salary issues had to be agreed together and outlined proposals along those lines. 'It is of the utmost importance,' Finance was warned, that

> before any settlement of the salary question or the pension question should take effect the INTO should be consulted. The failure to discuss the matter with the teachers in connection with the 1923 cut was followed by very grave results and, in the opinion of the Department, seriously delayed the Irishisation of the schools and generally damped the educational ardour of the teachers in other directions.[93]

At the end of March, Seán MacEntee introduced the Economies Bill in the Dáil. It introduced cuts in public service salaries, but teachers were by far the worst hit. Civil servants received no deduction if their salary did not exceed £300 and were subject to a two per cent cut thereafter, up to a maximum of 4.5 per cent on salaries of £700. However teachers were subject to graduated cuts beginning with a five per cent cut on the first £175 and increasing to eight per cent on anything over £450.[94] To add insult to injury, the government even issued a press release claiming the teachers had got an improved deal compared with what it had agreed in December 1931, and that they had also been treated leniently in comparison with other public servants.[95] Voted through on 31 March, the cuts took effect the following day. As the CEC met on 1 April to discuss what action they might take, an impromptu meeting of some 200 members gathered at the Teachers' Club on Parnell Square before marching to Head Office on Gardiner Place. Several Dublin teachers went before the CEC and urged that teachers use all means at their disposal to resist the cuts. They suggested a one-day strike and proposed that members should go on a work to rule of sorts abandoning 'all national activities outside their actual work as teachers', the teachers responsible for the GAA Primary Schools League matches already having postponed all matches until further notice.[96] Some days later, the CEC announced a one-day work stoppage, the organisation's first strike in 15 years.[97] Local meetings across the country endorsed the action, although a meeting of around 700 teachers from the Dublin city branch went further,[98] proposing an all-out strike but of Dublin teachers only, in an action which would create maximum impact, while allowing teachers outside the capital to continue working and contributing to the strike fund.

There was little appetite for this outside Dublin, though, and when the matter was discussed at the Easter congress, delegates voted to refer it back to the branches. There was also some controversy over who would be liable for the levy. H.A. McAuley of the Northern Committee warned that there was a danger of losing a section of the INTO if northern teachers were included in the levy. His words were echoed by a Belfast teacher, Miss McIlreavy, who pointed out that they had a rival organisation in the North and it was accordingly more difficult to collect subscriptions, and called on delegates not to include the North in the levy 'for the sake of preserving unity' in the six counties.[99] It was a debate that highlighted the regional differences within the organisation, with the Dublin teachers identifying themselves in the 'spearhead' of this fight, those outside Dublin taking a more cautious approach and some northern delegates wanting to opt out altogether. There was also disagreement over whether striking was appropriate. Some delegates argued that if professionals such as doctors or lawyers did not strike, neither should teachers, but this received short shrift from Dublin's David Kelleher. 'I know many of you think a strike is undignified and unprofessional,' he told delegates; 'that attitude is only pure and unadulterated snobbery. You say solicitors and bank clerks don't go on strike. They have no need to.'

The national one-day stoppage that took place on Wednesday 26 April resulted in the closure of most national schools in the 26 counties, with the exception of those under the management of religious orders. In all, only 324 members in the Free State did not observe the stoppage.[100] Teachers turned out at local meetings, and in Dublin 800 (of a possible 900) signed a strike roll of protest in the Teachers' Club before marching with banners near the Dáil.[101] The crowd was addressed by representatives of the Labour Party and Dublin Trades Council as well as the president, Cormac Breathnach, now a government backbencher, who took issue with the claim in the press that this was the first strike by national teachers, pointing to the anti-conscription strike of 1918.[102] If accurate, Breathnach was being a little disingenuous, since it was part of a wider political protest rather than an industrial dispute. This *was* the first strike of its kind by teachers and, unfortunately for Breathnach, it was taking place under the government of which he was a member. The presence of a large number of women members on the march in Dublin was a notable feature of the day. Angry as all teachers were at their treatment by the government, the women teachers had most reason to feel aggrieved; already paid less than their male colleagues, now they faced further discrimination with the introduction of the new marriage bar for women (see below), although the ban and the cuts were kept as separate issues during the campaign.

A success in its observation, the strike's impact was disappointing. As an *Irish Times* editorial put it bluntly, 'manifestly, the government is not frightened'. For one thing, the 'public's present sympathy with the teachers is real but mild'; but, more important, 'teaching, though a noble profession, is not, in the last resort, an essential trade. The only strikes for which success can be presumed are those that affect a nation's means of life.'[103] (This was why the Dublin teachers wanted a wider strike, for as one observed, 'There is no use in calling out the teachers in the countryside and the small towns because such influence would not be felt. But take a strike in any of the cities, say Dublin. If we take these out you will have 20,000 kiddies running around with nobody to teach them, or look after their moral or educational welfare.'[104]) The government remained as unbending as ever. Painting a grim picture of the position in which teachers found themselves in 1933, the *Irish Times* seemed almost to relish the disillusionment of teachers in the new state:

> We can understand the teachers' deep sense of grievance, for their dis-appointment is twofold. They find themselves the poorer not only by loss of salary but by the loss of an illusion … Yesterday the president of their organisation, who is also a member of Mr. de Valera's parliamentary party, declared that the teachers had been the standard-bearers in the fight for Irish freedom. There is no doubt, indeed, that the national teachers were an important force in the movement which began in Easter Week, 1916, and now has made President de Valera the dictator of their fortunes. They supplied a great part of the idealism on which Mr. de Valera has constructed his visions of republic; and we may believe that they were unselfish and sincere. The doctrine of a self-centred civilisation, in which they would renew the glories of Ireland's ancient bards and teachers, made a strong appeal to them. On the whole, the teachers' loyalty to this idealism has persisted.[105]

The Economies Bill passed through the Dáil and was passed in the Senate on 18 July after a Labour Party amendment to exclude teachers from the bill was defeated on a show of hands.[106]

Amid the attack on salaries, the teachers themselves took an important and long-lasting action. Accommodation for teachers had been one of the INTO's earliest grievances, its campaign resulting in the Residences Act of 1875, but funding for residences ended with the outbreak of the Great War and was not reintroduced subsequently. Alex McCabe was a former Irish Volunteer/IRA man, who subsequently joined the National Army and who served as Cumann na nGaedheal deputy and later as a teacher in St Canice's CBS in the North Circular Road in Dublin. In 1932 McCabe began to envisage a state-wide Irish building society. Having discussed the matter with some of his INTO colleagues, he collected funds to publish a pamphlet calling for a building society for teachers to be established. In February 1933 he held a meeting in the Teachers' Club, presided over by the president, Cormac Breathnach, which decided to set up the Educational Building Society. As T.J. O'Connell observed, a more inhospitable time to set up a building society among teachers could scarcely be imagined, but it received its certificate of registration in April 1935, with at least 80 per cent of its shares owned by INTO members.[107] The relationship between the EBS and the INTO remained close over the decades, with many INTO people sitting on its board over the years, although in 1941 it opened itself up to the general public. Almost 50 years after the EBS had been established, a group of INTO members established a credit union, Comhar Linn, whose birthplace was also the Teachers' Club. Both were examples of members taking the initiative to respond to practical issues themselves and finding the support of the organisation in so doing.

MARRIAGE BAR AND ENFORCED RETRIAL

It was through the *Irish School Weekly* dated 16 January 1932 that teachers learned of the Department of Education's proposal to withdraw teaching recognition on marriage for women teachers who had qualified after 31 March 1932. A marriage bar was already in force in most of Northern Ireland by 1932. First introduced in Down and Connor by Bishop John Tohill in the early 1900s, it was enforced at managers' discretion and had largely fallen into desuetude until the late 1920s, when not only was the practice revived but some local authorities in the state school sector followed suit,[108] but in accordance with the convention after 1922, since it was a uniquely Northern issue, it was left in the hands of the Northern Committee (see page 230). For some years, rumours had circulated that a marriage ban for lady teachers might be introduced in the Free State. One had been brought in for the civil service in 1924, which along with the ban in Northern Ireland (belatedly brought over from England) meant that the rumours were credible but, as Vice-President Michael Kearney put it in 1932, the idea was 'so harsh and unfair' that no one had taken them seriously.[109] In 1928, following a suggestion that a ban was being implemented at local level, the CEC wrote to the archbishop of Dublin, Dr Edward Byrne, to ask if there was a diocesan rule against the appointment of married women teachers and if he, himself, personally, was opposed to their appointment. The archbishop eventually responded that there was not, and said he did not hold a fixed view on the question: 'There are circumstances in which it would be a distinct advantage to have a married teacher appointed to a school and there are others in which the appointment of a single teacher is more desirable.'[110]

In fact the threat to women teachers came not from the Church but from the state. In the summer of 1929, on foot of a complaint about married women teachers, Pádraig Ó Brolcháin, secretary of the Department of Education, put the idea of a marriage ban to his minister, John Marcus O'Sullivan.[111] O'Sullivan said he would consider the idea, but nothing came of it until Ó Brolcháin raised it again, in October 1931. His argument for a ban was based on three grounds: 'first it would end an affluence that was undesirable, especially in country areas, second it would lead to greater efficiency and third, it would end emigration for young teachers'.[112] Notwithstanding this rather thin rationale and the prediction that the marriage ban would cost the state around £10,000 per annum in the short run, O'Sullivan gave his approval to the proposal in December, and informed O'Connell in a letter dated 1 January 1932. The proposal was roundly condemned by members at their quarterly branch meetings in January and on 6 February the CEC unanimously objected to the rule 'on economical, educational, and ethical grounds' and pledged its 'most uncompromising opposition to the introduction of any rule to that effect'. Its first action was to lobby the minister, O'Sullivan, for its withdrawal, and since it was being proposed on the eve of a general election, there was to be a meeting with de Valera to ascertain Fianna Fáil's position on the proposed rule.[113] There is no record of a meeting with de Valera on this subject but if the teachers did receive a response, subsequent developments suggest it was not the one they desired. The change in government in the February 1932 election only delayed the marriage bar's progress.

A couple of weeks after taking office, the new education minister, Tomás Derrig, sought the bishops' opinion on the matter, a process his predecessor had begun in January, although he waited a long time for a response. In the meantime, the INTO put its case to the minister at a meeting at the end of May, outlining eight points against the ban, namely that the regulation would be unconstitutional; it would make for inefficiency; it would involve the state in extra expense; married women are specially suitable as teachers of young children; parents favour married women teachers; there is no demand for such a regulation; the regulation will mean fewer marriages; and the arguments for the regulation are devoid of substance.[114]

The government ignored all these points, and once it had received word from the Catholic bishops that they would 'express no opinion' on the matter,[115] the ball was set rolling. On 2 December, the secretary of the Department sent a letter to this effect to O'Connell, outlining the 'strong reasons' for going ahead with the ban.[116] Far from strong, the rationale set out was a crude combination of sexism – albeit of its time – and petty resentment, with no evidential basis. As O'Connell observed, it was neither sociologically nor educationally sound. First, the letter observed:

> Generally speaking it is believed *that the continuance of women as National Teachers on marriage must mean some loss either to the school or to the home* … it is felt that *a considerable proportion of the absences of married women teachers is due to the fact that in addition to being teachers they are also wives and mothers.*[117]

Second, it went on:

> [I]n view of the present economic position of the country more weight is given to the theory of 'one man one job' and local irritation or jealousy is accentuated in a district by the comparatively large incomes received in households where the man and wife are both teachers, or where a woman teacher is married to a substantial farmer or shopkeeper.

This, as far as O'Connell was concerned, was the genesis of the ban. He later recalled how, during the 1920s, Minister O'Sullivan had 'more than once told me of the grumbling about teachers' "double salaries" which he and other TDs frequently heard' when they visited rural areas.[118] This conclusion may be rather reductionist (especially since the person responsible for pushing the ban initially was a civil servant), but it is likely to have lent weight to the argument in the eyes of the politicians. The other reasons given were: the difficulty in finding trained substitutes for women on maternity leave; and since the average age of women teachers on marriage was around 31 (once again, as O'Connell pointed out, there was no evidence for this), the state would still get ten years' return on the investment in their training and the ban would finance itself.

In a last hope, O'Connell went to lobby the bishops, but not only did he find they had already washed their hands of the issue – had they objected, it is inconceivable that the government would have pursued the ban – but also that the Catholic Managers' Association had given enthusiastic support.[119] The last remaining routes to stop the ban were legal or industrial actions. The latter was simply never considered: if there was going to be an industrial dispute it would happen over salaries and pensions. There is no record of legal advice being sought, but the failure to take recourse to law indicates that if it was given, it was to the effect that there was no case. The CEC had argued that the ban was 'contrary to the spirit if not the letter' of Article 3 of the Free State Constitution, which stated that 'every person without distinction of sex ... shall enjoy the privileges of citizenship'; but, as one constitutional expert has noted, that did not amount to 'some sort of free-standing equality guarantee'.[120] In the end, the only concession achieved on the ban was a delay in its implementation until 1934, so that no woman who had already entered her teacher training in the expectation of a lifelong career would be compelled to resign on marriage.

The marriage bar did not mark the end of the government's attack on women teachers; indeed for many women teachers what happened next was even more unjust than the ban. Pupil numbers had been decreasing throughout the 1930s: from 513,349 in 1933 to 472,145 in 1940, a fall of eight per cent.[121] At the same time, the teacher training and preparatory colleges had been producing more teachers than was necessary. The number of students admitted to training was cut, possibly as a result of INTO representations,[122] but the level of recently trained teachers unable to find permanent positions, or, indeed, any position at all, grew over the decade.

For a while, Head Office ran a list of substitutes, but by the end of 1937 there were over 500 trained teachers without employment.[123] In March 1937, the INTO in the South scored a major breakthrough when it secured an agreement with the Catholic clerical managers so that each diocese would have a panel of teachers who were at risk from declining averages. Any teacher at risk would be placed on the panel and any new appointments would be made from it.[124] This agreement was not easily won, and the INTO's success contrasted with the situation north of the border, where the managers resolutely refused to consider the idea, arguing that it interfered with their right to make appointments. The panel helped keep a lot of teachers in work, but it did not solve the problem of unemployment in itself, highlighted in August 1937 when a group of unemployed teachers from Kerry cycled from Tralee to Dublin to draw attention to their situation.[125] Their protest was well reported in the press, and when it was raised in the Dáil in November, the minister said the issue was being 'carefully examined' in the Department.[126] The Department's solution was announced quickly and cynically on the eve of congress. On 13 April, it wrote to O'Connell informing him of remedial measures to deal with teacher unemployment, the first of which was 'the retirement of women teachers at 60 years of age, or on completing 35 years' service, whichever is the later'.[127] Technically, this involved the enforcement of the existing pension rules, drawn up in 1914, which stated that the statutory age of retirement was 60 for women (and 65 for men). However, there was a provision in the 1914 rules whereby women could continue teaching until 65, provided they were efficient and had their manager's consent, and it had effectively become the norm.[128] Enforced retirement at 60 was a double blow for women, since not only did it deprive them of five years' salaried employment, but they were also forced to retire before they had reached

40 years' service – the minimum necessary to be eligible for the full pension. This creation of an insurmountable obstacle to the full pension for women who had laboured towards it all their working lives would be regarded as the gravest injustice.[129]

On Holy Thursday, the evening after receiving details of the Department's plan, a five-man CEC delegation met the minister and protested against the move. In the absence of Mrs Kathleen Clarke, the only woman on the executive, however, it is possible that the exclusively male deputation underestimated the level of anger which this proposal would generate among women teachers. Moreover, their cough might have been softened by the news that teachers could expect a five per cent pay increase. It was far from the restitution of 1920 pay scales that had been the demand since the cuts first began, but since it was the first time the government had budged upwards on salaries, it was a welcome move in the right direction. Accordingly, one account of congress reported that it 'opened on a cheerful note',[130] which, if it was accurate for the majority of (male) delegates, is quite unlikely to have been the case among the women. The timing of the announcement meant that there were no resolutions on the matter, and though an effort to put it on the agenda for discussion was approved by the Standing Orders Committee, according to some delegates, a discussion regarding the tactics of fighting the issue was barred.[131] Ultimately, congress condemned forced retirement and reduced pensions, but without giving consideration to what was to be done.

It was clear from branch meetings across the country that there was deep opposition to the move, and if, perhaps, the CEC had underestimated the enormity of the proposal at the outset, it soon became clear that it had 'aroused the greatest possible resentment amongst the profession'.[132] When another deputation met the minister to discuss the issue some weeks later, they were told that, having considered the unemployment issue from 'every possible angle', the decision was irrevocable, and the rule would become operative on 1 October.

A sub-committee to consider how to tackle the issue, with securing full pensions its priority, was set up by the CEC.[133] It sought the advice of two leading counsel, one of whom was a former attorney general and future taoiseach, John A. Costello, but the response was that legally they had no case: the 1914 agreement stated that the retirement age for women was 60 and there was nothing to stop the government from imposing that.[134] After the 1939 congress, they sought a third opinion but, once again, the advice was that the organisation had no case in law.[135] The INTO held public meetings in an effort to gain support and appealed to the opposition parties for backing, but the government refused to budge either on forced retirement or on making an allowance for this in the pension entitlements for women teachers affected. Forced retirement was described by one (male) teacher as the cause of the greatest indignation since

Blythe's ten per cent cut,[136] and this indignation only grew stronger after October 1938, when the first women were put out of their jobs. As one woman put it, 'apart from the monetary loss, I loved my work and I had hoped to be left teaching until December 1942. Now life seems over for me.'[137] In total 203 women were compelled to retire on 30 October. To pour salt on their wounds, the claim that it was done to end unemployment among younger teachers was a sham, as it emerged that in many cases, no new appointment was made in their schools.[138]

Some women complained that the organisation was not fighting their cause as trenchantly as it ought to, and there were suggestions that this was because their male colleagues had failed to take up their cause. One woman teacher wrote to the *School Weekly*, 'there are 6,360 women members and 4,110 men. Are you going to submit tamely to the crime of withdrawing the right to full pension from such a big percentage of the organisation?' Warning of a strong tendency in the country to put 'woman in her place', she urged her INTO sisters to stand against this, and encouraged them to write to the *ISW* to claim space for their grievances.[139] The old Lady Teachers' Own Page had been dropped during the 1920s, and a 'For women only' column appeared as a one-off. It gave fashion and grooming advice, and its publication in the issue dated 1 April 1939 suggests that it may have been included as a joke. Some male activists expressed frustration at the women themselves. Typical of this was one correspondent to *ISW*, who accused women of being indifferent. 'Ask any branch secretary to say what percentage of these lady teachers attended the recent quarterly meetings to voice their grievance or to show even the semblance of a fight. Less than one thirteenth of ours did.'[140]

Women activists were only too aware of this; as one told the 1942 congress, if women used their votes to vote for women, they could have a woman-only executive.[141] Instead, there was a single woman, Kathleen Clarke (not to be confused with the Lord Mayor of Dublin and widow of Tom Clarke), among 11 elected representatives. Some years earlier, around the time the marriage ban was being introduced, there had been calls at congress to rectify this by bringing in a designated women's seat in each district or introducing a women's advisory committee to the CEC,[142] but there seems to have been little support for anything of the kind. The general secretary, for one, was dead set against it. O'Connell argued:

> I would strongly deprecate any movement within the organisation that would have the effect of ranging the men and women into separate camps ... Full equality was accorded to the women members of the organisation [in the constitution written in 1918] ... No doubt women have their own problems – so have the men, but there is not great fundamental difference between both sets of problems any more than there is for instance between

those of principals and assistants or between the principal of a one teacher and a six teacher school. As teachers they are part of the one system and the only hope of success lies in unity.

His view had not altered when, in 1940, the Athenry branch tabled a motion that a lady delegate should be elected in each district in addition to the one designated place at CEC. Proposing the motion, Mrs Clune told delegates: 'women were in a majority of 2,674 in the organisation but they were shy to go forward for election in the usual way'. Describing the proposal as misguided, O'Connell said it was not in the 'interests of the lady Teachers that they should have a double vote. In other organisations they had something which develops into a sex war', and the motion was heavily defeated. If women could not be assured of representation through quotas, they would have to try the more conventional route. As Kathleen Clarke advised women teachers at the 1941 congress, 'Do your own work. Don't refuse to come to the meetings of your branches and to let your voices be heard. The days when men must work and women must weep are gone for ever.'[143] If hearts were set against quotas, minds were open to means of encouraging women in other ways, such as the special ladies' session at the 1942 congress, although, as O'Connell lamented, 'it brought no new speakers to the platform. All the ladies who contributed to the debate had, I believe, spoken at previous congresses', although another delegate observed that women teachers had played a 'prominent part in the proceedings'.[144]

Getting women to become active in the organisation was not easy. Whether it was for cultural reasons (reticence, a dislike of campaigning or a perception of a macho culture within the organisation) or for practical ones (many of them would have had families and prioritised their work at home), there were significant obstacles in mobilising women members – but there was some success. Mrs Kathleen Clarke, for several years the only woman on the CEC, stood for election as vice-president in 1944 and was elected unopposed. She was now joined on the CEC by two new representatives, Miss Nora Higgins of Castlebar and Miss O'Driscoll. The following year Mrs Clarke became only the second woman president of the INTO, more than 30 years after Catherine Mahon had left office.[145] By the mid-1940s there was a cohort of women who had become not only active but more militant, and who would put themselves to the fore in a renewed salary campaign after 1945.

THE INTO AND THE CATHOLIC CHURCH

When the Free State was established, the Catholic Church's main concern in education was that schooling would be left within its sphere of influence, and successive governments were content to do so. Many of the issues which had caused conflict between the Church and the INTO in the past had been largely resolved (tenure) or were no longer relevant (the Macpherson Bill) and the areas of greatest concern to the organisation – salaries and pensions, inspection, curriculum and averages – were under government control. This meant that in the years after 1922 there was seldom a time when the INTO was not at odds with the government of the day, but its relationship with the Catholic Church during this period was reasonably cordial, and with Catholic Actionists among the organisation's senior officials, potentially contentious matters were dealt with even before the clergy was aware of them (see the discussion of the Workers' Republic on page 95). The bishops had been unhelpful on the marriage ban but when asked to lend their weight to teachers' demands for salary increases (dealt with below) – something that cost the hierarchy nothing, financially or otherwise – the bishops had been happy to oblige. Nevertheless, as Noel Ward has pointed out, 'disagreements might have been relatively rare but they were unavoidable'.[146] Where they arose it was over concerns that the INTO was acting in a way that might diminish Church control, say in the running of buildings, or outside its sphere of influence, in the case of the Council of Education (see below). More often than not, they revolved around dismissal cases. Where these happened there would be 'a series of approaches and negotiations, the stuff of trade union life', but on occasions where the Church insisted in 'on the propriety of its action or belief, the INTO was left with little room for manoeuvre',[147] and the conflict would enter the public domain. This meant that while disputes were rare, when they did occur they could be lengthy and very fractious indeed.

COUNCIL OF EDUCATION

The fate of the Council of Education in 1934, an INTO initiative that fell foul of the Catholic Church, is a useful illustration of the parameters in which the organisation was allowed to operate and the methods used to enforce these limits. Mooted by Alfred O'Rahilly when he was helping draft the Free State Constitution, the INTO became the keenest proponent of a Council of Education which would bring together educational interests to advise the government. It became a keystone of the Labour Party's education policy and it also enjoyed the support of the ASTI.[148] However, while advisory councils existed in connection with the Departments of Local Government, Agriculture, Industry and Commerce, Fisheries, and Post and Telegraphs,[149] when it came to education, successive ministers were confident that they could manage policy perfectly well on their own. Among the opponents of the proposal was the influential UCD professor of education, Rev. Timothy Corcoran, who published several articles attacking the idea. Its biggest difficulty, as Corcoran saw it, was that 'certain bodies, "neutral in their constitution", might secure representation on the council by individuals influenced by English ideas and who might "challenge the principle of religious education, a principle which the Church is ever, and must be, on the alert to defend".[150] Were a council to represent only the Catholic interests in education, however, he did not see a problem.[151] While Cumann na nGaedhael ministers turned their faces against the idea, Fianna Fáil seemed more amenable. Speaking during the Education Estimates debate in 1931, Frank Fahy, its spokesman on education, proposed an education council, and de Valera argued that it could prove a useful resource for the minister. But when Fianna Fáil took office in 1932, Thomas Derrig did not share Fahy's enthusiasm, and spoke unambiguously against the idea in the Dáil in April 1933.[152]

In September 1933, the INTO took the initiative and began attempts to establish an independent education council, believing that 'though such a body would not be officially appointed by the Minister, no Minister could for long afford to ignore its views'. It invited organisations representing teachers and managers at secondary, vocational and third levels to a meeting to discuss the advisability of setting up such a council. Professor William McGuinness and the journalist and Gaelic League activist Shán Ó Cuiv were also invited to attend in their personal capacity.[153] When the meeting was held in the Teachers' Hall in November, it was attended by 40 representatives from 11 bodies.[154] Only the universities declined the invitation. Shán Ó Cuiv and T.J. O'Connell both felt the meeting went well and described its mood as having been broadly in favour of establishing a council but they failed to read the depth of opposition from certain sections. While most delegates expressed their unqualified support for the proposal, this did not include the Catholic Headmasters' Association (CHA), the Christian Brothers or the De La Salle Training College. The CHA chairman, Fr John Charles McQuaid, then headmaster of Blackrock College, had come with the intention of, at the very least, stalling the proposal.[155] Fr McQuaid had first met O'Connell two years earlier when they had worked alongside each other during the 1932 Eucharistic Congress, but they do not appear to have developed any particular rapport at that time.[156] Speaking after T.J. O'Connell had made his opening remarks, McQuaid led the charge against the council, giving four grounds: (1) it should only be set up in conjunction with the minister; (2) the ministry had 'always shown itself willing to receive the suggestion of the various associations'; (3) 'the constitution of such a council must prove unwieldy and be such that the CHA would of necessity be drawn into controversial questions that could not rightly be considered within the scope of the CHA'; and (4) problems of secondary education could be more equitably treated by the present machinery than by the majority vote of such an advisory council. McQuaid single-handedly managed to prevent the meeting reaching agreement on anything beyond a decision to hold another meeting.[157] Somehow, the INTO failed to appreciate the significance of this, and so did Shán Ó Cuiv. An enthusiastic and active proponent of the council, Ó Cuiv advised

T.J. O'Connell, 'go ahead … and all will come in, even those who might be inclined to be obstructive if they saw any hesitation on the part of those who really want to see the body established'.[158]

While Ó Cuiv and the INTO set about drafting a framework for 'an Dáil um Oideachas' for discussion at the follow-up meeting in March, McQuaid went about undermining the whole project and kept a grateful minister for education, who was unhappy at the 'big-stick methods of the INTO', updated on his sabotage.[159] McQuaid was not working alone – there was at least one meeting in Archbishop's House with, among others, a former minister, Professor Corcoran of UCD and senior clerics who regarded the matter with anxiety[160] – but he was entrusted with the heavy lifting. At the second meeting McQuaid stopped any agreement on anything until after the INTO put forward a draft document explaining the aims, constitution and actual function of the new body and by the time the INTO presented this to a third meeting, on 26 May,[161] any enthusiasm for the project outside the INTO had evaporated. Only 16 delegates attended.[162] McQuaid's only contribution at this gathering was to register protest 'on principle' against a paragraph giving nomination rights to the council to the Catholic Hierarchy, the General Synod of the Church of Ireland and the General Assembly of the Presbyterian Church.[163] O'Connell assured McQuaid of his 'complete respect for the Catholic hierarchy', but McQuaid was adamant that the offending paragraph had to be deleted. With 'a few desultory remarks' the meeting ended without reaching agreement on anything beyond calling another meeting for November and keeping the proceedings of this and previous meeting confidential.[164]

Afterwards, McQuaid was counselled by Archbishop's House to 'let the lay bodies drift for the present. Any attempt at propaganda against them might create bitterness.'[165] But while McQuaid was prepared to desist from propaganda, he could not allow things to drift altogether. Instead, he secured the support of the hierarchy to designate a day of the annual Catholic Truth Society week as a congress of all Catholic bodies involved in education and thus 'the proposed non-denominational Federation would be reduced to its true proportions in the eyes of the people'.[166] By the autumn, with the prospect of another meeting in November, McQuaid secured permission from his archbishop to hold meetings with the INTO and ASTI general secretaries. T.J. Burke of the ASTI 'agreed at once to secede from the proposed Federation' when McQuaid 'explained the situation' to him, and anticipated no problem with his executive, who, McQuaid noted, all 'happen to be Catholics'. Almost a week later, he met O'Connell (who had been away), who, 'on hearing the reasons put forward also agreed, at once, that the projected Federation must not be established'. Unlike his ASTI colleague, however, he said he feared 'some difficulty from certain members of his association, who may not readily understand the situation, for the project has been discussed at meetings and publicly commented on in the Year Book of the INTO. Nonetheless he felt confident that by deft arrangement and without giving all the reasons, he [would] satisfy at least the reasonable element and Association.'[167]

McQuaid's archbishop felt he had 'handled a very delicate situation with great tact and skill',[168] while Cardinal MacRory congratulated him for his valuable work. It had taken just over a year, but the Blackrock headmaster had managed to scupper the INTO proposals by delay and cajoling. He had been careful not to give offence to the INTO, because for one thing, it was a teaching organisation 'of lay persons, most of them Catholic', but he also operated from a position of strength since the CHA could make or break the proposal.[169]

It might seem logical that that during this era of vocationalism, far from sabotaging it, the CHA and the hierarchy should have actively supported a committee of this kind, but the problem was not with the idea of the committee, but who would be on it. The INTO and ASTI had proposed a non-denominational council; but, for the hierarchy and the CHA, it had to be a Catholic council or nothing. Writing to Archbishop Byrne of Dublin, McQuaid observed:

It has never appeared either from correspondence or conversation or the proceedings of the meetings that the INTO or ASTI consider it in any way opposed to Catholic principles to establish a federation of educational interests comprising any and every belief. There is serious evidence that the INTO (which in principle is non-denominational) is endeavouring to show itself the dominant educational actor in the country.[170]

McQuaid's opposition to the organisation of anything along non-denominational lines was partly about power; a wholly Catholic organisation would be easy to control, whereas a mixed organisation could prove more difficult. Perhaps equally disagreeable was an organisation in which Catholics and Protestants were encouraged to work side by side, which McQuaid observed was obviously objectionable to him, but had not even crossed the mind of the INTO. The INTO never saw the council as a show of strength, let alone dominance, but McQuaid's perception of this illustrates the sensitivity that existed towards the organisation having taken the initiative without first consulting the Church. The council of education may not have been the most pressing matter before the INTO at the time, but the determination of the CHA and the Catholic hierarchy to prevent it illustrates the narrow limits within which the INTO could operate without resistance. The organisation continued to support the establishment of a council for education but it abandoned efforts to establish one itself.

THE EDWARDS DISMISSAL AND THE WORKERS' REPUBLIC

A far graver threat than ecumenism was communism or socialism, which was almost as bad. The communist movement in Ireland during the 1930s was very small indeed, but in the early 1930s, the Cumann na nGaedheal government had run a red scare to boost its support, and the Catholic Church, concerned by events on the continent and guided by the Vatican, joined it against the red menace. The Church's antipathy towards the left and popular anti-communism grew stronger still with the outbreak of the Spanish Civil War in 1936, which was painted as an attack on the Catholic Church by anti-Christian communists.

One organisation identified at the time as communist and anti-clerical was Republican Congress, a movement that included those associated with the left in the IRA and a number of communists, and which ran a newspaper and organised campaigns such as rent strikes. One activist was a popular young teacher named Frank Edwards, who was from a well-known family in Waterford. Edwards' manager, Archdeacon William Byrne, had warned him against associating with the Republican Congress and told that if he attended a high-profile meeting of the Congress being held in Rathmines in September, he would be dismissed. Edwards went anyway and was served three months' notice. The INTO worked behind the scenes to try to have the dismissal withdrawn but it became a cause célèbre in the meantime, with Edwards receiving huge support locally as well as from republicans and leftists and at least two Fianna Fáil cumainn around the country. T.J. O'Connell and the president, Jerry Hurley, met Dr Kinane, the bishop of Waterford, but Kinane told them that he had approved the dismissal notice before it was issued, which meant it fulfilled at least part of the Maynooth Resolution. Kinane stressed that issue was religion rather than politics, since, he believed, Edwards was refusing to dissociate himself from a group whose objects were contrary to Catholic doctrine and principles. Kinane assured the INTO that if he changed his mind, the notice would be withdrawn. Edwards would not do so, however, and was read out from the altar as a result.

There were well-attended meetings in Edwards' support, which saw some of his pupils parading with banners,[171] and on Tuesday 15 January – the day the dismissal notice was to expire – some children at Mount Sion went on strike in protest. Waterford City was heavily policed, as supporters of Edwards and his opponents (many of them Blueshirts) faced off against each other, resulting in a baton charge outside the school gates.[172] At one public meeting in Dublin, Hanna Sheehy-Skeffington recalled that there had been a time when the present minister for education, Tomás Derrig, had had difficulty getting a teaching job because he would not sign an oath of allegiance, and she called on the Department to give Edwards a 'fair deal',[173] but the government had no interest in intervening. There was a lengthy discussion about the case at the INTO executive meeting in February (of what was said, unfortunately, there is no record), but, as the CEC report noted following the dismissal, there were 'no further developments in the matter so far as the Executive are concerned'.[174]

Subsequently, Edwards was given permission to address a private session of congress that Easter to state his case. He was greeted with 'some applause' by delegates, although one delegate was removed from the hall after repeatedly interrupting Edwards and calling for him to be thrown out. Edwards' case was simple: he had been dismissed for his political opinions, expressed only outside school; the principle that teachers could hold political opinions outside school was at stake.[175] But while there was clearly a great deal of sympathy for Edwards among the INTO officers and members, there was reticence at all levels of the organisation about showing support in this case: not only would it involve going against the Church as managers, as had been the case years earlier in Fanore, for instance, but the invoking of 'faith and morals' by the manager and his bishop added another dimension entirely. Edwards' dismissal was unjust, but it did not contravene any regulations, so legally there was nothing the INTO could do apart from publicly stand behind him.

Not long after, the Labour Party, to which the INTO was still affiliated, adopted a new constitution. Fianna Fáil's electoral support had kept growing since 1932, and Labour wanted to distinguish itself from the larger party, which had adopted many of its policies and was attracting much of its natural support base. Labour's new constitution was an effort to win back support by appearing more radical. Roundly criticised by many on the left of the party as being pale pink and lacking in substance, its support for a 'workers' republic' raised alarm bells in Catholic circles. Chief among its critics was M.P. Linehan, the INTO assistant general secretary and Catholic actionist. Linehan was personally opposed to the socialist rhetoric of the call for a workers' republic, despite Labour leadership assurances that it owed everything to James Connolly and nothing to the Soviet Union, but within the INTO there was concern over how the Catholic Church might react. After a flurry of excited coverage of the matter in the Catholic press, the INTO forwarded a copy of the Labour constitution to the bishops, seeking their advice. A special committee considered the document and reported that six sections involved 'a clear denial of the Catholic principles on private and individual ownership, as well as a denial of the essential liberty and natural rights of every individual under the state'.[176]

Eventually, following some careful groundwork, a motion drafted by Labour's administrative council was put before the 1939 party conference to remove the offending sections. There was opposition from some on the left of the party and at least one Protestant delegate, who complained that Catholic hierarchy was being allowed to dictate Labour policy, but a majority took the view that keeping the sections was more trouble than it was worth, and the motion to remove the workers' republic sections passed. The complaints about the INTO's affiliation to

Labour were voiced yet again around this time even though it had become obvious once more that the INTO had significantly more influence on the Labour Party than the Labour Party had on it. Nevertheless, the weight of opinion against affiliation was growing. In 1941 the ITGWU (Labour's largest union, ahead only of the INTO) disaffiliated and established a breakaway National Labour Party, claiming that Labour had been taken over by communists.[177] There was a failed attempt to table a motion to disaffiliate at the 1943 congress, during which there was reference to the malign influence of outside bodies on the organisation, one based in Ely Place, the other in Molesworth Street (home to the Knights of Columbanus and the Masons respectively), but the resolution was not moved.[178] In fact, while the Masons were said to have been influential in Tyrone House before 1922, their influence was virtually nil on the INTO, but the same could not be said of the Knights, who were said to have been well represented at various levels of the organisation, at least until the 1980s. Among them was John D. Sheridan, a former teacher in East Wall NS who edited the *ISW* between 1932 and 1941.[179]

Whatever influence they may have had, however, was not sufficient to inoculate the organisation from accusations of anti-clericalism at various junctures, especially from the 1950s. Moreover, it is worth noting that at the same time as the ITGWU disaffiliated from Labour, it also broke away from the ITUC and established a new umbrella group, the Congress of Irish Unions (CIU), which portrayed itself as a nationalist, anti-communist trade union congress, but if the INTO might have been a natural ally of the CIU's rhetoric, it remained with the ITUC. (The two congresses eventually reunited in 1959 to form the Irish Congress of Trade Unions, or ICTU.) Another effort to secure disaffiliation from Labour was scuppered at the 1944 Easter Congress, when T.J O'Connell called on the INTO to remain in the party and fight any malign influences as it had done before over the workers' republic,[180] but Labour scored a foolish own-goal later that summer, when votes it had promised to O'Connell in the Seanad election did not materialise and he lost the seat he had held as an independent since 1941. A furious O'Connell wrote to Labour informing the party that 'the relations between the INTO and the party would be a matter for grave consideration in the near future',[181] and having vigorously defended the INTO–Labour link at the congress in 1944, he raised no objections when the congress voted to disaffiliate the following year.[182] Subsequent attempts to woo them back proved unsuccessful.

THE INTO DURING THE EMERGENCY

On 3 September 1939, war was declared in Europe. Naturally, the experience of the conflict was rather different on either side of the border. Northern teachers lived and worked in a combatant state, while southern teachers operated in a neutral country, under a state of emergency. For the teachers, all the old problems remained, while Emergency conditions made others considerably worse, but there was one apparently positive development early on, when a government reshuffle saw Tomás Derrig leave Education, where he was replaced by the taoiseach. Derrig's removal was most welcome[183] and, unusually for an education minister, de Valera initially seemed eager to solicit the INTO's goodwill. The first meeting between the new minister and the INTO was at the minister's invitation – which was itself out of the ordinary – and over the course of four hours, he paid tribute to the work of teachers, complimented the INTO, referring to it as 'the most widespread and most influential union in the country', and promised to keep in 'constant touch' on all matters relating to education administration.[184] If de Valera's interest in education was genuine, it was not long before it became apparent that nothing would come of it. It was clear early on that de Valera would not yield on compulsory retirement for women and, at his second and final meeting with an INTO delegation, he made 'no secret of his own personal view' on the matter.[185] Neither was there good news on salaries.[186] De Valera attended congress in Killarney in March, where, speaking entirely in Irish, he spoke of the role of teachers, but promised nothing. Soon after, in June 1940, he relinquished his role, and Derrig returned to office, finding things much as he had left them.

Wartime shortages meant that prices soared, leaving teachers more discontented about their salaries. As Michael Moroney notes, 'the cost of living index increased from 173 in 1938 to 284 in 1943. Teachers were the only group of public servants that did not receive any increase in remuneration during the period, even though the INTO applied on a number of occasions for a war bonus.'[187] The treatment of their northern colleagues, who had been awarded a bonus, caused further bad feelings.[188] These were expressed by the president, Martin Leyden, in his address to the organisation's northern conference in Belfast in December 1939. Leyden delivered a litany of complaints relating to the South to the northern delegates, including high unemployment rates among teachers, low pay and high cost of living and the continued sidelining of teachers in education governance. He noted the dire housing conditions in which many of his pupils lived, and of how he had to share his lunch with many of them, most of whom had eaten no breakfast that morning. 'Can you expect in the Name of God, in the name of common sense, that you can make these children highly efficient in two languages – not one, but two!'[189] 'The twenty-six counties had nothing to offer the teachers of the North,' he continued, 'and if the northern teachers continued to receive good things as they had been, the inducement would be all on the Northern side of the border and the Southern teachers might join with them'.[190] It was a rather ill-judged speech. Its failure to appreciate the very particular problems faced by northern teachers was crass, but perhaps his greatest sin was that he had so unfavourably compared conditions of teachers of the South with their northern counterparts in public, and in Belfast of all places.[191] The speech, unnoted in the *School Weekly* but widely reported in the national and regional press, was discussed at the CEC's meeting on 3 February and, after prolonged discussion, it adopted a motion disassociating the executive from the president's statements.[192] There was almost nothing in the president's address with which many teachers in the South or members of the executive would disagree, but it was bad politics to say so. Resentment over teaching through Irish had been longstanding, but had come to the fore once again recently with the CEC's publication of the 'Report of the INTO Committee of Inquiry into the Use of Irish as a Teaching Medium to Children Whose Home Language is English' in the summer of 1941.[193]

Resentment was heightened further by the introduction of a wage freeze in the summer of 1941, but to add insult to injury, civil servants and the gardaí were given bonus increases with effect from 1 January 1942.[194] 'Why,' asked the general secretary, 'should the national teachers be always regarded as the Cinderellas of the public services?'[195] To be fair to the minister, Derrig did argue this point to the cabinet, but to no avail.[196] In fact, it is worth bearing in mind that notwithstanding O'Connell's low opinion of Derrig (shared, no doubt, by most teachers), he was not backward in putting forward the INTO's case for increased salaries over the years, but he was unable to overcome the implacable opposition to this from Finance.[197] Teachers had been instructed that they were not allowed to enlist in the defence forces because teaching was a work of national importance,[198] and had been plámásed by the minister at congress, but if they were told that their work was of great national value, their wage packets told them otherwise. Eventually, in December 1942, the government decided to award an emergency bonus to teachers earning less than £398 17s, but it was inadequate and not equal to awards made to other groups that had received more frequent increases. The award was also discriminatory, since male and female teachers ought to have received the same amount, but instead men teachers had been awarded seven shillings per week and women only five.[199] The INTO had just begun a new salary campaign, holding its first public meetings at the end of November, and it would appear that the decision to award this bonus, niggardly as it was, was, as Moroney has put it, an effort to defuse this 'and to influence public opinion against teachers. It was calculated to show that the teachers were being accommodated by the government and that they were malcontents, at a time when the country's economic circumstances were so grave.'[200] It succeeded, but only for a while and in July 1943, the CEC began putting together plans for a renewed campaign.[201]

THE SALARY CAMPAIGN AND THE 1946 STRIKE

Since the first cuts had been made to teachers' salaries in 1923, the INTO's key demand was the restoration of the 1920 pay scale. By 1940, however, that would not have been enough to compensate for the increased cost of living, leading congress to call for a new scale. Initially, though, the executive focused on securing an adequate war bonus, while working towards building support for the teachers' claims. When it put a claim for new scales to the government in June 1944, the minister was adamant that nothing could be done until after the Emergency, but in October the Catholic hierarchy wrote to the government recommending the teachers' claim. Responding to a question tabled by Patrick Halliden, a Clann na Talmhan deputy and national teacher, Derrig confirmed that he had received the bishops' recommendation and it was getting 'the closest attention',[202] but when he put the proposals to Cabinet the following week they were rejected outright by the minister for finance, Frank Aiken.[203] Instead, the teachers were awarded a wartime bonus of one shilling per week, widely regarded as little more than an insult.[204] Members were furious with the government and their own executive which, they felt, had utterly failed to push their claim.

The executive went into the 1945 congress expecting trouble,[205] but what happened that week in Galway came close to a coup. One member of the executive recalled how, by the time Congress met:

> [T]he rising tide of resentment had reached high water mark. The Executive, always regarded as fair game for attack, was of course, blamed for their lack of success during the year … There was a general feeling that the old method of sending deputations to the Minister was useless.[206]

The bad feeling was evident from the outset, when it looked as though the CEC's annual report would be rejected by a large majority.[207] Delegates, having concluded that the CEC had failed in its negotiations, in its propaganda and in running the salary campaign as a whole, decided to take matters out of the executive's hands altogether. Instead, in what O'Connell later described as a motion of no confidence in the newly elected incoming executive, an ad hoc committee of 32 delegates, one from each county, was selected to choose how the salary campaign should be pursued. After a few hours of consideration, it recommended that a Central Propaganda Committee (CPC) be established in Dublin. Consisting of the general secretary and eight members from the Dublin area (Dave Kelleher and Sean Sweeney of the CEC along with Seán Brosnahan, Dave Hanley, C. Sheehan, J. Kelly, Matt Griffin and P. Kelly), it was, in effect, given complete control of the salary campaign.[208] Despite its name, the CPC regarded propaganda as a waste of scarce resources from the outset and began, instead, to build up strike machinery and the organisation's fighting fund.[209]

In April the taoiseach reluctantly agreed to meet an INTO deputation, which told him that the teachers had reached boiling point. They provided family budgets for teachers, showing how they could not make ends meet, while the president, Kathleen Clarke, told him that more than 200 teachers in Dublin were in the hands of moneylenders. De Valera merely responded that he was familiar with their arguments but that he could not break the wages standstill.[210] A week later, 13 Dublin teachers staged a protest in the public gallery of the Dáil during the Education Estimates debate and were thrown out by gardaí.[211] As the *Irish Times* noted in an editorial, 'it is not very seemly, perhaps, that the proceedings of the national parliament should be interrupted by demonstrators who have to be ejected by the Guards; but it is far more unseemly that the teachers should be forced to take such steps in an attempt to secure their rights'.[212]

Plans for a strike began in earnest in the summer of 1945. On 1 June, the CEC approved the CPC's proposal to hold a regional strike in Dublin. The idea, first mooted by the Dublin branch in 1933, would see teachers in the capital take strike action, during which they would receive 90 per cent of their salaries, financed by a loan fund, contributions from branches and a ten per cent contribution from the salaries of teachers who remained in work.[213] This would enable the Dublin teachers to stay out for longer than a conventional all-out strike would allow, while providing for maximum disruption. The Dublin branch signalled its willingness to participate in the scheme at a meeting on 13 June and it was subsequently approved by the other branches at special meetings ten days later.[214]

On 6 October 1945 Dublin teachers met at the Mansion House, where they voted by secret ballot to go on strike if and when instructed by the CEC, by an extraordinary 999 votes to 47.[215] In November, there followed negotiations between the minister and the CEC, but the government's proposed scales fell far short of the teachers' demands and were rejected by the CEC on 17 November.[216] Further discussions proved largely fruitless, and eventually, on 10 December, O'Connell wrote to the minister to the effect that if the government didn't increase its offer by £350,000, the Dublin members would go on strike from 17 January.[217] Having issued the threat, O'Connell became quite anxious. Fearing that the long-anticipated action was actually going to happen, he sought advice from the keenest political operator he could think of, and telephoned the archbishop of Dublin, John Charles McQuaid. McQuaid listened as O'Connell explained that while the younger teachers were restless, the older teachers were very anxious to avoid a strike, and he set out the terms that the INTO would be prepared to accept.[218] Half an hour later, McQuaid met the minister, who, he recorded, was 'dubious about result with government but very happy door was not slammed'. Derrig was right to be dubious and the government rebuffed the approach on the grounds that no negotiations could take place after a strike had been threatened. McQuaid did not see a problem. Instead, as he explained to O'Connell, he would tell the government it ought to regard the letter as never having been sent, while O'Connell and Dave Kelleher would write to the minister to express regret that a paragraph in the letter had been 'regarded as containing a threat to strike' and unreservedly withdraw the offending paragraph. Informed of events at a special meeting a week later, the CEC approved of O'Connell's actions and agreed that the withdrawal of strike notice would be kept confidential until congress.[219] Negotiations with the Department resumed and O'Connell was able to write to McQuaid that 'all danger [of a strike] has passed' and thanked him for his 'help, advice and guidance in this crisis'.[220] The archbishop took the compliment, adding, 'we may all thank Our Blessed Lady to whom we had committed the care of this vexatious problem'.[221]

The problem of the new pay scale remained vexatious, however, and with no progress in sight, the executive decided to consult the members at a special conference in Dublin on 9 February 1946.[222] Writing to the minister on the eve of the meeting, Archbishop McQuaid noted that while it was 'impossible to forecast the result of the congress ... the information I have been able to gather is very disquieting. Passion may easily cause a total rejection of the new scales.' Between 400 and 500 teachers attended the conference at the Mansion House, at which, after a full day of stormy debate, delegates voted against the government's offer but in favour of a CEC resolution to keep talking. A Dublin amendment to call a strike immediately was narrowly defeated, but delegates did decide that in the event of a subsequent offer being rejected, the Dublin teachers would stop work within ten days.[223] Afterwards, the executive sought one final meeting with Derrig, who obliged, although he was clear that no improvement would come of it. The minister was true to his word, and when the delegation reported back to the CEC empty-handed, instructions were given to hold a referendum of members on the final offer, with a closing date of 6 March.[224] The result of the national ballot saw 55.7 per cent (4,749 to 3,773) reject the offer, with Dublin branch voting by 80 per cent (890 to 213) against. The CEC decided to call the Dublin teachers out on strike on Wednesday 20 March.[225] As Archbishop McQuaid put it to the minister after the strike had been called, 'There seems to be an inevitability about the matter, which will cause it to work itself out to the very bitter end. And, when the end will have been reached, it will be only a question of starting where one might have started long before, without acrimony'.[226]

Wednesday 20 March saw hundreds of Dublin teachers queuing in pouring rain outside the Teachers' Club, waiting to sign the strike register, 'watched appreciatively' by some of their pupils, who now found themselves on indefinite holidays.[227] The strike call had been virtually unanimous: 1,227 of 1,250 members signed the roll that day. Only three men and 12 women members in Dublin failed to go out, and by the end of the week the strike committee had reported that only six members were working.[228] A report by the Department's inspectors found that that while 85 schools had remained open (the majority under Catholic religious management), 96 had closed, and among the schools that did remain open, some did so with only a single teacher present.[229] The *Irish Times* reported that an important factor in ensuring the massive level of adherence was a letter written to the deputy general secretary by Archbishop McQuaid, which was published in the national press on the morning of the strike. In it he assured the teachers:

> [Y]our organisation must have no doubt that the clerical managers of this city and the religious superiors have full sympathy with the idea of a salary in keeping with the dignity and responsibility of your profession as teachers. Further, every member of your organisation must now clearly be aware of my own desire that you should obtain the best salary possible in the circumstances and of my unremitting efforts to secure such a settlement of your problem, as would keep negotiations open and avoid the decision to declare a strike. For these reasons, there is no ground for the fear expressed in your circular that a wedge may be used as an instrument for breaking the strike.[230]

The archbishop assured teachers that while clergy and religious were precluded from going on strike 'by reason of their office', no striking teacher would be penalised for their action during the strike or subsequently. It was, as Eugene McCormick notes, 'an invaluable morale booster for teachers'.[231] The *Irish Times* reported that 'some teachers who had not made up their minds whether to strike or not were, it was said, swayed in favour by the publication of the letter', further noting that 'a number of Protestant managers have expressed their sympathy with the teachers and Protestant schools were yesterday deserted'. Three Church of Ireland schools remained open at the beginning, with the manager of Rathmines asserting his opposition to the strike and pledging to keep it open with the help of 'volunteers' and pupils.[232]

The dispute was co-ordinated by a number of committees with rather similar names. As well as the CEC and the CPC (established at the 1945 congress to run the salary campaign), there was the Strike Administration Committee, set up by the CEC in March, which comprised six members of the executive and six members of the Dublin Branch. As Noel Ward notes, 'this met almost daily from 9 March ... with the Dublin Branch committee acting as an executive to carry out its decisions'.[233] Finally, there was a Strike Executive Committee and a Strike Payments Committee, which were charged with ensuring day-to-day operations such as taking care of the roll.[234] Initially, strikers were obliged to sign the strike register in the Teachers' Club weekly, but this was soon changed to signing on Mondays, Wednesdays and Fridays.[235] They also took care to ensure that the striking teachers did their share of picketing, and exercised vigilance over the schools that had remained open. From the second week, striking teachers were expected to go on picket duty outside schools where lay teachers were still working, unless instructed otherwise. At first, only men were expected to do picket duty, but as the strike went into its third week, women had to join them. Soon there were reports that at least half of the pickets were women teachers, and before long they had outnumbered their male colleagues.[236] With more grievances than their male counterparts, women were also well represented on the various strike committees and among the supporters of the strike nationwide, and two women who served on the strike committee, Bríd Bergin and Margaret Skinnider, would later serve as President (1950–1 and 1955–6 respectively). At least two of their male colleagues wrote to de Valera at the time, noting the women's role. One, a Fianna Fáil teacher in Dingle and critic of the strike, complained about the 'gullible and inarticulate "ballavawns" of rural women teachers' who had been 'dragooned into battle'. A more constructive point of view came from the chairman of the Paddy Moran cumann in Phibsborough, who advised that some 'small adjustments such as … a slight increase to the women teachers – who really caused the strike – would go a long way towards a solution'.[237]

One of the Strike Committee's preoccupations was the question of whether children were being accepted into religious schools and secondary schools, and it investigated a steady stream of alleged cases, visiting schools and interviewing principals on the allegations. Picketing officers in cycle squads ensured that pickets were where they were supposed to be, when they were supposed to be there, and a dim view was taken of slack time-keeping or smoking on duty.[238] Those not on picket duty were obliged to do clerical work such as addressing envelopes for the 'Weekly supplement' that was sent to public representatives, newspapers and so on.[239] Over time, fewer schools remained open. In the strike's second week, the INTO announced that more schools had been closed, with 108 schools completely closed and 66 open or partly open.[240] The following week the *Irish Times* reported that at most of the schools that had remained open, no pupils had attended, while the one pupil who had been attending the Model School in Marlborough Street (where one teacher was turning up for work) had stayed home.[241] By mid-April a reported 70,000 Dublin children were said to be off school.[242]

Archbishop McQuaid was eager to find a resolution, but he was determined to do so alone. Strike resolution was not an ecumenical matter, and when Church of Ireland Archbishop of Dublin Arthur Barton suggested they co-operate in seeking an agreement, McQuaid thanked him but lamented that 'at this moment, it seems just impossible for any person to intervene, each side is so set in its own position'.[243] The next day, however, he wrote to O'Connell asking if there was any chance of the CEC calling off the strike 'without prejudice'. O'Connell responded immediately that it would be prepared to do so if the government would reopen negotiations and appoint the archbishop as a mediator,[244] but the government was unwilling to talk. Still, if nothing came of it, the teachers had benefited from the government's refusal to negotiate in the face of McQuaid's apparent initiative, which became public when the correspondence between O'Connell and McQuaid was published on the morning the 1946 congress opened in Dublin.[245] The government's bullish attitude from the outset, with Derrig accusing the INTO of trying to 'hold up the community to ransom',[246] met with little sympathy, and its refusal to engage in any kind of mediation merely shored up support for the strikers, with popular sympathies firmly behind the teachers. This was reflected in the newspaper coverage. As one *Irish Times* editorial put it, 'the government is acting in an exceedingly high-handed manner. The national school teachers are not recalcitrant Communists, whose object is to wreck the state. To a man and to a woman, they are highly respectable citizens, charged with the greatest of all responsibilities – the education and training of the nation's youth.'[247] These sentiments were typical of the coverage, with the exception of the *Irish Press*, which, not surprisingly, took a view more similar to that of the government.[248] Support also came from local authorities across the country, trade unions and trades councils, and civil society groups such as the Women's Social and Progressive League, the Irish Housewives' Association, local tenants' associations and, crucially, from parents' groups. As the strike went into the summer the major Churches and parents' groups continued to plead with the government to re-open negotiations, but their calls were rebuffed; Derrig argued that the only people keeping the teachers out were the teachers themselves. It had become apparent that the government was playing a waiting game, anticipating that the country teachers would tire of paying their strike contributions and the Dublin teachers would be compelled to go back to work. The INTO *Quarterly Bulletin* warned that this would be a catastrophe, and every member would share in the organisation's 'humiliation and defeat', which they had in their power to prevent by paying their strike contributions on time, giving to the loan fund and showing solidarity at all times.[249]

As the summer holidays ended and the strike had gone into its sixth month, teachers returned to the picket lines with little prospect of a resolution in sight. September saw members of the CEC and the Strike Committee tour the branches in an effort to maintain morale, while various meetings and rallies were held in Dublin. The most famous action, however, was an unofficial one, Operation Shakespeare, named after the pub at 160 Parnell Street in which it was hatched.[250] It saw some 70 school teachers – some from Dublin, others up for the match – launch a pitch invasion at half time during the All Ireland Football Final on 6 October. Reports recorded how after the half-time whistle, a 'crowd of "black coats"' appeared, many carrying placards and banners with slogans such as: 'Public opinion demands mediation'; 'Teachers, fight for your place in the sun'; and 'Heed the voice of Church, press and people', and began to make their way across the pitch. It happened so quickly that many of the crowd were unsure what was happening, but by the time the protesters had made their way quickly to the Hogan Stand, where the taoiseach was seated, a man in the stand shouted, 'Good old teachers, there ought to be a settlement', and 'cheers came from thousands'.[251] It wasn't long, though, before gardaí rushed out and broke up the demonstration; photographs of teachers being manhandled by the police, their banners destroyed, filled the next day's papers. When one reporter asked a nine-year-old scallywag in town what he thought of the strike, he was told how 'a man showed me a paper this morning with a Guard beatin' up a teacher at Croke Park yesterday', before adding anxiously, 'I hope that won't mean the teachers will have to go back soon.'[252]

At the Fianna Fáil ard fheis held the weekend after the football final, de Valera gave no cause for optimism, and simply told the teachers to get back to school. This was not mere posturing; a secret effort to open negotiations with the government through the minister for lands, Seán Moylan, had been firmly rebuffed. Rumours began floating that the INTO was about to call off the dispute, but the executive responded with a statement confirming that 'the strike goes on'.[253] The following week, when the Dáil returned from its summer recess, the government allowed time for discussion on a motion tabled by Richard Mulcahy and Patrick McGilligan calling for the establishment of a conciliation committee. The motion was tabled without INTO consultation and O'Connell later wrote that had he been consulted the executive would have advised against it, since 'they realized that the government would use their over-all majority to defeat it, and this once done, there would be no further question of mediation'.[254] O'Connell had already concluded that enough was enough, but while he felt that the time had come to raise the white flag, he faced two problems. First, the Dublin teachers were as committed as ever to staying out. Second, if the teachers were to come back to work prematurely, he would have to engineer a way to do it that did not look as though they had been defeated or humiliated.

Happily for O'Connell, it was at this point that the archbishop of Dublin offered his services once again. On the evening of 28 October, the archbishop had asked the general secretary to come out to Drumcondra. When he got there, McQuaid told him that he would like the strike to end and would be prepared to write a letter asking the teachers to go back to work but would do so only if the CEC asked him. O'Connell returned to Head Office and called an emergency meeting of the CEC the next evening.[255] At 7.30 p.m. on Tuesday, the CEC met, along with members of the Strike Administrative Committee (SAC), to discuss the archbishop's proposal. Speaking personally, two of the eight SAC members supported the idea, while four were opposed. Seán Brosnahan, speaking as chairman of the Dublin branch, said his branch would be against going back. Having given their opinion, the SAC members withdrew and the CEC voted to 'accede to the request of the Archbishop'.[256] The archbishop was informed and he obliged by sending his letter, along with a draft press release for O'Connell to use, which had been drafted the previous evening.[257] At 9.30 p.m. the members of the SAC, the Strike Committee and the Dublin Branch committee were called in and told that the archbishop had been asked for his letter and the strike was off, just as the letter and the statement calling the teachers back was being sent to the press.[258] Many Dublin teachers discovered what had happened when they turned up for picket duty the next morning.[259] No one had seen this coming, and after seven months on strike it was, as the *Irish Times* editorial put it, a rather 'strange denouement', in which, 'in effect, the teachers have surrendered'.[260]

On Wednesday afternoon, on the instructions of the CEC, the Dublin teachers met at the Metropolitan Hall on Lower Abbey Street to discuss the turn of events. Chaired by Seán Brosnahan, the meeting began with the president, Dave Kelleher, giving an account of what had happened in the previous days, after which members made their views felt. Some expressed sympathy with the executive's actions; many more were deeply unhappy at the strike being called off. As Seán Brehony put it, the CEC had 'cut the ground from under our feet'.[261] Nevertheless, if many Dublin members were deeply resentful at being pushed back to work with undue haste, they reluctantly accepted the decision. The meeting ended with the passing of two resolutions, the first of which was published in the press:

That in the interests of unity and solidarity of the organisation, the teachers of the Dublin City Branch will loyally abide by the decisions of the CEC in acceding to the invitation of His Grace, the Archbishop of Dublin, Most Rev Dr McQuaid.[262]

The second resolution appeared in the *ISW* a fortnight later:

That while accepting the direction of the CEC that we return to work, we, the members of the Dublin City Branch, wish it to be placed on the record that we categorically disagree with their decision.[263]

The Dublin members had been completely committed to the strike, but they were more committed to the INTO. As one member later told congress, 'we accepted the executive decision to call off the strike rather than split the organisation and let this be clear, Dublin teachers were ready to go on and we would have refused to go to work but we intended to keep the organisation intact at all costs'.[264] Loyalty to the organisation came first, and if anything, the strike had shown how necessary it was, but if the Dublin members were committed to keeping the organisation intact, the strike had left unfinished business, not only with the government but also with the INTO leadership. The teachers had returned empty-handed but the exit strategy provided by the archbishop had allowed the strike to end without undue embarrassment. As McQuaid had put it months earlier, 'in last analysis, the teachers … must go back on the formula that *they*, not the archbishop will find suitable. When this government is forgotten, the church will still need the good will of the teachers. I will continue to do all I can to help.'[265]

Chapter 4 ~

THE POT BOILED OVER, 1946–1962

'A considerable section of the younger teachers ... with a strong tendency to be anti-everything.'

D uring the war, Britain had already begun to plan for a significant restructuring of its education system at primary and secondary level. These changes began to be implemented throughout the United Kingdom, including Northern Ireland, after 1945; but while teachers in the North saw reforms both in the education system itself and in their salary scales, there was nothing comparable in the South. Asked by the taoiseach in 1942 to come up with plans for education reconstruction after the Emergency, Minister for Education Tomás Derrig had taken the request literally, examining the need for new buildings. No one in the INTO would have argued against the need for new school buildings, but it was only one thing in an entire system that needed reform. In late 1944, de Valera suggested to Derrig that the recently published White Paper Educational Reconstruction in Northern Ireland might contain ideas that could be useful in the South, following which a departmental committee was set up to review the need for reform. With typical alacrity, it reported to the minister some two and a half years later.[1] As Seán Farren points out, its recommendations 'were never published, nor were any steps taken to implement them'.[2]

Some of the younger members of the INTO were particularly conscious of developments outside the 26 counties, and were keen to push for change. In 1947, after several years' gestation, the organisation published *A Plan for Education*, a 123-page document that considered every aspect of education policy, from the recruitment and training of teachers to inspection, curriculum, examinations, teaching methods, buildings, examinations, child welfare and the Irish language.

Four years in the making, it was primarily the work of Seán Brosnahan. It was put forward as a discussion document rather than a blueprint, but it became the foundation for INTO education policy for the next 30 years.[3] It fell on stony ground, however, and until the very late 1950s there was little movement on policy from within government. Notwithstanding the *Plan for Education*, the INTO's focus remained largely on teachers' conditions, particularly regarding school buildings and promotion, and, more particularly, pay. It was not until after primary teachers' pay was seriously addressed in the mid-1960s that the organisation was able to look at educational matters more broadly, but before that there were many false starts and disappointments during a period characterised by political change and instability.

THE ORGANISATION AFTER THE 'INTO WAR'

The 1946 strike cast a long shadow over the INTO for many years. There was considerable unhappiness in Dublin over how the dispute had ended. The fault line between Dublin and the rest of the country, evident before and during the strike, had deepened, although dissatisfaction was by no means confined to the capital. Solidarity seemed to have weakened. Between the years immediately before and after the strike, membership fell nationally by almost 20 per cent to its lowest level since 1914.[4] There was no official explanation for why this occurred, but it seems that disillusionment following the strike combined with an inability or unwillingness to pay the strike-related levies caused the drop. But if the years immediately after 1946 featured a continuation of internal rivalries and an effort to recover, they were also a time of significant political change, which seemed to offer hope of reform.

After the strike, there remained a great deal of anger towards the government, which had proved so hostile and unyielding throughout the dispute. Its decision, announced in January, to award a £10 bonus to teachers who had not gone on strike (£20 to principals) added further insult to injury.[5] There was particular antipathy towards the four Fianna Fáil teacher-deputies who had voted against Richard Mulcahy's motion on 23 October, and several branches demanded their expulsion. Called on to explain their actions, the four deputies argued that as elected members of Fianna Fáil, they were pledge-bound to 'sit, act and vote' with their party, and that 'as members of the INTO they had fulfilled the obligations as imposed on them by the organisation [i.e. the two Dublin members had gone on strike and the two others had paid their levies] and that they could not be held responsible to the organisation for the manner in which they discharged their political duties'. The CEC found their argument 'not without substance' – as a former pledge-bound teachta dála himself, T.J. O'Connell was particularly sympathetic – and decided to take no action, which proved unpopular.[6] Following a fractious debate, delegates at the April 1947 congress voted to demand their immediate expulsion.[7] The CEC remained reluctant to follow through but was less reticent in its attitude towards their party, and called on all teacher members of Fianna Fáil to 'withdraw their active support from the Fianna Fáil organisation until such time as harmony is restored between the teachers and the government'.[8] Some branches disapproved,[9] but others pledged their full support. For many teachers such an instruction from the CEC was unnecessary.

Though impossible to quantify, the government's behaviour towards the INTO cost Fianna Fáil significant support from the ranks of national teachers. Many of those who abandoned Fianna Fáil became actively involved in a new political party, Clann na Poblachta, which had been founded during the summer of the strike. Eithne MacDermott, a historian of that party, has credited the teachers with lending the new party 'a large degree of organisational gravitas' and assistance with policy-making, and helping to 'tone down, ever so slightly, the republican complexion of the party'. Four of the 11 members of the strike administrative committee became actively involved in the Clann, as did four of the 21 members of the strike executive committee.[10] One of them, the 1916 veteran Margaret Skinnider, was soon to be elected to the CEC, and would later serve as president. Another prominent teacher member of the Clann was Fionnán Breathnach, whose brother Cormac was one of the four condemned Fianna Fáil deputies. MacDermott has noted that:

> [The Teachers' Club] seemed to have become a virtual base camp, social centre and meeting place for Clann na Poblactha … Unquestionably, the INTO and Clann na Poblachta initially influenced each other, but in truth, despite the best that Fianna Fáil could come up with by way of paranoid conspiracies, the teachers' influence over the Clann was always far greater than the Clann's influence over the teachers.[11]

Clann na Poblachta would prove to be a classic example of a firework party, the kind that blazes on to the political scene with great energy and excitement only to burn out rapidly. Nevertheless, in a very short period, it would play a crucial role in challenging Fianna Fáil's dominance after 16 years in power.

While the government bore the brunt of members' anger, there was continued resentment, particularly in Dublin, towards the executive for its decision to call off the strike against the Strike Administration Committee's wishes. O'Connell played down this opposition, but the numbers of dissenters were not insignificant, and as 1947 began so too did preparations for the presidential election at the upcoming Easter congress. The convention was that there was an election for vice-president every year, and whoever won would be elected president uncontested the following year. To stand against the outgoing vice-president for the presidency was not the done thing at all. On this occasion, however, four candidates put their names forward. Three were based in Dublin – the outgoing vice-president Jeremiah O'Kelly, Dave Hanley and Seán Brosnahan – and from Kerry there was two-time former president T.J. (Tom) Nunan, whose INTO record dated back before the Dill Commission.[12] Seán Brosnahan (popularly known as Jackie) was also very much a Kerry man, though he was born in Clare and had taught in Dublin since qualifying from the De La Salle training college in Waterford.[13] Nunan's supporters suggested that a group from Dublin were making a power grab for the new executive, and that Nunan's candidacy was an effort to stop this, but of course the Dublin faction was more than geographical. As Nunan's supporter put it, 'fighting soldiers are essential in battle, experienced statesmanship is necessary to reap the peace'.[14] The 'fighting soldiers' were Brosnahan and his two running mates, C.E. Sheehan for the vice-presidency and Matt Griffin in the Eastern District, who had been among the foremost opponents of ending the strike. Hanley and O'Kelly were strong supporters of the CEC action.

Brosnahan and Nunan were the two front runners, and the contest divided between those who wanted a mature set of hands to guide the 'Old Ship' and those who favoured the young fighting soldiers.[15] There was an urban–rural divide, and an inter-generational division, but at the heart of the contest was disagreement over how the strike had ended. The Brosnahan group summed up their position in positive terms, arguing that they were forward-looking and that the time had come for the INTO to 'have a definite long-term and well-thought-out policy into which all its activities could be integrated to replace the pursuit of vacillating and haphazard policies which it has been following for so long'.[16] Those on the other side, however, maintained that this was hokum, and that their opponents were not motivated by policy but by revenge against the outgoing CEC.[17]

Brosnahan topped the poll with just under 40 per cent of the vote and was elected, but his fellow 'young men in a hurry' were unsuccessful in the contests for vice-president and Eastern representative.[18] The results were announced at Easter in Cork at a meeting described euphemistically by the *ISW* as 'a brisk, business-like congress'.[19] It was the first congress since the strike and much of it was spent going over precisely what had occurred to end it. There were several heated debates, but no meeting of minds. Perhaps the most important motion before delegates was the CEC proposal of a special levy of ten shillings per month, repayable on retirement, death or resignation, to build up a war chest.[20] Several delegates complained that ten shillings was too much and would risk losing members, and several northern delegates warned that it would see a mass defection to the UTU if it were applied in the six counties. Delegates eventually voted to impose the levy on members in the South only,[21] one delegate describing it as evidence the 'fighting spirit' had not left the organisation.

Another manifestation of 'fighting spirit' after the strike was the determination of more women to come to the fore. In 1939, Catherine Mahon had attended a function where INTO past presidents were awarded a newly designed presidential badge, at which she had noted that when she 'broke the ice' in 1910 she thought that the INTO would continue to elect a woman president at regular intervals.[22] In the meantime, there had been many women presidents in Scotland and England, but until Kathleen Clarke of Kiltimagh, who was President during 1945–46, Mahon remained the only woman president of the INTO. Mahon died in February 1948 so did not live to see the third woman elected to the position, Brigid Bergin of Herbert Place, who was elected vice-president in 1948. A veteran of the 1946 strike, in her election literature Bergin had asserted that she contested the vacancy

> not in a spirit of opposition but on the principle that men and women teachers should share the responsibilities of the higher offices of our Association. I believe that by a balanced representation the solidarity and unity of the INTO can be fully maintained … Only the combined efforts of men and women teachers can win justice for all; only a body a 100% strong and active can achieve the desired results.[23]

Her election as vice-president saw her join Margaret Skinnider, who had served alongside her on the strike committee in 1946, on the CEC.

As well as the increase in women representation in 1948, there was a revived attempt to remove the marriage ban. The minister, Richard Mulcahy, said he could 'promise no relief in the immediate future'. He did, however, hold out the possibility that 'if and when the school-leaving age is raised, the question of the supply of teachers would arise in an acute form and that would be an appropriate time to reconsider the ban'.[24] There was good news, though, during the summer, when the Department of Education finally decided that women teachers who were rated by inspectors as Highly Efficient or Efficient could stay on in their jobs until they were 65.[25] If women were finding their voices more in the organisation, however, it was not evident in the tone of the women's page in the *School Weekly*, which ran features on the 'feminine viewpoint' with injunctions such as how there was no need to look one's worst on a rainy day.[26] Moreover, while women like Brigid Bergin and Margaret Skinnider were formidable representatives, they carried too great a weight on their shoulders and few women were inclined to join them, with T.J. O'Connell suggesting that women members would not stand for election because they were 'not sufficiently thick skinned'.[27]

A NEW GENERATION TAKES CHARGE

After the 1947 congress there was a change to the make-up of the CEC and the rules to its election and for that of a general secretary. Instead of two representatives in four districts there would be one representative for ten, and all positions would be elected by proportional representation.[28] The method of electing the general secretary had arisen as T.J. O'Connell, who was 65 in November 1947, had announced that he would retire at some point in 1948. He had held the position since 1916, and the last years had been especially gruelling. Three people applied to succeed O'Connell.[29] They were William Keane, secretary of the Tipperary County committee; D.J. (Dave) Kelleher, the outgoing president from Dublin; and M.P. Linehan, the treasurer and assistant general secretary.[30]

Linehan and Kelleher were the better known of the three. Born near Macroom, Co. Cork, Kelleher had studied in St Patrick's College, Drumcondra, and on qualification, spent 25 years teaching in the practising school attached to the college.[31] His INTO record was substantial; he had served in the Dublin branch and on the CEC since 1932 and as president in 1946–47, and many members would have been familiar with his no-nonsense, sharply analytical mind. Linehan, on the other hand, was well thought of but, having joined head office more than 20 years earlier, he appeared too removed from the experience of the members and too much a bureaucrat to do the fighting job that members felt was needed, and his argument that the selection of general secretary should be based on the 'principle of promotion' badly misjudged the mood.[32]

In July 1947, the *ISW* announced that Dave Kelleher had been elected the general secretary designate, and he took up his role in Gardiner Place on 1 September. He did so with no clue as to how long he would hold that role since, as O'Connell reminded members, he had indicated that he would retire in 1948, but he had not decided when.[33]

O'Connell's was not the only departure, and 1948 could be characterised as a year of changing personnel. De Valera called a snap general election for 4 February, partly in an effort to put Clann na Poblachta to the test before it was quite ready. The CEC sent a questionnaire to the leaders of the six parties, seeking their parties' positions on salaries, pensions, equal pay for men and women teachers, arbitration machinery, the setting up of a council of education, and class size. They received responses from Fine Gael, Labour and Clann na Poblachta, but Éamon de Valera's personal secretary sent only an acknowledge-ment and Clann na Talmhan and National Labour did not reply.[34] Those who replied returned responses designed to meet a good reception among teachers; all said that teachers did important work and ought to be well paid, and so on. Only on the issue of equal pay for men and women did Fine Gael not answer in accordance with INTO policy, and in that case, the response was, 'this matter has not been examined'. The INTO gave no instruction on how to vote, but on the basis of the questionnaire at least, Fine Gael, Labour and the Clann were promising everything the teachers wanted and Fianna Fáil could not be bothered to reply.

The election saw Fianna Fáil lose its Dáil majority, and after negotiations all other parties and independents in the Dáil agreed to come together to form what became known as the first inter-party government. Fianna Fáil's loss of office after 16 uninterrupted years was a major change in Irish politics, which had grown increasingly stagnant after such a lengthy period of one-party government. Few tears were shed by teachers at the departure of Tomás Derrig. The new taoiseach was John A. Costello SC, who had long been the INTO's first port of call whenever it wanted a legal opinion, while Patrick McGilligan SC, whose advice had also been sought on occasion, was the new minister for finance. The new minister for education was the Fine Gael leader, Richard Mulcahy, who had been sympathetic to the teachers' plight during the strike but had no notable relationship with the INTO otherwise. In his attitude towards education, Mulcahy was cut from the same cloth as his predecessors. A devout Catholic with a Gaelic League background, Mulcahy saw Irish education as existing primarily to facilitate an Irish language revival and help turn out good Christian children, all with minimal interference by the state. Towards the end of his time as education minister, he outlined his vision of his role in a speech that has become infamous among educationists:

> You have your teachers, your managers and your churches and I regard the position as Minister in the Department of Education as that of a kind of dungaree man, the plumber who will make the satisfactory communications and streamline the forces and potentialities of the educational workers and educational management in this country. He will take the knock out of the pipes and will link up everything. I would be blind to my responsibility if I insisted on pontificating or lapsed into an easy acceptance of an imagined duty to philosophise here on educational matters.[35]

As befits a man who likened the role of education minister to that of a plumber, Mulcahy's ministry was never particularly dynamic or reforming. He was a bureaucrat, not a visionary, and as Robert Barton once observed of him, 'he was careful about details only. No imagination or sense, unobtrusive, but a hard worker.'[36] As the *ISW* observed, 'the new government has the advantage of succeeding a regime during which little or no heed was paid to the demands and advice of the teachers. It may do much better than the old, and we hope it will; but it cannot do any worse. So far as the relations between the teachers and the authorities are concerned we had already reached rock bottom.'[37]

The only commitment in the area of education that featured in the ten agreed policy points that passed as one of the earlier 'programmes for government' was that at long last an advisory council for education would be established,[38] something the INTO had been demanding for more than 20 years and which had featured most recently in *A Plan for Education.* It was April 1950 before the council for education was eventually set up, with such narrow terms of reference that it bore no relation to what the INTO had envisaged. Eventually, in 1954, it published a report on the function of primary schools and the curriculum, but it was, as Séamas Ó Buachalla put it, revealing of 'a conservative and reactionary value system which … did not see the need for change'.[39] Nothing came from it. On salaries, teachers had reason to hope to see some progress. Soon after his appointment, an INTO delegation met the minister on 5 March and discussed salaries, pensions, averages and allowances for teachers on strike. The INTO representatives pressed for a representative committee similar to the Black Committee in Northern Ireland to be set up to consider suitable salary scales and conditions of service and left feeling reasonably optimistic, with O'Connell detecting a 'genuine desire' on the minister's part 'to secure the goodwill and the cooperation of the teachers'.[40] Some weeks later, Mulcahy went to congress in Bundoran, where he gave a very well-received speech – deemed 'inspiring' by the *ISW* – which seemed to have quite an impact on the mood of teachers, with branch reports detecting an atmosphere of hopefulness among members.[41] One Dublin teacher sounded a note of caution, however. Noting how a 'wave of optimism permeates INTO meetings', he warned teachers against being 'lulled into a state of false security by carefully prepared propaganda', noting, 'we went on strike to get more money. We want more money. Anything else is merely throwing dust in our eyes.'[42]

The Industrial Relations Act 1946 had established the Labour Court, which provided arbitration to the private sector, but public sector workers, including teachers in primary and secondary schools, were expressly excluded from its remit under Section 4 of the Act.[43] Fianna Fáil opposed conciliation machinery for public sector workers. De Valera had rejected the notion outright when Richard Mulcahy had proposed setting up conciliation with the teachers during the 1946 strike. They could not, he said, 'have some outside body with no responsibility at all saying: "Oh yes, you can add another couple of hundred thousand". It would be an encouragement to strikes.'[44] A year later, the government had softened somewhat, and began to consider a scheme for civil servants, in which teachers were not included,[45] but there was no significant progress by the election in 1948, and such machinery was eventually introduced by the inter-party government, with a separate scheme also announced for primary teachers in the summer of 1948.[46] Finance opposed the move and managed to stall the introduction of the scheme, much to the frustration and embarrassment of Mulcahy, who had to turn up to the 1949 and 1950 teachers' congresses empty-handed. Determined not to do so again for the third year running, he managed to have a committee set up to consider the issue, and on 8 December 1950 it was agreed to set up the machinery for primary and secondary teachers along the same lines as for civil servants.[47] This was an important breakthrough but the length of time taken to bring it about caused a great deal of resentment among INTO members, especially after their expectations had been raised by the minister.

In 1949 the minister set up a committee 'to consider salaries and other grants, including provision on retirement, to be paid to teachers in national schools, and report thereon'. Chaired by Judge P.J. Roe, it would consist of 18 members, five representing the Departments of Education and Finance, six representing the INTO (including Margaret Skinnider, which ensured that there was a woman representative), three managers, and a representative each for business, farming and PAYE workers.[48] Its majority report, signed by the INTO representatives, was submitted to the minister in early May. It recommended, among other things, a common pay scale for men and women teachers with an annual marriage allowance for married men and additional bonuses for those with honours university qualifications. Several months passed, until at the end of September the minister announced he was prepared to concede the general recommendations such as the common scale, but not at the levels recommended, which would 'disturb the balance of the economy' and 'impose a burden of undue magnitude on the taxpayer'. The INTO was deeply unhappy that the government had, in effect, rejected the majority report in favour of a minority report written by the officials from Education and Finance, and had made a mockery of the whole process.[49] The government, however, was unyielding, and the revised scales came into effect on 1 January 1950.[50]

Resentment began to surface among different sections of the organisation and by the summer of 1950 there were several campaigns afoot. The salary scale proposed by the government following the Roe Report was universally un-popular, but among single men who were offered the smallest percentage increase and whose salaries were now equated with those of single women, there was particular resentment. A Men Teachers' Union was established in Mayo, which the CEC was quick to put a stop to, travelling to Mayo for meetings and refusing to publish their reports or advertisements in the *School Weekly*.[51] Women teachers were deeply unhappy at the single men's campaign, and in Dublin some 500 women teachers signed a circular calling on the executive to resist any sectional demands that ran counter to 'equality of pay and equality of opportunity for all'.[52] In the meantime, the Dublin branch had decided there should be a special salary scale for Dublin City teachers, an idea first mooted around the time of the Dill Commission and similar to the idea of London weighting, introduced for civil servants there in 1920. The Dublin teachers began independently to lobby ministers and Dublin deputies. After their activities were published in the *Irish Press*, the CEC issued a statement stating that their claim was not INTO policy and 'strongly condemning' their action.[53] However, while Dublin-based teachers faced a significantly higher cost of living, their colleagues in the rest of the country did not feel it was their problem, and a call for an inquiry into the cost of living in different parts of the country and whether different scales were needed as a result was roundly rejected at the 1951 congress.[54] Delegates resolved against, it arguing that 'if such a commission were set up nothing but further dissatisfaction and disagreement among the members of the organisation, nothing but further sectionalism and a break in the solidarity of the INTO would result'. A split in the ranks was avoided, but Dublin members remained far from happy, and continued to support regional scales. Meanwhile, the 1946 single men were intent on pursuing their case, notwithstanding the view of many women that it was wholly contrary to the organisation's support for equal pay for equal work.[55]

By the time of that congress in Easter 1951, relations with the minister had soured sufficiently that Mulcahy sent a representative rather than attend himself, having gone to the ASTI congress instead. It was all a very long way from the 'wave of optimism' three years earlier. As it turned out, Mulcahy was gone within weeks. A week after congress, the minister for health, Noël Browne, was compelled to resign over his proposals to introduce free pre- and ante-natal health care to mothers and to children under 16. Weakened by resignations following the Mother and Child Scheme crisis, the government was soon without a majority, and the Dáil was dissolved on 4 May 1951. In a contest between the outgoing government and Fianna Fáil, the INTO was disinclined to take sides. The inter-party government had undoubtedly introduced long-called-for reforms, but these were overshadowed by its refusal to implement the findings of the Roe Committee on salaries.[56] If the INTO was lukewarm about the outgoing government, however, Fianna Fáil remained unforgiven. As an *ISW* editorial concluded, whoever ended up in office, the teachers would get nothing if they did not fight for it and fight together, noting that the future depended 'not on the promises of politicians, but on the strength and efficiency of the INTO and on the loyalty of its members'.[57]

Fianna Fáil returned to office as a minority government supported by a handful of independents. Recalling the depths of poor relations between the INTO and the Fianna Fáil government between 1945 and 1947, D.J. Kelleher was distinctly unenthusiastic about the election result, but wrote, 'given fair treatment, teachers would be willing to forget'.[58] The appointment of Seán Moylan as minister for education seemed to bode well. The former minister for lands was a somewhat reluctant education minister, but his appointment was testament to de Valera's astuteness.[59] If there was one person in Fianna Fáil to whom the INTO was well disposed, it was Seán Moylan, who had worked behind the scenes to bring about a settlement in 1946.[60] If he was personally popular, however, Moylan's time as minister was not a very profitable one for national teachers.[61] The INTO's first application under the conciliation and arbitration scheme, made just after the election, resulted in an offer of approximately 12 per cent, significantly below the INTO demand. Assured they would do no better, and concerned about the political instability – the new Fianna Fáil government held office by the votes of a couple of independents – the CEC reluctantly accepted the 'grossly inadequate' terms, which pleased no one, the Dublin City branch being especially critical.[62]

The ongoing controversy over the 700 or so pre-1946 single men, which dominated the agenda of the 1952 congress, was even more vexed. The executive came under considerable criticism for not having initiated legal action against the men's treatment, but this was because three of the four legal advices they had on the matter said they should not take a case.[63] Despite this, the pre-1946 men insisted that 'all arrows pointed to the High Court'. Two men had begun steps, independently of the organisation, to institute legal proceedings, and despite the CEC's complete opposition to the action over the course of three days at congress, they eventually secured the INTO's financial and moral support for the case.[64] Apart from the CEC, almost the only opposition came from women delegates. As Margaret Skinnider, herself a member of the CEC, put it, women made up 64 per cent of the membership and single men only ten per cent, but the men were attempting to railroad something which was completely contrary to the INTO's policy of supporting equal pay.[65] Not only that but the previous day delegates had rejected an amendment supporting a test case against the marriage ban.[66] Later in the year, a Married Women Teachers' Organisation emerged, but the CEC refused to meet it, and it seems to have disappeared shortly afterwards.[67] The men's test case, which eventually went before the High Court in July, was dismissed with costs in September. After some consideration, there was an appeal, which was heard in February 1955, but the original judgment was upheld. If the organisation's support for the action had angered women members, it had also averted any split on the matter that might have otherwise arisen. The action did, however, halt the progress towards establishing conciliation and arbitration machinery, with the government refusing to deal with the teachers on the matter as long as the case was before the courts.

EQUALITY AMONG TEACHERS: THE CAMPAIGN FOR PAY PARITY

During the mid-1950s, the INTO changed tack in its pay demands. Rather than catch up with the rising cost of living and the sectional claims within the organisation, the INTO now demanded simply to be paid the same rates as other teachers. A common scale for teachers across all levels was introduced in

England in 1947 by the Burnham Committee, and this was replicated in the North soon after. Following this lead, the 1948 congress decided that pay scales should be based on four principles, including a common basic scale for all teachers and no discrimination on the grounds of sex,[68] but when vocational teachers were given parity with secondary teachers in 1953, it pushed the INTO to actively pursue the claim.[69] Moylan agreed to meet an INTO deputation in February to discuss the matter as well as the ongoing issue of establishing conciliation and arbitration machinery. The INTO delegation put forward its case for parity based on six points. It began by observing that:

> Unity in the teaching profession has for many years been an ideal aimed at by the INTO. This would involve an integrated system of education, with common professional training and a common professional standard for all teachers. It would mean freedom of movement within the profession and a removal of barriers and anomalies which are responsible for the existence of three distinct and watertight systems instead of one integrated whole. While parity in salary alone would not achieve the INTO ideal, it would nevertheless be an important step in that direction.[70]

The delegation emphasised the crucial importance of primary education, which provided a strong foundation and was the sum total of education that the majority of Irish people received. They set out the challenges faced by national teachers that made their role more difficult than that of those in the post-primary sector. These included the inherent difficulty of primary teaching because of pupils' age and development, the mixed abilities of children in primary level compared to post-primary, and the relatively small class sizes in secondary schools.[71] The minister's response, however, was not positive. He believed in a 'hierarchy' in the teaching profession and that there should be a particular status for each type of teacher, continuing that 'the same quality of effort was not needed for national teachers compared with secondary teachers, nor were they of the same calibre'.[72] He also maintained that parity would cost in the region of £1 million. Recalling the meeting at the 1954 congress, D.J. Kelleher noted that there 'was some pretty straight talk' over the minister's comments, but that they could see there was 'no use at that stage in trying to get anything from him', noting not least that there was 'a hidden hand behind the whole attitude of the Department and while that hand is there it [would] be extremely difficult to get parity'.

When a general election was called for 18 May 1951, Moylan, as he admitted himself, did not have a huge amount to show for his time in office.[73] The INTO made parity its key issue in the election campaign. Having written to each of the parties to seek their position on the matter, the INTO took out advertisements in the national press detailing the responses: Labour and Clann na Poblachta came out in favour of parity, while Fine Gael said it did not have a policy on the matter and could not be expected to formulate one in the weeks running up to the election.[74] The election resulted in the third change of government in six years, with a Fine Gael–Labour–Clann na Talmhan coalition taking office with outside support from Clann na Poblachta, and Richard Mulcahy returning to Education. Within days he had invited the INTO to discuss reviving the conciliation and arbitration scheme, but it would be December before the teachers' conciliation council first met.[75] In March 1952, the council rejected the INTO claim for parity, and when the claim went before the arbitration board in September, it did likewise. The arbitrator did advise that the gap between national teachers and secondary teachers should be reduced, but it upheld the principle of different scales.[76]

The ASTI was paying close attention. Its 1955 convention adopted a policy of opposing parity with national teachers, arguing that they spent longer in education and that teaching honours Leaving Certificate subjects required a level of specialism. They rejected the INTO's contention that, as John Coolahan put it, 'the pedagogic skills needed to teach in national schools were greater than for senior pupils, that the academic standard required for entry to training college was much higher than that required for university and that teacher training for national teachers was of greater duration and of greater pedagogic value than that for secondary teachers'.[77] The ASTI case was flimsy, but it was being made to a receptive audience. Maintaining the differential was cheaper for the state than conceding parity but it was also a case of social solidarity at the higher end of the scale, with the university graduates in the Department or the government open to the ASTI's contention that their degrees entitled them to a higher status and that a higher status should be identified by a higher salary. It is not unusual for sections of workers to become wedded to differentials, but what was unusual was that, for the primary and secondary teachers at least, status rather than money was the substantive issue. While it is obvious why primary teachers would wish to improve their status, the level of opposition from the secondary teachers is somewhat hard to fathom; but the observations by John A. Murphy, himself a secondary teacher during the 1950s, are interesting:

> I think that many lay secondary teachers had a complex sense of insecurity about their station in life. A large number, possibly a majority, had drifted into the profession with an arts degree which was, more often than not, of indifferent quality. ... Many secondary teachers propagated the graduate mystique, and sought the social and financial status to which, they claimed, their university education entitled them (this kind of elitism was especially directed against national teachers). At the same time they were uncomfortably aware that they were in an inferior graduate category to, say, doctors who

were accorded deferential preference by a society obsessed, then as now, with caste gradations. The secondary teacher did not have the same rooted and assured place in the rural and small town community as the national teacher whose status as 'master' was entirely independent of professional wrangles about hierarchical grading.[78]

It seemed extraordinary in retrospect, Murphy observed, 'that so much time and vehement energy should have been devoted to preserving a salary differential', and while a case could be made for it, 'there lingers a feeling that much of the Association's attitude towards the INTO was the product of snobbishness, insecurity and envy – envy, that is, of the superior promotional opportunities and the better professional training which were available to national teachers'.[79]

In January 1957 it emerged that the ASTI had been recommended an award which, though considerably less than it had sought, widened the salary differential with primary teachers. The government had discouraged the INTO from seeking a sizeable claim because of the terrible economic situation, and the INTO felt it had been duped, not only by the government but also by the ASTI. As a result a certain aloofness emerged. The ASTI withdrew its fraternal delegate from the INTO congress that Easter and informed D.J. Kelleher that 'the question of future relations between ASTI and the INTO will come up for discussion at our forthcoming convention'.[80] This was not likely to worry the INTO, not least because if either party benefited from co-operation between the two organisations it was the smaller, less professional ASTI. As Dave Kelleher pointed out, he had been asked to assist the ASTI on cases in the past and had been happy to do so, until now.[81] For his part, Matt Griffin, who as INTO president had led the campaign for parity from the start, was blunt when he told delegates, 'Not by as much as the black of my nail will we go away from the parity claim.'[82]

By this time, there had been yet another change of government after the election on 3 March 1957 saw Fianna Fáil return to office, this time with a majority. Fianna Fáil would remain in office for the next 16 years, uninterrupted, establishing a degree of political continuity after a decade of revolving governments. Nevertheless, while the same party remained in government, there was quite a turnover in ministers for education, with five ministers holding office in this time. The long sixties would be a decade of significant change in Ireland, as elsewhere. In 1959, Seán Lemass succeeded de Valera as taoiseach, and educational reform became a crucial part of the economic changes that were being undertaken. The fifties had been a wasted decade insofar as educational policy was concerned. Looking back on his time as minister, Richard Mulcahy lamented, 'I often feel ashamed of myself to think I was in the Department of Education for two periods of office and I ask myself what did I do there?'[83] His Fianna Fáil counterpart might have asked himself the same question. For the INTO, however, the introduction of conciliation and arbitration machinery marked one important advance, facilitating matters of pay and conditions to be dealt with on a continuous basis. The mood of the organisation was considerably less fractious than it had been as recently as the early 1950s, and if much was left to be done, Margaret Skinnider observed in October 1958 that comparing their circumstances with 1946 'gave one the hope and confidence that the spirit of the organisation would ultimately triumph in its fight for the teachers and especially the welfare of the children'.[84]

THE MARRIAGE BAN WITHDRAWN

One major cause for celebration at this time was the lifting of the marriage ban as of 1 July 1958.[85] Internationally, the Free State had been somewhat late in adopting the marriage ban in 1934, and was rather late in getting rid of it too. In 1947, the *Irish School Weekly* reported that in an international survey of 48 countries, Ireland was one of only four that did not sanction the appointment or retention of married women teachers, the other three being Australia, the Netherlands and South Africa.[86] By the 1950s the supply of primary teachers had become acute, and there was a particular shortage of trained women, with schools losing between 60 and 70 women a year when they married. Seán Moylan was committed to the ban on principle, however,[87] and rather than adopting the most logical solution by ending the ban, he suggested opening a new training college for Catholic women. The Department of Finance rejected this ridiculous idea, and suggested they either waive the ban for a limited period or re-employ, in a temporary and non-pensionable capacity and for a limited period, teachers who had been retired on marriage under the rule.[88] Finance and Education batted memoranda on the subject back and forth for some time, until eventually the new college was given the green light in December 1953, a decision rescinded shortly afterwards in favour of increasing the number of places at Our Lady of Mercy (Carysfort), Blackrock.[89] When Mulcahy returned as minister in 1954, he told the Dáil that he did not propose to change the rule, but by the eve of his departure as minister in February 1957, he had told an INTO delegation that the ban was 'being considered actively'.[90] Weeks later, Jack Lynch was appointed minister for education. He acknowledged early on the problem caused by the scarcity of trained women teachers. Lynch established a departmental committee on the issue, which recommended removing the ban,[91] and consulted with the Catholic hierarchy, which did not speak with one voice on the matter, although senior figures, including Archbishop McQuaid, supported its removal. Finally in June 1958 he announced his intention to rescind the ban.[92] Noting that the move was a necessary one, since even if two new training colleges were established it would have taken a whole generation before sufficient teachers would be trained, he continued, 'lest it be thought that the decision to rescind the marriage rule is one of mere expediency, I would like to stress that I am satisfied that on balance the long term effect of the Rule has been an adverse one, both educationally and socially'.[93]

'OUTSIDE THE PROVINCE OF THE TEACHERS'

Relations between the INTO and the Catholic Church had been reasonably cordial for the first two decades of the Southern state. Notably, there was a time when O'Connell was close to the archbishop of Dublin, John Charles McQuaid, seeing him as someone to whom he could look for guidance or help. McQuaid's relationship with O'Connell's successor, Dave Kelleher, was especially poor, however. There was none of the affinity that McQuaid and T.J. O'Connell shared, and Kelleher saw McQuaid as someone with whom he had to do business and showed little of O'Connell's deference, which McQuaid may have resented. Moreover, as someone who was very active in Dublin strike activities in 1946, it is possible that Kelleher resented the archbishop's involvement in ending the campaign. McQuaid's support for the national teachers in 1946 was in no small part an effort to keep them onside with the Church, but it was not representative of the relationship between the INTO and the Church as a whole, which had become strained the year before the strike began. This arose on the issue of school conditions which were frequently unsanitary and cold, particularly in rural or disadvantaged areas (see Chapter 3). Managers were proving unwilling to pay for or provide repairs, heating and cleaning, but neither they nor the hierarchy, with one or two exceptions, were willing to let the state take all responsibility for it. Tomás Derrig had looked to address the problem of school accommodation in 1942, when he commissioned a study into post-war needs, which came on the back of a succession of reports by county medical officers which had highlighted the dangers posed to children's health as a result of the poor conditions, and a survey conducted by the INTO's Cork county committee. The problem was starting to attract more public attention, and the INTO began to raise its voice on the issue.

The publication of the Beveridge Report in Britain pushed questions of state control of social services to the fore in Ireland in the early 1940s. The Catholic Church was deeply concerned with what it saw as creeping state socialism, which, it felt, would diminish parental responsibilities and push the Church out of its natural sphere of influence. Anything that increased state involvement in social services was seen as a threat, so that even something as apparently innocuous as suggesting that the state pay for the full cost of heating and maintaining schools was seen as a hostile act. The INTO had no interest in the principle of the matter; it just wanted its members to teach children in clean, warm schools. It was obvious that if the Church was not going to pay its full share, then the state should pay everything. Rather than accept this at face value, the Church decided that the INTO wanted to raise a red flag over every national school in the state.

The first skirmish took place around the 1945 congress in Galway, which was opened by Bishop Browne. Browne asserted that the functions relating to school building and upkeep rested with the clerical managers, and was adamant that nothing be done to interfere with that, suggesting that complaints about conditions had been exaggerated. Later that week, however, T.J. O'Connell remarked to delegates how, strolling through Galway, he had passed two schools: one was a vocational school in good repair, the other a national school, which was in a dire state of repair. The vocational school, he noted, was run by the state; but, he learned, the almost derelict national school was managed by none other than Bishop Browne. In those circumstances, was the current system really preferable to one that was secularised? The Church was on shaky ground on this subject, not only for its lack of care but also because its counterparts north of the border were demanding full funding for Catholic schools, to put them on an equal basis to the maintained sector.

Congress the following year called on the ministers of health and education to hold a special congress on school conditions along with the teachers and managers, and later that year the CEC issued a confidential questionnaire to schools on building, maintenance, heating and cleaning, to be sent to head office by the end of February 1950. A furious Archbishop McQuaid called the general secretary and the president to a meeting where he articulated his displeasure at the INTO's acting in an area 'outside the province of the teachers'. Kelleher and the president were unrepentant, however, and were backed up subsequently by the CEC, although, in deference to the hierarchy, it decided not to pursue the demand that the minister would hold a conference, but to try dealing directly with the managers.[94]

Predictably, the INTO found the managers wholly unforthcoming, but in June 1952 the issue was forced into the open once again when, for no good reason, the bishop of Clogher attacked the INTO's attitude from the pulpit. 'We are not going to give up our schools,' he warned. 'I want the INTO to know that and that they are treading dangerous ground.' Far from an apology or retraction, when the INTO complained about this to Cardinal D'Alton, he responded that the hierarchy objected very strongly to the INTO's campaign and the manner in which it had been conducted. As D'Alton put it, 'it has long been the considered view of the bishops that if the building, maintenance, heating and cleaning of the schools were taken out of the hands of the managers, the ownership of the schools by the Church and the right of the managers to appoint and dismiss teachers would also soon be lost'.[95] Furthermore, while the INTO was correct that certain Catholic bishops had supported this in 1919 when they were part of the Killanin Commission, they had done so in 1919 when 'the socialistic tendencies, now so widespread, had not yet made their appearance'. This correspondence took place just a year after the Mother and Child scheme controversy, and socialist tendencies loomed large in the bishops' minds. D'Alton concluded by expressing the bishops' confidence that now the INTO had been made fully aware of their views, it would discontinue its campaign. The letter appears to have had the intended affect. As Noel Ward notes, the motion on the issue passed at the following congress in 1953 was more in line with the bishops' wishes and contained no mention of full public funding. The issue of buildings and maintenance remained, but it was pursued in a manner less likely to attract the bishops' ire. Resentment on both sides remained nonetheless, but privately. Writing to Cardinal D'Alton in May 1954, Kelleher catalogued the INTO's efforts to solve the issue and the refusal of the managers or hierarchy to reply to its appeals, still less co-operate. 'Is it not to be wondered that this cavalier treatment has left a deep sense of grievance, and has led us to believe that the managers have no interest in a problem the lack of solution of which might well undermine and destroy the whole educational system, which they and we are operating.'[96]

The frosty relations between the INTO and the bishops during the early to mid-1950s deteriorated further afterwards over the Ballina dispute (discussed below), but it is perhaps worth noting the extent to which the antipathy became personal. Blunt and uncompromising, Dave Kelleher became seen as someone with whom the bishops could not or would not do business. In 1958, Archbishop McQuaid decided to inquire into the requirements for equipment – furniture, books, requisites – of Dublin schools, but notably he privately sought the assistance of T.J. O'Connell, by then 11 years retired from the INTO. When O'Connell suggested that the archbishop consult with the Dublin branch of the INTO, he was told, 'that would come later'. Crucially, McQuaid stated, any remedy would be forthcoming from the parish or diocese, but it would not come from state funds.[97] Clearly, O'Connell had misgivings, knowing that the task ought to have been given to the INTO, but he agreed to look into the issue, along with the principal of the Pro-Cathedral Schools, Rutland Street and an assistant teacher from Christ the King School in Cabra, and subsequently produced a report for the archbishop. Afterwards, in the summer of 1958, O'Connell told the general secretary of his dealings with the archbishop and his report and met with a predictably cool response. Kelleher bluntly disapproved of the whole approach, noting that if anything were to be done it should be done through the organisation itself. The present example was characteristic of a broader, sinister malaise since, Kelleher explained to O'Connell:

There seemed to be a general tendency by the Hierarchy, and individual members thereof, to ignore the Organisation in matters connected with schools, and to deal, if at all possible, with local teachers. He gave a number of instances of this tendency and said that even in the letter of the Hierarchy to the executive, there was a suggestion that the executive, in the views that they were expressing, did not represent the opinions of the rank and file of the organisation.

[Kelleher] said that he thought His Grace's approach to this matter was but another example of this tendency. He was getting a report on the position of the equipment provided in his schools and had brought in Dr O'Connell as ex-general secretary, who although not now directly connected, would always be linked in the public mind with the organisation. While using Dr O'Connell in that way he was at the same time endeavouring to by-pass the organisation.[98]

The timing here was significant, since these events took place during the first year of the Ballina dispute, where the INTO was fighting the handover of a lay school to the Marist Brothers, a dispute examined below. It would be going too far to read any actions during this period as a shift towards anti-clericalism, but there was definitely a chill between the INTO at official level and the hierarchy. In June 1958, the CEC decided after long discussion that the INTO would pay £100 to the Dublin branch's annual Votive Mass, but that this would be the last occasion a grant of this kind would be made. It might seem petty but it is indicative of the ill-feeling on the CEC. Later, in 1966, a short time before Kelleher retired, he and McQuaid had an altercation during a meeting over school building when the former accused the diocese's school building policy of 'pandering to snobbery and segregation'. The archbishop furiously objected to the use of the word 'pandering' as it applied to himself (but not snobbery) and the meeting wound up acrimoniously. McQuaid tried to arrange another meeting on the issue shortly afterwards but without Kelleher present.[99] The president, Eileen Liston, explained that she could not accept an invitation which curtailed the CEC's ability to choose its own representatives, and after a few days the archbishop relented, issuing an invitation for a full delegation, including Kelleher.[100] The irony was that the INTO generally, but especially in the 26 counties, appeared more Catholic than it had ever done, notwithstanding the fact that it was ostensibly a non-sectarian organisation. Nowhere was this more in evidence than in *An Múinteoir Náisiúnta* (*AMN*), which was filled with advertisements for religious orders and missions and which gave over pages and pages to articles on religious instruction or, for instance, accounts of the annual Votive Mass,[101] while at the same time, there was no evidence whatever in its pages of non-Catholic religious observance.

THE BALLINA DISPUTE

The greatest cause of trouble between the Church and the INTO arose from a dispute in Ballina. The principal of Ballina Boys' NS, D.F. Courell – a member of the CEC and one-time president – had retired before Easter. A number of the six assistant teachers in the school applied for the post, but over the holidays each received a note to say that Mr Courell's successor would take up duty after Easter, without any clue as to who this successor would be.[102] In April 1956, the six teachers returned from their Easter holidays to find that the bishop of Killala, Most Rev. Dr O'Boyle, had invited the Marist Brothers to establish a community in the diocese and had appointed Brother Alphonsus of Sligo to be the school's new principal.[103]

The number of schools controlled by religious orders had increased in the first decades of independence, and between 1926 and 1953 the number of lay schools in the Republic fell by 16.6 per cent, while the number of convent and monastery schools had gone up by 21.1 per cent. The schools run by religious orders tended to be larger, though, reflected in pupil numbers, which fell by 22.8 per cent in lay schools and increased by 28.6 per cent on the rolls of convent and monastery schools.[104] Some of these were new schools that had been built in cities following slum clearances, but others were transferred from lay control, a phenomenon referred to in the INTO as 'displacement'. When this happened, it was invariably larger schools that were transferred. Even when lay teachers remained a majority on the staff, displacement meant that the promoted posts – those of principal and vice-principal – were held by religious, which dramatically reduced the already scarce promotion opportunities for lay teachers. No agreement, formal or informal, existed between the Church and the INTO on the question. In practice, if a bishop wished to transfer a school to religious control, he would inform the INTO of his intention, the INTO would send a delegation to lobby against the move, and the bishop would proceed regardless. What happened in Ballina was rare, though not unique, but the 'discourteous and furtive' manner in which the bishop had carried out the transfer, as well as the action itself, helped fuel a crisis.[105]

As soon as the CEC heard what had happened in Ballina at Easter, it began arranging meetings to try to stop the transfer. First they met with the provincial of the Marist Brothers, then the bishop of Killala, the Ballina teachers, Archbishop McQuaid, the archbishop of Tuam, and the education minister, Richard Mulcahy; then, on 8 May, they once again met the bishop of Killala, who told them that he had decided to proceed with bringing in the Marists straight away.[106] The six teachers in the Ballina school voted unanimously to go on strike, and on 12 May a special meeting of the CEC gave them written instruction to go out on 15 May. That meeting also decided that an appeal to the Holy See on the matter was in order, and letters were sent to the archbishops of

Tuam and Dublin and the bishop of Killala to inform them of the appeal to Rome and to update them about the strike.[107] On their way to Ballina on the morning before the strike, an INTO deputation met Archbishop McQuaid in Drumcondra. He expressed sympathy and promised his full support to the teachers, while advising most strongly against holding a strike before the appeal to Rome.[108] The archbishop's account of the meeting to Cardinal D'Alton was slightly different, reporting that not only had he endeavoured to stop the strike but also that he had urged them to abandon their appeal to the Holy See, which the INTO appeared to have missed altogether.[109] The INTO delegation proceeded then to Ballina, where, swayed by McQuaid's argument, the teachers called off the strike to allow the appeal to Rome to proceed.

McQuaid's fellow bishops lacked his political nous. They were greatly annoyed at some of the INTO's public statements on the matter and wrote calling on the organisation to withdraw,[110] but the decision to go over their heads to Rome was intolerable. As a result, they refused to give any consideration to the Ballina case or that of lay teachers' displacement more generally, with the CEC left in no doubt over the depth of antipathy it had generated.[111] The legacy of the Killean dismissal controversy (see Chapter 8) was also evident, especially in the North. Early on in the dispute, INTO representatives were told by one northern cleric that that the Catholic managers in the six counties did not want to meet the INTO because they were 'nervous of the Organisation', or rather 'those at the top'.[112]

When the Ballina dispute began, the Catholic Church had been feeling rather vulnerable. Five years earlier it had fought off an attempt by then health minister Dr Noël Browne to introduce the Mother and Child scheme, which would have introduced free pre- and ante-natal care for women and health care for children under the age of 16 years. The Church had viewed the scheme as a case of creeping socialism, and interfering in their sphere of influence, since religious orders controlled most of the hospitals in the state. The campaign against the Mother and Child scheme had succeeded, but at a great cost. Noël Browne had made public the Church's role in bringing the scheme down and public opinion had tended to go against the bishops, making it a pyrrhic victory. Having lost a lot of goodwill for its politicking, they were reticent about engaging in similar controversies in public, but they were also especially sensitive to anything that might be regarded as an attempt to limit their powers. This meant the INTO's willingness to clash with them over Ballina was perceived as a grave affront and a symptom of a worrying trend in Irish society to tell the Church its place.

A document written for the bishops at the start of the dispute gives an idea of the Church's perception of the INTO at the time. It noted that the CEC was very much under the influence of three men, Seán Brosnahan, Alfie Faulkner and Liam O'Reilly (who was a teacher in Ballina), and 'all three are anti almost everything; managers, government, work'. It went on to say that there was a 'considerable section of the younger teachers, especially those from the Gael-teacht with a strong tendency to be anti-everything' and suggested these may have picked up something from the 'mild secularism of the preparatory colleges'. The prominent coverage of the dispute on Radio Éireann was attributed to the fact that two of the station's news editors were ex-teachers. The author of the note observed that some had attributed its prominence in the *Irish Press* and *Sunday Press* to the 'lightly anti-hierarchical policy of the paper', which they felt was 'hardly a fair explanation … though it is quite probable that it gave a certain amount of pleasure to have a safe wipe at the Bishops'.[113] However, when the hierarchy sent its response to the INTO complaint to the Holy See, they emphasised that the executive and the general secretary were not representative of the teachers as a whole. 'Like all similar organisations it is the vocal and con-niving few who assume leadership and oftentimes express views which do not reflect the feelings of the members.'[114] Recalling the INTO's support for the Macpherson Bill 40 years earlier, the bishops concluded that it was issuing veiled threats to the bishops, but:

> The Irish people under the leadership of their Bishops fought for their schools before and they are not going to part with them without a struggle. The bishops feel that they will have the support and active cooperation of the vast majority of the Catholic lay teachers with them in this fight.

Locally, things became very unpleasant for the teachers. As one teacher told congress a year into the dispute, 'we were the subject of talk, not least by what I call the "craw thumpers" of Ballina. They are the same as they are in every town … Some people possibly expected us to sprout horns.'[115] The atmosphere only got worse as the dispute dragged on. The teachers were subjected to petty changes in their working conditions, such as being made to go home for lunch instead of eating in school as they had done previously; there was a smear campaign against the men; and, following a complaint from the principal, their school manager wrote to the Department complaining about the conduct of the lay staff.[116]

The respective positions became increasingly entrenched. The hierarchy would not consider the matter because the INTO had approached the papal nuncio; the papal nuncio would do nothing because a report of the INTO's intention to write to him had leaked in the *Irish Times* before he had been approached.[117] Meanwhile ministers for education (Mulcahy and, later, Lynch) said the dispute was none of their business and refused to get involved. Having tried every possible avenue and been rebuffed at every turn, the INTO executive took a number of decisions which were unlikely to improve the situation.

Brother Alphonsus, the new principal in Ballina, was expelled from the INTO and other Marist members were told that their subscriptions would no longer be collected. Two years into the dispute, in the summer of 1959, the INTO executive issued a 'non-fraternisation' order calling on members to have nothing to do with Marist Brothers. The secretary of the hierarchy wrote to the general secretary protesting in 'the strongest manner' to the circular, which was described as 'contrary to Christian charity', while the archbishop of Dublin made his opposition to the document known on a number of occasions.[118] Around the same time, D.J. Kelleher convinced Paddy Crosbie, a national teacher and the host of *School Around the Corner* on Radio Éireann, to pull a proposed show in Ballina in which children from the school were to participate, since there was a danger it would 'result in a boost for the Marist brothers'.[119]

There were various efforts to end the impasse, such as the INTO's suggested compromise towards the end of 1959 that, perhaps deriving inspiration from Solomon, the school would be divided in two, a senior school and a junior school, with a layman appointed principal of one school while a Brother remained principal of the other.[120] This, however, was ultimately scuppered by Bishop O'Boyle (described euphemistically by one journalist as a man inclined to be 'very emotional'[121]), but not before he had dragged out the dispute for a further two years.

In January 1961, the INTO secured a meeting with Taoiseach Seán Lemass and Minister for Education Dr Patrick Hillery, who was now the third minister to preside over the affair, only to be told by the taoiseach that it 'would be impossible' for the government to interfere since 'the state recognises the managerial system, and the question of intervention would imply that the state would assume a right which it did not possess'.[122] With no prospect of a solution, the CEC's thoughts turned once again to a strike. When congress met in Bundoran at Easter 1961, it was exactly five years since the dispute had begun and patience had worn thin. Speaking for 90 minutes, the general secretary gave a detailed account of events to date, and finished to prolonged applause. Although two Dublin delegates spoke against the executive's behaviour, complaining that the non-fraternisation policy was a 'serious breach of Christian charity', they were in a minority. Moreover, as Seán Brosnahan pointed out, the clergy were in no position to condemn when they themselves had participated in a boycott against Protestants in Wexford only a couple of years earlier.[123] The Ballina men having earlier decided that they would strike if instructed, delegates voted to hold a special congress to make that call and increase subscriptions to pay for the strike, which was approved by a 90 per cent margin at the special congress, held on 20 May. The only opposition came from delegates from Belfast and Derry, followed by a number of other northern delegates, but they were not well received,[124] and later the executive took grave exception to the 'biased and damaging' account of the debate that was published in the Northern Committee's monthly journal the *Northern Teacher*. The journal was made to publish a statement to correct 'many of the untruths incorporated in the report', and soon after the northern secretary, Gerry Quigley, was appointed controlling editor to ensure that 'matters which were contrary to the interests of the organisation should not be published in the journal'.[125]

With a strike on the horizon, efforts to resolve the dispute revived. The INTO president, P.J. Looney, and Cardinal D'Alton arranged a secret meeting between Bishop O'Boyle, along with his fellow bishops from Achonry and Elphin, Dr James Fergus and Dr Vincent Hanly, and a deputation from the INTO comprising the president, the general secretary and deputy secretary. This took place in Sligo at the end of September. There was no room for compromise; the INTO delegation later recorded that Bishop O'Boyle was 'in a most self-righteous mood', and that 'repeatedly at intervals, and especially when the argument wasn't going as they would wish, and when discussion tended to come to close quarters they reverted to what they regarded as the fundamental – *the right and authority of the bishops to do what they wished to do in school control, staffing and education matters generally*'. The meeting was shambolic. Bishop O'Boyle reluctantly agreed to consider the idea of splitting the school, but then went back on this, with Fergus and Hanly accusing the INTO of having bullied O'Boyle. It may have been that the meeting was over-refreshed but the whole thing was a fiasco, and with the INTO leaving empty-handed everything was set for the strike to begin on 10 January 1962. Two teachers did not go out: one was not an INTO member; the other refused to take part and was expelled.[126] D.J. Kelleher reiterated that the strike was 'not a question of being opposed to religion or religious. We are striking over … the principle of a denial of lay teachers of promotion.' They had tried everything, he said; this was the only thing they had left.[127] Finally, Minister for Education Patrick Hillery stepped in, and eventually a solution was found where the Department would pay one of the lay teachers an allowance that would make his salary equivalent to that of a principal, and the minister would secure a letter from the hierarchy that would acknowledge 'the normal expectations of the national teachers in regard to posts of principal teacher'. Cardinal D'Alton agreed to this, as did the executive and then the teachers of Ballina, who voted by ten votes to three to call off the strike.[128] There was considerable unhappiness among members at the terms, not least among the Ballina strikers, who wanted to stay out, but while the Marists held the school, the principle for which the teachers fought had been established; the prospects of lay teachers would no longer be threatened by the installation of a religious order. No other lay school was subsequently handed over to an order, and as new schools were built in Dublin during the 1960s, they were all put under lay control from the outset, even if, as Breandán Ó hEithir pointed out, the irony was that it happened just before the teaching orders began to run out of recruits.[129]

The INTO may not have emerged victorious from Ballina, but it did show itself to be in muscular form. In taking on the issue, and in not relenting from it for so long, it had shown its mettle. The campaign's abrupt beginnings had contributed to poor tactics. In turning to Rome before advancing every possible avenue at home, for instance, it had not only ignored protocol but had put several hierarchical noses out of joint; but, as Archbishop McQuaid's unsuccessful effort to reach a compromise in 1959 illustrated, even had the 'proper channels' been taken from the outset, the result would have been the same. Ballina was the most open conflict with the Catholic Church since the Killean dismissal which had occurred in the north some 20 years earlier (see Chapter 8), but it went far, far deeper. For such a respectable part of Irish society to wage such an uncompromising campaign against the Church at all, still less to carry it on for six years, was unprecedented. Few people outside the organisation could understand it, or how such an apparently minor dispute had managed to go on so long, but, as Dave Kelleher explained to the taoiseach when he asked why the controversy had arisen, 'the pot had boiled over'.[130]

Chapter 5 ～

THE SLEEPING GIANT?
1962–1978

*'Because their pupils are drawn in the main from the
poorer and under-privileged classes in town and
country, the value placed on their service is less than
that placed on the service of those who teach the
children of the richer and privileged classes.'*

During the 1960s Ireland tried to catch up with the post-war development
that had so far failed to materialise. These were years of great social and
economic change in the Republic, and one of the greatest areas of
modernisation was in education. Given its social impact, it's not surprising that
the introduction of free secondary education is the best known advance in
education during the period, but the changes at primary level, while relatively
overlooked, were really important in what was taught and how it was taught,
while the perennial issue of school conditions was brought to the fore.

A new attitude towards education within government was emerging in the late
1950s, whether evidenced by an acknowledgement to reduce class sizes, ending the
marriage ban, ending the recruitment of the untrained junior assistant
mistresses, or the closing of the preparatory colleges. These were piecemeal
reforms, however, and the buzzword in Irish politics in the Lemass era was
'planning'. The First Programme for Economic Expansion had been introduced
in 1958, with its successor, the Second Programme, to run from 1964 to 1970,[1]
and it was natural that a similar approach would be taken in education.
Education was not included in the First Programme but would represent a
standalone project, albeit one seen as fundamental to the project of economic
expansion. As the minister for education, Patrick Hillery, put it in November
1959:

If we are to overcome the degree of underdevelopment at which we find ourselves we must have more and more education. A large part of the State's responsibility was to foster the country's economic interests and the first essential in this regard was that the system of education should, as far as possible, fit the pupils to face the modern world by, for example, promoting the teaching of science.[2]

In October 1962, Hillery appointed a survey team, partly financed by the Organisation for Economic Co-operation and Development (OECD), to investigate education funding. Crucially, the government was now looking at education as an economic good, rather than a social one. To put it crudely, now that all children were future contributors to GNP it was not enough for them to leave schools fully versant in the catechism and with a basic level of literacy and numeracy.[3] At first, however, the INTO failed to notice the shift and failed to adapt accordingly. This was evident from its submission to the commission on teachers' salaries. It began by asserting that 'in any Christian society standards of remuneration should be governed by certain ethical principals' before quoting from the Programme of Primary Instruction, which stated that 'of all the parts of a school curriculum Religious Instruction is by far the most important, as its subject-matter, God's honour and service, includes the proper use of all man's faculties, and affords the most powerful inducements to their proper use'.[4] The submission did include sound economic arguments for establishing pay parity between national and post-primary teachers, but the INTO was out of step with the time in framing its case even partially in terms of 'ethical principals' or on religious grounds. What would have been normal, maybe even expected, ten years earlier just looked incongruous. The language of politics and education had moved on and the INTO appeared to be stuck in the past. Moreover, if it was the case that the 1947 *Plan for Education* had stood the test of time, there had been no efforts to revise or update it, so by the early 1960s the INTO's most recent policy document on education was 16 years old.

At an institutional level, the INTO had become rather tired and lacked vision. Its energies were being poured into salary campaigns or other issues as they arose, such as its successful fight against increasing the length of the school day by half an hour,[5] or side-tracked by disputes such as Ballina. The INTO's journal, *An Múinteoir Náisiúnta* (*AMN*), was lacklustre and not fit for purpose, with one member complaining, 'the whole set-up of the journal is wrong. A monthly journal is next to useless, when it is a month late [as it frequently was] it is useless.'[6] The journal did not reflect the lively debates on education at the time or the enthusiasm of its members; instead its pages were filled with historical recollections by T.J. O'Connell and obituaries of activists of old. Sometimes its efforts at innovation merely made it look more old-fashioned.

The summer of 1963 saw the appearance of a Women's Page, but it consisted entirely of fashion and lifestyle tips and compares unfavourably with the campaigning women's journalism that was beginning to appear in the national press, or, for that matter, with the Lady Teachers' Page in the old *Irish School Weekly*.[7] The editor was periodically invited before the executive to discuss the journal's many problems, among them editorials contrary to INTO policy, irregularity of publication and the numerous mistakes in every issue – including incorrectly naming the minister for education and former INTO presidents – but the publication remained poor.[8]

If the organisation looked increasingly out of touch, this did not reflect the young people entering the profession, many of whom took a keen interest in progressive educational ideas. In 1961 a group of those based in Dublin set up what became known as the Teachers' Study Group, whose aims included the study of problems in primary education and promoting policies that might remedy them. One of their early meetings featured a debate on the topic 'Is the INTO Asleep?', which they bravely invited Seán Brosnahan to preside over. D.J. Kelleher was also in attendance, and lively exchanges ensued. Brosnahan, by now, was working full time in head office, having succeeded M.P. Linehan as treasurer when he retired in 1961.[9] By the autumn of 1963, the study group had some 230 members, mainly in Dublin.[10] The younger teachers did not have a monopoly on policies, however. The 1964 congress adopted a CEC motion calling on the Department of Education to establish a schools psychological service to assess 'mental handicap' and advise on remedial education. Proposing it, Alfie Faulkner recalled the INTO's support for special needs education going back decades and observed that during the 1950s, the INTO had donated £300 to the Departments of Psychology in UCD and UCC to help train graduates in the field, but having completed their training, the graduates found there was no work for them and they had been compelled to emigrate.[11] Another CEC motion called for the establishment of a National Council for Education Research which would work in close co-operation with university departments of education and psychology and with training colleges and other agencies. Perhaps not unreasonably, the INTO was trying to put the onus for educational research on the government and universities rather than itself, but the absence of any concerted development of policy by the official organisation, particularly at a time when it was involved in a protracted campaign over salary parity, was not good for the INTO's image. As a CEC memorandum published in September 1964 conceded, in recent times the INTO had 'concentrated on salary and social security questions to the neglect of the professional side'.[12]

SUB-COMMITTEE ON REORGANISATION

By the mid-1960s, the centenary of the INTO was looming into view. If the organisation was feeling its age, the prospect of marking its first 100 years spurred reflection. At the 1964 Cork congress, delegates gave the green light for a special committee to be set up to examine and report on a number of matters, including the structure of the Executive and Finance Committee, the role of the organisation in educational matters, head office staffing and accommodation, updating the rules of the organisation and any other matter which might modernise the working of the organisation and increase its prestige.[13]

Although it was supposed to report by the end of the year, it was October 1966 before it completed its investigation, during which branches across the country made submissions on the future of the organisation. Some were more detailed than others, but the same issues arose again and again, which could be summed up by the North Clare branch's observation that 'teachers are interested in more than salaries [and] our image does not reflect this'.

Branches highlighted the need for a dedicated education committee and called for a new declaration of educational principles by revising the *Plan for Education* on modern lines. With this in mind, several branches called for the appointment of a full-time education officer. As the Dublin City branch submission argued, 'if we are sincere in demanding "status" and "prestige", and the right to be considered "professional" people, then we must be prepared to introduce a new and revolutionary system, and be prepared to pay for it'. In the end a special congress in November 1966 approved the proposals of a conservative report. It found that the number of district representatives on the CEC – which had been drawn up when the organisation had a considerably smaller membership – was insufficient to deal with the growing burden of organisation work. It recommended revising the district boundaries, and dividing the Dublin branch, whose membership had grown significantly, in two. This increased the number of districts from 10 to 13, hardly likely to have any meaningful impact on the executive's capacity to do its work or make the CEC more representative of the membership. Of potentially more impact was the recommendation on staffing, but even then the report did not go far, only recommending that an executive officer be appointed, which would bring the number of officials in the organisation to three.[14] More notably, the new rules also provided for the setting up of a new education sub-committee of the CEC, which would be appointed by the CEC from a list of members, aided by an official who would act as secretary. The education committee would develop into one of the most lively parts of the INTO, organising conferences and publications and placing an important focus on the professional aspects of the organisation's role.

If the rule changes proved cosmetic overall, the decision to make the northern secretary an exofficio member of the CEC was more significant, and remedied an astonishing state of affairs, which had existed since the creation of the role over 40 years earlier, where the northern secretary played a semi-detached role in the running of the organisation. There were other changes afoot. The INTO was on the move. It had bought 35 Parnell Square, adjoining the Teachers' Club, from the ITGWU when the Transport Union moved into the new Liberty Hall in 1965, and in 1967 head office moved there from its premises in Gardiner Place, where it had been since 1918. Just as head office had moved, but not far, similarly there was a change in personnel, although one that signified more continuity than change. In October 1965, D.J. Kelleher informed the executive of his intention to retire on his 65th birthday in October 1966, but he subsequently agreed to stay on for a further year 'to facilitate the executive in appointing a successor'.[15] There was never any question about who his successor would be. There may not have been any natural succession from the position of deputy general secretary to general secretary, as M.P. Linehan had discovered in 1947, but Seán Brosnahan's position in the organisation was unrivalled. His was the only nomination for the position and he was formally elected secretary designate, unopposed, at a CEC meeting on 29 January 1966.[16] In the summer of that year, Matt Griffin, Brosnahan's long-time friend and colleague from the Dublin branch and CEC was elected treasurer and deputy general secretary by a five to one majority.[17] Twenty years after the 1946 strike, two of its foremost figures were at the organisation's helm, and the next ten years became the era of 'Matt and Jackie', with the new leadership in head office representing more continuity than change. They were joined by a new official, Michael Moroney, bringing the number of officials in head office to three.

THE McGAHERN AFFAIR

One of the INTO's more notorious controversies occurred around this time, when John McGahern, a teacher in St John the Baptist Boys' National School in Clontarf, later Belgrove, was dismissed. Teaching since 1955, he was a talented writer whose first novel, *The Barracks*, was published to great acclaim by Faber & Faber in 1963. It won various prizes, among them a one-year fellowship worth £1,000, which stipulated that the holder travel abroad for a year.[18] McGahern was given leave of absence without pay to take up the fellowship, during which time he lived in Europe and married Annikki Laaksi, a divorced Finnish theatre director whom he had met in Paris. In May 1965, towards the end of his fellowship, McGahern's second novel, *The Dark*, was published. On the day it was due to go on sale in Ireland, it emerged that a consignment of the book had been seized by Customs two days earlier, pending a decision by the Censorship Board.[19] As with so many of its literary predecessors on the banned list, *The Dark* was not, to quote the legislation, 'in its general tendency indecent or obscene', but Customs had been ordered to seize the consignment without anyone having read it. This was overzealous in the extreme, and the bizarre circumstances of the seizure caused quite a furore, prompting questions in the Dáil, all the more so because, in the more liberal climate of the mid-1960s, the impromptu act of the Censorship Board to impound a work of literature seemed like such an anachronism.

In early June, *The Dark* officially joined the banned list, and the controversy carried on over the summer.[20] McGahern was still out of the country throughout this time and had remained silent during the fuss, but with his fellowship coming to an end, he wrote to the school regarding his intention to return and was advised by his headmaster not to return but to seek a job in London, and that if he tried to return to the school, it would be 'difficult'. McGahern had no interest in becoming part of a row about censorship, but he was determined not to go quietly from the place that had been his work and his livelihood for years.[21] When McGahern reported for work on 11 October he was met by the headmaster, who gave him his marching orders. A month later, at a meeting with his manager, Fr Carton, McGahern was told that he had been excluded from school at the behest of Archbishop McQuaid, who took particular exception to impure books and could not countenance a writer of banned books teaching in a school in his diocese.[22]

Given an oral dismissal by the school manager, and unable to secure a written copy outlining the reasons, McGahern turned to the INTO, of which he had been a member for almost eight years. By his own account, McGahern left his meeting with the INTO having 'more or less agreed' to let the case drop and was 'congratulated on being reasonable', but immediately he had a change of heart and the following day he wrote to head office asking it to discover the exact reason for his dismissal.[23] An entirely inadequate explanation was offered a month later, asserting only that McGahern knew well why he had been dismissed – but when it was considered by a CEC meeting on 8 January 1966, no action was taken.[24] McGahern attended that meeting and later gave an account of it in his memoir, which did not reflect well on the executive.[25] Recognising there was nothing further he could do, insofar as the INTO was concerned, McGahern asked that it seek for him the three months' severance pay to which he was entitled, but it never did. When the story of McGahern's dismissal broke in the *Irish Press* on 4 February 1966, the INTO informed journalists that McGahern was no longer a member of the organisation 'within the union rules',[26] but this was rather disingenuous. Having joined the INTO immediately on beginning teaching, he had never been in arrears in eight years but his membership had lapsed when he went on his leave of absence. He could not have paid his subscription while he was abroad since they were usually collected in school – it was the 1970s before they were deducted at source – and McGahern had planned to pay his arrears on his return. While the INTO had handled his case, insofar as it had, it had regarded him as a member, but, he said, 'it seems

they used a technicality to escape their responsibilities and avoid the embarrassment of clashing in any way with the Church'. He thanked journalist Peter
Lennon and the *Irish Times,* which had devoted considerable attention to the
case, 'for initiating what I believe should have been the responsibility of the
INTO to make public in the first place'.[27]

Kelleher, for his part, declined to comment, and the INTO remained mute
on the controversy thereafter.[28] Privately, McGahern heard that Archbishop
McQuaid had warned the INTO that it could not rely on his support in
forthcoming pay negotiations with the Department, but that he would 'back
them to the hilt if they would have nothing to do with [his] case'; but, as he
acknowledged, there was no way this could be proved.[29] There is no evidence of
this, though it is quite plausible, but while the motivation for the INTO's
behaviour may not be known for certain, there is no doubt that its treatment of
McGahern was shabby and unedifying. For McGahern, that was the end of the
matter. While writers and liberals promoted his case, and he was offered
financial backing were he to take his case to the High Court – although he was
advised he would lose – he was reluctant to become a pawn in a struggle
between liberal and conservative Ireland.[30] Instead, McGahern moved to
London, where he worked as a labourer and supply teacher before ultimately re-
establishing himself as a highly regarded and very successful writer. He displayed
a remarkable lack of bitterness about his treatment, and was gracious in
accepting an invitation by the INTO to perform a reading at the Teachers' Club
in 1991, when the president, Jimmy Collins, acknowledged that for the INTO,
the occasion of his presence was both 'pleasurable and penitential'.[31]

THE CAMPAIGN FOR DECENT BUILDINGS AND THE
AMALGAMATION QUESTION

In 1965, there were 4,948 national schools in the Republic. Of these 2,409 were
two-teacher schools and a further 750 had one teacher, so almost two-thirds of
the state's schools had only one or two teachers. Falling averages caused by rural
depopulation, whether through emigration or migration to the cities, meant
that some three-teacher schools in the west were in danger of losing a teacher as
a result of falling averages.[32] Among policy-makers and commentators there was
a growing belief that the era of the small school was at an end. It was not merely
that they were uneconomic, but that they did not provide the best education for
the children attending them. This was a view put forward by the Labour Party in
its 1963 policy document on education and by the London Tuairim group in its
1965 pamphlet on education, and it enjoyed some support in Fine Gael. At the
INTO's 1965 congress, the Dublin City branch tabled a motion proposing a
special committee to look into the question. The motion was passed, but the
committee was never established.[33]

In April 1965, George Colley became minister for education. In June, he averted to amalgamating small schools in the Dáil during the Education Estimates debate, but he did so in Irish and it received little attention. Some months later, this time in English, he told the Dáil that he had been 'having another look at the problem' of small schools, which he argued held back pupils' educational attainment and stopped them getting a fair chance.[34] Colley said he had made up his mind to take action. He recognised there would be considerable opposition, most of which would be based on 'misguided sentiment', but appealed to the opposition 'not to support this kind of agitation', pointing out that it was Labour and Fine Gael policy anyway. Colley had been acting on his own initiative but had secured the support of the taoiseach by the end of September, although Lemass warned him to proceed cautiously and bring the public with him since the plan had not been sufficiently publicised.[35]

The opposition soon manifested itself. In September, the bishop of Galway, Dr Michael Browne, opened a new two-teacher school in County Clare, lamenting that it might be the last time he would do so. He painted Colley's policy on small schools as an attack on rural Ireland and asked if the one- and two-teacher schools were all to be 'abolished and merged just as it was proposed to merge the small farms'.[36] A number of opposition deputies echoed Bishop Browne's concerns in the Dáil. Oliver J. Flanagan, with the sagacity for which he was well known, asserted that the minister's motives were 'evilly disposed', and that he was hiding something extraordinary that had not yet been disclosed. When Colley jokingly suggested that he was engaged in a communist plot, Flanagan was almost reluctant in agreeing with him, but 'bearing in mind that the State are taking over, may I say in a Communist fashion, the education of the people, the next step is the taking over of the complete lives of the people by the state'.[37] In fairness, this paranoiac red-scaring was atypical of the scheme's opponents in rural Ireland, however. As John Coolahan has put it:

[F]or many communities the school had come to symbolise their continued well-being. The daily routines of children going to and coming from school, the noise of children at play in the playgrounds, the sentimental attachments of some parents to the school of their own schooldays, the use of the school for aspects of adult education or community occasions, all tended to emphasise the close ties of the school with the daily life of a district. As well as inconveniences arising from closure, the very fact of closure could be seen by communities as a vote of no confidence in their future, and this tended to hurt deeply.[38]

The INTO executive met Colley twice to discuss his plan, keen to ensure no jobs would be lost. They also secured an assurance from Colley that it would not lead to any infringement of the Ballina agreement, so that no lay schools would be forced to amalgamate with religious schools unless there was no alternative. As a result, Colley felt able to tell the Dáil that he had discussed the issue with the INTO, which had no objection in principle. That was not true since the matter had never been discussed at congress but it dominated proceedings in Killarney at Easter 1966. There was considerable division on the matter, falling largely on lines of Dublin versus the rest, while, speaking for the executive, Alfie Faulkner noted that the majority of inspectors and school managers were in favour of the scheme and urged delegates to 'think of this progressively, for the sake of the country. It is inevitable that sacred cows are going to go to the educational abattoir. Far from saving money this will cost a vast amount and don't let it be said that the INTO is going to be … obstructionist and not progressive.'[39] In the end, delegates voted by 200 to 121 in favour of a motion approving of amalgamation in principle. The *Irish Times* education correspondent, John Horgan, reported:

> [T]owards the end … it became obvious that the supporters of the motion were in a distinct majority. In the circumstances it is clear that the majority of the 121 negative votes were cast not specifically to defeat the motion, but to register a strong warning that national teachers, while willing to cooperate, were also on their guard. They were, in fact, declining to sign a blank cheque.[40]

Opponents of the plan felt that was precisely what had happened,[41] and there was a sense of resentment among rural teachers who felt they had been outgunned by people who were not affected by the policy.

The opposition from the small-school teachers or parents counted for little against the forces who either favoured the move (the taoiseach and the rest of the government, the Department and the Dáil opposition, apart from a handful of Fine Gael deputies) or were not opposed in principle (the INTO as a whole, the Catholic hierarchy as a whole, and their school managers).[42] Colley and Bishop Browne of Galway continued to clash on the matter in public, but although Colley moved to Industry and Commerce in July 1966, his policy was implemented successfully by his successors, and by 1972 over 900 small schools had been closed. As John Walsh notes, 'the policy of amalgamation delivered a radical reorganisation of primary education within a decade of its introduction' and, significantly, the clash with Bishop Browne 'marked the first open conflict between the Minister for Education and a Catholic bishop concerning the reform and expansion of the educational system'.[43] Twelve years later, in 1984, the number of one- and two-teacher schools had been reduced to 900 (from 3,194 in 1962), with the school stock reduced by a third overall.[44]

Related to the question of school amalgamations was the condition of the buildings, which continued to be a dire problem. When Jerry Allman, principal of Killury school in Causeway, County Kerry, was elected president for the year 1967–68, he identified school buildings as the priority for his presidential year. Having begun to hold local meetings on the subject, from November, the CEC operated a policy where complaints over substandard accommodation would be investigated by two members of the CEC and a doctor with public health experience. In cases where the complaint was substantiated, the staff in the school would be instructed to withdraw. Several schools in Allman's local area were first identified for investigation and in January 1968 the 12 teachers in Ardfert voted to withdraw their services from the five parish schools in the area, complaining of deplorable toilet facilities, with pupils refusing to use the dry toilets in the school, inadequate heating, unwashed floors, unpainted walls and dirty playgrounds.[45] The teachers had the parents' support, and the dispute was immediately front-page news. Within days, there was a statement that improvements would be carried out in the schools in the parish, and before the week was over contractors were on site to make temporary repairs.[46] The teachers in Ardfert returned to work after a fortnight on strike but not before the manager of the closed schools had resigned.[47] It had forced the issue on a matter that was widely known to be unacceptable, while remaining stubbornly unresolved. Even the minister for education, Donogh O'Malley, had described between 600 and 700 schools as 'hovels' that were 'unfit for pigs'.[48] In the annual report for 1968–69, the CEC reported that in nearly every instance where the INTO had issued a complaint about substandard accommodation, improvement works had begun in a very short time. By the 1968 congress, an estimated 500 schools had been tackled since the campaign had begun in the winter of 1967–68.[49] This was in some ways an impressive testament to the power of the INTO, now in its centenary year, but on the other hand it was a shocking indictment of the unwillingness of Church and state to fulfil their responsibilities to the school children – and their teachers – forced to spend their days in these conditions.

In his presidential speech to centenary congress, Jerry Allman recalled the teachers' early struggles to be recognised, and how in its early years the INTO had been frowned upon by authority, both lay and clerical. Today, though, there was no limit to their activities, and they were to be found in all areas of Irish life, with teachers prominent in cultural and athletic movements and in organisations involved with rural development. Allman noted that 'the sons and daughters of teachers are to be found in religion, in the professions, in the higher rungs of the civil service and in the banking services. At least five members of the Catholic hierarchy are sons of teachers. This is all a far cry from the days when teachers' social status was deliberately depressed.'[50] True as this was, it also pointed to a phenomenon whereby many teachers discouraged their children from following them into the profession. The centrepiece of the INTO centenary in 1968 was its hosting of the World Confederation of Organisations of the Teaching Profession (WCOTP) biannual conference in Dublin in July and August of that year. It was an opportunity for the INTO to celebrate the occasion among around 600 delegates representing 149 organisations from almost every country in the world, and of which the INTO was among the oldest.

SALARIES AND PARITY CAMPAIGN

The INTO's campaign for parity with post-primary salaries, which had begun in the mid-1950s, continued throughout the 1960s. It was a decade that saw the state side make a volte face on its attitude towards the INTO's claim, while the ASTI's opposition hardened, and it ended in a largely successful outcome for primary teachers. Such a result had seemed very unlikely in the summer of 1960, though, when the Teachers' Salary Committee presented its report to Minister for Education Patrick Hillery. His predecessor, Jack Lynch, had appointed the committee in December 1958 'to examine and report on the principles which might guide the Minister for Education in determining the relationship between the remuneration payable to trained National teachers, recognised Secondary teachers and permanent whole-time Vocational teachers, respectively'. Comprising 15 men – a chair, four clergymen representing school managers, two representatives from each of the three teacher organisations (INTO, ASTI and the Vocational Teachers' Association, or VTA), a principal officer each from Finance and Education and two representing business interests – the committee met in full on ten occasions between January 1959 and May 1960.[51] It heard submissions from the three teacher organisations and looked at international practice.

It soon became evident to the two INTO representatives, D.J. Kelleher and Gerry Hurley, that the deck was stacked against the primary teachers. By its third meeting in May 1959, they had concluded they were 'talking to stone walls', as Kelleher put it.[52] The two found 'no sympathy' with anything that would disturb the status quo and the whole weight of the committee was against them on parity.[53] The INTO had been honing its case for several years by now, and its claim was in many ways a strong one. Kelleher had also expected that the argument that national teachers had so much responsibility for children's moral and religious training might strike a chord with the four clergymen on the committee, but it seems that, if anything, it had the opposite effect. As Kelleher told congress afterwards, '"The Rev. Mr. Looney" teaching in a seminary did not want "ordinary Dave Kelleher" teaching in a National School to have the same salary as he had. They brushed aside that aspect of the National Teachers work ... As far as the clergymen were concerned, you can be sure that they were no friends of yours.'[54] It is unlikely that the Ballina dispute, then at its height, did anything to predispose the clergy either to the interests of the INTO in general or to their task in religious instruction in particular, but it seems as though they were merely taking the same point of view as their colleagues, which was, in Kelleher's view, based on 'snobbery', not towards the teachers themselves, but towards their pupils.

As expected, the committee flatly rejected the case for parity, but also recommended machinery which would copper-fasten the teaching hierarchy through a unified conciliation and arbitration scheme for the three groups.[55] The majority report was signed by 13 members, with reservations from the ASTI and VTA representatives, while the two INTO representatives submitted a 14-page minority report. The authors of the minority report did not mince their words when they asserted their belief that the majority report expressed 'in the twentieth century a Victorian attitude towards the education of what used to be called "the lower orders"'.[56] Summing up, it observed:

> The National School system was originally intended for the 'deserving poor', to make them 'good farm labourers and servants' and this tradition continues in the Majority Report. No matter how high the qualifications of National teachers may be, no matter what subjects, or age-groups they may teach, because their pupils are drawn in the main from the poorer and under-privileged classes in town and country, the value placed on their service is less than that placed on the service of those who teach the children of the richer and privileged classes, and must be remunerated accordingly. The mentality which conditions such an approach to the problem might be appropriate to the France of the anti-clericals or the Russia of today. It should hardly apply to a country under whose constitution all children are cherished equally and whose citizens claim to be followers of a religion whose distinctive characteristic is that it teachers the Gospel of the poor.[57]

In March 1961, the government announced that it would accept the report's recommendations.[58]

While parity remained the ultimate goal, the INTO continued to make salary claims under the existing conciliation and arbitration machinery. The process was far from smooth. INTO members rejected a number of offers and came close to striking in 1963 and 1964. When status increases were awarded to the national teachers in 1964, the ASTI was aggrieved that their differential was closing and when the arbitrator refused to increase the secondary teachers' salaries to restore it, the ASTI congress advised members to boycott the state examinations in protest, requesting the INTO to ask its members not to co-operate in superintending or marking the Intermediate and Leaving Certificate papers.[59] When the CEC discovered why the ASTI was taking this action, it released a statement to the press, which it also sent to the minister and the ASTI, observing that the INTO regretted the ASTI's protest and that while it could have counted on INTO support if it had based its protest on the broad issues of the inadequacy of teachers' salaries generally, 'the INTO cannot, nor can it reasonably be expected to, lend support to a campaign which, if successful, would have the effect of depressing the salaries and status of its own members'.[60]

The curtness of the INTO's statement, as John Cunningham has observed, 'gave a carte blanche to primary teachers to act as supervisors and examiners. Many were to do so, and this would be a cause of considerable bitterness between these two arms of the profession'.[61] Furthermore, that autumn it emerged that the ASTI had been in secret negotiations with the Catholic Headmasters' Association (CHA), which ended in a very generous deal that agreed a new basic salary of £200 plus an additional 12.5 per cent of the state salary. It also provided a mechanism for automatic increases in subsequent years with increases linked to length of service and cost of living.[62] The deal upended all the recent moves towards parity for national and vocational teachers, and the INTO and VTA were most unhappy when they became aware of it.

The three organisations continued to make their separate claims at conciliation and arbitration, the ASTI endeavouring to stay ahead while the other two tried to catch up. This leap-frogging, or attempted leap-frogging, was wholly unsatisfactory to the government, which wanted a common conciliation and arbitration scheme for all teachers, but this was unacceptable to the INTO without salary parity. In the end, then, it was practical matters rather than any principle of equity that convinced the official side that parity had to be the way forward. Afterwards George Colley, who became minister after the election of April 1965, pushed for the common scale, but it was October 1967 before the three unions came to consider the proposal for a tribunal on teachers' salaries suggested by Colley's successor, Donogh O'Malley.[63] Over six weeks or so, the three organisations and the officials negotiated the committee's structure and personnel. There was strong resistance within ASTI to participating in the tribunal, which would, given its task, mean giving de facto support to the common scale, but eventually its executive decided by a narrow majority to co-operate,[64] and on 15 December 1967 the five-man tribunal was established. Chaired by Louden Ryan, professor of industrial economics in Trinity College, its terms of reference were straightforward: 'to recommend a common basic scale of salary for teachers' and 'to recommend what appropriate additions might be made to the basic scale in respect of qualifications, length of training, nature of duties etc.'[65]

The tribunal met some 20 times between January and March 1968 and in April submitted its report to the minister, which recommended a common basic scale set at the current rate for vocational teachers, with 17 increments. (To be accurate, there were two scales, one for single men and women, and another for married men.) The entry points were based on length of time in training, which

Vere Foster (1819–1900), first president of the INTO.

W.J.M. Starkie, resident commissioner of national education, 1899–1904.

Catherine Mahon summed up Starkie's period in charge of national education as years of civil war between himself and the INTO. *(Courtesy of Dublin City Library & Archive)*

Irish National Teachers' Organization.

The members of the Sligo Congress Committee present their compliments to — Pesse B L. and request the favour of his attendance at the opening proceedings of this year's Irish National Teachers' Congress, which will be held in the Town Hall, Sligo, on 27th inst.

Chair to be taken by Alderman Flanagan, J.P., Mayor of Sligo, at 11 o'clock, sharp, when the President's annual address will be delivered.

P. KILFEATHER,⎫
                   Secs.
T. HORAN,   ⎭

Town Hall, Sligo, April 11th, 1905.

Patrick Pearse's invitation to the 1905 INTO congress in Sligo, as representative of the Gaelic League. *(Image courtesy of the National Library of Ireland)*

Members of the CEC and Reception Committee at the Waterford Congress 1906: (*front row, L to R*) George Ramsay, Michael Doyle, John Moore, Mr McDiarmid (EIS), D.C. Maher (President), Mr Macpherson (EIS), Terence Clarke (Central Secretary, 1898–1909), David Elliott; (*centre row, fifth from the left*) Edmund Mansfield, (*sixth from the right*) John M. Thompson.

Catherine Mahon (*far left*) with the staff and pupils of Carrig School in 1903, four years before she became one of the first women representatives on the CEC.

JOHN BULL'S GENEROSITY.

JOHN BULL—"For your long and magnificent services in the cause of Irish National Education, accept my best thanks and this well-earned reward of twopence-halfpenny per day."

The recent statement of Mr. Ginnell, M.P., in connection with his appeal for the remedy of National Teachers' grievances, that a teacher of 29 years' service received the princely annuity of £3 17s. 6d. or 2½d. per day, is not calculated to cause overcrowding amongst these "spoilt children" of the Treasury.

INTO campaigning managed to secure pensions for national teachers in 1879, but the payments were very small. Eventually, in 1914, the INTO negotiated a new scheme where the pension depended on the average salary at retirement. *(Courtesy of Dublin City Library & Archive)*

To all Trades Unionists

The Irish National Teachers' Organisation have ordered a cessation of work

On 2nd October,

and a General Strike from

4th November,

if the demand for a War Bonus on Civil Service Terms be not conceded in the meantime.

They appeal to all parents to keep their children from school on those occasions, and thus refuse to act as Strike-Breakers.

They confidently claim their support in this fight for mere justice.

The Teachers of English and Scotch Children are infinitely better paid than the Teachers of Irish Children. Why should this be so?

Curtis, Printer, Temple Lane, Dublin.

Bill poster for the INTO's first industrial strike in 1918. Many members had gone on strike earlier in the year for the general strike against conscription. *(Image courtesy of the National Library of Ireland)*

A cartoon anticipating public service cuts in 1931. In the end the axe was to fall on the national teachers. *(Image courtesy of the National Library of Ireland)*

Teachers attending compulsory Irish classes during their summer break, 1923. *(Courtesy of British Pathé)*

INTO Strike Committee 1946: (*front row, L to R*) Miss B. Bergin, Miss Mairead Skinnider, Miss McBride, Miss McGrath, Mrs Breen, Mrs P. Byrne, Mr Sean O'Grady, Mr M. O'Doherty, Mr E. Regan; (*back row*) Mr W. Mullarkey, Mr B. Wright, Mr Sean Brehony, Mr Sean Kennedy, Mr P. O'Reilly, Mr Dan Rinn, Mr Kevin Costelloe, Mr Leon Ó Dubhgaill, Mr Tom Roycroft, Mr C. Clandillon.

Picket outside the Convent of Mercy School near Gardiner Street Church: (*L to R*) Dan Gillespie, Mrs Murphy and Noel Giles, 1946.

In 1946 many Dublin teachers learned that the strike had ended from the front pages of the newspapers.

CEC, 1948–9, featuring the outgoing and incoming general secretaries: (*front row, L to R*) M.P. Linehan (General Treasurer), D.J. Kelleher (General Secretary), Liam Forde (outgoing President), T.J. O'Connell (ex-General Secretary), J. Mansfield (incoming President), S. Brosnahan (ex-President); (*second row*) P. Gormley, S. Sweeney, Capt. H.F. McCune Reid, D. Ó Scanaill, I.H. McEnaney, G. Hurley; (*back*) Liam O'Reilly, P. Carney, W. Keane (D. McSweeney not present).

Officers and officials, 1955. Margaret Skinnider (Vice President) in the centre, flanked by Matt Griffin (President, 1954), H.J. McManus (President, 1953), D.J. Kelleher (General Secretary) and M.P. Linehan (General Treasurer).

Mr J. Ryan, Frank Cunningham (President, 1981), Liam O'Reilly (President, 1957) and Seamas Doyle picketing Ballina Boys' School, 1962.

Pádraig Faulkner, the first INTO member to be appointed Minister for Education, addressing the 1970 Congress.

Newly elected president, Fiona Poole, addresses congress in 1978, with CEC members John White, Tom Gilmore, Gerry Quigley, incoming General Secretary Gerry Keane, Brendan Scannell and outgoing General Secretary Seán Brosnahan.

Twenty presidents and officials from 1910 to 1968 (taken in 1971): (*back row, L to R*) H.J. McManus (1953), P O'Riordan (1962), D. O'Scanaill (1963), S. McGlinchey (1960), L. O'Reilly (1957), G. Hurley (1958); (*middle row*) A.J. Faulkner (1968), M.P. Linehan, (General Treasurer 1927–1961), S. Brosnahan (1947, General Treasurer 1961–7, General Secretary 1967–78), L.H. McEaney (1951), Miss M. Skinnider (1956), J. Mansfield (1949), P. Gormley (1952), P. Carney (1964), W. Keane (1959); (*front row*) L. Forde (1948), J.D. Sheridan (editor *Irish School Weekly*), E. Mansfield (1910), T.J. O'Connell (General Secretary 1916–1948), Miss B. Bergin (1950), Mrs K.M. Clarke (1945), T. Frisby (1926 and 1944), J.P. Griffith.

INTO press conference 1985: (*L to R*) Michael McGarry (CEC), Séamus Puirséil (Vice President), Roisín Carabine (President), Gerry Quigley (General Secretary), John Carr (CEC), Charlie Lennon (official) and Bernice Nunan (Research Assistant).

In August 1985, education minister Gemma Hussey told teachers to address themselves to the morality of their pay demands, which 'turned moderate teachers into raving Bolsheviks.'

Members of INTO, TUI and ASTI at a rally in Croke Park, 1985.

The Lord Mayor of Dublin, Michael O'Halloran (*L*), at the Mansion House with the 'belligerent Northerners' President Roisín Carabine, General Secretary Gerry Quigley and Northern Secretary Al Mackle, 1985.

First meeting of the Equality Committee, 1987: (*back row, L to R*) Liam Moran, Marjorie Murphy, Nora Mac Cinna, Máire Ní Chuinneagáin, Nora Murphy, Teresa Murphy, Eamonn Ó Murchú, Kathleen Ryan, Mary Gallagher, Rosemary Gallagher, Fran O'Grady, Noreen Queally, Anne Madden, Helen Kennedy-Martin, Jim Magee; (*front row*) Michael Drew (Vice President), Gerry Quigley (General Secretary), Catherine Byrne (Equality Officer), Tom Honan (President) and Michael Moroney (General Treasurer).

Tadhg Mac Pháidín, Henry J. O'Dwyer (Chairman EBS), Tom Gilmore, John Joe Connelly and Michael Drew at the plaque to mark the founding of the EBS in the Teachers' Club, 1988.

Education Conference in 1991: Declan Kelleher, Don Herron (Education Committee members) with General Secretary Joe O'Toole and Education Officer and future General Secretary John Carr.

Ministers for Education from both jurisdictions – Michael Woods and Martin McGuinness – with President Joan Ward at INTO Congress 2002.

INTO Executive Committee 2008: (*back row, L to R*) Frank Bunting (Northern Secretary), Helen O'Gorman, Mary Cahillane; (*second row from back*) Máire Ní Chuinnegáin, Seamus Long, Anne Fay; (*third row from back*) Emma Dineen, Claire Byrne, Noreen Flynn; (*fourth row from back*) Jim Higgins, Brendan O'Sullivan; (*second row*) John Boyle, Tony Lappin, Sean McMahon, Gerard McGeehan, Donal O'Donoghue; (*front row*) John Carr (General Secretary), Denis Bohane (ex-President), Angela Dunne (President), Sheila Nunan (Deputy General Secretary and Treasurer), Declan Kelleher (Vice President).

INTO LGBT celebrating its tenth anniversary at Arás an Uachtaráin with President Michael D. Higgins in 2014.

Officers at the 2017 Congress in Belfast: Noel Ward (Deputy General Secretary and Treasurer), Rosena Jordan (outgoing President), Sheila Nunan (General Secretary), John Boyle (incoming President), Gerry Murphy (Northern Secretary), with Anne Horan and Joe McKeown (CEC Representatives).

The current INTO Presidential chain of office, in use since 1957.

Equal Pay Demo: A demonstration as part of a general pay campaign and a campaign for pay equality, North and South respectively, at INTO Congress 2017.

meant that primary teachers, who trained for two years, would begin on the first point, while secondary teachers, who trained for three or four years, would begin on the second or third point. The report recommended allowances for certain degrees and diplomas and for 'posts of responsibility' to be set up in larger schools, in effect topping up the basic salary scale for secondary teachers. After some 15 years of campaigning for a common scale, the INTO had at last got what it wanted. There were a few 'objectionable features' to the report, but these could be dealt with privately with the Department.[66] While a pleased INTO remained 'diplomatically mute', the other two unions were quick to spurn the proposals.[67] The VTA was first to formally reject at a special congress in mid-June by 64 votes to 18,[68] while for the ASTI, the question was not whether the report should be rejected but how to fight it if it was adopted.[69] A special conference in July voted to establish a strike fund and to ballot in the event of Ryan being implemented.

By now, there was a new minister. Donogh O'Malley had died suddenly on 10 March and his successor in Education, Brian Lenihan, was in no hurry to act, apparently saying of the report, 'I didn't want it; I don't want it; I never wanted it; and now I'm stuck with it.'[70]

The delicate situation was not well managed by Lenihan. Charles McCarthy of the VTA suggested afterwards that had there been subsequent negotiations, done with skill and sensitivity, an agreement could have been reached,[71] but Lenihan just let it sit over the summer recess, and when it was picked up in the autumn, 'far from aiming at a consensus, [Lenihan] seemed to be caught up in a highly complex, devious business of balancing one group against another for the purpose of following their own view of what should be done'.[72] An improved offer on pay scales and degree allowances was made in October but it fell far short of the secondary teachers' demands, and ASTI members rejected it by 92 per cent. INTO members voted to accept it by almost the same percentage, while VTA members also agreed to the revised proposals in a ballot in November.[73] Negotiations saw all offers rebuffed by ASTI, and on 1 February its members went out on an all-out strike, which ended a fortnight later when ASTI accepted new proposals from the minister.

As long as the government engaged in separate negotiations with individual unions or threw money at one union over the others, the parity issue could not be resolved, and the VTA's and the INTO's response to this latest sop to the secondary teachers was predictably hostile. After the VTA went on strike for two days in May, followed by the INTO the next day, the Department invited the two unions to new salary discussions. These were chaired, once again, by Louden Ryan, and when Ryan issued his second report on 13 June, the INTO had reason to be pleased. Reiterating the need for a common basic scale, it noted that the ad hoc decisions of recent months had seriously breached the framework set out by the first Ryan report.

The publication of the second Ryan report coincided with the general election on 18 June 1969. Fianna Fáil returned to office in its fourth successive victory, but there was a new minister for education. Unlike his predecessor, Pádraig Faulkner was unshowy and diligent in his ministerial duties, and where Lenihan had shown little sympathy for national teachers, in the new minister they had a comrade. Not only had Faulkner worked as a national teacher from 1938 until his election to the Dáil in 1957, he had also been an active member of the INTO and one-time chairman of the Drogheda branch, and was still a member when he became minister.[74] It would be crude to suggest that Faulkner was playing favourites, but he had a natural sympathy with the national teachers' case. By mid-September, the minister issued proposals to the three teacher unions that accepted the second Ryan report. The ground ceded by Lenihan on parity had been recovered,[75] which led the ASTI to plan a series of strikes from February 1970. It was another year before the ASTI eventually, and controversially, came on board with the joint scales. The INTO had finally won the battle for parity, having first fought the government and then its fellow teachers for the right.

TRAINING COLLEGES, THE BEd AND STRIKING STUDENTS

The question of university degrees for national teachers had been inextricably tied in with the parity campaign, which saw secondary teachers argue that they should be paid more, in part, because they held degrees. For its part, since 1908, it had been INTO policy that national teachers should study for university degrees, rather than the two-year NT (national teacher) qualification awarded by the training colleges, but although Eoin MacNeill had indicated a willingness to move towards this when he was minister around 1924, nothing came of it, and none of his successors was supportive. During its campaign for parity, the INTO had argued that the NT qualification was worth more than a Bachelor of Arts since the entry requirements were higher, the contact hours heavier and the examinations more difficult, but despite this, the INTO still wanted degrees. The organisation put its case to the government's Commission on Higher Education in a written submission in 1961 and in oral evidence to the commission the following year. In the course of his evidence, Seán Brosnahan was asked if national teachers felt that the present system did not qualify them sufficiently for teaching. He responded that on the contrary, the opposite was the case, but 'they do feel that they should have this status symbol'. Asked if it was the case then that degrees were simply a status symbol, Brosnahan replied 'yes'.[76]

Whatever its reason for wanting degrees, the INTO had a number of allies on this issue, most notably the president of St Patrick's College of Education, Dr Donal Cregan, along with his staff and students, who were becoming increasingly vocal on the matter. In May 1969, more than 350 student teachers and their instructors from St Patrick's staged a protest march to the Department of Education calling for improvements to primary teacher training, including the extension of the course from two to three years.[77] By then the newly established Higher Education Authority was considering the question, and in December 1970 it was announced that it had suggested a three-year course with a degree to be awarded by a new body rather than by one of the universities. This fell short of the basic demand for a university degree and was roundly rejected by the INTO, the training colleges and the student representatives.[78] The following year, when Pádraig Faulkner arrived at St Patrick's for the conferring of diplomas, hundreds of students from the college held the minister 'prisoner' in his car outside the grounds in a protest demanding three-year university organised course and grants for all teacher trainees. Faulkner got in eventually, but the ceremony was boycotted by some students.[79]

It was the second time in six months that the minister had received a hostile reception from students in St Patrick's; the earlier occasion related to the closing of a school in Dún Chaoin. By the late 1960s and early 1970s, student protests were not uncommon in Ireland, as elsewhere. These included UCD's 'Gentle Revolution' of 1969, a dispute in the National College of Art and Design, and one occasion when an education minister (Brian Lenihan) was pursued by Maoists at an event in Trinity College and had to escape through a toilet window. Trainee teachers were traditionally more conservative – Joe O'Toole recalled going to St Patrick's for his interview, and sitting in a waiting room which 'seemed full of besuited seventeen- or eighteen-year olds, all wearing a Fáinne, or Pioneer pin, or both'[80] – but if many of them may still have been wearing Fáinní as they barracked the minister in excellent Irish, the type of deference towards authority that might have been expected some years earlier was no longer in evidence.

This was also apparent a couple of years later in Carysfort, when 650 trainee teachers went on strike from November 1973 until mid-January 1974. The dispute began over college authorities' refusal to allow the students to change elective subjects, but there were other grievances caused by the rapid expansion in student numbers as well as the authorities' unwillingness to treat them like adults. Not that the nuns were alone in this, with at least one newspaper portraying the student strikers as 'curfew girl rebels', which made them sound like characters from a St Trinian's story.[81] The main union involved in this dispute was the Union of Students in Ireland (USI), which the Carysfort students had joined, but the college authorities refused to recognise. The then USI president, Pat Rabbitte, complained of a 'methodical campaign of vilification and slander being carried out by individual members of the religious' against USI generally over the dispute, which included his having been denounced from the pulpit as 'a Dublin communist'.[82] However, while the dispute was between the

USI and Carysfort, as it continued into the Christmas holidays the INTO attempted to intervene. Seán Brosnahan arranged a meeting with the leader of the Carysfort students, Catherine Byrne. Acting as an intermediary for Archbishop's House, Brosnahan came with an offer that the principal of Carysfort would be removed if the students would return to college, but nothing came of this. The dispute was settled on 10 January, when the authorities agreed to recognise the USI; and when four students were appointed to the college's board at the beginning of the next academic year, it gave Carysfort the highest student representation in the state.[83]

On the question of degrees, as is often the way, a change of minister resulted in a change of policy. In March 1973, a Fine Gael–Labour coalition took office and Richard Burke replaced Pádraig Faulkner in Education. Addressing congress in Kilkenny a few weeks later, he announced that the training course was being extended to three years from the following September, and that, subject to the agreement of the universities, it would carry a university degree. He also promised to use his influence to secure a favourable response and that the new teacher training course would be drawn up. In May, it was announced that the senate of the NUI had approved a new Bachelor of Education degree, and that the teacher training colleges were being invited to apply for 'recognised college status' in the National University.[84] St Patrick's College, Carysfort and Mary Immaculate College became colleges of the NUI, while the Church of Ireland College, Marino College and Froebel College became associated with Trinity College Dublin.[85]

THE TEACHING OF IRISH AND THE NEW CURRICULUM

Though the education system as a whole was undergoing re-evaluation during the 1960s, the content of what was taught and how it was taught in primary schools was not vastly different from four decades earlier. The national schools curriculum had not been significantly revised since 1926, although the curriculum was narrowed somewhat in 1934 to make more time available for teaching Irish.[86] The Primary Certificate, first introduced in 1929 and compulsory for pupils in sixth standard from 1943, with its emphasis on written work in Irish, English and arithmetic, further limited the work in the senior classes. This trend was exacerbated where pupils studied for the written county council scholarships in order to attend secondary school.[87] The INTO had long criticised the curriculum and the Primary Certificate, but, as it acknowledged in the 1947 *Plan for Education*, there could be no real discussion of reforming the curriculum without examining the use of a non-vernacular language as a teaching medium.[88] The 1947 plan called for all aspects of the curriculum to be modernised and the Primary Certificate abolished, with child-centred learning at its heart, observing 'the needs of the child must take precedence over all other interests, motives or aims. If we build about the child, and for the child, we cannot go far wrong.'[89] It was not until the mid- to late 1960s that serious reconsideration of the curriculum was undertaken at official level. This discussion occurred in the context of economic development and the government's aim for Ireland to join the European Economic Community. The curricular review was also informed by educational thinking outside Ireland, most notably the 1967 Plowden Report in Britain, and important new research on the educational standards of Irish school children. However, as the *Plan for Education* had noted back in 1947, serious reform of the curriculum was impossible without looking at the position of Irish in the classroom.

The prevailing attitude in the INTO towards the teaching of and through Irish had changed over the decades. After compulsory Irish was introduced in 1922, there was considerable resentment among teachers, who had had to learn the language themselves and teach through it. Shouldered with full responsibility for the language revival at the same time as their salaries were being cut by successive governments, for many of those teaching when the Free State was established, Irish was a burden. This grievance was evident each year at Easter congress, in the pages of the *Irish School Weekly* and in INTO pay claims throughout the 1920s, 1930s and into the 1940s. By the 1940s, however, a generational shift occurred. Part of this was due to the high proportion of teachers who had come into training via the Gaeltacht preparatory colleges – a route of entry the INTO opposed – which meant that more and more teachers had Irish as a first language, but others from outside the Gaeltacht were learning it from school anyway. By the mid- to late 1950s, the amount of Irish that was being used in *An Múinteoir Náisiúnta* was considerable, and sometimes its editorials were entirely in Irish; and D.J. Kelleher observed in 1957 that not only was congress younger but more Irish was being used in debates.[90] Not only had Irish ceased to be a grievance – no longer held up as a reason why national teachers should be paid more – but by the 1950s, the INTO asserted that the main aim of primary education was the restoration of the Irish language.

Ironically, this shift had taken place just as the debate on the role of Irish and its impact on pupils' general learning was taking off.[91] By the 1950s it had become quite clear that the Irish language revival, pursued almost uniquely through the primary education system, had not worked, but perhaps more important were the changes of personnel in government. There could be no diminution of Irish while de Valera was taoiseach, but his successor, Seán Lemass, did not share his enthusiasm for the revival and, indeed, had almost no Irish himself. The issue remained hotly contested, but there was, for the first time, a possibility of reform. In 1960, Minister for Education Patrick Hillery made two crucial decisions which had significant impact on the teaching of Irish. In January, the Department issued a deceptively bland circular (11/60) that informed teachers that inspectors would place a greater emphasis on oral than on written Irish, so teachers were free to transfer the emphasis from 'teaching *through* Irish to the teaching of Irish Conversation', which was taken as an invitation to teachers to abandon teaching through Irish for infants.[92] Then, later that year, Hillery closed the preparatory colleges, which had established a supply of fluent Irish teachers into the national schools.[93]

In 1967, as part of the broader changes in education, including the intro-duction of free post-primary education and the planned increase of the school-leaving age to 15 years, the hated Primary Certificate was finally abolished. Around the same time, a review of the curriculum began which was completed in the autumn of 1968, which the INTO welcomed in principle, although the Teachers' Study Group observed that it was odd that the national teachers were not consulted during the drafting stage, unlike a similar review of the secondary school curriculum a couple of years earlier.[94] Of the new curriculum, introduced in 1971, John Coolahan later observed that it had been 'the single greatest factor in changing the life-experience of both teachers and pupils within the schools. Its philosophy, content and methodology have helped to make schools more interesting, varied and satisfying places for those who spend a significant portion of their lifetimes in school.'[95] But if the curriculum was a vast improvement it was also seriously under-resourced, and the INTO's 1974 review of the new curriculum noted, among other things, the failure to establish machinery to evaluate and review the curriculum, as had been promised; the 'continued failure to meet the need for a sustained and ambitious programme of in-service training'; and the delays in providing suitable classrooms with adequate equipment to teach the new curriculum. It also noted the failure to address the widespread large class sizes, particularly in the larger schools, and the failure to give schools in under-privileged areas more generous treatment with regard to the numbers required for appointment and retention of teachers.

SCHOOL GOVERNANCE AND MANAGEMENT

By the early 1970s, the last thing which remained untouched in education was governance, but that changed after a national coalition of Fine Gael and Labour took office in March 1973. The taoiseach, Liam Cosgrave, was adamant that Fine Gael should hold Education, believing a Labour minister would lead to conflict with the Catholic Church, and appointed Dick Burke to the role.[96] Before his election in 1969, Burke had been an ASTI activist in south Dublin, but, according to one contemporary profile, 'had not a great deal to say about education' since entering the Dáil.[97] A Christian democrat on Fine Gael's conservative wing, he was put into Education 'in the knowledge that there would be no surprise attacks or dangerous policy initiatives'.[98] Nevertheless, while initiatives under his guidance were few, his proposals to change the management structure were potentially far-reaching and caused considerable concern within the INTO.

School management had been an INTO grievance since its foundation, and it might seem obvious that, offered the prospect of ending the system of clerical managers running schools and replacing them with local boards of management, the INTO would grasp it with both hands, while the Church would reject it outright. In fact the opposite was the case. The Church's change of heart came largely from two factors. First was the influence of the Second Vatican Council, which encouraged greater lay involvement in the Church and education, but there was also a much more practical reason for the Church's attitude; as the Catholic Managers' Association admitted to the INTO, 'they knew that the younger priests will not accept the full responsibility of school management, and the raising of funds for the upkeep and maintenance of schools'.[99] The INTO, on the other hand, found the managerial system as it stood less than ideal, but it was the devil it knew. Dealing with the local parish priest was one thing; being managed by a committee including parents was something else entirely. What role would parents play? Might the local butcher end up responsible for hiring or firing teachers or be privy to confidential information such as inspectors' reports? There were alarmed suggestions that boards of management would become 'stomping grounds for aspiring demagogues', and while INTO members north of the border, who had been working under similar management regimes for some time, counselled that there was nothing to be worried about, resistance remained. The CEC dragged its feet on an agreement. Often, if negotiations could be prolonged enough, the minister would be replaced or the government might fall and that would be the end of it, but if that was the plan here, it did not work. Eventually, in October 1974 the CEC put the government's proposal on management to a ballot and it was passed by a 3:1 majority. This established the basis for further talks with the minister and the managers, and eventually a scheme was arrived at that the INTO was prepared to engage with for a three-year period (the lifetime of one management committee) before reviewing the situation. When there was no review in 1978, the INTO withdrew from the process, although restructured management boards eventually came into operation in October 1981, eight and a half years after the idea was first proposed.[100]

The INTO did not cast itself in a good light during the process. Relations with the managers had deteriorated so badly by September 1975, when the decisive ballot finally took place, that a representative from the managers told the *Irish Times* that 'we get no information from them at all. We can't understand what their game is. I and none of the managers I know have any trust in the INTO at the present. Confidence seems to have vanished.'[101] Notably, the article containing this observation did not feature an INTO response. It had long had a stand-off relationship with the press, but by now senior officials were barely on speaking terms with the education correspondents in the national newspapers.

The executive was deeply unhappy with the INTO's press coverage, particularly on the management issue and especially in the *Education Times*, the new weekly education paper published by the *Irish Times*, but for the CEC to pass a motion deploring the 'inaccurate and mischievous reporting and comment in certain sections of the press' was truculence unlikely to improve the situation.[102] Senior officials' contempt for the press was quite open. At least one education correspondent was denounced from the congress platform by name, and John Horgan recalls one congress where a member actually ran away from him mid-conversation when he caught sight of the general secretary, for fear of being seen speaking to the press. However, where the general secretary was unwilling to speak to papers, others, whether opponents outside the organisation or critics from within who were increasingly frustrated with its lack of direction, were not.

Horgan had attracted the wrath of Brosnahan for a critical article published in the *Education Times* before the 1975 congress. It observed that 'for a union which is actually the largest and potentially the most important organisation of teachers on this island, the INTO is in a curious state of disarray at the moment', and pointed to its hesitant approach towards management and its failure to 'think constructively about education structures'. 'Rather than being in the vanguard of a new system,' Horgan wrote, 'the organisation ... has left its shop-floor workers effectively rudderless ... The INTO is a giant, but it is a sleeping giant, lulled into dreamland by the now comparatively smooth-running salary and negotiations structure, and only intermittently raising a sleepy eyelid to gaze at the world around it. Perhaps it needs someone to come up and shake it.'[103] Horgan noted, 'in more senses than one, the INTO stands at a cross-roads today'.

To the INTO leadership this analysis would have seemed churlish. There had been great changes in Irish education during the long 1960s, and for the INTO it was a remarkably successful period, when so many of the things for which it had campaigned for decades were finally brought about. If draughty, rat-infested buildings had not disappeared altogether, they had become unusual rather than the norm. The hated Primary Certificate had been abolished and there was a new curriculum which had much in common with the INTO's *Plan for Education*. Teachers had greater autonomy over their teaching and child-centred learning was placed at the heart of education, replacing the prescribed rote learning of before. Teacher training changed, with modernised training colleges now teaching three-year degree courses, and with research facilities and study centres set up to facilitate trainee teachers and continuing professional development through in-service training. After a lengthy struggle, primary teachers' pay was now pegged at the same levels as for those teaching in post-primary, and together they were part of a conciliation and arbitration mechanism.

Nevertheless, for all of the INTO's successes, there was a sense of drift and, indeed, complacency by the mid-1970s. At a time when the membership was growing – the result of more teachers being appointed and a higher level of membership – there was a growing sense of alienation between the new, younger teachers and the INTO establishment, a natural generational tension which had been most clearly evident before in 1946; but now the young Turks had become the old guard.

Chapter 6 ~

TEACHERS UNITED, 1978–1990

'We are the gentle, angry teachers.'

THE GENERAL SECRETARY CONTEST, 1977

In November 1976, it was formally announced that the general secretary Seán Brosnahan would retire on 30 June 1978, and with him the general treasurer Matt Griffin. The election for a general secretary designate would take place in 1977 and the successful candidate would take up the post on 1 January 1978.[1] This brought into the open the surreptitious campaigns that had been going on for several years, and in February 1977 three candidates formally declared. They were Michael Moroney, executive officer in head office since 1968; Dublin-based Tom Gilmore, who had been on the executive since 1966; and Gerry Quigley, northern secretary since 1953. This was the first contest for the position since 1946, when Dave Kelleher had beaten M.P. Linehan, and there was particular interest in the campaign, and not only in the INTO itself: the keen press interest illustrated the INTO's status by this time.

The 1977 congress in Fermoy was taken over by the election. One INTO veteran had deemed it all 'most unseemly', observing that 'it looks like the New Hampshire primary in full swing'.[2] Gerry Quigley recalled later how 'a lot of the lads who were backing me wanted the razzmatazz business', but razzmatazz and glad-handing did not come naturally to the rather reserved northerner.[3] As Christina Murphy observed, 'many of the old guard still find canvassing and lobbying most unseemly. But the younger ones and the liberals love it.'[4] Her light-hearted ribbing prompted a complaint to Murphy's editor for 'slanting news concerning the election and with being offensive to Tom Gilmore in particular', and of generally belittling the proceedings of congress.[5] Once again the INTO's reputation for adroit politics failed it when it came to the press.

From the outset, it was a two-horse race between Tom Gilmore and Gerry Quigley, with Gilmore starting as the favourite. Over the previous ten years, he had worked closely alongside the out-going Brosnahan/Griffin leadership, and had proved himself a very able negotiator. He played an important role in securing some of the INTO's most important gains in recent decades, including the removal of the Primary Certificate and the introduction of a common basic scale for teachers.[6] Gilmore's experience was to be his weakness, however. He was closely identified with the old regime at a time when many members, especially the younger members, thought it was time for a change. Gerry Quigley, for his part, had the benefit of over two decades of experience as northern secretary, but he was seen as an outsider, partly because he worked from Belfast, but also because he was not close to the outgoing leadership. Quigley had an immensely strong record as an organiser, having rebuilt the INTO in the North from some 1,250 members when he took over in 1953 to four times that by the mid-1970s, and was a skilled negotiator for the INTO and with the Northern Committee of ICTU and other representative groups in the North, in the UK and in Europe.

With the three candidates all identifying similar aims, including equal pay, smaller class sizes, better promotion prospects and resolution of management issues, the main difference between them was how the INTO would work as an organisation in the future. For many, there was a sense that the INTO had become too casual, and that there was a dearth of openness and accountability in how it was run. Quigley's promise of 'modern trade union procedures to resolve individual and collective disputes' and an end to what he privately called the 'huggermugger' way of doing things was very attractive. Disaffection with the old regime, which could be seen from the outside as something of a clique, was widespread, but especially strong among younger members, who put their weight behind Quigley as the candidate for change. By the time the branch nominations started arriving into head office in May 1977, the groundswell of support for Quigley was unmistakable. By the close of poll, he had been nominated by 109 of 178 branches and won almost two-thirds of the total votes.[7] Subsequently, Michael Moroney successfully ran for the position of treasurer designate, while Al Mackle of the Armagh branch, a CEC representative and close colleague of Quigley's, was appointed northern secretary designate.

It was the end of an era, and the 1978 congress had the air of a wake about it. There were emotional speeches and glowing tributes to Griffin and Brosnahan, with Griffin telling delegates, 'I owe my whole life to the INTO. No other life would have suited me.'[8] Noting that the retirements marked a watershed in the INTO's history, Christina Murphy observed that there was no other figure in teaching as legendary as Seán (Jackie) Brosnahan:

He has seen 13 Ministers for Education come and go since he first took up national office for the union. He has negotiated with two Cardinals of Armagh and several archbishops. His name is prominent in the accounts of all major activities of the union since the Second World War.[9]

If it was a watershed at the very top, the CEC remained largely the same. In 1978, all but two districts returned their representatives unopposed, something which belied a certain unhappiness with the executive, in Dublin at least.[10] The changes to the CEC that year included a new member for Dublin, Joe O'Toole, and a new president, Fiona Poole, both of whom represented a more liberal, and often younger section among the national teachers.

WOMEN IN THE INTO

Fiona Poole's election as president in 1978 is noteworthy and should be understood in the context of the place of women in the organisation up to and around that time. The INTO was not unusual in being male-dominated, but the absence of women at a leadership level in a sector where they were numerically superior was a problem, and issues affecting women specifically, such as equal pay, were not pursued with the same vigour that might have been the case had they affected men. In 1959, the Irish Congress of Trade Unions (ICTU) established a Women's Advisory Committee, on which Margaret Skinnider and Eileen Liston represented the INTO, which pressed for women's issues in the trade union movement and pushed through a motion demanding equal pay in 1963, but the INTO was slow to follow its lead. In the early to mid-1960s, the women's case was put forward by a triumvirate of Dublin-based women delegates: the past president, Margaret Skinnider; and Eileen Liston and Alice Brennan, both future presidents. When the three found themselves facing a wall of opposition on the question of equal pay at the 1963 Easter congress Alice Brennan observed that, 'because the women had no representative on the executive they had to be grateful for the crumbs which fell from the master's table', but she continued that it was up to the women themselves to put themselves forward and get elected to fight for themselves. In 1964, Eileen Liston stood for vice-president and was elected. She served on the executive for three years. When she stood down, Alice Brennan, who taught in St Laurence O'Toole GNS in Seville Place in Dublin's north inner city was elected District VIII representative. Alice Brennan was elected president in 1971, but died after a long illness, in January 1972.[11] Her death was deeply saddening for her many friends and colleagues, but it was also a particular loss for women members, whose cause she had championed.

No woman stood in the CEC elections of 1972, in which most districts were uncontested, or the following year. In fact, between 1972 and April 1978, there was not a single woman on the executive or among the organisation's officers. When Kathleen Day (née McDonagh) was elected to the Education Committee in 1973, she was the only woman member of any of the INTO's four national committees, including the Northern Committee, whose record of female representation was worse than that of the INTO as a whole. As Alice Brennan had told the 1963 congress, the problem of representation could be boiled down to women not asserting themselves in the organisation, but there was little interest among those running the INTO in asking why this was the case, still less in changing it. The reasons why women tended not to run for office were the perennial practical and cultural ones. As Fiona Poole put it at the time, women's lack of eagerness to be nominated for office was:

[P]artly because many are being teachers, mothers and housewives simultaneously. And partly because Irish women are not traditionally notorious for becoming involved in union activities. In this country we tend to think of union work as men's work ... men look on office-holding as part of the power game, as rungs on the ladder of ambition. Women don't.[12]

Kathleen Day pointed out that women were well represented at branch level, but observed, 'we have no such thing as a women's lobby, although it would be a formidable one if we had'. The culture of the CEC during the 1970s was rather macho and hard-drinking and not an especially welcoming environment for a woman; and in the absence of any women, this culture only became more entrenched. When two fraternal delegates from the NUT and the Scottish Education Institute went to the 1976 congress they expressed amazement at the situation, and urged the organisation to actively encourage women to seek office, pointing to the important role that women leaders had played in their own unions.[13]

This is not to say that women's issues were ignored entirely. Together, the three teaching unions pursued paid maternity leave through the conciliation and arbitration process. Until the end of 1974, the Rules for National Schools compelled teachers to absent themselves for not less than two calendar months on maternity, when they would have to employ a substitute at their own expense. Through the conciliation process, the unions secured maternity leave for permanent teachers of not more than 12 weeks on full pay, with the same arrangements for paying substitutes as for sick leave (1 January 1975). The scheme was not perfect, but it was a good start and preceded by six years the Maternity Act 1981, which provided for maternity leave for workers in other sectors. The teachers' conciliation council also ensured that from 1975 maternity leave would no longer be treated as sick leave, and that the entitlement to leave was increased to up to 14 weeks.[14] This would prove unpopular in more reactionary circles. After Gay Byrne spent a number of programmes on his morning radio show railing against teachers taking maternity leave, the INTO reported him to the Employment Equality Agency, which in turn issued a formal complaint to the RTÉ authority and the director general for his discriminatory campaign.[15] It was not unusual for Byrne to have a go at teachers generally, and this was not the only time members took issue with his outlook, which became common in the press over the 1980s as public sector workers came increasingly under attack.

Improved maternity provision was not followed by adequate childcare provision and attitudes towards working mothers generally could still be very negative. For instance, the January 1977 edition of *An Múinteoir Náisiúnta* had discussed mothers who worked outside the home and suggested that placing young children in pre-school would lead to a weakening of the family, which would be disastrous for society and damage the children.[16] The next issue featured a letter from a woman member, criticising the editor for attacking women members with families, along with his patronising response: 'No dear, no attack. Working mothers are to be admired but mothers working with their families are to be admired most.'[17] The editor was admonished by members of the South County Dublin branch, but no apology appeared in the journal.[18] The editorials were subsequently criticised at congress and the CEC established a sub-committee to examine the journal more broadly.[19] *An Múinteoir* did not improve noticeably in the short run, but the overt sexism did not reappear. Michael Regan retired as editor in June 1978 and the role was left unfilled pending a complete review of INTO publications.[20]

Tired of the lack of women in the INTO leadership, Fiona Poole, a south Dublin teacher, decided to run for the presidency, breaking the convention that there was a contest for vice-president but the president was elected unopposed. Breaking this convention was rare and usually done to prove a point – the last time anyone had done so was some 30 years earlier, when the young Seán Brosnahan ran after the 1946 teachers' strike. Poole was a somewhat unorthodox candidate. Having taught in Dublin city since 1954, she had spent two years in Singapore from 1966, and on her return became active in her local INTO branch in south Dublin and set up the Returned Emigrant Teachers' Action Group (RETAG). Poole was also separated at a time when marital breakdown carried a stigma and, as she later noted, 'the climate of the time was hostile to separated teachers at a professional level' since the majority of teachers of primary school worked under Catholic religious management.[21] Active in INTO, but not an officer, she was not well known in the organisation nationally. Her opponent was Seamus McArdle, a Cavan teacher who had served 11 years on the executive. Described as publicity-shy, his campaign was based on his experience and the convention that it was his turn.[22]

The contest would probably have just made a small paragraph in the education or perhaps newspaper women's pages, but it became front-page news when it emerged that hundreds of anonymous letters had been sent to priests and teachers stating that Poole ought not be elected. Poole had been a volunteer with the Irish Family Planning Association for several years, at a time when the provision of contraceptives was mostly illegal. Charles Haughey's Health (Family Planning) Bill, which proposed the famous Irish solution to an Irish problem – doctors providing married people with access to birth control – was only before the Dáil at this point. Poole was accused of being part of the 'contraceptives lobby' and, one letter claimed, she wished to introduce sex education in schools.[23] Lest anyone fail to be convinced by its moral arguments, the letter explained that sex education and contraceptives had reduced the number of school-aged children in Britain, and that teachers there had lost jobs as a result. The letter was from the Irish Family League, a small conservative Catholic lay group with links to the Knights of Columbanus.[24] Its secretary, Mary Kennedy, admitted to the *Irish Press* that she had written the letter, but her claim that it was not anonymous – rather, she had been in a hurry and had forgotten to sign it – was generally found unconvincing. The press branded it a smear campaign and a McCarthyite witch-hunt.[25]

Whether the controversy had anything to do with it, turnout in the election was significantly higher than it had been for years, and Poole won with 54 per cent of the vote, becoming the seventh woman president as the INTO entered its 110th year. Looking back at the letter and surrounding controversy, Poole observed that it 'undoubtedly cost me some votes, but it won me many more'.[26] It would be crude to paint the contest in terms of a challenge by urban, younger, liberals and older, rural, conservatives, however, even if there was an element of that. Poole's election was symbolically important, but it did not usher in a new wave of CEC representatives. The following year the number of women on the executive doubled to two when Róisín Carabine was elected a representative for District I, while women contested the vice-presidential elections in 1980 and 1981, albeit unsuccessfully.[27]

THE INTO MODERNISES
On 1 July 1978, Gerry Quigley and Michael Moroney assumed office as INTO general secretary and treasurer respectively. In the first six months, Quigley made a number of changes in the running of the organisation, such as organising the CEC meetings on a more professional, streamlined basis. Dates for meetings were agreed well in advance and no new matters were allowed on the agenda unless they constituted an emergency and were cleared with the president before the meeting. Individual cases were not to be raised unless they required a new policy decision,[28] and three standing sub-committees were

established to take some of the weight of the executive's work, meeting prior to the full CEC meetings.

Following Michael Moroney's promotion, a new executive officer was appointed, Charlie Lennon, a young activist in the South County Dublin branch then working as a remedial teacher in Monsktown.[29] Among other duties, Lennon was made ad hoc editor of the organisation's publications, which were under review and which Quigley was determined would have to be improved.[30] It was decided to keep *AMN* as a quarterly, alongside a new monthly information bulletin, *Tuarascáil*, an annual handbook for members, and, it was anticipated, a serious educational journal.[31] It was not until October 1981 that an editor was finally appointed to *AMN*, Michael McKeown, originally from Belfast and now based in Dublin.[32] In 1980, a new position of general executive officer was established, and Catherine Byrne was appointed. This brought the number of officials in head office to four, with Byrne becoming the first woman official in the organisation since Mairead Ashe had retired as treasurer on her marriage in 1927. Byrne had been teaching in Dublin since the mid-1970s and was active in the organisation, but she remained best known for her role in leading the Carysfort strike in 1974. Though it was not made explicit in her role, Byrne's appointment would prove crucial to the INTO's efforts to modernise its policies on gender, which Quigley identified as a priority from the outset.[33] As well as publications and staffing, there were other practical issues, such as the question of the ownership of the Teachers' Club, to which the INTO had loaned substantial sums, which became a contentious issue between Quigley and members who were closely identified with the club.[34]

DRIMOLEAGUE

One of the most pressing matters before the new general secretary was the Drimoleague dispute, a localised but lengthy strike that became infamous, and cost the organisation millions. Once again, its origins were in the managerial system. The problem began in mid-1975 over a principal teacher's post in Drimoleague National School in west Cork. After the Department decided that none of the applicants was suitably qualified, the manager, Fr Crowley, appointed a teacher, Nicholas McCarthy, as principal in a temporary capacity. McCarthy had less than five years' experience, which made him ineligible under Departmental rules, and it was Crowley's intention to employ him in a temporary capacity until he had reached his five years and was eligible.[35] One of the unsuccessful candidates, Jimmy Collins, who was a principal teacher in Dromore NS, a three-teacher school in the next parish, took exception to this. Not only had he seniority as a principal, and was highly qualified, holding a BA awarded by UCC while he was working as a teacher, but he was CEC representative in the area. Locally, the conclusion was that the failure to appoint Collins was a case of blatant victimisation due to his INTO activities.[36]

There was considerable unhappiness in Cork on the matter and the CEC came under pressure to intervene. In November 1975, the CEC decided to call the teachers in Drimoleague NS out on strike, but following a special meeting a couple of weeks later, it reversed the decision.[37] A majority on the CEC supported taking a legal approach to the matter, but locally, opinion favoured industrial action, and notwithstanding the CEC's reluctance, an all-out strike began of seven schools in the Drimoleague area on 1 April 1976, although the teachers subsequently returned to work in four of them. Local parents came out against the strike and the dispute became increasingly entrenched. The teachers involved determined to continue as long as McCarthy remained principal and until the committee of management was disbanded. There were various attempts at arbitration and intervention including an investigation initiated by the Labour Court on Bishop Lucey's suggestion, but no form of compromise could be reached, and on 20 August 1976 the dispute escalated further, after the CEC issued a circular to teachers in schools adjoining Drimoleague parish instructing them not to enrol Drimoleague pupils. The circular, which in effect boycotted Drimoleague students, was not withdrawn until June 1977, almost a year later.

Parents of the children affected took legal action against the INTO and the Department of Education for having had their constitutional rights to education withheld, and the case, taken on behalf of six of the children, went before the High Court only days after Gerry Quigley took office. On 21 July Mr Justice McMahon gave his judgment, which fully vindicated Jimmy Collins but found that the INTO had acted unconstitutionally in depriving the children of the educational facilities guaranteed under Bunreacht na hÉireann; the teachers were entitled to withdraw their labour, but the CEC's directive to members in nearby schools not to accept pupils from Drimoleague was not legal.[38] He also found against the minister for education during the period March 1976–December 1977, when the decision was made to provide buses. In light of legal advice, the CEC and Finance Committee agreed not to appeal the judgement.[39]

The strike continued, as did efforts to resolve the dispute. On New Year's Day 1979 Gerry Quigley visited Dr Michael Murphy, coadjutor bishop of Cork, at the bishop's request. While they seemed to be in agreement about a solution, the parents remained opposed, and no agreement was possible anyway, since Nicholas McCarthy, who it was proposed would leave Drimoleague and transfer to the principalship of Castledonovan NS, did not accept the terms.[40] The dispute remained deadlocked throughout 1979 and dragged on into 1980, when further efforts to resolve it failed. At the end of 1981, with the strike somehow in its sixth year, there was a fresh attempt to end the dispute. There was a new bishop of Cork and Ross, Dr Murphy, and, crucially, a new parish priest in Drimoleague, Fr Eugene Cashman.[41] Once again, the proposal centred on the division of the school, either on a boys/girls or a junior/senior basis.[42] Finally, on the eve of the 1982 congress,

Gerry Quigley and Michael Murphy held a joint press conference announcing that the dispute had been resolved, and that the Drimoleague, Cnocbui and Castledonovan national schools would re-open after the summer holidays.[43]

The six-year-long strike proved very costly indeed. The £70,000 the INTO paid in strike pay each year it went on strike was a pittance compared with the legal costs and damages paid to the children who had been affected by the dispute. By the time the last cases had gone through the courts in 1991, the INTO had amassed over £1 million in damages and legal costs. There was also the amount of time the case had consumed, but also the reputational damage done to the INTO. Notwithstanding the justice of the original case, the dispute was incredibly bitter and no one came out of it with their reputations enhanced, the INTO included.

TEACHERS' SALARIES 1979–1982

Politically, the late 1970s and 1980s were characterised by two periods of relative stability with an unstable 18-month period in between. Between 1978 and 1989 there were six different administrations and six ministers for education.[44] Economically, it was a difficult time. Fianna Fáil had won the 1977 election on a give-away manifesto and the government's ill-timed pump-priming, followed in 1979 by the second oil crisis in six years, resulted in soaring inflation. This meant that the last years of the 1970s saw teachers, like other public servants and workers in the private sector, concerned with maintaining their purchasing power as prices rocketed. After the mutual antipathy of the 1960s and early 1970s, the three teacher unions had established good relations from 1973. Efforts by then Minister for Education Dick Burke to set up a teaching council proved unsuccessful, so there was no formal structure for co-operation between the three, such as there was between teacher unions in the North. More important, they had established good working relationships in recent years, and this was given further impetus when Gerry Quigley took office as general secretary. Quigley had experience of working well alongside the UTU in the North and identified inter-union co-operation as a priority, telling the *Irish Times* that he was 'interested in setting up structures which would minimise conflicts between them, so that they could come together and hammer out a common policy',[45] which was especially important at a time when the ASTI and Teachers' Union of Ireland (TUI, formerly the VTA) had been in discussions about a merger.[46]

Teachers' salaries were subject to national wage agreements negotiated through the ICTU, of which there were three between 1977 and 1979, and specifically through their own conciliation council.[47] In September 1978, the three unions lodged a status claim of 15 per cent, with the arbitrator awarding a total of 7.8 per cent, applicable over two phases, in April 1979.[48] A further claim, lodged a couple of months later, was rejected in October 1979. Although the three teacher unions had voted against the revised terms of the National Under-standing Pay Agreement in July 1979, they were bound by the ICTU's majority acceptance.[49] In December 1979, the TUI and INTO submitted a joint request to the government to establish a Salary Review Body,[50] which the government acceded to but it recommended only a seven per cent increase for those at the lower end of the scale, and long-phased increments which would mean that a teacher would have to be at least 56 years old before they could benefit from the top increment. The three unions were unanimous in rejecting the recommen-dations, arguing that, far from raising teachers' salaries, they would make things worse.[51] Facing the real prospect of strike action, the minister for education, John Wilson, met the unions and agreed to start new negotiations on teachers' salaries the following week, the three unions promising that strikes would follow should the talks fail.[52] By 23 October, settlement proposals had been agreed, including increases of between 12 per cent on the common basic scale and 29 per cent for those at the top end of the scale, which would be awarded to teachers with 25 years' service, rather than 35 as the review body had recommended.[53]

In the end, INTO members accepted the proposals by 76 per cent,[54] while the TUI and ASTI also accepted the proposals, by slimmer margins. A number of issues remained outstanding, including qualification allowances, specialist teachers, posts of responsibility and payment for posts generated by the points system, which were jointly presented in an agreed claim at the conciliation council in January 1981. When the conciliation council failed to reach an agreement, the claim was referred to arbitration.[55] The arbitrator's report, presented to the government in November 1981, was largely supportive of the unions' case, offering an increase of 25 per cent on qualification allowances and 30 per cent on responsibility allowances with effect from September 1980. In addition to the deal arrived at with Wilson, there was also the latest agreement as part of the ICTU's negotiations on pay in the public service, which offered increases in three phases over 15 months. This looks like a very substantial pay increase, but with inflation running between almost 16 per cent and 20 per cent annually at this time, it was barely keeping up. Summing up this period in his history of the ASTI, John Cunningham wrote:

> The three-year period between the spring of 1979 and the spring of 1982 … was incredibly complex from the industrial relations point of view. It was a period of proto-social partnership, marked by frequent ballots, during which the ASTI representatives [and those of the INTO and TUI] had been involved in negotiating three national agreements, one re-negotiation of a national agreement, and the negotiation of a public service pay deal, as well as engaging with a pay review body and Department of Education officials and processing several claims on salaries … through conciliation and arbitration. There was

not complete agreement on every issue between the teachers' unions during the period but the nature of many negotiations made it desirable and strategically sensible that there be close co-operation between them.[56]

While it was 'strategically sensible' for the teacher unions to work well together, the personnel involved helped things to run smoothly. In 1980, the former Irish Federation of University Teachers (IFUT) secretary, Kieran Mulvey, was appointed general secretary of ASTI.[57] Like Gerry Quigley, he was committed to coalition-building among the teacher unions and in the trade union movement more broadly. Moreover, while the three unions had been co-operating well informally, the TUI congress in 1981 had proposed a group to regulate relations between the teacher organisations; and during that summer, IFUT, which until now had not been aligned with the other three, suggested establishing a 'federal arrangement to provide a forum for discussions among the teachers unions'.[58] Talks during the autumn between the INTO, ASTI, TUI, IFUT and the National Association of Teachers in Further and Higher Education (NATFHE), the Northern Ireland section of a British union (affiliated to ICTU), led to the setting up of a Council of Education Unions (CEU) in December.[59] Though a positive development, the formation of the CEU was not quite the 'momentous occasion for all concerned with education' that was flagged at its launch,[60] and it ultimately proved to be of secondary importance to the, as yet, informal triumvirate of the INTO, ASTI and TUI.

AGE OF ENTRY

In John Wilson, the teacher unions had had an ally in a government which was generally inclined to spend money that it did not have. Public indebtedness had been increasing steadily, but despite Taoiseach Charles Haughey's now infamous 1980 television address that 'as a community we [in the Republic] are living way beyond our means', there was no political will to cut spending for the time being.

That changed in 1981. Following a general election in June, a minority Fine Gael–Labour coalition formed a government and remained in office until the following February. The minister for education during the nine-month life of the government was John Boland, a one-time sales representative and auctioneer on Fine Gael's right wing who was first elected in 1977.[61] Described by one of his cabinet colleagues as 'difficult though clever',[62] Boland took an abrasive attitude towards the INTO. As one INTO representative who faced him across the table observed, 'He was an obnoxious kind of a man in negotiations, it was confrontation all the way. I was never at a civilised meeting with him.' If it had been a long time since the teachers had faced such a hostile minister, the economic circumstances made relations even more fraught. Within a month of taking office the minister for finance, John Bruton, had introduced an emergency budget, and as teachers went back to school at the beginning of September, some of its effects on education began to become apparent. There were to be extensive cutbacks in education spending, including capital expenditure on buildings, reductions in teacher training places and in the recruitment of ancillary staff at second level.[63] For the INTO, the most worrying aspect was Circular 24/81. Issued without any prior consultation at the height of the school holidays, the circular outlined revised dates of entry and increased the minimum age of enrolment in national schools to four and a half with effect from 1 October.[64]

There had been some debate over the appropriate age for children to start school, but while individuals had different views, the INTO wished to maintain the age of entry at four years.[65] On 7 September, an outraged INTO delegation outlined its objections to the minister, among them: that there had been a lack of consultation on the matter, which ran contrary to stated INTO policy; there was no indication of such a policy in the manifesto of either government party and it had not been in the coalition's programme for government; it would result in a reduction of teaching posts and cause unemployment among teachers; it would have a particularly damaging effect on rural communities; and it would have serious social consequences for low-income parents.[66] The INTO prepared various documents for politicians and the media and an information leaflet for parents. Using data collected through a survey of branches, it showed that, contrary to the minister's claim that the policy would not result in job losses, the new age of entry would lead to 921 posts being lost over a two-year period.[67]

Boland was unyielding, but while he tried to justify the decision on education grounds, arguing that he had not introduced the measure for savings alone, the press was broadly against the move, as was the National Women's Council, among others, which opposed raising the school-going age without any improvements in childcare provision for working parents.[68]

A special congress in Limerick in November authorised the CEC to organise regional one-day strikes and a national one-day strike, if appropriate, and voted to take legal action to establish whether it constituted breach of contract. Crucially, the conference directed members to disregard the circular and continue to enrol and teach pupils until the issue had been determined in the courts. When the new year began, the INTO placed advertisements in national newspapers advising parents that its members would continue to enrol four-year-old pupils in defiance of the order. When the schools re-opened the following week after the Christmas holidays, the press featured various reports of four-year-olds being enrolled.[69] This prompted a haughty editorial in the *Irish Times* asserting that it was 'time it was made clear that it is the Minister for Education who runs the education system, and not the INTO president'.[70] The editorial noted that 'the government may indeed be entirely wrong in this matter ... but they are still the government. They were elected by the people to run the affairs of the country, among them the school system' – overlooking the INTO's contention that government had no mandate for it from either party's manifesto and that it was absent from the programme for government. The leader had argued that 'if they have made a bad decision in this case, then it is up to the electorate to take this into consideration at the next election' and happily for the teachers the next election was to be sooner than the *Irish Times* might have envisaged.

A week later, the government's budget was defeated and an election followed on 18 February 1982. This time, the INTO's pre-election questionnaire was much shorter and more precise than usual. Parties were asked about their attitude towards parents' right to send their children to school aged four; and about the creation of teaching posts to provide employment for the estimated 300 trained teachers who were then unemployed. Fine Gael's policy was that four years old was too young for formal schooling, Labour was somewhat divided on the matter, while Fianna Fáil's campaign prominently featured its promise to withdraw the circular.[71] Once again, no party or bloc secured a majority, although Fine Gael attempted to woo independents by promising to change the age of entry to four years and two months, rather than the six introduced in Circular 24/81.[72] In the end, however, Fianna Fáil secured the support of independent deputy Tony Gregory, thus forming a short-lived minority government, one of the first actions of which was to restore the school entry age to four.

CORPORAL PUNISHMENT

If his attempt to raise the age of entry was cursory, Boland's lasting legacy was the abolition of corporal punishment. The regulations for its use were first codified in 1907 when a corporal punishment book was introduced to national schools. Principal teachers were required to enter each instance of punishment, the reason for it and the extent of the punishment, but the book had fallen into disuse in 1922 and dropped altogether in 1932.[73] From that point, the regulations were included in Rule 96 of the rules for national schools and were relatively stringent, with punishment only to be administered for 'grave transgressions and only by the principal teacher or other members of staff duly authorised by the school manager; only a light cane should be used, whereas boxing children's ears, pulling their hair, and similar ill-treatment was forbidden'.[74] The INTO did not have an explicit position on the matter but tended to take a dim view of the occasional reformers who wished to put an end to corporal punishment, the *Irish School Weekly* observing in 1933 that 'the school is a little community of men and women in the making and their delinquencies must be early checked if we are to produce men and women of character ... Corporal punishment is as old as the days of Solomon'.[75]

If this attitude seems cruel, it was of its time. As Maguire and Ó Cinnéide have pointed out,

[H]istorically there was little understanding that corporal punishment was potentially harmful or that it could have lasting negative effects on children; indeed, the view prevailed that 'a good beating never hurt anyone,' and that some corporal punishment was necessary to instil respect for authority, to maintain discipline and to rear 'good citizens' and the 1909 Children's Act specifically upheld the right of parents and teachers to administer corporal punishment.[76]

In a society where the idea of 'spare the rod and spoil the child' held weight, the idea that teachers should not have recourse to corporal punishment was a minority view among teachers and parents alike. There was concern in instances of excessive punishment, where teachers had clearly exceeded the regulations outlined in the rules for national schools and had caused serious injury to the children. Most of the time, these cases did not attract a great deal of attention but they were too common and as Maguire and Ó Cinnéide note from looking at the Departmental complaint files that it is clear that 'the rules were often broken, and that the Department of Education usually turned a blind eye'.[77] However, in the early 1940s, inspectors had raised serious concerns that there had been 'an alarming growth of punishment' administered in schools lately, with T.J. O'Connell countering that it was merely a stronger tendency among parents to complain.[78] The inspectors had observed that many of the cases had arisen in the context of Irish lessons, and it may have been with this in mind that in 1947 Tomás Derrig amended the rules, specifying that 'in no circumstances should corporal punishment be administered for mere failure of lessons' and that the cane should be used only on the open hand.[79] It was not until the mid-1950s that an organised campaign against corporal punishment emerged, a group called the School Children's Protection Organization, formed in 1954,[80] but it met with a broadly hostile response from the political establishment, and was described by the minister for education, Richard Mulcahy, as 'anti-religious, malicious and an attack by people reared in an alien atmosphere'.[81] If the majority view favoured the status quo, however, voices were emerging within the INTO wanting an end to corporal punishment altogether, with the Dublin City, South Dublin, Athlone and Moate branches tabling motions to that effect at the 1955 congress.[82] Similar motions appeared periodically thereafter but never passed.

In the short term, things worsened when, in 1956, Richard Mulcahy issued a circular permitting use of the strap as well as the cane.[83] Ten years later, in 1967, a new campaigning organisation, Reform, was established and received a significant amount of attention in the media but while the campaign against corporal punishment waxed and waned over the following years, it remained a minority issue, although Labour's 1969 manifesto pledged its abolition.[84] By the 1980s, Ireland, along with the United Kingdom, was one of the last states in Europe to permit the use of corporal punishment, but with cases being taken on behalf of British children in the European Court in Strasbourg, it looked as though the writing was on the wall. However, the INTO failed to take the initiative, so that when the time came for corporal punishment to be removed, the INTO had had no input into the sanctions that would exist in its absence. Labour and Fine Gael had both pledged to abolish corporal punishment at the 1981 general election, and in October, John Boland met the unions and managers and told them of his intention to act on this promise. The INTO expressed its opposition to the move before suitable alternative sanctions were provided, since national schools were not entitled to expel difficult pupils and suspension was difficult, but they found the minister unco-operative.[85] The ban began on 1 February 1982, leaving Britain the only EEC country which still allowed corporal punishment in schools.[86]

CUTS AND CO-OPERATION, 1982–1987

Out of the blue, on 30 July 1982, the government announced a series of spending cuts, a pay freeze, an extension of the public service embargo on filling vacancies, and education cuts amounting to £7.5 million.[87] Within three months there was a new government which faced similar problems.

The November 1982 election resulted in a majority Fine Gael–Labour coalition led by Garret FitzGerald and ended what felt like a merry-go-round of governments in the early 1980s, lasting close to a full term and bringing a degree of governmental stability that had been absent of late. Politics remained fraught, however; the Troubles in the North were ongoing and moral issues were bitterly contested, most obviously in referendums on abortion (1983) and divorce (1986). Around that time, the case of Eileen Flynn came to public attention. A secondary teacher of Irish and history in New Ross, she was dismissed from the Holy Faith Convent School in 1982 after she became pregnant by the separated man with whom she was living, the nuns who employed her arguing that her 'lifestyle ran contrary to Catholic morals and opinions'.[88] The Flynn case was difficult for the teacher unions because she had refused to become a member of the ASTI, but a sense of solidarity and a recognition of the principle that was at stake meant that many INTO members assisted her campaign on an individual basis. The INTO also issued a statement to the effect that a teacher's private life was not a matter for the board of management of their school and warned that any attempt to dismiss an INTO member because of circumstances relating to their private life would be strenuously opposed by the organisation.[89] A few years later, Maurice Kearney, from the Navan Branch, Tadhg MacPháidín, then of the Benevolent Fund Committee and later of the Teachers' Club, and former president, Fiona Poole, came together and in November 1988 founded the Separated Teachers' Support Group (STSG) to cater for separated primary school teachers who felt especially vulnerable around this time.[90]

Then there was the economy. National debt was at record levels, and unemployment and emigration reached levels that had not been seen since the 1950s. In early January 1983, only weeks after the new government took office, the first round of cuts in education funding were announced. The minister overseeing this was the recently elected Fine Gael deputy for Wicklow, Gemma Hussey. She was on the liberal wing of her party, and having come from the Seanad, was somewhat inexperienced. On her appointment, John Boland, her party predecessor in Education, told Hussey that she had got the 'dog' ministry, which was 'never good even in prosperous times' and would be 'purgatory' this time around. The January cuts saw post-primary hit worst, and while the TUI was alone in calling a one-day strike in protest, the INTO backed the protests against them, co-signing letters of protest and demonstrating outside the Dáil.[91] The minister responded by accusing the teachers of over-reacting, and added that they should 'thank God that they have a highly paid, high-status, secure profession'. In an ironically provocative statement, she appealed to them 'not to down tools at the smallest provocation'.[92] Hussey was not unique in her idea of teachers as pampered public servants, however. Partly because they had won a series of pay increases in recent years and then staved off efforts to claw these back or freeze them, the teacher unions were seen by some commentators as being too powerful.

The Republic's national debt had been growing steadily for some time, and in 1983 it passed 100 per cent of GNP and kept growing.[93] There was an economic imperative to reduce borrowing, and this dovetailed with the increasing dominance of neo-liberalism around this time as the Keynesianism of the 1970s yielded to 1980s monetarism.[94] Where the USA had Reaganomics and the UK Thatcherism, Ireland had the Doheny & Nesbitt School of Economics, which advocated swingeing cutbacks. The minister for finance, Alan Dukes, took a similar view, but while he was in the minority in government for the speed and depth by which he wished to cut, the government's view – especially among its Fine Gael members – was that a pay freeze was required, but failing that any increases would have to be below the cost of living.

An 18-month public service pay agreement was reached between John Boland and the public service committee of ICTU, which was approved by the unions in September 1983, but in October the following year the government published its economic strategy document *Building on Reality*, which stated that the government would pay salary increases which had been sanctioned up to then, but indicated that there would be little to come after that.[95] This was an arbitrary line in the sand and put claims that had been held up in the less-than-speedy arbitration machinery at risk. One of these was that of the status claim, lodged by the three teacher unions in December 1982 in an effort to catch up with civil and public service salaries, which was about to conclude at long last. On 7 August 1985, while the relevant ministers and several of the union officials were on holiday, the arbitrator sent his preliminary findings to the unions and the government on a confidential basis. The arbitrator found that teachers had slipped behind the professional grades in the public service and that the government's case that the state of the exchequer finances was so bad and the high cost of teachers' pay so great that the claim must be rejected constituted 'a quite unjustified discrimination against teachers as distinct from all other professional grades in the public service'.[96] He recommended an award of ten per cent to be paid in two tranches, which was less than half of the unions' claim of 22 per cent, although it was better than had been expected. This was unacceptable to the government, which leaked the arbitrator's interim recommendation along with its intention not to pay the award,[97] and a week later the government announced a 12-month pay freeze for all public servants.

On 19 August, the press reported that three teacher unions were to meet shortly to co-ordinate their opposition to the pay freeze, including the possibility of short strikes in key ministerial constituencies.[98] That evening, the minister for education made a speech to a Young Fine Gael meeting in Bray in which she repeated her previous observations about teachers' very favourable conditions and accused them of trying to improve their condition at the expense of 'some weaker sectors of the economy'. 'It is vital that all those organisations that publicly clamour for increases should address themselves to the morality of what they are about; are they so bound up in self-justification and media attention that they can't stand back for the sake of the country?'[99] She then repeated her remarks on *Morning Ireland* the next day, ruling out any payment of the arbitrator's award. It is a brave person who tries to lecture or admonish teachers, and whatever her intention, the minister's words provoked a strong response. One national teacher observed afterwards that she had known 'some teachers who were vehemently against the strike, but Gemma Hussey's "morality" speech changed their minds' or, in the hyperbole of the *Sunday Independent*, it 'turned moderate teachers into raving Bolsheviks'.[100]

TEACHERS UNITED

On 26 August, representatives of the three teacher unions met and agreed a joint position. First and foremost, the arbitrator's award was non-negotiable, and they would not enter into any discussions to amend it. Each union would vote on a series of joint industrial actions that would include a series of one-day regional strikes designed to attract the maximum press coverage,[101] and in September the three unions, now operating under the banner 'Teachers United', announced the schedule of strikes. These would take place over 11 days in November, with a national stoppage organised for 5 December, with the exception of primary schools designated as special schools, which were exempt from strike action.[102] Before this round of strikes began, teachers also participated in a one-day strike on 15 October called by ICTU protesting at the government's refusal to appoint a public service arbitrator.

The ICTU, especially general secretary Donal Nevin, was firmly behind the teachers. It regarded the government's refusal to pay the arbitrator's award not so much as a response to the current economic circumstances but rather as ideological, part of a wider desire to dismantle the industrial relations machinery that had been hard won over decades. But while the unions saw this as Thatcherism Irish-style, they were largely alone; many more voices were raised in criticism of the dispute. These included Catholic Auxiliary Archbishop of Dublin James Kavanagh, who accused public servants and teachers in particular of 'national sabotage' at a time of high unemployment, in a rather vivid illustration of how the INTO's relationship had changed from the days of Archbishop McQuaid. His counterpart in the Church of Ireland, Donal Caird, was also critical.[103] The CPSMA was not supportive and the media was almost universally hostile.

The Teachers United campaign was by far the most professionally run dispute the teachers had ever organised. At a national level, there was a 'group of nine' national co-ordinators from the three unions, including the three general secretaries, Gerry Quigley, Kieran Mulvey and Jim Dorney, and the deputy secretaries and presidents, which was increased to 12 the following March. The campaign was organised on almost military lines. At local level, a campaign co-ordinator was appointed for each county except Dublin, where there were four representatives from each union.[104] Local groups were instructed to use local media, lobby local TDs and senators and make arrangements for one-day strikes and teacher meetings. They were also given instructions on how all this should be done.[105] With the Dáil due to resume in the third week of October, co-ordinators instructed that lobbying politicians was to be the absolute priority and that reports of how this had gone were to be forwarded immediately to the relevant head office.

The teachers found opposition representatives from Fianna Fáil and the Workers' Party predictably supportive.[106] Notwithstanding the cabinet's position towards the teachers, the government TDs and senators were generally sympathetic, though extremely cautious. Part of this was a natural fearful reaction towards such a well-organised campaign, especially one that came at a time when the government was feeling particularly vulnerable since the local elections that summer had seen the government parties perform very badly, Labour especially. Elected representatives were reminded that at a local level, 'many teachers take a keen interest in politics and between them they have

40,000 votes and then perhaps three times that number in their families and close relatives', and that they were the type of people who do vote rather than abstain.[107] There was particular concern among teacher deputies, there being 20 government members in the Oireachtas who were current or former teachers; they formed an important lobby within Fine Gael and planned to approach Alan Dukes to try and secure an agreement. When a local INTO delegation met five members of the Parliamentary Labour Party, which included Brendan Howlin, another national teacher, they were told that Labour had been responsible for setting up the conciliation and arbitration schemes for the public service, and they would maintain them and recommend that the integrity of the award be upheld.[108] Whatever soft words were being said at these lobbying meetings, however, the government was unyielding, not least the education minister herself. Many at cabinet felt the government had to stand firm, with Hussey lamenting in her diary, 'will no government ever face up to the unions?'[109]

The pièce de résistance of the campaign took place on 5 December, when some 20,000 teachers from across the state made their way to Croke Park for a massive display of strength. Croke Park was chosen as one of the only venues big enough, but it was also symbolic, with its echoes of Operation Shakespeare, the INTO's pitch invasion at the 1946 All-Ireland final during the great national teachers' strike almost 40 years earlier. This demonstration was on a completely different scale. It was a massive logistical exercise, with 100 coaches and 15 special trains needed to bring many thousands to the rally. There were two hours of speeches and music at Croke Park. The entertainment included the Connolly Folk Group, who performed a song written especially for the occasion:

> We are the gentle, angry teachers, and we're singing for our rights
> Where are the teaching TDs today – are they marching for their rights?
> Garret and Gemma are you listening? We're singing for our rights.[110]

The whole thing was filmed, and a video featuring a voiceover by Niall Tóibín was later distributed to branches under the title *United We Stood*. Afterwards, the teachers marched across the city centre to Leinster House. The gathering was generally good humoured, but at one point, as the demonstrators filed past Christina Murphy of the *Irish Times*, they started chanting 'Out, out, out.' Murphy reported that 'it was not the most comfortable day on which to be a reporter. The anti-media feeling was almost palpable.'[111] Certainly feelings among the teachers at every level ran high. Murphy and her paper had taken a hostile line against them but they were by no means alone, with the Independent group also seen as especially antagonistic, and teachers felt demoralised by constant bashing.[112]

Eventually, after unfruitful meetings in the new year, the Dáil met on 6 February and voted to set aside the arbitrator's report and substitute it with a ten per cent award in three phases, beginning in December 1986, without retrospection. Significantly, it passed not only with government votes but also with those of the Progressive Democrats, the new party that had been launched just before Christmas. Socially liberal and fiscally conservative, its economic policies were viewed with considerable concern by the trade union movement, which feared that it might bring Thatcherism to Ireland in earnest, notwithstanding the unions' view that the current government had moved uncomfortably far in that direction already.

Following the Dáil vote, special congresses of the three unions voted to continue the dispute, with ballots approving strike action by over 80 per cent. These took place in designated areas over three consecutive days in three consecutive weeks in March, with more scheduled for May,[113] but when the post-primary union congresses voted to boycott examination work, including supervision, correcting and examining practicals, it brought a new sense of crisis to the dispute. Fianna Fáil had tabled a motion for 15 April calling for the government to bring in a mediator, but there was a growing sense of crisis in the government on the matter. There followed talks between the government and the unions at the Employer–Labour conference, but these collapsed after ten days and nights of negotiations.[114] By then, with the state examinations looming on the horizon, there was growing anxiety over the exam boycott. Some members in the post-primary unions were profoundly reticent about using the tactic, and it was naturally very unpopular with parents. Polls commissioned by the INTO showed that the parents had not been firm supporters of the teachers in the first instance – although they believed the government was more to blame for the dispute – but they were becoming less supportive. There were even instances of pupils striking in a number of schools, although some of these were in support of the teachers.[115] Eventually, on 5 May, direct talks began between the ministers for education and public service (Labour's Ruairí Quinn having replaced John Boland in the February reshuffle), and the three teacher unions, which concluded on 9 May.[116] The proposals that emerged were put to a ballot of members of the three unions and each voted to accept. The INTO's support for the deal was the lowest of the three, but was still almost three to one in favour, at 72 per cent of the ballot. There was considerable anger at what was billed by its negotiators as an 'interim settlement', when congress had voted for full implementation of the arbitrator's report and to consider nothing less.[117]

CUTS AND CORPORATISM

The Republic's fiscal and economic crisis reached its height in 1986–87. The national debt had doubled in four years and was at £28,000 per head, while the official unemployment rate was 18 per cent.[118] Disagreements over how to deal with the economy had hastened the end of the Fine Gael–Labour coalition, and following a general election in February 1987 Fianna Fáil formed a minority government with the casting vote of the ceann comhairle. The government, led by Charles Haughey and with Ray MacSharry as minister for finance, began to implement a programme of swingeing cuts to public services that earned MacSharry the nickname 'Mac the Knife'. The minority government was supported in this by the largest opposition party, Fine Gael, whose Tallaght Strategy committed its support for Fianna Fáil's economic policies in the Dáil as long as Fine Gael judged they were in the national interest. MacSharry's first budget, brought in only weeks after he took office, was harsh and included a hiring freeze in the public service. If shadow finance minister, and former teacher, Michael Noonan predicted it would 'make our education cuts look like the teddy bears' picnic', the worst of the education cuts were inflicted on higher education,[119] for the moment at least, while Health bore the brunt of the initial round of retrenchment.

The government began its programme of cuts with the support of the majority of the opposition, but as Brian Girvin noted, 'this right wing consensus on fiscal policy was not an example of Thatcherism Irish style'.[120] As Girvin observed, 'the Thatcherites (Fine Gael and the Progressive Democrats) were outside the cabinet and were not able to influence the details of government policy',[121] so while the government began slashing public services with one hand, it reached out to the unions with the other. Since Seán Lemass's time, Fianna Fáil had favoured national wage agreements between the government, unions and employers, but there were no subsequent agreements after the 1980's second National Understanding had run its course. In 1987, the model, which became known as 'social partnership', was revived, and it would be the industrial relations framework for the next 20 years. It was a model that had trenchant critics on the political left and right, but among the majority of the trade union leadership at the time it was seen as giving organised labour an influence on economic policy. This was particularly appealing after being sidelined by government in recent years and even more so because of a widespread fear of neo-liberalism among Irish trade union leaders, which had been heightened by the relative success of the economically right-wing, anti-union Progressive Democrats in the recent general election.[122]

Initially, talks began between the government and the ICTU on a bilateral basis. There was a ministerial ICTU group that met monthly 'to deal with pay and other income matters and three joint government-ICTU working parties, meeting at least weekly, [which] were established to deal with employment and development measures, taxation and social welfare'.[123] The ICTU negotiations were led by Peter Cassells, ICTU's assistant general secretary, and Gerry Quigley, then ICTU vice-president.[124] Subsequently the employers' representatives were brought into the negotiations, and by early October details of the proposed arrangement began to emerge in the media.[125] INTO members were balloted and voted 66.7 per cent in favour of accepting the deal, which was ratified by 181 votes to 114 at an ICTU special delegate conference on 19 November 1987.[126] The agreement, known as the Programme for National Recovery (PNR), included very modest pay increases over two years after a six-month pay pause.[127] The PNR also included agreements beyond pay and conditions, including employment equality, social equity, tax reform and education. A commitment was secured that 'in implementing whatever adjustments are necessary' in education 'the burden of adjustment does not fall on the disadvantaged', with Travellers and the mentally and physically handicapped noted in particular.[128]

By August, after several months of rumour and speculation, it became apparent precisely what the 'burden of adjustment' would entail when the education minister, Mary O'Rourke, confirmed there would be an increase in the pupil–teacher ratio, and the age of entry was to be raised from four to five years old.[129] In addition, when the education estimates were published on 13 October, there was a reduction in capitation grants, with spending on primary school buildings halved. Circular 20/87, published soon after, set out the changes in the pupil–teacher ratio with effect from 1 January 1988.[130] Its objective was to remove 1,300 national teacher posts by the end of 1988, bringing in classes of 40 pupils, which would reverse two decades' of progress on class size.[131] INTO's president, Tom Honan, described the plans as 'the worst attack on the education services since the hungry thirties'.[132] The INTO used every means at its disposal to prevent 20/87 being implemented. Under the slogan 'Give Kids a Chance', teachers marched alongside parents in local demonstrations across the country. In one, some 12,000 parents, teachers and children marched to the minister's home in Athlone, and another almost twice the size took place in Dublin on 11 December.[133] Meanwhile, as ever, a campaign of political lobbying continued, and while an opposition motion against the circular was defeated in the Dáil in November, a government amendment supporting it was also defeated. As the *Irish Times* editorial noted the next day, 'it proves once again what a formidable lobby the teachers' unions are, and they played a large part in mobilising the parents'.[134]

If O'Rourke was personally sympathetic to education, she did not have an especially good working relationship with the INTO, and while little progress was being made negotiating with the minister, informal side-bars began separately between individual CEC members and Taoiseach Charles Haughey, and Minister for Labour Bertie Ahern.[135] On 22 December, at the taoiseach's invitation, an INTO delegation met him and the ministers for labour and education for 'talks about talks'. Haughey put to the INTO a proposal for a whole-scale review of primary education, which would include class sizes and would examine the implications of the substantial decline in pupil numbers over the coming years.[136] A month later, on 22 January 1988, the government announced that a Primary Education Review Body (PERB) had been established, which was launched the following month with former UCD president, Professor Tom Murphy, in the chair.[137] No official statement on Circular 20/87 was ever released, but privately education officials admitted it had been 'buried'.[138] The INTO alone among the education unions had scored a victory against its cuts.

On 21 May 1988, a special INTO congress voted by 487 to 194 to accept the PERB's proposals, which would reduce the number of teachers in primary education by 800, which was a lot but significantly fewer than the 1,800 teachers the government had planned.[139] The diocesan review panels were used to redeploy teachers, and some 375 teachers accepted voluntary redundancy.[140] Teacher unemployment and under-employment would be a major source of anger for several years. There were some 850 substitute teachers working around this time, and low pay rates and poor conditions, including delayed payments and no sick leave or holiday entitlements, meant that they led a highly precarious existence. The INTO appealed to the Department for a pay increase and substitutes' inclusion in the conciliation and arbitration machinery, but they were rebuffed.[141] There were complaints among substitutes, who had a 40 per cent membership rate, that the organisation was not doing enough on the matter, but at the 1989 congress significant time was devoted to a debate on the problem, which Gerry Quigley described as a 'festering sore' in education,[142] and a motion was passed demanding the CEC take action on substitutes' pay and conditions. Eventually, the INTO secured the appointment of an independent arbitrator, who recommended an increase in substitutes' daily rate from £38 to £50 with effect from 1 May 1990, and found that there should be a link with any increases in the common basic scale. The Department of Education eventually agreed to the direct payment of qualified substitutes from 1 September 1990.[143] These were important though modest improvements, and substitutes' pay and conditions remained an issue over subsequent years. The service given as a substitute was eventually recognised for superannuation purposes in 1993.[144]

TEACHER UNITY

By the late 1980s, the relationships between the three teacher unions were closer than they had ever been. During the 1970s, there had been suggestions that the two post-primary teacher unions should merge,[145] but in 1985 delegates at the INTO congress passed a motion instructing the CEC to engage in 'the closest co-operation with the other teacher unions with a view to presenting proposals for amalgamation into one large organisation to Congress at a future date'.[146] In the short term, the emergence of Teachers United to fight for the arbitration award was as far as things got, but its success prompted thoughts of putting this co-operation on a firmer footing. Outside the teaching unions themselves there was encouragement from the ICTU, which had advocated trade union rationalisation for decades and was promoting it particularly vigorously by the mid-to-late 1980s, particularly in the context of social partnership. The ICTU was especially keen for the smaller unions to amalgamate, but it also put its weight behind attempts to merge some of the largest unions on the island. In 1988, the ICTU had 82 affiliated unions, but if things progressed this could end up as about six sectoral blocks of large unions.[147] Most notable of these unions were the country's two largest, the Federated Workers' Union of Ireland (FWUI) and ITGWU, which began merger negotiations in 1987, which led to the formation of the Services, Industrial, Professional and Technical Union (SIPTU) in 1990. The ICTU initiated talks on teacher unity in December 1986, but nothing came from them, and it was after March 1988, when a meeting between representatives of the three unions took place, that matters proceeded rapidly. An interim sub-committee was set up, with three representatives from each union to draw up proposals for a united teachers' organisation, and there was a meeting with the minister for labour, Bertie Ahern, to discuss practical matters arising from any merger, or more accurately to see what funds might be forthcoming to pay for it.[148]

Following negotiations, chaired by Donal Nevin, towards establishing a Council of Teachers' Unions (CTU), the CEC considered Nevin's recommendation that 'immediately following its establishment, the Council should address itself to the drafting of a constitution and rules for a single union for teachers in Ireland'. An administrative officer would be appointed on a temporary contract and the council's costs would be borne by the three unions roughly according to their membership.[149] By the time they were published, slightly revised, in the March edition of *Tuarascáil*,[150] it was too late for them to be considered at many branch meetings before congress, and at the 1990 Easter congress there were complaints that the matter was being pushed through with undue haste. Moreover, where some felt that things were moving too quickly, others were unsure about the wisdom of the idea at all, believing the INTO had all to lose and nothing to gain from such a merger, one delegate likening their situation to the members of Grattan's Parliament being asked to vote themselves out of existence.

In the end, there was a two-to-one vote in favour of holding a special congress on the question.[151] Held in Dublin on 23 June, it voted in favour of the new council by an overwhelming majority.[152] The ASTI had already done so at Easter and once a special conference of TUI approved the document in October, the CTU finally held its first meeting on 4 December 1990.[153] Differences between the three had emerged even before the first meeting, though, when the

ASTI and TUI released a joint statement against common training for all teachers, which did not bode well for the future.

In March 1990, Gerry Quigley announced he would step down as general secretary the following year. He was only 61, but after almost 12 years he felt he had achieved most of what he had set out to do in relation to modernising and professionalising the organisation. The somewhat casual decision-making of old had been replaced by a more systematic approach, and the work of the CEC had been streamlined by using sub-committees. There was a greater emphasis on the education side of the organisation, with the INTO beginning to take a hand in professional development and training, and there was a steady publication of policy documents on areas including special education, disadvantage, the teaching of Irish, maths and other curriculum issues, early childhood education, computers and the elimination of sexism in school, whether against pupils or teachers. There was a new emphasis on gender equality. When Catherine Byrne was designated equality officer in 1982, the INTO became one of the first trade unions to have a full-time equality post. As the INTO's own research showed, the situation at the end of the 1980s was that women remained seriously under-represented at all levels of the organisation. But there was a will to resolve this, evident in the creation of an Equality Committee in 1987. As the 1991 pamphlet 'A Decade of Progress' put it, 'the level of progress made by the INTO during the last decade in achieving general equality in primary education can only be fully appreciated when considered against a background of inequalities which existed in the teaching profession in previous decades up to the mid-seventies'.[154]

The organisation also became more adept at working with other groups, whether its sister teacher unions, other stakeholders in education (specifically parents, through the National Parents' Council) or the media. In the past, it had mistrusted the press to the point of refusing to talk to journalists; now, not only did it have a press officer, but it also gave media training to local activists. The INTO certainly did not get an easy ride from the press – what unions do? – but at least the organisation was better able to deal with them. Finally, outside the organisation, Quigley, as vice-president and then president of ICTU, 1987–9, had been a central figure in the building of social partnership in which the INTO would play a prominent role in future years. Teachers had been left some-what bruised by the cuts of the 1980s, but Quigley left his successor an organisation that was organisationally strong and politically formidable, although, with the prospect of a united teachers' union on the horizon, would they be secretary of the INTO for long?

Chapter 7

CHANGE, CONSULTATION AND CRISIS, 1990–2018

The transformation of Ireland, North and South, since 1990 has been extraordinary: most notably, there was the peace process in the North, the economic boom and bust of the 'Celtic Tiger' which saw mass emigration replaced with sustained inward migration to Ireland from 1996 until 2009, with people coming from within the European Union – which expanded in 2002 – and beyond, including the USA, Nigeria, China and the Philippines. Irish society became more outwardly diverse in other ways. It became increasingly secular. The authority of the Catholic Church, for so long all but unshakable, was gravely undermined in the wake of a succession of scandals, most seriously the coming to light of multiple cases of child sexual abuse by members of the clergy and abuse in Church-run institutions. Slowly, some of the Republic's moral legislation was liberalised, with homosexual acts being decriminalised in 1993 after a lengthy campaign and, following a referendum in 1995, divorce being legalised, while the X Case in 1992 reignited the question of abortion. It is worth remembering that religious vocations had been declining since the 1960s, and had long since passed the point of sustaining the numbers of clergy, the number of new priests having fallen from a high of 412 in 1965 to only 44 in 1998.[1] This had a massive impact on the face of teaching in Ireland. Having provided a large proportion of teaching staff over several decades, by 1997 the Conference of Religious in Ireland (CORI) predicted that within 25 years there would be no religious left in Irish schools.[2] Nevertheless, the Catholic Church remained a powerful force in the management of primary schools, even if demand for non-denominational or multi-denominational education increased, while teachers increasingly began to question their role in the teaching of religion.

On top of these social and cultural changes, there was the technological leap forward. Schools went from using blackboards to interactive whiteboards, and from a time when a high proportion of schools did not have a telephone to one where every teacher, not to mention many pupils, had their own mobile. Technological developments were rapid and far-reaching. All in all, it is difficult to exaggerate how different the Ireland of the new millennium was compared with the Ireland of 1990. As John Carr noted in the INTO's 2004 publication *Change in Primary Education*:

> Teachers, perhaps more than any other profession, appreciate the need for change … The profiles of our pupils have changed. Many classes now include pupils with special needs, non-Irish pupils and pupils with different learning abilities. Society has changed. There is a greater variety of family structures. Authoritarian relationships are less acceptable, attention spans appear to be shorter and pupils are more exposed to a culture of entertainment through computers and television.[3]

Once Gerry Quigley had formally announced that he would retire, Joe O'Toole signalled that he would put himself forward as successor. It had been widely anticipated that he would succeed Quigley, and there was no surprise when nominations closed and O'Toole was the only candidate. O'Toole was only 42 at the time, but had represented north Dublin on the CEC since 1978 and had been brought into INTO head office when Gerry Quigley was elected president of ICTU to help ease the general secretary's workload. Significantly, his position as an independent member of Seanad Éireann since 1987 gave him a high profile, and O'Toole was already an established, well-known voice in the media before taking office. During his time as general secretary, he became notorious for his colourful turns of phrase and memorable sound bites, even if sometimes they might have been better forgotten. O'Toole took office as general secretary designate in September 1990 and took over as general secretary on 1 January 1992 when Gerry Quigley retired. The two men differed considerably in their style of working; where Gerry Quigley placed a great deal of emphasis on procedures and formality, and was known as 'Mr Quigley' to the staff in head office, 'Joe's' style of working was considerably more informal. They shared a view of the INTO as an important player in the ICTU and its use of social partnership as a way of securing some of the organisation's long-term demands as well as pursuing salary increases. Over a period of just under 20 years there were seven national agreements, beginning with the Programme for National Recovery (PNR) in 1988 and ending with Towards 2016. These agreements were often controversial, and over time became the source of friction between unions as well as within them, but they provided the framework on which the work of the unions was based for the best part of two decades.

TEACHER UNITY

When Joe O'Toole was elected general secretary designate, there was press speculation that he might find himself the head of a new teachers' 'super-union', but that soon proved misguided, as divisions emerged between the primary and post-primary unions. The system for allocating promoted posts in schools had been established in 1970 in order to get around post-primary teachers' opposition to the common basic scale established by the Ryan Report. Under the system, schools were entitled to promoted posts (known as A posts and B posts) based on a points system, where a child aged between nine and 13 years old was worth two points, while a child aged 17 years was worth eight.[4] This severely limited primary teachers' chances of promotion, so that in 1992, for instance, there were 342 A posts in primary schools compared with 2,923 in post-primary, while there were 1,846 B posts in primary schools compared with 5,798 in post-primary.[5] A motion calling for all pupils to be worth the same points, and looking for ASTI and TUI support for this, was passed at the 1990 Easter Congress, but the two post-primary executives rejected the INTO's position outright, and that meant that the INTO could not proceed with its claim under conciliation and arbitration. Eventually, the deadlock on points resulted in the 1993 congress voting by 209 to 188 to effectively withdraw from the unity process, so long as the other two unions refused to support the INTO on points. The post-primary teachers would have lost nothing by supporting the INTO, merely lifted some of their primary colleagues up, but their insistence that the post-primary teachers were to keep their differential made unity impossible. Joe O'Toole observed that the vote at the 1993 congress had put teacher unity and the points system back five years but, as it turned out, insofar as teacher unity was concerned, it was more permanent. The INTO gave notice that it was withdrawing from the Council of Teachers' Unions in May 1993, and the office was wound up in August, when the contractual commitments had ended.[6] In the following years, there were tentative approaches towards unity by different unions, but none bore fruit.

There was still co-operation on a number of campaigns, nevertheless, such as the effort to bring about a scheme of early retirement for teachers, with teachers at all levels complaining about the stress of the work. Many older teachers observed a decline in discipline over the years, and morale was becoming increasingly poor. Teachers were pilloried constantly in the media, Gay Byrne once again leading the charge against teachers on his morning radio programme.[7] Reflecting on the mood in 1989, Roddy Day, whose teaching career went back to the 1960s, observed that a sinister attack on the idea of public service had taken root during the 1980s, with teachers harassed, adding that 'the new god was the selfish entrepreneurial idea of success'.[8] Early retirement was not a cure for the attack on teachers' status and certainly was not seen as a solution to the problem of stress, but it became a priority for the three teacher unions, and one on which they were (briefly) able to achieve a joint position in 1994, putting a joint claim to the conciliation council that teachers be entitled to retire on a pension from 50 years of age,[9] although the TUI later withdrew from this position. There were negotiations on the subject with the government but they collapsed in April 1995, leading to a one-day strike by the INTO and ASTI in May.[10] Negotiations resumed afterwards and eventually resulted in a deal in February 1996 which offered early retirement at 55 with 35 years' service (capped at £300 per year) and a bonus of £1,000 a year for those who stayed on after that age.[11] It was rejected by the two post-primary unions, but a clear majority of the INTO approved.[12]

The INTO also scored a massive victory on promoted posts at this time, which resulted in the creation of some 3,500 extra promoted posts, but it did so in a fairly unorthodox manner. ASTI and TUI opposition to equalising the points system had prevented any progress on the matter through conventional means, but now, with the government trying to negotiate a successor deal to the Programme for Competitiveness and Work (PCW), the INTO informed the Department in December that it would vote against the new arrangement, Partnership 2000, unless the promoted posts were sanctioned by the government.[13] There had been genuine concern in government that the unions would not pass Partnership 2000, with the majority in SIPTU, the country's largest union, among those against the deal.[14] The threat worked, and the government immediately agreed to implement the proposals on the promoted posts as soon as possible. The INTO met its end of the bargain by putting its 17 votes behind Partnership 2000 at the ICTU's special delegate conference, which met with angry responses from the other teacher unions, fuelling a sense of cynicism among the unions more generally. The TUI's Jim Dorney attacked 'side deals', but Joe O'Toole only responded that the INTO 'took nothing belonging to anyone else and we didn't eat anyone's dinner along the way'.[15] As Padraig Yeates noted at the time, 'it is hard to be overly critical of the INTO general secretary, Senator Joe O'Toole. All he did was engage in a brilliant bit of brinkmanship. He maximised the negotiating ability of his union at a crucial moment in the Partnership 2000 process to win his members something they have sought for 26 years. Nice work, if you can get it.'[16]

LEGISLATIVE CHANGE DURING THE 1990s

As a 1991 OECD report into Irish education had put it, 'the first point to be made about the Irish Education system is that it is difficult to understand. It was not planned methodically but expanded in a piecemeal fashion in order to respond to importunate pressures. There have been no grand designs in the classic mode of centralised government.'[17] The Irish education system had a quasi-legal status, with various ministerial orders, circulars and a small number of Acts of the Oireachtas providing its framework. This rather ramshackle approach to the system was at odds with international practice, and the INTO had long sought the introduction of an education Act that would provide a legislative framework for the system. There was momentum towards the introduction of an Act during the 1980s,[18] and in November 1990, the then taoiseach, Charles Haughey, announced that the government intended to introduce a comprehensive education Act,[19] but it was a further eight years before the Education Act 1998 finally established a statutory basis for primary and post-primary education. Its long gestation was partly the result of a lack of political stability or continuity in the Department. There were six ministers for education in five governments between 1990 and 1998, and changes in personnel had come at critical times. The first effort to draw up a White Paper on which the legislation would be based was undertaken by Mary O'Rourke, who was minister from March 1987 to November 1991. O'Rourke had made good progress after bringing in Professor John Coolahan to assist in drafting a Green Paper, but a reshuffle in November 1991, when Albert Reynolds became taoiseach, saw O'Rourke replaced by Fianna Fáil deputy Noel Davern, who was succeeded by his party colleague Séamus Brennan three months later.

Brennan was sympathetic to the economically right-wing Progressive Democrats, and his free-market liberalism and belief that the role of education was to best prepare people for work informed his attempts at policy-making during his short time in Education. Having landed in Education on 11 February 1992, he was determined that he would have his own Green Paper ready in time for the teachers' congresses six weeks later, and the result, 'Education for a Changing World', got the shortest shrift imaginable at Easter. The INTO was its most vehement opponent; delegates gave Joe O'Toole a standing ovation when he bluntly told the minister he would have to 'go back and try again', with his proposal to test pupils at seven, 11 and 15 described as 'Thatcherite proposals being dumped on the Irish market'.[20] As one report noted, 'there was no menace in the INTO attack but the clear message was that change would have to have union support. The INTO is celebrating its 124th congress and is in a powerful position to either impede or expedite change. It is as aware as the next of the frailty of the government and the likelihood that Mr Brennan has little more than a year in office – if the government lasts that long.'[21] True enough, Brennan's first round of teacher conferences was his last, but the lesson for his successor was clear enough: there had been an implicit agreement from government, through bodies such as the National Council for Curriculum and Assessment (NCCA, established November 1991), that the unions were partners in education and their input into policy-making was not optional.

Fianna Fáil formed a coalition with Labour for the first time after an election in November 1992. In the past, where Labour had coalesced, Fine Gael, the majority partner, had held Education, lest the communists or liberals of the

Labour Party attempt to dilute the Church's influence in the sector. This time, Fianna Fáil was content to give Labour whatever ministries it wanted, and when Labour leader Dick Spring suggested his party take Education, Taoiseach Albert Reynolds agreed.[22] Mervyn Taylor was initially considered for the post, but he went to the new Department of Equality and Law Reform,[23] and Education went to the Dun Laoghaire deputy Niamh Bhreathnach, who was appointed a minister on her first day in the Dáil.[24] Holding the portfolio until the June 1997 general election, Bhreathnach was the longest-serving education minister during this period. Her background was in education. Froebel-trained, she had taught at the School for Deaf Boys in Stillorgan and in Dublin's inner city at St Audeon's before training as a remedial teacher, but she was careful not to be drawn on her policies at the outset. Her colleagues painted her as a safe enough pair of hands, 'a pragmatist … something in the same mould as Mary O'Rourke and Gemma Hussey', 'hard working', 'cautious' and 'won't set the place on fire with radical ideas'.[25]

One of her first tasks was to try to recover some of the ground and the goodwill lost by Séamus Brennan and to publish a new Green Paper. The INTO welcomed Bhreathnach's appointment and she received a friendly enough reception at her first INTO congress, held in Waterford in April, where she arrived promising new school buildings, no compulsory formal testing in primary schools and expressing a preparedness to enter discussions on early retirement.[26] Where Brennan's Green Paper had been written in six weeks without any consultation with the education partners, Bhreathnach engaged in a consultation process that was unprecedented. This was reflected in the four years it took for the Education Bill to finally emerge.

Bhreathnach established a consultative convention on education which would inform the new Act.[27] It included school managers and parents but the unions were lukewarm, and the INTO was especially unenthusiastic at the prospect. The teacher organisations felt that they ought to be given greater weight in the process and be included in the secretariat, believing that the Department had 'lined up a series of third-level experts from universities and flashed in a few more experts from Paris and New York, and they will tell primary and post-primary teachers how to do their work', but eventually, less than a fortnight before the convention began, the unions announced they would participate fully.[28] The convention reported to the minister in January 1994, the INTO welcoming its report as 'an indication of support for well-established INTO policies', particularly its recommendation to establish a Teaching Council,[29] and the convention report helped inform Bhreathnach's White Paper on Education, 'Charting our Education Future', on which much of the Education Bill was based, albeit with several significant changes. The process from White Paper (April 1995) to the presentation of the draft heads of bill to the cabinet

(March 1996) to the bill's publication (January 1997) took 21 months. The INTO was broadly supportive of the White Paper since, as Joe O'Toole put it, some 95 per cent of it was progressive and the result of years of consultation, and any differences they had could be sorted out through negotiations.[30]

There was no negotiation, however, on the first action to arise out of the White Paper. This was the 'Time in School' circular, which sought to lay out the amount of teaching and non-teaching time for primary and post-primary teachers, something which had been imposed on Northern teachers some years earlier.[31] Though clearly flagged in the White Paper, the circular was issued at the beginning of August 1995 without any consultation with the unions.[32] The INTO responded with a survey which showed that teachers worked over the regulation hours anyway, and following a series of meetings with management bodies, they achieved a consensus that the 'Time in School' circular would in effect be ignored.[33]

ETHOS, MANAGEMENT AND DISCRIMINATION

Not surprisingly, school patronage had been the most controversial topic for the convention and continued to be so afterwards. Among the recommendations of the National Education Convention's report was that the composition of school boards would change so that patrons, teachers and parents would be represented equally. This was supported by teacher organisations and parents' groups but roundly rejected by the Catholic hierarchy and the CPSMA as well as Catholic post-primary managers, who wanted patrons to have a majority. Furthermore, the Catholic bishops declared that the boards of their schools would have to have a majority of 'active and committed' Catholics in order to ensure the ethos of Catholic schools.[34] Representatives of the Protestant churches were also opposed, albeit less trenchantly.[35] In a July 1994 position paper on the governance of schools, the minister outlined a compromise: patrons would retain the right to nominate the majority of the board, but there would be 'equivalence of membership', so that the patron's nominees would have to include a parent and a teacher.[36] In September two days of talks on the matter, attended by representatives of the school owners, parents and teachers, failed to reach agreement. The Catholic representatives remained deeply hostile, characterised by Bishop Thomas Flynn's assertion that 'the ideology behind some of these proposals is seen by some bishops as an attempt by the state to push the Church out of education'.[37] Shortly afterwards, Labour withdrew from the government, but soon, on 15 December 1994, Bhreathnach returned as minister for education, this time in a 'rainbow coalition' alongside Fine Gael and Democratic Left. Her return to the same portfolio meant that the change in government had little impact on education policy, but with some of the most religiously conservative deputies and convinced secularists in the Dáil now sitting side by side in Cabinet, tensions were inevitable.

Direct negotiations on school management having proved fruitless, Bhreathnach appointed an economist, Dr Tom McCarthy, as a facilitator. He spent two years endeavouring to seek a resolution and eventually, in November 1996, the minister announced an agreement on governance, outlined in a 'historic document',[38] which would see boards consist of two nominees of the patron, two parents, a principal and another member elected by staff; these six could co-opt two others if they agreed unanimously.[39] The INTO was very unhappy with the deal, taking grave exception to a section relating to Church of Ireland schools that asserted that nothing should oblige them to accept as pupils children who were not members of the Church of Ireland, and that the two co-opted board of management members would themselves be Church of Ireland,[40] but after two years of negotiating, it said it would 'not veto the document' if it was found acceptable by all other parties. Notwithstanding its reluctant acceptance, the INTO remained vocal in its opposition, with Joe O'Toole's description of the clause as 'sectarian' deeply resented by the Church of Ireland.[41] Ultimately, however, questions over the constitutionality of the agreement meant that a final wording was not worked out until October 1997, a full three years after Dr Tom McCarthy had begun the process.[42]

School admissions was a question of principle for the INTO, but an issue of more immediate relevance was on what basis they would make appointments in the context of their 'ethos'. The vast majority of schools in the South were under religious management, and whether they were Catholic, Protestant, Muslim or Jewish, they were determined to retain control of running their institutions and were vigilant against any legislative threats to their status. These threats came not only from Bhreathnach's attempts at education reform but also from the new Department of Equality and Law Reform. As the first minister for equality, Mervyn Taylor introduced several ground-breaking pieces of anti-discrimination legislation, but the two pieces of legislation that had particular significance for schools were the Equal Status Bill, which outlawed discrimination on nine grounds including gender, marital status, family status, religion and sexual orientation (the bill decriminalising homosexual acts having been passed in June 1993),[43] and the Employment Equality Bill. The former would remove schools' ability to discriminate against pupils on the basis of religion and the latter would remove their ability to do the same against teachers and other members of staff. The religious-run schools lobbied to exclude themselves from both pieces of legislation, while the INTO wanted schools to be prohibited from discriminating against pupils or teachers on the basis of religion or other aspects of their private lives.

The two issues – pupil admission and employment – were inextricably bound up with the question of ethos and equality, with the INTO's primary concern the Employment Equality Bill, which would have a direct impact on its members. Until this point, religious schools were able to take teachers' religion into account when they were making appointments and, as the High Court found in the Eileen Flynn case (1985), they were in their rights to fire anyone they felt did not live their private lives in accordance with Church teaching.[44] Following the Flynn judgment, the CPSMA issued guidelines that included the following criteria for appointments to Catholic schools:

> A principal teacher must be a person of integrity; be exemplary in carrying out religious duties; and be a model to the community at large. An assistant teacher must be a practicing [sic] Catholic committed to handing on the faith.[45]

At the time, the CEC made the INTO's objections known to the then minister, Gemma Hussey, but her response was that it was a matter for the management authorities of the schools, and the CPSMA's guidelines remained unchanged.[46] Any changes to this state of affairs would prove highly controversial. When the minister for equality began the process of drawing up his employment equality legislation in 1994, he was advised to leave matters relating to education to the relevant department, where they would be better dealt with in an Education Bill.[47] Taylor obliged but he had not seen the last of the matter. In the summer of 1996, it was reported that Bhreathnach had decided not to give the churches a legal veto over appointments (with a report published in the *Independent* at Easter announcing, 'Churches to get "religion veto" on hiring teachers' having met with a predictably angry response[48]), but all this meant was that the question of a veto was passed to Mervyn Taylor for inclusion in the Employment Equality Bill.[49]

Catholic educational interests were keenly interested in the issue, but though they were far from inactive on the matter, they left the brunt of lobbying on the issue to the Church of Ireland. For many in minority faiths, schooling was an important part not only in the retention of religion or faith formation but also of fostering a community among co-religionists. The Church of Ireland argued that excluding schools from the legislation would protect minority interests, and that to force the equality legislation on all schools would be detrimental to the well-being of Irish minorities. As the Church of Ireland archbishop of Dublin put it to the minister, who was himself an Orthodox Jew, as a member of a minority religion he would be 'keenly aware of the importance of preserving the religious traditions of minorities', observing that 'members of the Jewish Congregation often elect to send their children to a Protestant school as they find their tradition and ethos preferable to schools of the majority faith'.[50] Similar representations were also made in medicine, with representatives from the Adelaide Hospital expressing their anxiety to the minister.

As well as this lobbying, there was advice from the attorney general, Dermot Gleeson, pointing to a number of legal cases and the Constitution. Gleeson told the minister that 'not only [was] the State allowed to give an exemption for discrimination in employment which is essential for the maintenance of the religious ethos of an educational institution … it is *probably also constitutionally obliged to give such an exemption*'.[51] This exemption found its way into the legislation in Section 37 of the Bill. A number of representative bodies expressed concerns about Section 37, including the Gay and Lesbian Equality Network (GLEN), which argued it could 'provide a pretext for and perhaps even legalise discrimination',[52] but the INTO was the section's loudest and most vociferous opponent. Section 37 was an example of an issue where teacher unity might have strengthened the teachers' hand, but in this case, there was none, at an official level at least, although a group called Teachers for Pluralism in Education, ostensibly an umbrella group but mostly INTO members, held a number of meetings and arranged a petition, which was signed by some 10,000 teachers.[53]

There was lobbying of the minister and of government and opposition politicians. INTO representatives attended several meetings with the minister, while members who were politically active were encouraged to lobby their elected representatives against legislation which Fintan O'Toole described as state-sanctioned sectarianism.[54] Attacked by the liberal commentators, under fire from his Democratic Left colleagues at cabinet,[55] and with some of his Labour colleagues worrying about the principles involved and the unhappiness it caused among left-wing teachers in their own party,[56] Taylor complained to a meeting of Roman Catholic and Church of Ireland bishops that he had no idea how he had got himself into education policy, but that he had to strike a balance because 'teacher unions are powerful', adding that the INTO had accused him of 'marching to the tune of the bishops'.[57] In the end, the section was revised so that if an employee or prospective employee appealed against a discriminatory action, the burden of proof of that argument would fall heavily on the institution to show that it was necessary to prevent its religious ethos being undermined.[58]

The draft that went before the Dáil in February 1997 explicitly allowed religious-run schools to favour co-religionists in appointments or promotions 'where it is reasonable to do so in order to maintain the religious ethos of the institution'. Having failed to secure Fianna Fáil support to table an opposition amendment against the bill, Joe O'Toole tried to introduce it at committee stage in the Seanad, but without success. The bill passed both houses of the Oireachtas by 5 February, and after consulting with the Council of State on 1 April 1997, President Robinson referred it to the Supreme Court, which found three of its parts unconstitutional but upheld Section 37.[59] Only a few weeks later, the Rainbow coalition was replaced by a Fianna Fáil–Progressive Democrat government. The new government published a revised bill in November 1997, with Section 37 substantially unchanged, which was eventually enacted in June 1998. Teachers who felt that they had been discriminated against under the section were advised to inform the INTO, which would support them, through the courts if necessary,[60] but the legislation's effect was subtle and hard to prove, with LGBT (lesbian, gay, bisexual and transgender) teachers the most affected by its chill factor. In November 2004, the INTO hosted the first meeting of the LGBT teacher support group (it officially changed its name in November 2012 to INTO LGBT Teachers' Group). With 14 members present, there were almost as many officials as LGBT teachers[61] – an indication of their sense of precariousness – but their numbers and their visibility increased in subsequent years. The Northern INTO LGBT group held its inaugural meeting in October 2010. Eventually, after a number of abortive efforts, legislation was passed at the end of 2015 which amended Section 37.1, but fell short of its deletion, which the INTO had demanded.

The Education Bill was finally published in February 1997. Broadly welcomed by the INTO, which, along with the NPC, had been consulted on the penultimate draft,[62] the bill came under sustained attack from religious groups, which accused the minister of engaging in a state takeover of education.[63] The Progressive Democrats were of a similar view. Michael McDowell TD, a senior counsel and former Gonzaga pupil, was quick to question the bill's constitutionality, and other eminent senior counsel followed.[64] By the end of April, the minister had announced some 60 amendments to her bill, while Fianna Fáil, for its part, submitted over 200,[65] but by then, time had run out. The Dáil was dissolved on 15 May and the June general election saw a Fianna Fáil–Progressive Democrat government take office.[66] Before the election, the PDs' spokesperson on education had asserted that her party would ensure that Labour's Education Bill would 'never see the light of day', while Fianna Fáil had already pledged to remove key policies, most notably the setting up of Regional Education Boards.[67] The bill, with its emphasis on devolved education administration, had run aground.

The new minister for education was a young Fianna Fáil deputy, Micheál Martin, a former secondary school teacher who had been his party's education spokesman in opposition. In September, he announced that he would introduce a new education bill before Christmas that would not feature Bhreathnach's Regional Education Boards, and which would include statutory recognition of the National Council for Curriculum and Assessment (NCCA) and legislative recognition of the professional status of teachers,[68] something which the teacher unions had complained was absent from the original bill. Opposition deputies complained that the new bill was 'devoid of vision' and a wasted opportunity, but it was more 'teacher-friendly' than its predecessor, and it included a more acceptable approach to dealing with complaints about teachers.[69] Noting that the teachers had been consulted about the legislation, Joe O'Toole observed that 'every change I have seen has been an improvement in the bill'.[70] With the most controversial aspects of the bill erased in the new version, including administrative devolution, the bill passed easily through the Oireachtas and was signed into law on 23 December 1998.

JUST LIKE AN ATM

Reforms tended to mean more work. The 1990s had seen significant changes in what was being taught in classrooms, from the new computing technology to the sensitive area of sex education, prompting complaints of curriculum overload, but there were also changes in how schools were run and principals, in particular, complained about the workload. Towards the turn of the millennium, there was also growing discontent among teachers that incomes were falling behind as private sector incomes were rising, and the cost of living was increasing sharply. This was felt most keenly among younger teachers, as house prices soared beyond their reach (albeit not for the first time), especially around Dublin. After nurses and the gardaí negotiated special increases in 1999, the teachers' sense of injustice became acute, and in the autumn of that year, the three teacher unions established a working party to work towards a pay increase for the 'early settlers'.[71] When attempts to secure an early settlers' claim had not concluded by the time Partnership 2000 had expired, it carried over into negotiations for what would be the fifth partnership agreement. Before the 1999 congress, Joe O'Toole outlined a three-pronged approach to pay negotiations that the INTO would take over the next year: first, the early settlers claim; second, the payment of the final two per cent of Partnership 2000 to every teacher; third, and most important, the pay increases in the next agreement, which, he said, would 'have to be the highest award in ten years if wage war [was] to be avoided'.[72]

Crucially, the context had changed. Where the early agreements had aimed to stabilise the economy and manage a crisis, they were now geared towards 'managing growth and rising expectations', but as Joe O'Toole put it, 'after ten years of belt-tightening, we now want our share'.[73] Negotiations on the new agreement began in December 1999, and it did not take long before differences emerged between the teacher unions. The division arose, ostensibly, over the idea that there would be a performance-related element to any pay deal. Joe O'Toole supported a productivity element in the programme, or 'benchmarking' as it was called, arguing that performance-related pay was 'more an opportunity than a problem'; teachers who obtained extra qualifications or training would be rewarded financially.[74] Infamously, he likened the process as being 'no more than going to a different ATM: we will punch in the formula and collect the pay-out'.[75] There was a degree of scepticism among INTO members, but among the post-primary unions, the productivity idea was anathema, since it raised the prospect of individual appraisals and teachers' pay being based on exam results. The level of opposition within the ASTI was such that on 22 January 2000 a meeting of its executive voted to withdraw from the ICTU and pursue a 30 per cent pay claim outside the ICTU structures.[76] Over the next few years, the ASTI took a militant stance over pay outside the social partnership arrangement and operated on its own.

The deal itself – the Programme for Prosperity and Fairness (PPF) – was concluded in February 2000. It included a cumulative pay increase of 19.2 per cent over 33 months, which, along with changes in taxation, would amount to a 29 per cent pay increase overall. Among the non-pay-related aspects of the deal, there would be 1,500 additional teaching posts and the implementation of strategies to combat illiteracy and disadvantage. It fell somewhat short of what the INTO had hoped for but, perhaps as important, partnership fatigue had set in. There was a growing sense of resentment that partnership held some sectors back while others benefited; limited promotional prospects and no overtime payments put teaching in the first camp, although primary teachers were spared the fate of some of their post-primary colleagues who saw some former students earning more than them after only a couple of years in the workforce. There was also a fear that the deal would not keep up with the cost of living; the Irish rate of inflation was the highest in the EU, having ranked among the lowest only two years earlier.[77] Previous partnership agreements had passed easily in the INTO but it became apparent early on that there was a very real chance that members would reject the PPF, with Dublin branches voting against it in early ballots.[78] The INTO leadership mobilised in support of the deal, lobbying members and holding meetings around the country to sell it, and when the result was announced it passed but by fewer than a hundred votes, or half a per cent.

The level of opposition to the deal among teachers was not reflected in the wider union movement, however, and PPF passed comfortably with a 69 per cent vote in favour overall. In the short term, there was some disquiet in the INTO at the result, and the narrow margin by which it had passed, resulting in a change in voting in agreements from branch meetings to postal ballots. This was an important and overdue reform that made it considerably easier for members to vote, as was evident from the two-thirds turnout for the subsequent agreement (Sustaining Progress) in March 2003.[79] The PPF vote was the high-water mark for opposition to partnership. A consultation process during 2002 found that for the most part there was 'a general feeling that partnership was worth pursuing, providing it did not include extra workload for teachers', while there was also 'some concern that partnership had not delivered on the social issues'.[80] There was some political opposition to social partnership from the left (though not restricted to the left), as there was in every union, but despite significant differences in opinion the organisation was never riven by disagreement on the matter. At a time when the ASTI was embroiled in a bitter internal dispute (which ultimately led to the departure in 2004 of its general secretary, Charlie Lennon, after a lengthy legal process), the INTO, for the most part, avoided any debilitating splits on the matter.

THE INTO IN THE NEW MILLENNIUM

After a little over a decade in the position, Joe O'Toole announced that he would step down as general secretary in 2002. It had been a period of unparalleled change. Unlike the 1980s, when the organisation had had to battle cutbacks and pay freezes, the apparent new prosperity had enabled the creation of new posts. The ending of the points system meant that half of all national teachers were given promoted posts, and incomes generally were rising, although the rising cost of living, and of housing in particular, was a very real problem. Social partnership had its critics, but it had helped put the teaching unions in a position of influence over policy in a way that was without precedent. The INTO was well aware how different this could be; its influence on policy south of the border contrasted with its position in the North, where teacher unions were largely side-stepped in policy-making under the UK regime. From the first programme in 1987 education reforms were included in the agreement, and many of the INTO's demands to tackle areas such as educational disadvantage, remedial teaching and special needs were being put in place by successive governments. Social partner-ship also had an effect on the nature of the INTO's work. As more of the pay issues went into the remit of the national collective pay agreements, negotiated formally through the ICTU, the organisation became more focused on its role as a professional organisation. Throughout the 1990s, a succession of policy docu-ments outlined the INTO's position on every conceivable aspect of primary education, with a view to informing government policy. In 1993, the INTO's Professional Development Unit was established, funded by EU structural funds, which set up a programme of continuing professional development for teachers, run by teachers. The critics who devoted column inches every Easter to complaining that teachers spent their annual conference talking about money instead of education overlooked the fact that the INTO, at least, also held annual education conferences, special conferences and regular seminars and courses on education, which the media was content to ignore. Whether it was in training or case work, more and more of the work of the organisation was run from head office, where more officials had been appointed over the course of the 1990s as the organisation professionalised, and their role in the running of the INTO became more central. The days of branch reps or the CEC representatives doing all the case work for the members were all but over.

The INTO had modernised, but had it done so at the expense of its strength as an organisation? During the debate on the PPF, there was criticism that the leadership was out of touch with the rank and file; certainly, they were at odds on that deal. But it was also the case that teachers, especially principals, felt that the education and administrative reforms were unrelenting, leaving them exhausted and unrewarded; and that the CEC and officials saw change as inevitable and its role as being to manage it, or, in many cases, to lead it.[81] The idea that the INTO was managing change was not always consolation to an over-worked teaching principal who just wanted it all to stop. As one critic noted at the time, while the INTO's research and advocacy on education matters was laudable, the organisation had become too close to the Department of Education and had put this before members' rights, pay and conditions. The INTO had always had a dual role, they complained, but 'I feel the balance has been completely lost'.[82]

Ultimately, the INTO had become one of the most influential organisations in the state because of a variety of factors. It was a large union – though there were others much larger[83] – whose members had traditionally enjoyed a particular status in their communities because of their jobs and, frequently, their participation in local sports and so on. Teachers were often politically active, across the parties, and the INTO continued to encourage members to use their political contacts to lobby on particular issues, notably on the question of Section 37.1. At a higher level, the INTO had established itself as a leading voice in the ICTU and in the partnership process, and notably the 1990s began with Gerry Quigley serving as ICTU president and ended as Joe O'Toole became vice-president. If, by the end of the decade, there was criticism that the INTO was inclined to be the 'good boy' in class when it came to partnership, in contrast with the ASTI as troublemaker, the organisation could point to a number of important gains for primary education and for primary teachers that had been secured through the process, not least the ending of the points system in a controversial side-deal to Partnership 2000, a fine example of the kind of adroit political bargaining for which the general secretary gained a reputation. Throughout this time (or to be accurate, between 1987 and 2011), Joe O'Toole served as an independent senator, which gave him regular informal access to ministers and people of influence, allowing him to formulate bargains and deals away from formal negotiations. This was very effective in terms of outcomes, but it was not always the most transparent or, indeed, democratic way of doing business; and there was a degree of friction between the high-level political fixing on the one hand, and the INTO as an organisation on the other. By the 1990s, INTO membership had never been higher, but there was concern about levels of engagement and communication. Notwithstanding the succession of studies into how the INTO might improve the participation, primarily of women, but later more generally,[84] there seemed a decline in engagement. The internet changed how things worked too, prompting Joe O'Toole to pen an editorial for *InTouch* headlined 'Seriously, do we need to go to meetings at all?'[85]

Joe O'Toole had been elected unopposed in 1990; the election of his successor was the first contest for general secretary in 21 years and, perhaps unsurprisingly, it was strongly contested. With six candidates securing nominations, twice as many ran compared to the last election in 1978; of those, three were women. Three of the candidates were long-time CEC representatives: Noel Ward, who had represented South Dublin from 1989 to 1995; his successor, Sheila Nunan, who was then president, and who, like Ward, was from the Tallaght branch; and Tom O'Sullivan, a principal in Limerick City who had represented District 13 (Kerry and Limerick) on the CEC since 1989.[86] Brenda Ní Shúilleabháin, the principal of a Gaelscoil, was on the committee of the Tallaght branch, its third candidate in this contest, and described herself as a 'non-establishment candidate'.[87] This time, the two front-runners from early on came from head office: John Carr, the general treasurer and deputy general secretary; and Catherine Byrne, assistant general secretary. John Carr had been a full-time official since 1989 and had succeeded Michael Moroney after he retired in 1997. Catherine Byrne had worked as an official since 1981, apart from a period working with the trade union movement in Europe. Of the two front-runners, John Carr was tipped by some as the favourite to win, but while Catherine Byrne predicted he would win on first preferences, she hoped to overtake him on transfers.[88] With the exception of Ní Shúilleabháin, who expressed support for the ASTI's demands, there was broad consensus among the candidates, who identified better salaries as the organisation's priority, as well as better resources and smaller class sizes, and recognised the need to establish a leadership that listened to and acted on the needs of the members. In terms of tactics, none of them argued that any of this should be outside the partnership process.[89] After a hard-fought campaign, John Carr was elected on the fifth count, having received 9,218 votes to Catherine Byrne's 7,559.[90] Subsequently, Catherine Byrne was elected unopposed as general treasurer designate, becoming the second woman to hold the position, and the first since Mairead Ashe retired more than 70 years earlier.

The new INTO leadership took over at a time that in retrospect could be seen as the calm before the storm. Where the pace of reform during the 1990s had been unrelenting, it slowed down markedly going into the new decade. For classroom teachers, the most significant reform was the launch of the revised primary school curriculum in March 1999, which was phased in over a period of years at the INTO's insistence, with extra course days and in-service training to help with the preparation.[91] In the early to mid-noughties, the INTO had the space to develop a number of campaigns including pay, which was pursued through the benchmarking process, as well as school modernisation and the perennial issue of class size. These campaigns were pursued in a generally favourable economic context. The period between 2000 and 2008 was ostensibly one of continued national prosperity[92] (although growth levelled off between 2002 and 2004) and a degree of political continuity, with Fianna Fáil-led coalitions in office throughout the decade. The May 2002 general election resulted in the return of a Fianna Fáil–Progressive Democrat government, which remained in office for its full term. Following the general election of 2007, Fianna Fáil returned to office with a new junior partner, the Green Party, in government for the first time. There was somewhat less continuity in the role of minister for education and skills, with three ministers holding office between January 2000 and May 2008.

The first two, Michael Woods and Noel Dempsey, each held the portfolio for 28 months. A political veteran, Woods moved the focus to implementation after eight years of unrelenting innovation. His most notable reform was of the running of the Department of Education and Science (DES), which was widely regarded as ill-equipped to fulfil its role in planning policy. Former secretary of the Department of Finance, Seán Cromien, was appointed to examine 'operations, systems and staffing needs' and, following the Cromien report, many of the Department's responsibilities were devolved to new external agencies, including the State Examinations Commission and the Special Education Council, but it had another direct impact on primary teachers. As Deirbhile Nic Craith notes, 'responsibility for day-to-day administration has also gradually shifted from the Department of Education to school level – to principal teachers and boards of management', an evolution that brought about significantly increased administrative and bureaucratic workloads for principal teachers in particular.[93]

When Fianna Fáil and the Progressive Democrats returned to office following the 2002 general election, the education section in their programme for government looked like an INTO shopping list, including a reduction in class sizes (below 20:1 for children under nine); an increase in teacher supply; specific policies to target disadvantage; and a programme to improve the condition of school buildings.[94] By the time the estimates were published in November, however, it was a different story. The global downturn which followed the dotcom bubble bursting in 2002 inevitably affected the Irish economy, and by the autumn budgetary figures showed an 'unexpected' deficit. There were spending cuts across the board and the school building programme was slowed down considerably. Building work on almost 400 primary schools was frozen because of the cuts, which saw an allocation of €147 million in a total education budget of €5 billion for the following year.[95] Following considerable lobbying and threats of strike action, by the time the estimates were published in November 2003 they featured an extra €23 million for primary school buildings, with an extra €30 million for primary and second-level school buildings included in the budget shortly afterwards.[96] This was all part of a €1 billion school modernisation fund to upgrade primary schools over five years, and represented a significant INTO success at a time when government spending was being tightly controlled.

Noel Dempsey, a former teacher, had been appointed minister for education in 2002, and he had a reasonably good working relationship with the INTO, which he found sincerely concerned about education. 'Within ten or fifteen minutes of a meeting with the INTO, we ended up talking about education and children,' he recalls, 'even if it started with pay and allowances.'[97] One of the major areas of co-operation between the minister and the INTO during this time was special needs education. The 1998 Education Act had confirmed the policy of promoting the inclusion of pupils with special needs in mainstream schools, which had begun in the 1970s and gained momentum during the late 1980s and early 1990s.[98] Legal actions, including the 2001 Supreme Court judgment in the Sinnott case, had added to the impetus for change. The question of special needs education had been part of the INTO agenda since the 1950s, when Seán Brosnahan had been one of its earliest champions, and during the 1990s it held a dedicated conference on special education and issued reports on special needs teaching.[99] As inclusion became more widespread the issue itself became more mainstream, and by the mid-2000s, as one education correspondent noted, some 20 per cent of the INTO's Easter congress agenda was devoted to special needs education. The INTO was engaged both publicly and behind the scenes in campaigning for resources and promoting policy.[100] In January 2004, the National Council for Special Education (NCSE) was established, taking the responsibility for the area from the DES, and subsequently the Education for Persons with Special Educational Needs Act 2004 was passed. The INTO worked closely with Dempsey when he was drafting the bill, and the minister credited the organisation with helping him understand the practical necessities involved. Resources, as ever, remained an issue, but this was an area where significant advances were made in a relatively short time. In 1998, there were fewer than 300 special needs assistants in place in Irish national schools; by 2005 there were some 6,000.[101]

During Dempsey's time as minister, there were negotiations for a successor agreement to the controversial PPF. The negotiations themselves were sometimes fraught. Dempsey, a combative individual who, in the words of one colleague, 'could start a fight in an empty room',[102] went into the Sustaining Progress talks intent on securing a number of 'modernisation' reforms, notably standardising the school year and securing extra hours in school from teachers. Finding Dempsey entirely unwilling to budge from his insistence that all parent–teacher meetings be held in the evening, the INTO secured a climb-down by taking the issue directly to the taoiseach, Bertie Ahern, who was happy to oblige.[103] Dempsey's attempt to standardise the school year was also unpopular, still more so his decision to send inspectors into schools two days before Christmas to make sure they were still open, which inevitably raised teachers' hackles, and made the talks more difficult.[104] When the deal was finalised, though, Sustaining Progress proved nowhere near as divisive as its predecessor, not least since the cumulative increase of the pay deal, at seven per cent, and the benchmarking award would mean a 21.67 per cent increase for teachers in just over two years, and over a year's worth of back money from the benchmarking award would be payable as soon as the INTO signed on. The largest increase in such a period since national agreements began, it was approved by 77.3 per cent.[105]

After the summer of 2004 there was a government reshuffle, and Noel Dempsey was moved from Education. He was succeeded by the Dun Laoghaire TD and government chief whip, Mary Hanafin, a former history and Irish teacher in the Dominican College, Sion Hill in Blackrock, where she had been ASTI school steward.[106] In his account of that government, Pat Leahy records how the taoiseach's instructions to her on her appointment were simple: get the unions back onside. While Hanafin was told to rebuild relations and go to the teacher conferences, there was no specific instruction beyond a general injunction to 'keep the unions happy'.[107] Education was Hanafin's prized portfolio. First elected in 1997, it had not been that long since she was in the classroom herself, and she was naturally sympathetic towards the teachers, with a style that was considerably less abrasive than that of her predecessor. At a time when morale among teachers was not good, particularly after the fractious ASTI dispute, this was welcome. Her appointment coincided with the INTO's third major campaign of the decade. As one education editor noted shortly afterwards, 'the INTO is a formidable lobbying machine. Its campaigns have already helped to achieve minor miracles on issues such as special needs and school buildings. Now it is turning its sights on class size.'[108] Class size was the priority over the next number of years, but while classes were considerably larger than those in many EU states, the number of teachers had increased vastly since the 1990s. Between 1996 and 2006, the number of primary teachers had increased by one-third, from 21,000 to 28,000, and they were teaching fewer pupils.[109] This had been done at the same time as their salaries had increased significantly, going from the seventh best paid in the OECD region in 2002 to the third best paid in 2008.[110]

The good times were very nearly at an end, however. In June 2006, the social partners agreed Towards 2016, the last agreement of its kind. By the following year, the Celtic Tiger bubble reached its highest point and the period of growth and apparent prosperity came to a catastrophic end in 2008. In March 2008 Lehman Brothers collapsed, beginning the international banking crisis, and by September, when the schools went back, Ireland was officially in recession, and the government – a Fianna Fáil–Green coalition elected the previous summer – had announced an emergency budget, the toughest in at least two decades. By the end of the month, the government had introduced the ruinous bank guarantee scheme which ultimately led, two years later, to the €85 billion bailout by the Troika in November 2010.

ELECTION

Sheila Nunan was elected general secretary in 2009, becoming the first woman to lead the INTO. She was joined by Noel Ward as deputy general secretary and treasurer. They took office at the most difficult time for the INTO in living memory. Like every public-sector union at the time, the INTO now faced two main problems: the prospect of job cuts; and cuts to members' incomes. In September 2009 the Financial Emergency Measures in the Public Interest Act 2009, or FEMPI, was introduced. Along with other public servants, teachers were hit with a pension levy averaging 7 per cent, pay cuts averaging 7 per cent the following year and the introduction of the universal social charge. The combination of salary cuts and levies or extra taxes meant that by 2010 teachers' take-home pay had fallen by an average of 17 per cent. In March 2010 the Public Services Committee of ICTU and the government reached the Croke Park Agreement with the aim of halting further cuts and ensuring that there would be no compulsory redundancies. It was to run until 2014, with annual reviews. The CEC recommended its acceptance, making the INTO one of the first unions to do so, despite the ASTI's and the TUI's rejection, and in May 2010, members voted yes by 65 per cent to 35 per cent against.[111]

Croke Park was hugely controversial among all public-sector workers, and was attacked both by the left, who felt the unions needed to take a more militant approach, and on the right by those who wanted to take full advantage of the crisis to slash public service numbers and pay as much as possible. For teachers with permanent jobs, it gave stability of income and security of employment, which was welcome. For those who entered the service subsequently – teaching had been almost alone in not having an embargo on recruitment, although there was one on promotions – things were difficult. Teachers appointed on or after 1 February 2012 were not entitled to the same salary allowances as existing teachers. Around this time, the government introduced a job activation scheme, JobBridge, whereby people on the live register would work in jobs as interns while keeping their social welfare payment and receiving an extra €52.50 per week. In December 2011, the INTO issued a directive against participating in the scheme. But if the use of JobBridge at primary level was largely avoided, the inequality in income of new entrants remained a problem. Not for the first time, the demand for equal pay for equal work became a catch cry among members. Partly because of the relatively high numbers of new entrants to the profession affected by this, the INTO has been one of the most vocal public sector unions on the matter. In May 2013, the Haddington Road agreement was put to members and passed by a margin of three to two. The Lansdowne Road agreement in September 2015 was passed by almost three to one, but the CEC recommended the rejection of the Public Service Pay Agreement, in June 2017, mainly because of its failure to progress the issue of pay equality.

The government treatment of public servants after the crash wiped out many of the financial gains that the INTO had made in the previous ten years. Much of the organisation's work as it reaches its 150-year anniversary inevitably continues to involve challenging government resistance to restoration of austerity cuts and to implementing equal pay for equal work. At the same time, the INTO also runs campaigns such as Stand up For Primary Education, focusing on class size, among other issues. Despie the cut backs, the INTO can still point to areas where its campaigns and positions succeeded during the period from the 1990s to the crash, particularly in the areas of special needs supports, educational disadvantage and Traveller education. Section 37.1, which the INTO had consistently opposed, was severely curtailed. Towards the end of the 2010s, the INTO remains an important and influential organisation not only in education but also in Irish public life. The union continues in its role as an advocate for teachers and primary education as a whole, as well as for members on an individual basis, and it acts as a professional body, whether through developing education research and continuing professional development or through working with the statutory regulatory body, the Teaching Council.

Chapter 8

THE INTO IN NORTHERN
IRELAND, 1922–1950

*'We in Northern Ireland are making a tremendous
fight for the INTO.'*

S ince 1868, the INTO had organised and worked for teachers across the
island of Ireland. Now that Ireland was to be divided into two jurisdictions,
was that to change? Had the organisation as a 32-county entity run its
course? While the idea was mooted, it was never seriously contemplated. The
INTO had strong roots in the North. In its early years, the INTO's largest
association by far had been the one in Belfast, where Vere Foster also lived. The
INTO had a committed, active membership in the north-east. A number of
Protestant teachers had broken away since the Ulster Teachers' Union (UTU)
was founded in 1919. However, by the beginning of 1921 (see page 64) and as the
new northern state came into being, the UTU numbered only around 500 while
the INTO had around 2,100 members in a state which had 2,040 primary
schools. What were they supposed to do now?

FOUNDATION OF THE VIGILANCE COMMITTEE, 1921
At the end of June 1921, the INTO held a meeting in Clarence Place Hall in
Belfast for teachers in the six counties, at which they discussed what might lie
ahead for the organisation.[1] Welcoming them, INTO president John Harbison
noted suggestions that the INTO had 'served its day' and could do no more for
the teachers in the North. Harbison pointed to the example of other unions that
organised successfully in more than one jurisdiction. Irish railway workers, for
instance, were members of the British-based National Union of Railwaymen,
but had an Irish executive. They could consider a similar type of set-up, with a
small executive to look after the interests of teachers in the northern area, which

would co-operate with the teachers in the 26 counties on common issues.[2] The most important thing, though, was the absolute necessity to preserve the INTO intact. As a non-political and non-sectarian organisation, the INTO offered a broad platform to all teachers. Most of the senior activists in the INTO at this time (most if not all of those reported as speaking at the meeting were Protestant) saw the mixed, non-sectarian character of the organisation as of fundamental importance, not least while the UTU was recruiting Protestant teachers only. George Conaghan from Derry pointed out that there had been previous splits in the organisation between North and South which had failed to benefit either side. Following his proposal, the meeting voted unanimously in favour of a motion stating that:

[W]e, representing the teachers of the six Northern counties of Ireland, while proclaiming our adhesion to the INTO as a distinct Irish educational unit, recommend that the CEC sanction the appointment of a vigilance or interim committee to safeguard the interests of primary education and of the teachers in the Northern area, and we request the CEC to ask the various associations in the area to nominate the members of such a committee.

A four-man Vigilance Committee was set up on an interim basis, consisting of three members of the CEC and one from the finance committee. Soon after, its membership was expanded to include the chairman of each county committee, and an additional member of the Belfast committee, and its powers were extended.[3]

Because of the disturbed state of Belfast city and its surrounding areas, the full Vigilance Committee did not meet very often at the beginning, and most of its work fell to its members who lived in or near the city.[4] The sectarian violence and civil conflict that had broken out in Derry during the summer of 1920 spread to Belfast and continued until 1922. Over a two-year period some 23,000 people – mostly Catholics – were driven from their homes in the city. Many Catholics were put out of their jobs and some 500 people were killed as a result of sectarian violence. The IRA had also been active in Belfast at this time, a number of national teachers among its membership, some of whom would end up interned.[5] It was in response to its killing of two soldiers in the city in April 1921 that one national teacher, Paddy Duffin, and his brother Dan, who had been the quartermaster of IRA B Company, were shot in their home in Clonard Gardens by the RIC in a reprisal. Their older brother, John, was himself a teacher in St Paul's NS.[6] He would become one of the stalwarts of the INTO, remaining active in the Belfast branch for decades and serving on the CEC. Around this time, however, John Duffin was particularly notable for his activities in co-ordinating what became known as 'the rebel teachers'. Dáil Éireann had responded to the sectarian violence by instituting the Belfast

Boycott in 1920, but its policy towards the new northern state once it had been established was one of non-recognition. It was a strategy followed not only by Dáil Éireann but also from within the six counties. Apart from the Catholic MPs who did not take their seats in the new parliament, crucially for education, the Catholic Church refused to deal with the new government from the outset, and a large section of teachers followed suit.

The INTO was one of the few organisations to continue to operate on a 32-county basis after partition, but where, say, the GAA or the various churches were civil society organisations, able to continue on much the same basis as before, that could not be said for teachers north of the border. In at least one important way, the northern teachers had a greater level of continuity than their colleagues in the Free State, who were having to adjust to the new policy of bilingual teaching in national schools. Nevertheless, northern teachers could be confident of a significant structural, and possibly political, shake-up in the educational system, not least because the greatest support for the education reforms contained in the Macpherson Bill had come from unionist politicians. While the INTO had supported the Macpherson reforms, there was concern among Catholic teachers in the north-east about the form that any changes implemented by a unionist administration might take, fearing that it might 'interfere with their idea as Catholics and Irishmen'.[7] While the government of Northern Ireland, and the new ministry for education, was inaugurated in June 1921, it was not until 1 February 1922 that responsibilities for education were transferred from the Board of National Commissioners in Dublin to Belfast, which would also mean that the northern government would now become responsible for paying the northern teachers' salaries. A significant section of Catholic managers and teachers in their schools supported a policy of non-recognition of the new regime, but they would require practical support.

Joseph MacRory, bishop of Down and Connor, had been keeping the Dublin government informed about events in the North, and in the days around the transfer of Education to the North, he had met with the provisional government to explain the northern Catholic teachers' concerns.[8] He ultimately secured its financial support, so that Catholic teachers in the North would continue to teach in the schools there, but would be paid from Dublin. T.J. O'Connell was approached privately to see if the INTO would give its support to the action, but O'Connell suggested that this would be very unlikely, since it was an explicitly political act, and he was not approached on the matter again.[9] It would have been impossible for the INTO to involve itself in such an action without losing most of its remaining Protestant members in the North, but as it was, its support proved unnecessary. Instead, the 29-year-old John Duffin managed for ten months to run a clandestine administration which saw him collect the salary forms from over 800 teachers in 283 schools across the six counties – about a third of the Catholic elementary schools in the province – and send them back across the border with the help of a restaurant attendant on the Dublin train.[10] The non-recognition programme continued until November, some teachers having resisted the provisional government's efforts to end it in August, amid growing alarm at the cost of the endeavour, the practical problems it had created and concern over the consequences if the northern government established the source of the teachers' salaries, which would have been a breach of the Treaty. The school teachers' boycott of the northern administration was a notable act of resistance, although it is difficult at this stage to establish the level of support it enjoyed. John Harbison of the Vigilance Committee had made representations to the new ministry, explaining that in at least one case, the school teachers had filled in their salary forms, but when they submitted them to their manager for his signature, the forms were then dispatched to Dublin.[11]

THE NEW STATE AND EDUCATION

The constitutional framework for Northern Ireland was set out under the Government of Ireland Act, which became law on 23 December 1920. It provided for a devolved administration, subordinate to the parliament in Westminster, to which Northern Irish constituencies would continue to elect some 13 MPs. The Government of Ireland legislation placed various limitations on the northern government's powers; it could not make laws aimed at religious discrimination, for example. The greatest limit to its powers, however, was financial. The London government retained a number of important functions, including tax-raising powers. The financial provisions were restrictive enough that they seriously clipped the northern government's wings and 'heralded two decades of frustration, irritation and a hand-to-mouth existence'. The northern government was responsible for allocating four-fifths of the spending in the province, but four-fifths of its revenue came from London, with only death duties, motor licences, entertainment and stamp duties falling within its remit.[12] While the economy in the north-east enjoyed a post-war boom, this was short-lived and was followed by a period of massive unemployment. Moreover, the social infrastructure in the North was inadequate, with poor housing, poor roads and, crucially for the teachers, poor school buildings.

This was all ahead of the new government. The North's first elections were held in May 1921 and parliament was opened the following month by King George V. The opening was attended by the Unionist MPs, who had won 40 of the 52 seats, and members of the upper house, but was boycotted initially by the 12 MPs who had been elected as Nationalists or Sinn Féin. There was uncertainty in the early years of the new state; would partition last? If so, would the border remain the same? But if among nationalists there was a hope that the border would be a temporary imposition, the Unionist government led by Prime Minister Sir James

Craig (later Lord Craigavon) began to establish an administrative framework which ultimately remained unchanged for the next 50 years.

It was clear from the outset that education would be one of the major areas of contention between the new Unionist government in Northern Ireland and the Catholic Church. The Catholic Church was satisfied with how the education system operated; it had control over its schools without significant responsibility for contributing to their upkeep. The Church had only recently fought off efforts to reform the administration of education in the Macpherson Act. Considering the broad support among Protestant politicians, Churches and media for the provisions of the Macpherson Bill, it was inevitable that there would be an attempt to introduce something very similar into Northern Ireland, so the Catholic Church faced the prospect of another battle. This time, however, the Church came from a position of relative weakness as a minority in a mainly Protestant state, which also meant that the stakes were higher, since any dilution of Catholic power in the particular circumstances appeared to be an attack on the nationalist community as a whole.

The man in charge of education from 1921 until the end of 1925 was Lord Londonderry, an aristocrat educated at Eton and Sandhurst before being elected as MP for Maidstone and serving in France during the Great War.[13] A liberal unionist in his politics, he was invited by Craig to become education minister and leader of the senate in the northern parliament. The new minister faced considerable challenges. As Sean Farren observes:

> In educational terms, Northern Ireland inherited nothing more than the schools and colleges which had been operating within its six counties. This amounted to 2,040 national schools, 75 intermediate schools, 12 model schools, 45 technical schools, one teacher training college (St Mary's, a Roman Catholic college for girls in Belfast), Queen's University, also in Belfast, and the quite small Magee College in Derry. Because the Boards of National and Intermediate Education had been based in Dublin, no local administration existed in Northern Ireland. The task facing the new Ministry of Education was, therefore, an enormous one. It virtually meant starting to build from the ground up and it was a task which the first Minister for Education seemed to relish, at least to begin with.[14]

In September 1921, Londonderry appointed Belfast MP Sir Robert Lynn to chair an enquiry into education services, known as the Lynn committee. The major Churches were invited to nominate representatives on the committee. The Catholic Church was alone in refusing, and Londonderry's appeals to Cardinal Logue failed to change his mind. Logue responded that he had 'little doubt that an attack is being organised against our Catholic schools', and that the Lynn committee would be used as a 'foundation and pretext for that attack'.[15] This meant that there was only one Catholic on the committee, but that he was there as a government official: A.N. Bonaparte Wyse, who had come up from Tyrone House to join the education ministry in Belfast as assistant secretary.[16] It is difficult to say whether the refusal of the Catholic Church to co-operate with the Lynn committee had significant consequences for how the school management system in the North was established and how it would run thereafter. Perhaps Logue was correct, and the Catholic Church's co-operation would have had no influence on its findings, but merely given the committee a cross-community veneer. Their absence meant that Catholic voices played no role in the design of the new administration although, as the Lynn committee's interim report stated, its members had tried to make allowance for the Catholic point of view in education and had tried to refrain from 'recommending any course which might be thought to be contrary to their wishes'.[17] The opinion of one eminent historian of Irish education, Donald Akenson, however, is blunt:

> In all probability the refusal of the Roman Catholic authorities to join the Lynn committee was the single most important determinant of the educational history of Northern Ireland. By refusing to sit they surrendered their last shred of influence at the very time when the basic character in Ulster's educational development was being determined. From the recommendations made by the Lynn committee emerged the principles of later developments.[18]

For its part, the INTO co-operated with the committee, with the Vigilance Committee deputing its chairman, John Harbison, to appear before it and submit a statement of evidence. The INTO found few faults in the interim report, which was published in June 1922,[19] and which Londonderry used to draft his Education Bill, presented to parliament in March 1923. In effect, the bill attempted to roll back the education system towards the kind envisaged when the national school system was set up in 1831. It promoted a system of non-denominational schools under community management, in which religion was not part of the curriculum. The key reform in the Education Bill was the creation of local education committees which would act as education authorities. School managers would transfer the management of their schools to these local committees, which would be secular. Managers, however, would not be compelled to hand over control of their schools. Instead, there would be three categories of school, each with different types of management and funding. Class I schools were those provided by or transferred to the local education authorities. These schools would be non-denominational and fully funded by the state, with any religious instruction to be provided outside school hours. Class II schools were managed by 'four-and-two' committees, which were four former managers, trustees or representatives of the old management and two representatives from the local education authority. These schools would receive funding for all salaries, half of maintenance (heating, cleaning and so on) and could apply for capital costs. Finally, there were Class III schools. They were voluntary schools which remained independent of local authority control. They received full salary costs, half of heating, lighting and cleaning but no capital costs. This meant that there was no compulsion for managers to hand over their schools to the local authorities but there were significant financial consequences if they did not. A minor, though not insignificant, change was that 'national schools' would henceforth be known as elementary schools. This was only a small change in terminology but it meant that the 'Irish *National Teachers*' in 'Irish National Teachers' Organisation' was no longer an accurate description for teachers north of the border, and, over time, the term 'National Teachers' increasingly came to equated with '*Nationalist* Teachers', which some members felt had become a barrier to Protestant participation.

The Northern INTO held a special one-day conference to discuss the Education Bill, which was described as their 'first congress in Belfast'. 'Ulidia', who wrote the *Irish School Weekly*'s 'Notes from the North', reported that the bill was 'generally acknowledged to be an excellent measure and one which if properly administered would do all that the earnest reformers of the last 40 years hoped to see accomplished'.[20] The Education Act of 1923 introduced 'significant structural change affecting the ownership, management and financing of schools in Northern Ireland', and repealed in whole or part 17 earlier pieces of legislation.[21] In many ways it was a progressive Act, which sought to remove religion from schooling and attempted to establish a secular, state-run school system. However, it met with sustained opposition from Protestants, who accused Londonderry of trying to remove the Bible from education. They also argued that giving local education authorities power to appoint teachers in maintained schools, but not allowing them to take the applicants' religion into consideration when making the appointment, could lead to Catholics being appointed to teach Protestant children. Eventually, after considerable lobbying, the Protestant Churches managed to secure amendments to the 1923 Act which meant that religion could be considered when making appointments and that the Bible could be taught in school. In effect, therefore, the state-maintained elementary school system was no longer strictly non-denominational, but it was open only to Protestants.[22] Catholic schools that wished to teach the Catechism and other religious topics outside Bible studies would have to remain in the voluntary sector, thus ensuring that a two-tier education system was established, with Protestant schools funded entirely by the state and Catholic schools paid for only partially. A few Catholic schools transferred to Class II, or 'four-and-two' schools, but most did not. This meant that Catholic schools in Northern Ireland were run much in the same way as they had been before the 1923 Act, but with the financial penalty of having to pay half the running costs for the school and any capital costs for the building, something which inevitably meant that pupils and teachers in Catholic schools had to work in very unsatisfactory conditions. It was another 40 years before there was any significant change to the situation. The Catholic managers continued to jealously guard control over the schools, not least in hiring and firing teachers. This became the source of considerable tension between the Church and the INTO over the years, and the cause of more than one long-running dispute.

THE ORGANISATION IN THE NORTH

At the beginning, the president, John Harbison, who was principal of St Enoch's School in Belfast, was chairman of the Vigilance Committee, with Joseph Boyce the honorary secretary, but the committee had no separate apparatus, and the northern teachers found themselves somewhat separate but by no means equal within the organisation. Northern affairs had a single page in the *School Weekly*, Ulidia's 'Notes from the North'; similarly, northern concerns took up relatively little time at the Easter congress. The Vigilance Committee, as its name suggested, had been designed to oversee rather than administer or decide, and northern teachers found themselves frustrated by the arrangements.[23]

A number of changes adopted at the 1923 Easter congress put the organisation in the North on a more business-like footing. Number 12 Bridge Street was secured as a northern office where the Vigilance Committee could hold its meetings and, more important, where Joseph Boyce could be found from 4.30 to 6 p.m. on Monday to Thursday and on Saturday mornings. Not that teachers were merely expected to come to the INTO, for at the same time W.W. McFetridge, a well-known activist from Ballymena, began work as an organiser in the North, and 'proved his earnestness [by] becoming the possessor of a very fine new two-seater motor car' with which he could tour the six counties.[24] The *School Weekly* encouraged members to help him get in touch with those who had never joined and those who had strayed.

At a time when the UTU was boasting of increased membership – it was claiming 2,000 members in 1924,[25] a couple of hundred fewer than the INTO at the same time – the INTO did a remarkable job of holding its own in the circumstances, and while McFetridge worked hard to bring people into the organisation, he recognised that this was not his primary task. As he told delegates at the Easter congress in 1925, 'I hold you cannot measure my work by the number of [new] names I can hand in but you must try and remember the number I have prevented from falling out ... which requires a good deal of tact and experience.'[26] McFetridge held the position for the next ten years, working alongside the secretary, Joseph Boyce, until the two retired in 1934.

The INTO's most significant rival was the UTU, although it was interested in poaching only the INTO's Protestant members, and had decided to focus mainly on recruitment in the border areas, since these were where 'the tensions are strongest and where our organisation may be needed most'.[27] Naturally enough, there was a certain amount of bad blood between the two organisations. In December 1923, 'Notes from the North' in the *School Weekly* printed without comment a letter from the Educational Institute of Scotland turning down the UTU's request for recognition 'on account of the more representative character' of the INTO.[28] The Belfast branch gave the letter to the *Northern Whig* the following month, to the UTU's great annoyance; it deemed the action 'worthy of men who are directly affiliated through the Irish Trades congress with the Third or Red International, and who are doubtless well acquainted with the methods of their Russian allies'.[29]

In fact, by 1924 the red flags were few and far between, and the ITUC's enthusiasm for Bolshevism had largely abated, but that was of little consequence to the UTU, for whom it was a useful device to distinguish itself from the INTO without appearing explicitly sectarian. It created a significant problem for the INTO in the North. If members in the South differed on the value of the INTO's affiliation with ILP & TUC, the majority supported it, not least because it had afforded them direct representation in the Dáil after the election of T.J. O'Connell. For northern members it was a different story. Labour was not organised in the six counties and teachers were prohibited from standing for election, but not only was politics of no benefit to them, it was actively used against the organisation by the UTU. Tabled at congress in 1924, when the northerners successfully had it sent back, the idea of a political fund was tabled again in 1925, when there was strong disagreement between representatives from the two parts of the organisation over whether the INTO should establish such a fund, with most of the southern delegates supporting the move and all of the northerners speaking against it, some of them questioning why it had been tabled at all and asking why the Vigilance Committee had not been consulted on the matter. One after the other, the northern men told congress that if they adopted the political fund, the organisation in the North would be 'wiped out', that 'if the INTO is not dead it soon will be and you will have to change the title to FSINTO [Free State INTO]', while T. Stanage from Banbridge complained that 'we in Northern Ireland are making a tremendous fight for the INTO and we are fighting against a far bigger enemy than the people in the Free State have any idea of. We are fighting against people who can give us tons in the way of propaganda. We are fighting against people who are not fighting an up and down, straight fight.'[30] For all that some of the southern delegates expressed sympathy with the northern delegates' position, Stanage was clearly correct in asserting that the Free State teachers had no comprehension of their northern colleagues' problems. When Eugene Caraher read from a piece in the *Northern Whig* about the INTO's association with the importations from Russia and red flags, there was laughter in the hall, but, however ludicrous, it was a serious problem for the INTO in the six counties nonetheless. Eventually, the political fund was put to a division and was passed by 175 votes to 116 against, the northerners' concern being roundly ignored for the benefit of the southern organisation.

Later during the same congress, the Tyrone association proposed a motion which would change the organisation of the Vigilance Committee to comprise the committee as it already was (i.e. the members of the CEC and finance committee residing in Northern Ireland, and *ex officio* northern district representatives), and a number of elected representatives with a secretary to be elected by members in the six counties. Speaking against the motion, T.J. O'Connell said he opposed it 'in the interests of the unity' of the organisation, since the Vigilance Committee was set up by the CEC and subject to its rules, and this proposal would end that arrangement, but when he observed, 'if you want to have an all-Ireland organisation, you must have an all-Ireland executive', one northern delegate retorted, 'whether it suits us or not'. The motion was lost.[31] The proceedings, ironically held in Belfast, highlighted the extent to which the organisation as a whole was deaf to the pleading of northern members on issues of concern but was unwilling, nevertheless, to give it a meaningful degree of autonomy.

TEACHER UNIONS IN THE SIX COUNTIES

The INTO and the UTU were not the only primary teachers' unions in the North. During the 1920s, there was a third, the Principal Teachers' Union (PTU), but over subsequent years, teachers' representation in the North became more fragmented, as micro-organisations emerged to represent sectoral interests, and came to resemble the situation in England and Wales more than it did the position in the 26 counties.[32] This was something the INTO had worked hard to prevent for many years, and it had done so successfully, but once the principle of the 'one big teachers' union' had been breached, it proved difficult to stop or reverse. If relations between the different organisations were less than cordial, particularly in the early years after partition, they at least shared something of a common enemy in the government.

In April 1926, faced with the prospect of a programme of school amalgamations and a seven per cent salary cut, the UTU executive decided it would be wise to secure the co-operation of the PTU and the INTO to safeguard the teachers likely to be affected. As a result, representatives of the three groups met to discuss the question of forming a Federated Council of Teachers and, in the meantime, the three took a joint deputation to the minister for education.[33] Initially, however, the idea of a federated council was held up by the INTO. At a meeting on the proposal in November 1926, representatives of the UTU and the PTU came with mandates to proceed to form the council, while the INTO representative had failed to do so, and said they could proceed no further without the approval of either the Vigilance Committee or the CEC.[34] There was no progress from the INTO side when the three met some months later, and it became apparent that the INTO was not enthusiastic about a federated council of elementary teachers, prompting the UTU to take a wider approach and establish a council that would span from elementary level to technical schools. The Federal Council of Teachers was established in 1927 with an executive committee including representatives from each of the member organisations, including three from the Northern Committee (NC) which the INTO had by then formally established. The executive held its first meeting on 10 December 1927 and its first general council meeting in Belfast the following month, but was effectively dormant until it was revived some six years later.[35]

The need for co-operation became apparent when in 1931 the education minister Lord Charlemont announced that he planned to cut teachers' salaries because the cost of living had fallen. At the time, he advised that it would only be a small cut, but several weeks later he announced it would be 7.5 per cent; coming after the seven per cent cut in 1926, this meant northern teachers' pay had been cut by almost 15 per cent in the space of five years.[36] Immediately after the NC met on 7 March to discuss the cut, it contacted the UTU, which was also meeting that day, and they agreed to take joint action, subsequently approaching the PTU. The result was that a joint executive committee of the three unions was established to co-ordinate a campaign against the cuts. The joint committee put out statements, lobbied MPs and 'other public men' and held joint public meetings against the cut.[37] Subsequently, the three unions co-operated to support 'full civil and political freedom for teachers'. In April 1932 they submitted to the prime minister a joint petition, signed by 3,600 elementary teachers, calling for teachers to be given the same political rights as teachers in the rest of the UK (as indeed they were in the South), and later published their case in a pamphlet.[38] On that occasion, Craigavon refused to meet the teachers to discuss the issue and referred the matter to the minister for education, who said that the time was not opportune to revive the matter.[39] But while the government had no intention of enabling teachers to become politically active, a political alliance among the teachers on a political matter was also intolerable. Members of the government held a series of extraordinary informal meetings with the UTU that were designed to isolate the INTO, the government explaining to the UTU that if they granted full civil rights it would mean granting nationalist teachers the right to publicly endorse nationalist causes.[40] Subsequently, the UTU withdrew from the Joint Committee, which was then dissolved. The government's resolve not to concede political rights to teachers remained firm. The INTO continued to campaign on the issue, but to no avail. When, some years later, the INTO approached the different teacher unions at all levels on the matter, several of them expressed their support for the issue, with the UTU alone in refusing to support the idea, responding that it was not their problem.

If co-operation on more political issues had proved problematic, there was an appreciation nevertheless that they were better off working side by side on other matters, not least salaries, so the Federal Council of Teachers, which had been effectively inactive since its foundation at the end of 1927, now took on a 'new lease of life'.[41] The council took quite a broad remit for itself, from holding meetings for teachers on professional pedagogical issues, such as the use of films and physical training in education, to occasional lobbying. For many years, it served primarily as a useful forum to maintain contacts between the different organisations at executive level and to discuss and respond to education policies and reforms, notably the raising of the school-leaving age to 15, a reform which was to be introduced in 1939 until the outbreak of war intervened.[42]

NEW NORTHERN SECRETARY

In April 1934, the CEC decided to appoint a new combined secretary/organiser to the NC to allow the two incumbents to retire. An advertisement for the post received 200 applications; six applicants were interviewed and at the beginning of August it was announced that Jack Beattie, the Labour MP for the east Belfast constituency of Pottinger in the northern parliament, had been appointed organising secretary, a position he would hold for almost the next 20 years. An announcement of the appointment in the *Belfast Newsletter* observed that it would 'not interfere with his parliamentary duties' and this indeed proved to be the case.[43]

Aged 48 on his appointment, Beattie was the first INTO office-holder to come from outside teaching, having started out as a blacksmith before becoming full-time organiser of the Associated Blacksmiths', Forge and Smithy Workers' Society, a post which was abolished after partition. Born into a liberal Presbyterian family, Beattie's politics were more Labour–Home Rule and, later, anti-partitionist than Unionist Labour. Elected to Stormont in 1925 for the Northern Ireland Labour Party (NILP), he found himself among the few opposition MPs in the House. During the summer of 1934, he was expelled from the NILP on a disciplinary matter, but the party agreed not to make it public until the competition for the INTO job was announced, lest his expulsion interfere with his chances.[44] Though appointed as secretary/organiser, Beattie's main work for the INTO was in parliament, where he gave an important voice to its members. This was particularly so on the restoration of the pay cuts, on which he was supported by the nationalist MPs, while local INTO branches ran local campaigns and a postcard campaign.[45] In contrast, the UTU took a much less aggressive position, and lobbied quietly behind the scenes.[46] There was a partial restoration of the cuts in May 1936, with a full restoration secured the following year, allowing the INTO to launch a campaign against the UTU in which it could portray itself as 'the major instrument in the restoration'.[47] This may account for a small and short-lived spike in INTO membership in 1937. Membership had been on a downward trajectory since 1930, having increased, albeit only slightly, each year since 1921. The six-county membership had fallen from 2,418 in 1930 to 1,706 in 1936, a decrease of almost 30 per cent.[48] If the INTO could capitalise on the pay restoration of 1936–7, however, it was only temporary, and the numbers continued to fall the following year. The increases in the cost of membership did not help. In 1933, congress ignored the warnings of northern members that it was on its way to losing a section of the INTO when it approved a strike levy across the 32 counties to fund a campaign in the South.[49] The following year, congress voted to increase the price of subscriptions, despite the concerns of northern delegates who pointed to the UTU giving better sickness grants.[50] There was also a fourth union on the scene by now – the Women Teachers' Union – but it is not clear whether it attracted any erstwhile INTO members.

One concession that congress did make to the North, however, was to change the rules so that teachers in the six counties who joined the INTO from another union would be given credit for that membership up to a maximum of three years, which made it possible for UTU members to join the INTO without losing their benefits.[51] INTO activists were acutely aware of the problem of falling numbers, the Belfast branch especially so. The matter regularly came up at branch meetings, even though, as one activist noted, it was 'a matter for the Northern Committee but since the Executive apparently did not interest itself in the membership of the organisation' the branch would have to take on the task itself.[52] One area where the NC was accused of being slack was in trying to attract student teachers in the training colleges, in contrast with the UTU at that time. The INTO had long held an annual dinner dance for students from Stranmillis and St Mary's, but that appears to have been the extent of engagement. It was, perhaps, an example of how the lack of a dedicated organiser put the INTO at a distinct disadvantage, for, despite his job title, Jack Beattie was not working as an organiser, and the membership continued to decline. Speaking in 1940, the president, who was a member of the NC, said of Beattie that he devoted all his attention to INTO interests once he had been given instructions by the NC, but he prefaced this by saying that he was a 'new man, feeling his way still'.[53] By then he was almost six years in the job, perhaps not a veteran of the organisation like many others, but certainly not 'new'. By

1947, his performance remained under scrutiny and unfavourable comparisons were drawn between him and the UTU's general secretary of the previous two and a half years, Joseph King-Carson.[54] Though there was a school of thought that his greatest service to the organisation was as a parliamentary representative rather than an organiser, the northern executive felt that he should travel around the six counties recruiting members, which was part of his job.[55]

By the autumn of 1948, Beattie seems to have conceded that he had been slack in the area of organising, and in September an assistant organiser, Miss M. McCallister, a recently retired teacher in Avoniel Primary School in Belfast, and who had been active in the organisation for many years, was appointed.[56] By this time, the matter had become quite acute, as there had been a particularly steep fall between 1946 and 1948 during the period of the Dublin strike. Although membership fell in every INTO district, it was particularly pronounced in the six counties, which saw a fall of one-eighth, from 1,600 to 1,403, in two years. There were several reasons for the decline in the whole island, principally apathy, strike levies and dissatisfaction over the strike,[57] but the strike levies were particularly problematic in the North. Once again, northern delegates warned congress about the consequences of making northerners pay for industrial disputes in the South – in this case a compulsory £5 levy towards a striking fund – and once again their concerns were overruled.[58] During the summer, the president, Seán Brosnahan, attended an NC meeting to discuss the issue of the levy, but John Duffin reported afterwards that Brosnahan did not understand the problem and was unsympathetic to their concerns.[59] This type of encounter led to a not unreasonable feeling that there was little reciprocity on the part of southern members. This sense was highlighted by particular instances, such as the time the INTO president travelled to Belfast in December 1939 to complain to the Northern Conference about how Northern teachers had been given a war bonus when conditions in the South were so bad, in a speech regarded as tactless, at least;[60] or when Seán Brosnahan gave a speech to the 1947 northern conference, reported in the *Belfast Newsletter* under the headline 'Ulster Leads Eire in Education', which resulted in him being accused by the *Derry Journal* of being a propagandist for the Stormont regime. Brosnahan complained afterwards that he had been misrepresented, and the chairman of the NC vouched for his president, but it was deplored in private by those who had been present, and it made for an embarrassing incident.[61]

In any case, Miss McCallister had an office which was opened every Wednesday and otherwise travelled around recruiting using a circular she had written herself. In her first two months, she enrolled 84 new members; in the following two months, she had signed up 71 members – 36 in Belfast (22 Protestant and 14 Catholic) and 35 from elsewhere.[62] She also visited Portadown, the branch having left the INTO en masse, apparently at the instigation of the senior members. McCallister was highly thought of and appeared to be doing well, but if Jack Beattie was somewhat ungenerous when he suggested that some people would sign anything to get rid of an organiser, the figures seemed to bear out his caution, with only 20 more members in 1949 than the previous year. McCallister remained in the post until she resigned in October 1950. No successor was appointed at that point. Jack Beattie's retirement was on the somewhat distant horizon by this time, but when it came the new post was clearly specified as the northern organising secretary.

KILLEAN DISMISSAL

The circumstances of Catholic teachers in the North meant that INTO tended to act quite gingerly towards the Church in the six counties. There was one notable exception to this – a long-running dispute known as the Killean dismissal. It was the first significant breach between the INTO and the clergy in almost 20 years and illustrated that conflict with the clergy was not wholly out of bounds for the organisation. Significantly, though, the controversy did not involve politics or accusations of irreligiosity but was a relatively straightforward clash over power and procedure.

Mrs Eleanor Keenan was the teacher at the centre of the row. In 1926, she was appointed assistant teacher in Killean Girls' School, Newry,[63] and seven years later, in 1933, following the death of the school's principal, Mrs Keenan was appointed as her successor. However, since there was a likelihood of the school being amalgamated with the local boys' school, her appointment was made in a temporary capacity pending any future amalgamation. In October 1938, the manager, Canon McNally, called a meeting of teachers from the two schools in Killean, at which he announced that he would be making some changes: the lady assistant teacher in the boys' school would become the new principal of the girls' school, and Mrs Keenan had a choice of working as an assistant teacher in either the girls' or boys' school. She was counselled by colleagues to approach her union on the matter, and the INTO advised that she was entitled to the protection of the Maynooth statute in any move to dismiss her from the principalship. The manager, on the other hand, insisted that it did not apply since he was not dismissing Mrs Keenan, merely moving her. In a remarkably spiteful move, he declared that if the INTO insisted on pressing its claim to a hearing under the statute, not only would Mrs Keenan be removed as principal but the offer of an assistantship would be withdrawn.[64]

Undaunted by this threat, the INTO insisted that the case be heard by the bishop of the diocese, and on 27 December 1938, Mrs Keenan and the general secretary went to Ara Coeli, the residence of the archbishop of Armagh, where they expected to put Mrs Keenan's case to Cardinal MacRory. Instead, the cardinal had deputed Dean McDonald to meet Keenan and O'Connell, although he did condescend to say a few words to O'Connell as he was leaving Ara Coeli. O'Connell was rather taken aback when the cardinal told him that, though he had not had the opportunity to speak to Dean McDonald, he had been made fully aware of the facts of the case by the manager and that unless some agreement were arrived at, he would serve the required three months' notice on Mrs Keenan. He then hinted that there were 'other reasons' for removing Mrs Keenan from her position; pressed by O'Connell as to what these might be, the cardinal claimed that she had called the roll at the wrong time.

The next day saw Mrs Keenan receive her three months' notice of dismissal from Canon MacNally. The INTO protested that by merely going through the motions at the hearing, it had departed from the spirit of the Maynooth statute, but on 28 March 1939, on the eve of congress, Mrs Keenan was ordered to surrender her keys to the school and the new principal was installed next day.

The INTO had made strenuous efforts to prevent the dismissal from coming into effect. Naturally, O'Connell had lobbied the cardinal directly; but, significantly, the organisation had used all the influence at its disposal, noting that 'various influential people, among them high ecclesiastical dignitaries, had been approached, both by the executive itself and by others at its instigation with a view to having the decision reversed', but MacRory would not yield.[65] With an emergency motion on the matter scheduled for debate on the Tuesday of congress, there was one final effort to resolve the situation before it became public after 'delegates who belonged to a well-known Catholic social organisation [presumably the Knights of Columbanus] had met and appointed one of their number to act as their representative'. The teacher did meet the cardinal, but nothing came of their discussion, and a resolution condemning the dismissal was put before congress on Thursday morning.[66] The next day, the national newspapers featured lengthy reports of the motion that had criticised Canon MacNally's behaviour as 'a harsh, unwarranted and arbitrary exercise of managerial authority'.[67]

When the matter was considered by the Armagh Provincial Council of the Catholic Clerical Managers Association on 29 May, it issued a public statement supporting the manager, describing the congress' criticism of Canon MacNally as 'undeserved' and its statements on the application of the Maynooth statute as 'not sustainable'.[68] It also published Canon MacNally's account of events, in which he put the blame for Mrs Keenan's dismissal firmly at the feet of the INTO and O'Connell (a tract which was distributed to teachers in the area, among others).[69] There was subsequently a volley of correspondence in the press between Rev. Donnelly and O'Connell. The correspondence from the Armagh clergy to the press, and to O'Connell privately, was remarkable in its tone. If the teachers were incredulous that one of their colleagues could be sacked in such an arbitrary fashion, it was nothing compared to the reaction of the manager, the cardinal and his fellow priests that the INTO would have the temerity to question their right to run their schools as they wished. As the cardinal's secretary put it to O'Connell, 'He [the cardinal] feels that this unfortunate case … is entirely due to the fact that you butted in and attempted to force a venerable and justice-loving manager to forego his right to appoint his own teacher.'[70] Perhaps even worse than this 'butting in' was the idea that the INTO would make public its displeasure at what had occurred and to do so at a congress in Belfast, of all places.[71]

Ultimately, there was little the INTO could do, however. Persuasion had come to naught, a further appeal (in late 1940) had been ignored,[72] it had ruled out recourse to the northern administration on the issue and the CEC had concluded that no good would come of an appeal to Rome.[73] The issue was kept alive at congress and in the pages of the *School Weekly*, but by 1941 the organisation was prepared to admit defeat, in private at least. As O'Connell told congress that year:

[T]he very fact that this has happened in this case may be a very good thing because it may possibly be another thirty five years before we will have another Killean Dismissal case or anything like it. Of course there are always wounded soldiers in every war. Mrs Keenan happened to be wounded in this war and it is our duty to see that she does not suffer.

To this end, the INTO produced a booklet, 'The Killean dismissal: a harsh, unwarranted and arbitrary exercise of managerial authority', to counteract a pamphlet on the case produced by the managers; and while actively working to secure her alternative employment in her area, the organisation continued to pay her salary. This arrangement continued until the summer of 1955, when she was paid a lump sum in lieu of further payments.[74] Recording the settlement and Mrs Keenan's thanks to the CEC, the general body of teachers and her northern colleagues, David Kelleher, then general secretary, concluded: 'Thus ends, as far as the INTO is concerned, what they regard as one of the most unhappy chapters in their relations with the clerical authorities.'[75] As Noel Ward has noted, 'in his handling of this case, T.J. O'Connell displayed a masterly ability to oppose publicly and strongly the actions of a church to which he and most of his membership declared themselves loyal. His marshalling of the support of Congress and of the branches was a decisive factor.'[76]

THE SECOND WORLD WAR AND REFORMS IN NORTHERN EDUCATION

Naturally, the Second World War affected Northern Ireland to a much greater degree than the neutral 26 counties. The North was a fully active part of the

British war effort, and its role in manufacturing made it the target of German air raids in April and May 1941. Areas of Derry, Newtownards and Bangor were hit, but by far the worst afflicted was Belfast, where there was devastation. There was massive property destruction in the city, particularly in densely populated areas, and a number of elementary schools were damaged or destroyed. Bridge Street was one of the areas to be hit; number 12, where the NC had its office, was completely destroyed and almost all the NC's official records with it.[77] There were some 960 civilian deaths, and perhaps twice as many people were injured. Many teachers volunteered in the rest centres that provided shelter and food in the raids, while some 500 elementary teachers were assigned to schools in reception areas, set up to cater for the children who had been evacuated after the blitz, where, in some cases, they had to work double shifts in existing schools or work in makeshift hired halls.[78]

In addition, many teachers volunteered for service at home and abroad. According to official figures, in all 102 men teachers and 27 women teachers joined H.M. Forces during the war, of whom 14 were killed in action.[79] While the very immediate practical challenges caused by the war were ongoing, the British government was planning social reforms to pursue after the conflict, among them reforms in education. The 'Northern Notes' of the *ISW* reported on these 'in view of the tendency of the authorities in Northern Ireland to follow England in educational matters'.[80] By 1943, however, there was a White Paper on Education in England and no sign of movement on the question in the North. In the absence of any official policy, the Federal Council of Teachers produced its own report on educational reform, which was published in August 1943.[81] By the following year, the northern government began to prepare for reforms similar to those under consideration in England, and these were published as a White Paper in December.[82]

The proposals broadly followed the lines of the Education Act of 1944 for England and Wales. There would be compulsory schooling between the ages of five and 15 (raised from 14). Transfer to secondary schooling would take place at 11 following a qualifying examination, or what became known as the 11+. Those who passed it would be admitted to grammar school, while the others would transfer to what would be called intermediate schools. This was opposed by the Northern Ireland Labour Party, the UTU and the INTO. It was opposed sincerely on the grounds that selection at such an early age was not appropriate, but there was also concern in the unions about the impact the reforms would have on teachers' employment if pupils were leaving elementary schools at 11. Following a special conference at the end of January 1945 to discuss the proposals, the NC released a statement welcoming the White Paper and endorsing features such as the extension of compulsory attendance, reductions in class size, supply of free books, changes to scholarship schemes, the extension of health and welfare services and assurances about religious instruction, but it expressed serious misgivings about the 11+ and demanded security of tenure for teachers.[83] Another source of INTO concern was the White Paper's proposals for the funding of voluntary schools, which offered increased grants – in maintenance up to 100 per cent and capital costs up to 65 per cent – on condition that they adopt the four-and-two committee first.[84] When the Education Bill was eventually published in September 1946, the teacher unions were unhappy to find that the proposals for selection at 11 remained, although otherwise, the Northern Conference stated that the bill met with its 'general approval'.[85]

The 1947 Education Act was effectively the Northern Ireland version of the Butler Act in England. Under it, elementary education would end at age 11, which presented the prospect of elementary teachers losing their jobs as a result of pupils transferring to second level at a younger age. Naturally, the elementary unions were concerned for their members' job security and the Federal Council of Teachers expressed its grave concern that the ministry had refused to give assurances that teachers would not suffer loss of employment, income or status as a result.[86] There was a difference of opinion within the INTO on the matter, however. While the NC was almost unanimous in its demand that teachers of senior classes should be eligible to teach in intermediate schools, the Belfast branch was adamant that all elementary teachers, including those in junior classes, should be recognised. The Belfast branch sought to override the NC's stance by introducing an emergency motion at the 1948 congress in Bundoran that all elementary teachers would be eligible, which, naturally enough, was opposed by the members of the NC present, except for John Duffin, who had proposed the motion.[87] The motion was never put to a vote, however, following the general secretary's intervention. It was, he said, 'a purely domestic question in the North', and it was the 'first time in thirty years that Congress [had] been asked to review a decision of the NC affecting purely northern matters'; his proposal to move to next business was passed by a show of hands.

Teachers sought to have their qualifications recognised to teach in intermediate schools, or at least that they be given the opportunity to attend any requisite course which would enable them to get recognition.[88] To this end, the ministry organised summer schools for teachers in Stranmillis for those seeking to qualify to teach in intermediate schools, although eligibility was restricted to people aged over 30, or whose training had been completed no later than 1939.[89] Much of the elementary teachers' concerns over the impact of the intermediate schools arose because there was no redeployment panel for teachers, unlike their Catholic counterparts in the South who had fought for and secured one ten years earlier. It was not a concession that the Catholic managers in the South wished to make, but the INTO was in a somewhat stronger position on that side of the border when it came to the teacher–managerial relationship. That is not to say that the INTO had a good relationship with managers in the South, but in the North there was a greater reticence to confront the Church because of the political situation, which made Catholic teachers and the INTO wary of 'letting the side down'.[90] The Northern INTO lobbied for a panel, but found themselves up against Catholic managers who had set their faces firmly against it. In May 1941, the provincial Catholic managers had passed a resolution asserting that they could not 'see their way to recommend the acceptance of the panel system in Northern Ireland', apparently without conveying this to the INTO. The following year, Jack Beattie was dispatched to raise the question with Cardinal MacRory, but while the cardinal expressed his willingness to help, he said that he could not oppose his managers, and that the other bishops were in the same position.[91] (This was discussed at the standing conference in 1943 but generally accepted to be dead.)

The final Black Report in February 1947 had recommended the introduction of a panel, but it was up to the managers to adopt it; not surprisingly, they chose to ignore the suggestion. The issue of displacement was not as acute as it might have been, however. Though the Act came into operation in 1948, with the first 11+ exams taking place that May, there proved to be no rush to establish the new intermediate schools in the short run. But if the feared upheaval to the system did not quite materialise, the existence of intermediate schools posed the question of who would organise their staff. Expanding eligibility for INTO membership seemed a logical conclusion.[92] When the new CEC met for the first time after the 1948 congress, it invoked Rule 3 of the INTO's constitution to declare that 'hereby … teachers engaged in Intermediate or Grammar schools in Northern Ireland are eligible for membership of the INTO', and the decision was recorded in the *School Weekly* the following week.[93]

Beyond specific post-war reforms in education, the establishment of the welfare state in the United Kingdom under the Attlee government in London had important consequences for residents of Northern Ireland. Teachers were now the beneficiaries of a National Health Service and, from 1948, were compulsorily insured under the National Insurance Act 1946. This resulted in changes to the teachers' pensions, with new entrants beginning service after 1 July 1948 having their pensions and, correspondingly, their contributions reduced by over £2 a year.[94] Under the National Insurance Act, teachers were also eligible for unemployment and sickness benefits, maternity allowance, widow's allowance and a death grant.[95] At the 1948 Congress, it was decided that teachers in Northern Ireland could decide whether they wished to avail of the INTO's Illness and Mortality Fund, with members voting by four to one in favour of discontinuing to pay into it.[96] Although stopping contributions to that fund was a clear case of northern members not paying for services twice, it was also tied up with the continually vexed question of northern subscription rates.

When a motion was tabled for the 1950 congress to impose a 15-shilling levy on members in the six counties, to be paid to head office, the Belfast branch tabled an amendment for it to be deleted. They succeeded in having their amendment passed after working behind the scenes to secure it was carried, but Belfast members were angry that they alone had been responsible for this because no one from the NC had been available to speak.[97] Only two members of the NC had attended congress that year, both of whom were also members of the CEC, and so were not in a position to speak against the original motion. Although the NC could have sent two more members, none attended, an act regarded by some in the Belfast branch as indicative of the NC's apathy.

When the question of subscription rates arose again two years later, however, the NC was noticeably more active. It held an emergency meeting to discuss the matter, and sent a deputation of John Duffin and R.J. Megaw to a CEC meeting before congress to explain the situation in the North and discuss matters of funding. They, along with the rest of the CEC, were treated to a lengthy explanation from the treasurer, M.P. Linehan, of the North's income and expenditure, with which the northerners were 'not quite in agreement'. In the end, it was decided that the original motion would go ahead, and the NC could submit an amendment that 'the rate of subscription to the Management and Defence Funds be the same for all members of the INTO'.[98]

One voice speaking against the proposal was a young first-time delegate from Belfast city branch named Gerry Quigley, who noted a ten per cent fall in membership in the North since 1947, and warned that were the proposal to be carried, it would have a very adverse effect on the younger members.[99]

SALARIES

The Northern Committee's main demand had been to secure the same rates of pay for teachers in Northern Ireland as in England and Wales, where teachers' salaries were arrived at under the Burnham Committee system. Set up in 1919, the Burnham Committees were made up equally of representatives of the teachers and their employers, the local authorities. Originally there had been committees to set different scales for elementary, secondary and technical schools, but these had been reformed under the Education Act of 1944. Their functions were consolidated into a single committee that set a common scale for teachers at all levels, which came into force on 1 April 1945. The scales were generous and teachers in the North united in advocating that they be applied to teachers in Northern Ireland. But while applying Burnham to the North would, as the *Belfast Telegraph* pointed out, have been in keeping with the northern government's 'step by step' policy of keeping pace with welfare benefits in Britain, the government had no intention of doing so.[100] However, despite mass meetings of the three unions and the work of the joint campaign committee, set up to push for Burnham, the minister for education, Lt Colonel Hall-Thompson, flatly refused to consider such a thing. Instead, in May 1945, he finally established the long-anticipated, and generally unwanted, committee under Mr Justice Black that would inquire into matters relating to the teaching professions.

Consisting of a number of teachers, ministry officials and other interested individuals, the Black Committee was an advisory committee with no power to refer back, unlike Burnham, which fixed salary scales that the minister for education would accept or reject in their entirety.[101] The Black Committee submitted its interim report in November and shortly afterwards the government agreed its recommendations, which would operate retrospectively from 1 April 1945.[102] The committee's report set out a common scale for qualified teachers in primary and secondary schools which began at scale 1, for those with a qualification from a course of less than three years, so it applied to many elementary teachers, whose training was two years. The rate was £280 for men and £250 for women, to a maximum of £650 and £520 respectively, and the Highly Efficient rating was abolished.[103] The NC found the scales 'on the whole satisfactory' since they were broadly based on the Burnham scales. The greatest dissatisfaction was felt by the younger teachers at the lower end of the scale, whose salaries began at a lower level than Burnham (which were £300 and £270) with longer periods between increments.[104] There was less attention given to complaints about the different scales between men and women teachers; it took a woman teacher 22 years to reach the maximum of her scale, compared with 14 years in England.[105]

Another significant area of contention was the differentiation between intern and extern degrees. At that time, where primary teachers had a degree, it was invariably an extern one. When it was established in 1880, the Royal University of Ireland allowed students to sit its examinations without attending lectures in its colleges, which enabled a generation of teachers to be awarded extern degrees after studying in their own time. When the Royal University was dissolved in 1909, however, neither the Queen's nor National Universities chose to continue the practice, but in 1928 Trinity College Dublin agreed to begin awarding extern degrees to anyone who had passed their final examination in a recognised training college in Ireland or Great Britain.[106] The lesser financial benefit given for extern degrees was raised during the debates on the teachers' salaries in Stormont, and was the only part of the report to be referred back to the committee. It decided unanimously to double the increment for external degrees but to maintain the advantage of the internal qualification.[107] The recommendations were finally passed by the Commons on 15 January 1946 and became law the next day.[108] On 10 March 1948, further recommendations from the 1948 Black Committee were introduced to Stormont, bringing northern salary scales into line with the recent revisions in Burnham and the Teviot scales in Scotland.[109]

In January 1950, Hall-Thompson was succeeded as Education Minister by

Harry Midgley. Born in 1892 into a working-class Methodist family in Belfast, Midgley had begun his political life as a socialist in the Belfast Labour Party before joining the Northern Ireland Labour Party, for which he was elected in the Dock constituency of Stormont in 1932. He had become increasingly anti-Catholic and pro-unionist during the 1930s, however, and by 1947 he had joined the Ulster Unionist Party, with which he shared little politically beyond a commitment to the Union.[110] Significantly, he had some familiarity with education when he was appointed, having spent time as the UTU's parliamentary secretary, appointed to give it a voice in Stormont to match that of Midgley's one-time party rival, Jack Beattie, for the INTO. In terms of education policy, then, Midgley seemed to offer the prospect of a sympathetic ear insofar as pay and conditions were concerned, but a hard line against any concessions to voluntary schools.[111]

His appointment came around the time of growing discontent among the teachers about salaries. The cost of living had been steadily increasing, and dissatisfaction among the teachers had been heightened by the Burnham Committee's rejection of an English teachers' pay claim at the end of 1949. Pay was the most pressing issue, with the northern conference voting for immediate action to increase teachers' salaries and an immediate cost of living bonus.[112] Naturally, the other unions shared the INTO's desire to see teachers' salaries rise, and there was a united front when a mass meeting of teachers across all sectors was held in Belfast in January 1950, but once Midgley had announced he would set up a committee to inquire into salary revisions, divisions soon emerged.[113] When the Federal Council met in March, it was unable to reach a decision on scales because, while the primary unions favoured a single scale, the secondary and technical teachers felt there should be one scale for primary and intermediary teachers and another, higher scale for everyone else.[114] The INTO representatives felt that agreement at the Federal Council was most unlikely, and approached the UTU with a view to the possibility of the primary teachers dealing directly with the salary review committee. A breach in the Federal Council seemed to have been averted after a sub-committee from the different branches met twice and managed to reach an agreement to seek an all-over increase for all teachers, which was then approved by an extraordinary meeting of the Federal Council, but by the end of May, the decision had been made that the Federal Council would take no further part in the salary negotiations.[115] After that, the executives of the Northern INTO and the UTU held a joint meeting to establish a solid primary position to salaries and the allocation of places on the salary commission, while the INTO also approached the PTU and WTU to join a united primary front which styled itself the United Primary Executives.[116] In mid-June the Ministry wrote to the unions to outline the terms of the new Standing Committee on Teachers' Salaries and Conditions of Service. The committee, it

said, would 'approximate as closely as possible in composition and responsibilities to the Burnham Committee', and as such would consist of an independent
chairman, an employers' panel and a teachers' panel.[117] Negotiations followed as to
the make-up of the teachers' representatives, with the primary teachers ultimately
securing seven of 14 seats shared between the four organisations. But in November,
the minister announced a change to the composition of the committee after the
grammar schools' boards of governors and teachers had decided that the
Burnham-style committee was unacceptable and refused to serve on it. The UTU
and the INTO were outraged that a minority had managed to override the wishes
of 'five sevenths' of the teachers, with Midgley's response that the teachers'
opposition to his changes did 'not present a very edifying spectacle to the
community' unlikely to soothe tensions.[118]

While there was a great deal of anger over Midgley's change of heart, the
unions were deeply divided over whether they ought to co-operate with the new
committee. The INTO's Belfast branch passed a resolution that they wanted 'a
statutory committee of the same type as Burnham and nothing else', a motion
proposed by a young teacher named Gerry Quigley. Quigley was also active at
this time in a group called the Young Teachers' Action Council (YTAC). The
YTAC held its first meeting in the Ulster Museum on 18 November 1950, where
an executive committee of INTO and UTU members was set up. Members of the
Belfast branch of the INTO, notably Gerry Quigley and John Duffin's elder
daughter Mary, had been involved in setting it up – indeed, there had been some
concern that it might just look like a recruiting tactic by INTO – but it seems to
have avoided being seen as such.[119] The YTAC's primary demand was a permanent
negotiating committee on salaries and conditions of service and the application
of the Burnham scales in Northern Ireland,[120] but its primary role was to be both
an umbrella group for young teachers as well as operating as ginger groups
within their own unions. It held mass meetings, distributing a petition for a
Burnham-type committee, and Young UTU members protested outside a
meeting of their union held to discuss its attitude towards Midgley's proposals,
where the older members were more inclined to reluctantly accept the revised
committee.[121] The extent of division on the matter within the INTO became
apparent when it was discussed at the northern conference on 5 and 6 January
1951, when delegates voted by 27 votes to 26 not to participate in the new
committee. Conference was 'somewhat shocked' at the vote, prompting the
Derry branch to object in writing that the vote was illegal, not least because the
motion had not been printed in the final agenda for conference. The chairman
ruled that the vote was legal, but afterwards the NC overturned his ruling and
arranged for an emergency conference on the question in Belfast on 27 January.[122]
The meeting was heated, with Gerry Quigley 'howled down' after he argued that
the decision to overturn the conference decision was illegal and called for them

to get legal advice. In the end those present voted by 44 votes to 30 that 'the INTO take part under protest in the Committee'.

The whole episode was something of a fiasco, and when Quigley proposed to a meeting of the Belfast branch that they call on the NC to resign, it was passed by 15 votes to five.[123] It was indicative of some of the tensions and problems faced by the INTO in the North at that time. Just as there had been in the South around the time of the 1946 strike, there was something of a generational divide between younger, more radical members of the organisation and the more conservative older members. More specifically, though, there were structural problems with how the North operated. For one thing, the lack of a full-time dedicated secretary led to a lack of professionalism that had resulted in the most important motion before conference being left off the agenda, but, as the NC's annual report noted, the 'malpractice' of failing to send an adequate agenda in a timely fashion had 'grown out of the fact that the NC has never had any specially suited Rules or Constitution to guide it. While it is merely a subordinate Committee to the CEC yet it requires rules specially designed to suit its work.' In effect, it had continued to operate as an ad hoc committee for 30 years, but it was inconceivable that it could continue in such a fashion.

Chapter 9 ~

THE INTO IN NORTHERN IRELAND SINCE 1950

'The INTO is a non-political, non-sectarian organisation.'

GERRY QUIGLEY AND THE NORTHERN REVIVAL

J ack Beattie retired as northern secretary on 30 June 1952, but it was eight months before his successor was appointed. In May 1952, just six weeks before he was due to leave, the CEC had asked the NC to give further consideration to Beattie's successor, and was told that 'the efficient organisation of the INTO in the North should be the chief consideration in the selection of a Northern Secretary Organiser'.[1] The following month, the CEC set up a sub-committee to look into the organisation in the North and the role of the northern secretary. It reported its findings on 1 November,[2] suggesting the division of the North into four areas: one, the Belfast and South Antrim area, would be organised by the incoming northern secretary, who would be appointed on two years' probation; the other three areas would each be organised by a local organiser, with the situation to be reviewed after the new organiser-secretary's initial two years. The NC agreed to the plan, suggesting that the probation period be one year, to which the CEC agreed.[3] Advertisements for the job in the Belfast and Dublin daily papers and the *ISW* specified an upper age limit of 45, John Duffin and others from the North having impressed upon the CEC that the INTO would lose the North if they did not appoint someone who was young and prepared to do the necessary work in rebuilding the organisation.[4] There were 17 applications for the position, with one clear favourite. At its meeting on 10 January 1953, the NC agreed unanimously to appoint Gerry Quigley as the new northern organising secretary, initially in a 12-month temporary capacity.

Belfast born and raised, Quigley was just 26 when he was appointed. He had ruffled a few feathers within the organisation since becoming active in the INTO a few years earlier, and was inclined to be blunt rather than political – somewhat like his mentor, John Duffin – but he was energetic, serious and committed, with a fierce intelligence. A job specification was drawn up, which set out regular work hours and tasks that included: writing monthly organising reports for the NC and CEC; establishing 'regular and systematic contact with branch secretaries in the North'; drafting the NC's annual report; keeping a cuttings file of press reports relating to all references to teachers in the press; making 'timely and full preparation for all NC meetings and for Northern Conference'; and dealing with all correspondence to the Northern Office.[5] In effect, it established a full-time working northern district office for the first time, based at 83 High Street, with Quigley's first request to the CEC being a bookcase, filing cabinet and duplicating machine, refurbishment of the office itself and the employment of a part-time typist. Quigley also secured a loan of £400 to buy a new Anglia for organisation work.[6]

He had his work cut out for him. Membership had been declining for two decades: in 1951, INTO membership was 1,288, less than half that of the UTU at the same time (2,730), and Quigley was keenly aware that recruitment had to be his priority.[7] Later, he recalled how he spent his time on the road, day and night. 'I went to the schools. I went after school hours, but during school hours I would pass a school and go into it and get chatting to them and try to recruit them.' Róisín Carabine, a future president, would remember being called to the office when she started teaching in 1956 to find Gerry Quigley waiting there to sign her up.[8] Slowly but surely, the numbers increased. Where there had been 1,531 in 1953, the year of Quigley's appointment, by 1960 there were 2,276 members, a nearly 50 per cent increase in seven years, and the first time in almost three decades that the organisation in the North had over 2,000 members. Apart from the professionalisation of the office and Quigley's organisation work on the ground, another important development around this time was the NC's decision in February to establish a quarterly journal for members in the six counties. The lack of northern focus in the School Weekly had long been a source of unhappiness, and as the INTO's first dedicated six-county publication, The Northern Teacher, would provide not only an important source of information for members, but help to give a sense of identity to the northern section as a distinct area.[9] The first issue was published in April 1953 and featured an editorial by T. Jamison, then in his eighties, who had first joined the INTO as a student member in 1893, a reminder of the organisation's deep roots in the North.[10]

These were necessary and long-overdue changes, but the governance of the organisation in the six-county area remained less than ideal. In an effort to make the NC more effective and more representative, John Duffin had proposed to the northern conference that the NC would draft a scheme which would have to be approved at the Easter congress, but while delegates approved it there was a certain reticence about the idea.[11] The proposals for the necessary rule changes put before the 1957 congress included direct elections to the NC, but no increase in the NC's powers. It was something the Belfast members, at least, felt would help in the drive for recruitment while improving the calibre of representation on the NC.[12] The proposals, however, were opposed by the Dublin City branch, with Seán Brosnahan expressing the belief that it would 'provide a form of CEC in Northern Ireland and consequent danger of autonomy in the Six Counties'. Matt Griffin added that, like Brosnahan, he could 'not claim any first-hand information as to the running of things in the North but he had noticed over the past few years a rather marked tendency to create within the INTO an autonomous organisation. That was a tendency which should cause disquiet.'[13] Griffin suggested that giving the NC more representatives would set it up to make a complete break, but he failed to address the idea that keeping it so clearly subordinate to the 32-county CEC could hinder its efficacy or its appeal. John Duffin expressed himself 'positively astounded' at the trend of the discussion and noted his surprise at finding 'so much suspicion harboured about the people of the benighted north'. Addressing Brosnahan and Griffin and the members in Dublin City whom they represented, Duffin was blunt:

> If you are sick of us, tell us. If you feel suspicion say so. You are always pointing the finger and wondering what is our next dangerous move. To all of you who share that outlook I will say, 'for heaven's sake, kick us out if you don't want us or trust us. If you want to trust us tell us so.'[14]

After a lengthy and often heated debate, the NC's proposed rule change, along with some minor procedural amendments, was passed by the necessary two-thirds majority on a card vote, with 157 voting for and 67 against.

In fact, the vote on direct representation to the NC was the second occasion Griffin had criticised the northern organisation during that congress. Earlier, he had taken issue with references to the UTU in the NC report and wanted them removed. Recalling that the UTU was a splinter union, which the INTO had never recognised – and INTO had 'gone out of their way' to make this clear in international forums, specifically at teachers' conferences in Scotland and England over the years – Griffin accused the NC of conceding equality of status to the UTU by mentioning it by name in its report. He was adamant that the entire section in which it featured should be deleted.[15] The report was only supposed to be a record of what had taken place over the course of the year, and to excise all mentions of salary policy and the Federal Teachers' Council because the INTO had served alongside the UTU was clearly ludicrous. With enormous patience, northern members had to explain that notwithstanding the UTU's origins as a splinter union, it was recognised by the northern government, and the INTO in the North was obliged to work alongside the UTU on negotiating bodies. If 'the INTO and members were to put into operation an ostrich-like policy of non-recognition of reality it would be impractical and unworkable in the extreme' and might be 'heroic or noticeable' but would have no benefit to the members and would ultimately lead to members leaving the organisation. Griffin was unyielding but when his proposal that the references be removed from the report was put to the floor, it was beaten by a large majority on a show of hands.[16]

The nature of the debates at the 1957 congress had highlighted an anomaly in the organisation. While the general secretary and the treasurer could attend and participate in congress debates, the northern secretary was not accorded the same status and could not reply to debates or make statements of fact. When the NC met again after congress in 1957, it discussed the issue and agreed to raise it informally with the CEC in the autumn.[17] The northern secretary was unrepresented not only at Easter congress but also at the CEC, and it was not until the INTO revised its rules at the 1967 congress that the northern secretary became an *ex officio* member of the CEC and was expected to attend meetings.

If it was obvious to the vast majority of delegates that Griffin's proposal was neither feasible nor advisable, it was indicative of a particular school of thought in the South, which was ostensibly nationalist but which had little appreciation for the practical day-to-day issues facing people living in the North. As one northern delegate had pointed out during the debate on the NC Report, the UTU was only one of nine other teacher unions with which the INTO had to co-exist (in fact, as the northern chairman noted at the Northern Conference in 1959, there were 14). The idea that keeping the INTO in the northern region as clearly subordinate to the rest of the organisation might strengthen it against its rivals was fanciful. The organisation, with Quigley as organiser, was doing well to increase its numbers; and in 1960 the INTO expanded its membership in the North further to include teachers at all levels, leading at least one member to suggest that the organisation should change its name to something more inclusive, such as the Teachers' Association of Ireland, which was the English translation of Cumann Muinteoirí Éireann.[18] The issue of the fragmentation of teachers' representation was further exacerbated by the arrival of the National Association of Schoolmasters (NAS) in the six counties in the 1960s. At the beginning of 1961, there were eight members in the North who had returned from teaching in Britain, but at a meeting in May it was decided to start recruiting, and by the end of the year there were 161.[19]

The historian of the NAS noted that at its 'founding meeting' for Northern Ireland it made 'a crucial decision to recruit teachers irrespective of religion, political affinity or school type', but his assertion that its 'strictly non-sectarian approach' was a distinctive feature in the North was not really correct. Recruitment across religious or political lines had always been INTO policy. During the 1920s, much of the INTO's NC had been Protestant, and there was still a strong Protestant contingent into the 1950s, one of whom, H.F. McCune Reid from the Belfast branch, was elected INTO president in 1955. McCune Reid was a Presbyterian who had served as a captain in the RAF during the war. Forty-two years a member by the time he became president, Captain McCune Reid was part of the old guard of Protestant INTO loyalists, but as that generation retired they were not matched by new members, despite the organisation's best efforts. On the proposal of the Belfast branch, the 1957 congress voted to insert the statement 'the INTO is a non-political, non-sectarian organisation' into the constitution, in order to 'put into print what was already accepted as a fact' and to help the INTO organise among Protestant teachers and trainees.[20] That they felt it was necessary was due to a growing perception that the INTO was a Catholic, nationalist organisation. This perception arose from a number of factors, not least its name, which was incongruous in a place where the term 'national teacher' no longer existed, and where, as a *Northern Teacher* article pointed out, the organisation represented teachers at all levels of schooling.[21] But if the INTO in the North took its non-political status very seriously, the same was not always true of its southern colleagues, such as in 1955 when the then president Matt Griffin told the northern conference that he did not recognise the unnatural partition of the country. Afterwards, Harry Midgley told a UTU conference that he regarded this as tantamount to not recognising the northern government, and that, partly because of this, he regarded the UTU as 'the premier teachers' organisation in our area'.[22] Two days later, an affronted Captain McCune Reid, the incoming president, told delegates that in his 42 years in the organisation, with experience in almost all its positions 'up to this, the highest', he had never found the INTO to be other than a non-political, non-sectarian body.[23] Nevertheless, recruitment outside the voluntary sector remained a challenge, and the perception of the INTO as a Catholic organisation remained, and would deepen further after the outbreak of the Troubles in 1969.

MARRIAGE BAN AND EQUAL PAY

Equal pay had long been official INTO policy nationally, though the organisation was certainly not as robust in pressing this as it might have been. Nonetheless, in January 1954 the northern conference passed a resolution demanding equal pay for men and women.[24] The issue had been higher on the legislative agenda in Britain than it had been in Ireland, where it was entirely absent. There had been a number of abortive attempts to introduce equal pay before it became a reality. In 1936, the Commons had voted to introduce it for civil servants, but this was reversed when Prime Minister Stanley Baldwin forced a vote of confidence on the issue. Then, in 1944, something similar happened when, by a single vote, the Commons passed an amendment to the Education Bill, opposed by the government, requiring equal pay for women teachers. This was soon reversed after Churchill forced a vote of confidence on the question.[25] In 1946, the Royal Commission on Equal Pay, appointed two years earlier by Herbert Morrison, reported on the question for workers in central government services including the civil service, the post office and teachers, and concluded that women working for government services should be paid the same wages as men, but that women in industry should not.[26] In 1955, the British government eventually began to act on this recommendation in the case of teachers, beginning a process of equalising salaries between men and women, but doing so over a period of six years, which would conclude in 1961. Since Northern Ireland salaries policies tended generally to follow Britain, this seemed to bode well. Responding to a question in the House in March 1955 on whether he planned to introduce equal pay for women teachers, Minister for Education Harry Midgley said he hoped to make an announcement on the subject 'in the near future'. In September of that year, the Stormont government conceded the principle and, predictably enough, announced that it would bridge the pay gap over a six-year period, with parity to have been reached by 1 April 1961.[27]

It was around this time that the INTO began again in earnest to press for the removal of the marriage ban in the North. While the existence of the marriage ban in the South is well known, little or no attention is given to its operation north of the border, in part, perhaps, because it was not a policy of the Northern Ireland government. As noted in Chapter 2 (see pages 84–90), the first marriage ban for women teachers in Ireland existed under the Union, having been brought in to the diocese of Down and Connor by Bishop Tohill. It continued to operate at the discretion of individual managers under Bishop MacRory when he succeeded Tohill in 1914, providing the background to the dismissal case of Mrs Flanagan in Kilkeel in 1916. Under Bishop Daniel Mageean, who succeeded MacRory when he translated to Armagh in 1929, the ban was made compulsory once again, and was later introduced into the neighbouring diocese of Derry under the Most Rev. Dr Farren from 1939.[28] These bans affected women teaching in Catholic schools in the two dioceses, but there were also occasional cases of women being dismissed on marriage elsewhere.[29] The 1923 Education Act established local education authorities (LEAs) along the same lines as those in England and Wales. The LEAs in Britain had the right to enforce marriage bars in their own areas, and freely did so, so that by 1926, only one-quarter of LEAs did not operate some sort of marriage bar.[30] The Northern Ireland LEAs lagged behind by a few years, but by 1929, the NC was being approached by increasing numbers of women teachers who were being asked to sign new agreements that would compel them to resign on marriage. Jack Beattie raised the issue of the new agreements in parliament but was told that they were at the discretion of local managers.[31] The INTO sought legal opinion,[32] but were advised that legally there was nothing that could be done. Anyone qualifying from teacher training in the North was obliged to teach there for at least five years or else pay back the full cost of their studies. In an especially egregious interpretation of the rules, women who married within five years of graduating and had to resign were chased for their fees. There was an appreciation among government depart-ments that this was unfair and in February 1932 (around the time the ban was being considered in the South) the Departments of Education and Finance agreed to a graduated scale of repayments for a woman who was compelled to resign on marriage after she had served two years. But the change in the regulations was not generally made known 'so as to discourage as much as possible [women] teachers from entering into the marriage contract before the completion of five years' service'.[33] That the numbers involved were low (16 between 1922 and 1929) suggests this strategy may have been largely successful.

The North Antrim Education Committee was the first public body to bring in a ban,[34] and was followed over the next couple of years by Ballymena, Coleraine, Derry, Limavaddy and County Down, Belfast (which voted for a ban by 11 votes to four), Fermanagh and Dungannon.[35] The Lisburn and Belfast Regional Committee was an exception, its members arguing that married women were the best qualified people to have the care of children.[36] The NC passed a resolution declaring that the INTO 'emphatically' opposed the ban, which it said was a 'distinct violation of the vested rights' of women teachers. Northern conference in February 1932 passed a strong protest against the policy, which was afterwards relayed to the minister.[37] The UTU was making similar representations and there were a number of joint meetings on the matter, but nothing came of this; neither did anything come of the resolution passed at congress over subsequent years.

The question came to the fore once again when the Education Bill was being drafted in 1946, and teachers pressed to have the ban lifted. Though it was not included in the original bill, the minister agreed somewhat reluctantly to an amendment tabled by Harry Midgley that no woman should be disqualified from employment in any county or voluntary school or be dismissed from such employment by reason only of marriage.[38]

Notwithstanding the legislation, however, Catholic managers continued to operate a ban in Derry and in Down and Connor, where they made women teachers sign a supplementary agreement promising that they would retire on marriage. There was a reticence within the organisation about taking on the Catholic managers on the question, but when Gerry Quigley was appointed northern secretary in 1953, he was determined to achieve a resolution. During

1954, the NC identified a woman teacher who might take a test case. She was brought to Carndonagh in Co. Donegal to meet with the president and Dave Kelleher, who agreed that the NC could get counsel's opinion, but made it clear that the organisation would be under no obligation to proceed with the case.[39] Counsel, James McSparran QC, advised that the supplementary agreements were legal and teachers had no case.[40] Quigley was convinced this was in error and that the weight of the law was with the teachers, but he had to wait before seeking another opinion.

Nevertheless, the issue of a marriage ban was officially reopened when the 1955 northern conference adopted a resolution from the Tyrone County Committee to 'investigate' the matter,[41] and, at the end of the year, the INTO tried to raise the practice with the ministry, but its response was unsatisfactory. In January 1957, the NC sent a deputation to meet with Mageean and Farren, bishops of Down and Connor and of Derry respectively, to appeal for the ban's removal based on its injustice to the women concerned, its detrimental effect on the schools and its waste of public money, but the two men were unyielding. Indeed, Farren went so far as to issue a threat to the deputation: if it were legally established that he had no power to require women to resign on marriage, he would staff the girls' schools in Derry City with members of religious orders.[42] By that time the INTO was a year into the Ballina dispute, and replacing lay teachers with religious was a serious threat, as well as being ill-advised.

The INTO was in no mood to be blackmailed, and the lifting of the marriage ban in the South in July 1958 brought the issue to the fore once more. Once again Quigley sought, and was given, the general secretary's permission to secure counsel's advice on the legality of the ban. He had also identified two women teachers who might be used in any consequent test case.[43] Quigley prepared the brief carefully and counsel, Mr McGonigal, gave him the response he wanted: (1) The agreements which managers in the two dioceses compelled women teachers to sign, in which they agreed to resign on marriage, infringed two sections of the 1947 Education Act (20(7) and 84(3)); (2) The managers' forms were invalid under the teachers' contracts with the ministry; (3) When the forms were signed was of no material consequence – section 20(7) could not be contracted out of, and under section 20 any teacher being dismissed in the circumstances had a right to appeal. The NC having considered the advice at a meeting on 14 November, Quigley then wrote to the two bishops to inform them of counsel's advice. His tone was diplomatic but firm: the NC had a duty to take such steps as were necessary to defend the interests of their women members; the law was with them; and the ban had been lifted in the South some months earlier. However, the NC was anxious to avoid any further publicity on the matter and therefore respectfully requested their lordships to abandon the ban.

When, after several weeks, neither bishop had deigned to acknowledge the INTO's correspondence, Quigley was instructed to write again.[44] Subsequent letters had become more explicit about the INTO's threat, namely that while the NC was keen to secure a voluntary settlement, if this was not forthcoming it would have to lodge a formal complaint with the ministry, and indeed had been instructed to do so by the northern conference in January 1959. Farren took the threat as a fait accompli, and despite subsequent politicking by intermediaries, he refused to negotiate or yield in the face of what he regarded as a hostile move by the INTO. As a result, the NC submitted a formal complaint to the ministry on 23 March 1959. Eventually, on 4 August, the ministry wrote to the NC to say that it had been in touch with their lordships and had been assured that the practice of requiring women teachers to enter into a supplementary agreement to retire on marriage was to be discontinued, and that all existing agreements were to be withdrawn at the earliest opportunity.[45] The effort to remove the marriage bar had succeeded through good preparation and steely resolve, and the Armagh County committee, at least, was unanimous in placing the credit for the success with Gerry Quigley, although he attributed it to a group effort.[46] But while the campaign ended successfully, not everyone approved of the manner in which the matter had been managed, with the Derry City branch complaining about the treatment of Dr Farren in the course of events.[47]

As significant an achievement as this undoubtedly was, the lack of female representation in the INTO in the North was a significant problem, and was even worse than the organisation in the South, with no women on the NC until 1974, when Miss M.B. McFadden was elected as an area representative for Belfast. By 1977, two of 15 seats on the NC were held by women, a poor show but better than the UTU, whose 19-member executive was entirely male.[48] Two years later, in 1979, Róisín Carabine won the election for District 1 and became the first northern woman on the CEC.

However robust the Northern INTO's pursuit of an end to the marriage ban may have been during 1958–59, it tended to be reticent about any action that came too close to anti-clericalism. During the Ballina dispute, delegates from Belfast and Derry were the only voices at the special conference held in May 1961 to speak against the strike and the *Northern Teacher*'s 'one-sided' critical account of the meeting prompted a rebuke from the CEC. An apology from the editor appeared in the next issue, while Gerry Quigley was appointed controlling editor to ensure there was no repeat. (See Chapter 4, page 132.)

But if the Northern INTO was particularly sensitive towards the minority position of the Catholic Church in the six counties, its relationship with the Church was difficult nevertheless. In addition to the campaign against the marriage bar in the North, and the Ballina dispute in the South around the same time, there was residual resentment in the North about the organisation's position during the Killean dismissal. As NC representatives had found in 1957 when they tried to establish a formal relationship with the Catholic managers, the managers did not want meetings with them, largely because they were 'nervous of the organisation – those at the top', and they could not forget the Killean case.[49] In 1960, the NC resumed efforts to establish consultation with the Catholic Voluntary Managers. In February it secured a meeting with Dean Quinn, the chairman of the Catholic Managers' Association in Northern Ireland, at which there was a 'frank discussion' on the issue, after which the NC heard nothing further from Quinn.[50] The following year, the NC tried again, writing to Quinn in January, but while Quinn responded to say that the INTO's selection of topics could 'form the basis of a useful and fruitful discussion', when the NC wrote back to try to arrange a meeting, it received no response.[51] By now it had turned into an annual event; every January the new NC would meet and write to the Catholic managers to seek a meeting, which would invariably be rebuffed indirectly or directly.[52]

By 1964, however, there had been a change in personnel. William Philbin had succeeded Mageean as bishop of Down and Connor in August 1962, and a year later, on 9 September 1963, William Conway was appointed archbishop of Armagh and primate of all Ireland following the death of Cardinal D'Alton. Mageean and D'Alton had both had bad relations with the INTO, over the marriage ban and the Killean dismissal respectively, but their successors did not have the same strong antipathy towards the organisation. The spirit of the Second Vatican Council may also have encouraged Philbin and Conway to co-operate with lay associations. In any case, when the NC approached Philbin directly with a view to discussing the establishment of a Catholic Education Council, among other things, he indicated his willingness but told the NC to contact his brother bishops since the matter also concerned them. The NC did so and received a somewhat mixed response, including a very blunt 'No' from Dr Farren in Derry. On 14 March, however, Quigley and three members of the NC met Cardinal Conway to discuss various NC proposals. Eventually, in September, Conway wrote to inform them that the bishops 'warmly [welcomed] the principle of mutual co-operation and friendly consultation' between the INTO and representatives of the Catholic school authorities, although it was not until April 1965 that discussions on a framework actually began, the first meeting of the consultative body taking place in September.[53] The setting up of the Catholic Education Council was long overdue and marked, perhaps, a belated realisation that the teachers in county schools could be allies in their efforts to secure much-needed funding from the state, rather than seeing them as enemies of the Church. Furthermore, the arrival of the NAS in Northern Ireland, which had become an official district with a representative on the NAS executive in 1965, saw the Catholic managers facing the prospect of their staff being represented by an English union.[54] But if setting up the body represented a formal advance, this was not reflected in any new spirit of co-operation among the bishops or the managers. The INTO tried to use the body to lobby for the establishment of a protocol for appointments in Catholic schools, which would include advertising all vacancies, including vice-principalships and principalships.[55] Long sought by the INTO, the managers were wholly opposed to anything that would interfere with their ability to make appointments as they wished. In 1959, the INTO had asked the ministry to intervene, and legislate for compulsory job advertisements, but while the officials were sympathetic to the teachers, in the end they proved unwilling to fight the managers over it.[56] Returning to the matter directly with the bishops again in 1967, the INTO found them as unco-operative as before, and INTO complaints about bad practice and jobbery in appointments continued.[57] The question of members of religious orders being appointed to promoted posts was another area of conflict between the INTO and the Church. The replacement of lay teachers with religious had largely ended in the South after the Ballina dispute. During 1967 there were still cases in County Armagh of principalships in new or amalgamated schools being given to members of religious orders, prompting INTO intervention. Rather than try to overturn the appointments, the INTO sought assurances from Cardinal Conway, the archbishop of the diocese, that the posts of vice-principal and any posts of responsibility would go to lay teachers.[58] In the end, the INTO succeeded in securing one lay vice-principalship in a new girls' secondary school in Portadown and posts of responsibility for teachers in the boys' school. Two years later, a dispute arose in St Eugene's Girls' School in Derry over the appointment of a vice-principal. The lay members of staff unanimously voted to strike when a nun was appointed to the post. During the summer, INTO representatives met the bishop of Derry, the school manager and the reverend mother to discuss what would happen next, and, as a result of the meeting, the position of vice-principal was advertised. A number of the lay teachers in the school applied for the job and one was successful, while the nun who had been removed from the role was transferred to another school.[59]

It was two years after the consultative body began its meetings that the voluntary schools underwent the greatest change in governance since the northern system had been established. In October 1967, Education Minister Captain W.J. Long published his White Paper on 'Local Education Authorities and Voluntary Schools', which proposed to create a new category of voluntary school, called 'maintained' schools.[60] In return for representation by the LEAs on governing boards on a 'four and two' basis (i.e. a board of management with two-thirds appointed by the Church and one-third by the LEA), schools would be entitled to an 80 per cent grant rather than 65 per cent, while the LEA would be responsible for all maintenance, equipment and day-to-day running costs. In this way schools went from being fully voluntary to semi-voluntary. The NC held an emergency meeting on the afternoon of the White Paper's publication and afterwards released a statement welcoming the proposals. It noted that the organisation's concern was to 'ensure that equal educational opportunity is provided for all children in accordance with parental wishes'; that was not the case as things stood, since 'generally the standards of equipment, cleaning and maintenance of voluntary schools [had] fallen behind those of county schools' because of the financial burden. It was an important show of support for the proposal from an organisation representing some 3,000 teachers in Catholic schools, and was remarked on approvingly by Prime Minister Terence O'Neill.[61]

The northern bishops as a whole were slower to comment. Philbin had come straight out to describe the proposals (in a 'personal reaction') as 'the first step towards the disappearance of Catholic schools in the province', but the early signs were that Catholic opinion was not with him. Certainly, Queen's University Belfast's New Ireland Society, a progressive nationalist forum, passed a motion (by 355 to 36) expressing regret at his comments.[62] Cardinal Conway, who had been in Rome when the White Paper was published, took a somewhat more measured tone on his return to Ireland, although he was worried about the proposals.[63] On the whole, though, Conway was inclined towards being pragmatic. On 8 November, the bishops of the Northern Province issued a statement welcoming the proposal to increase the grants for voluntary schools while opposing the changes to management. Subsequently they attempted to negotiate with the ministry, and eventually announced that they accepted the principle of public representation on management committees but wanted the nominations to come centrally, from the minister rather than the LEA. The minister considered this request before turning it down, at which point the NC rowed in to support the bishops, now that they had conceded the principle of public representation. The NC released a statement and, over two days, lobbied MPs on both sides of the House, before securing a meeting with the minister on 14 December. The Education (Amendment) Bill was published on 7 January, passed its final stages on 19 March, and became operative on 1 April 1968, with the new boards to have been appointed six months from then.[64] Efforts during this time by the INTO, the bishops and nationalist politicians to secure amendments proved unsuccessful. If the Catholic authorities had been unhappy with the turn of events, they did not find them so objectionable that they could not overlook them in order to apply for maintained status. Cardinal Conway ultimately expressed the hope that in practice, and with goodwill on all sides, the scheme would work satisfactorily for the greater good of the children.[65] As the ministry had no doubt anticipated, they couldn't afford to do otherwise. The 1968 Education Act made a significant change to the material quality of Catholic schools in the North and changed the management structure some ten years before it happened in schools in the South. Southern teachers were anxious about the impact of having outsiders (or more accurately neighbours) participating in the running of schools; but in the North, the prospect of adequate funding was sufficient to off-set any such concerns. The episode also provided an illustration of the NC political nous in action, in its speed and clarity in supporting the White Paper while politically supporting the managers once they had given their support to the substantive issue. If the INTO did not secure any concessions to the legislation, it was not of any significant concern, and ultimately, the changes were to their benefit and the benefit of the pupils in their schools.

The timing of the Education Act was fortuitous, coming as it did only a few months before the outbreak of the Troubles. The first civil rights march, between Coalisland and Dungannon, took place on 24 August 1968. Six weeks later, on 5 October, the civil rights march in Derry was broken up by the RUC, who baton-charged the crowd in front of television cameras, and was followed by days of serious rioting. O'Neill introduced what he later described as a 'small, timid reform package' in November, but tensions escalated in the new year and the events of 1969 would transform Ireland.

The civil rights marches continued, as did the violent reaction from loyalists. A general election on 24 February 1969 saw O'Neill returned to office, but following a loyalist bombing campaign of electricity and water services, he lost the confidence of the Unionist Party and was replaced as prime minister by James Chichester-Clark on 1 May. There had been serious rioting during April but it was during marching season that summer, after a year on the brink, that ferocious violence broke out in Derry and Belfast, including the Battle of the Bogside from 12 August and the attacks on Catholic homes in Belfast beginning the next evening. By 15 August the British army had been deployed, eight people had died and thousands were displaced, the majority of them Catholics, some of whom fled to the South as refugees. In its first issue after the summer, the *Northern Teacher* observed how 'the even tenor of our lives has been shattered by the awful eruption of violence in August and the subsequent sporadic orgies of destruction', noting how 'many teachers in the Belfast area have had direct experience of the consequences of this cataclysm both through participation in relief work and in the evidence of depleted numbers in their classes'.[66]

At the end of August, Home Secretary James Callaghan visited the North on a fact-finding trip along with his minister of state, Lord Stonham. Stonham held one-to-one meetings with the teacher unions, and during its meeting the NC outlined what it said was 'the organisation's views on the steps that should be taken to secure completely impartial educational administration'. Afterwards, at Stonham's request, Gerry Quigley, Al Mackle and Michael McKeown drafted a memorandum on the matters they had discussed, which was sent to the minister on 19 September and subsequently to members in the North.[67] After a historical overview and an outline of some of the main education controversies, including the 1968 Act, the memorandum raised a number of concerns, including the sectarian imbalance in the inspectorate; prohibitions on the use of school texts; the oath of allegiance; and integrated education.

Integrated education had been the dominant issue for Northern Ireland's education system since the late 1960s. Supported by liberal unionists such as O'Neill, and by the UTU, which likened segregated schooling to apartheid, by September 1969 the home secretary, James Callaghan, and the Cameron Report on 'Disturbances in Northern Ireland' had joined in criticism of denominational education. Integrated education was broadly opposed by Catholics, however.[68] On 14 October, shortly after the publication of the Cameron Report, the NC gave a well-covered press conference in which it published its submission to Stonham the previous month, but with most of the focus given to integrated education, which the NC had suggested was 'unrealistic' because it would be resisted by both communities.[69] This statement proved controversial among membership, however, and when the northern conference met in January there was criticism from delegates over the NC's remarks at the press conference. After a 'lengthy and tortuous debate' on whether the word 'unrealistic' was too strong or, indeed, accurate at all, a majority voted to remove the paragraph from the NC's report for the year.[70] Afterwards, the *Northern Teacher* summarised the NC's policy as follows: '1. We would oppose any attempt to impose integrated education on those who do not want it; 2. We would support any voluntary experiments to promote integration and 3. We would encourage our members to co-operate in any acceptable schemes of in-school or out-of-school activities.'[71]

In April 1970, the NC reiterated the recommendations in its memorandum to Stonham to officials from the Ministry of Education at a meeting in Stormont, which took place on the recommendation of then minister of state at the Home Office, Shirley Williams, but nothing came of it. There was a 'frank exchange of views' on the denominational imbalance in the inspectorate, textbooks, and the removal of the oath of allegiance, while matters to do with the organisation of education were not discussed since they were being examined by the Local Government Review Body, chaired by Sir Patrick Macrory.[72] The NC sought submissions from its 31 branches across the North, and submitted a memorandum to the Macrory Review Body based on the responses, recommending the establishment of a single education authority for the whole of Northern Ireland, rather than the present system with its eight LEAs. The Macrory Report included among its recommendations that education be administered on a regional basis from Stormont.[73] Described by Michael McKeown as something of a curate's egg, the NC welcomed its recommendations, which would 'do away with the present petty dictatorships' of LEAs, although the consequences of transferring responsibility to Stormont, and what was later dubbed the 'Macrory gap', were far away on the horizon (see below).[74]

NORTHERN REORGANISATION

The 1968 northern conference passed a resolution authorising the appointment of a special committee to examine the nature of the organisation in the North. It was set up to look at the Northern Committee's constitution, electoral areas, branch structure, provision for sectional interests and any other administrative matters. At the time, the Northern Committee was not elected. That option had been rejected by the CEC immediately after partition. The executive had felt that giving the Northern Committee a mandate would invest it with too much authority and make it a rival to the CEC. Instead, it would have mainly *ex officio* members: the two CEC representatives for the North (districts 1 and 2), the finance committee representative, the northern secretary, area representatives from Belfast and two secondary school representatives. One of the latter was to be from Belfast and the other from outside Belfast, which meant that at least two members of the NC had to be post-primary teachers. There could also be more than that, and in 1968 four of 13 members of the NC were post-primary. The committee of 11 men and one woman decided upon a scheme which would include the CEC and FC representatives, six area representatives and two representatives each from the primary, secondary and grammar school sectors.[75] The recommendations were approved first by the northern conference in 1970. The national congress in Galway voted to change the rules and the newly constituted committee came into office at the end of December 1970. Just before then, in September 1970, a new administrative officer, Seamus White, joined the northern office after the CEC had given permission for the post. Northern members' subscriptions were increased from five guineas to seven guineas to pay for it.[76] As well as changes to the make-up of the Northern Committee, there were also efforts to amalgamate branches in Castlederg and Strabane as well as Ballymena and South Antrim. Members successfully held out against the moves and the branches remained as they were.[77]

Around this time the northern office found a new home. Having operated out of rented accommodation at 72 High Street since the war, in September 1971 the NC moved to new rented property at 23 College Gardens. It eventually purchased the property on the proviso that the owner, Mrs Hall, who occupied the flat in the building, should be able to remain there rent-free during her lifetime. Following her death there were major renovations and the flat was incorporated as part of the main building.[78] The building would not get hot running water, however, until a massive refurbishment in 2003.[79]

THE ATTEMPTED UTU–NUT MERGER

During 1970, the UTU executive wrote to the NUT seeking a merger between the two. Referring to 'the tendency of Northern Ireland to move closer toward the rest of the UK', the UTU had a 'need to merge with a larger parent body with whom there is an identity of views'.[80] For many years, the NUT had refused to recognise the UTU as a fraternal union due to the INTO's insistence that it was a splinter union, but after the war, in 1946, the two had established a relationship and had begun to send fraternal delegates to each other's conferences.[81] There was good logic for a merger; since the NUT was, in effect, fighting for salary agreements in London that were then implemented in the North, it made sense to consolidate the operation, not least when the NAS/UWT had set the precedent of an English union operating in the North in 1961 and was posing a threat to the UTU's position. If the NUT agreed to the merger, however, the INTO would be alone among the large teacher unions in not having a base in London. This might reasonably leave its members to wonder what they were doing being part of an all-Ireland union when their salaries were effectively decided by negotiations in London.[82]

As Gerry Quigley and the NC saw it, a merger between the UTU and the NUT could have been fatal and it was imperative that it was stopped. Notwithstanding a certain embarrassment among southern officials at the prospect of the INTO locking horns with its sister union in England, the NC raised its objections directly with the NUT. It secured permission from the CEC to attend a meeting in London in October, where the NUT maintained it was perfectly in order in moving into the North as other unions had done, and was only responding to the UTU's approach.[83] With the NUT unwilling to withdraw, the NC decided to invoke the terms of the Bridlington Agreement, a set of principles agreed on by the British Trade Union Congress (TUC) in 1939, which had been drawn up to stop unions poaching each other's members (although this applied only to the NUT in this instance, since the UTU was not then affiliated to the TUC), and to take the matter up with the ICTU and its northern committee.[84] A three-man delegation from the NUT, including its president and general secretary, travelled to Dublin to meet with the INTO on 29 November, and by mid-December the NC felt that the threat had subsided somewhat, suggesting that the NUT's silence after the meeting meant its enthusiasm might have slowed down somewhat. However, in January 1971 the NUT invited both the UTU and the INTO to London for talks, at which point the matter entered the public domain.[85]

Though the UTU was less than happy that the invitation had been extended to the INTO, it agreed to go nonetheless, and on 5 February representatives of the three unions met in London. At the meeting the INTO stressed the desirability of securing the greatest possible measure of teacher unity in Northern Ireland, and its commitment to the principle, as long as it would not involve the INTO fragmenting its own organisation. The INTO would not accept segregation of teachers, whether on the basis of sex, religion, race, status or type of school. The INTO delegation also pointed out that while a friendly settlement of the INTO/UTU problem would be 'a milestone on the road to reconciliation' in the North, an NUT/UTU merger would put the INTO in conflict with the NUT and would 'set back indefinitely the achievement of teacher unity' there. As well as putting essentially a moral case to the NUT, the INTO deputation warned the English union that it would be in conflict with its own policy on professional unity, adopted in 1960, and that putting itself in direct conflict with the INTO would cause a deep sense of resentment among the *thousands* of Irish teachers working in England, many of whom were themselves members of the NUT.[86] This was a scenario that offered nothing but trouble to the NUT and the meeting ended with the NUT declaring that they would prefer that the problem was settled between the UTU and the INTO, and that the UTU should give serious consideration to INTO proposals regarding teacher unity. This meant that the NUT had effectively withdrawn from the issue, for the time being at least. Having returned home, the UTU distanced itself from the agreement. It wrote on 16 February that it was only interested in a 'complete merger', not any kind of affiliation, but this could only be considered with a six-county organisation, which the INTO could not consider.[87] There were more meetings and correspondence during the summer but by June the UTU wrote to thank the INTO for its part in the 'frank and sincere' discussions, but it was proceeding to hold a referendum on a merger with the NUT.[88] As the UTU later put it in a letter to the INTO:

> We would value very highly a union with the INTO provided such a union could be formed based entirely in Northern Ireland ... the separation of the UTU from INTO some fifty years ago arose not from any wish for fragmentation but due to the same ideals as led to the separation of Northern Ireland from the rest of Ireland in order to preserve the feelings of identity and common citizenship with the people of England and Wales under the Crown ... we acknowledge the sincerity of the INTO's republican aspirations.[89]

Ultimately, the UTU's executive had concluded that 'an INTO completely divorced from Dublin would be acceptable but we are not going to listen to any blandishments from the South'.[90] There were some dissenting voices on the matter, with the UTU vice-president warning that refusing to accept the INTO's invitation would mean the UTU isolating themselves 'as a union of bigots'.[91] The NUT was 'not in the slightest bit enthusiastic about' getting involved in Northern Ireland, but the INTO reiterated its position, writing once more to pledge to fight any merger. Gerry Quigley was quoted in the press as saying, 'I am opposing the incursion of the British union into Ireland, the whole move is an exercise in neo-colonialism.'[92]

At the end of January, Quigley travelled to London with Al Mackle and Seán Brosnahan and left a meeting with the NUT optimistic that they had convinced the NUT deputation that it would not be in the union's best interests to pursue the merger, although they would still have to convince the other members of the NUT executive. Following another tripartite meeting in London in February, the INTO men on the deputation could report that it now appeared that the NUT was 'not enamoured' with the idea of establishing itself in the North.[93] Following this meeting, the UTU wrote to the NUT noting that there was no purpose in continuing a dialogue and that the merger would have to be shelved, although 'as long as Northern Ireland remains part of the United Kingdom, members of this union will always cherish the ambition of being part of the NUT'.

Quigley and the NC had used every means available to them with great success, whether invoking trade union protocols, accusing the NUT of colonialism or threatening the alienation of its Irish members working in England, while showing the INTO to be open to a merger itself, albeit under conditions that the UTU would never agree to. A few months later, in May, a delegation from the NUT visited Dublin as the INTO's guests, and arrangements were made to 'improve communication and to avoid any future strain on relations' between the two.[94] Naturally, the issue did nothing to foster good relations between the INTO and UTU, but the following summer, the two sides had decided that the time had arrived when some effort should be made to promote unity between the two organisations.[95]

In July 1973, after several informal discussions, the UTU and INTO agreed to significant co-operation on a number of important areas. These included establishing a joint central standing committee which would hold regular meetings, including an annual joint meeting of the two executives; establishing a joint educational journal based on the *Northern Teacher*; and, where possible, issuing joint statements on matters of educational or professional concern. They also discussed determining a common level of subscription for the two unions.[96] By the end of 1974, the NC could report that the two unions' close working relationship had continued throughout the year, noting that since the two together represented about three-quarters of the organised primary and secondary teachers their combined influence was considerable. It was 'clearly desirable that the two should always act together where possible'.[97] In June 1977, the INTO invited the leaders of unions from England and Wales (NUT), Scotland (Educational Institute of Scotland, EIS) and the North (UTU) to Dublin for a joint meeting. Fred Jarvis from the NUT observed afterwards, 'the main reason for coming together at this stage is the European community. But over and above that there is a common interest. It's just that it took the EEC to provide the motivation.' And one report noted afterwards, 'there wasn't much work done really'. The real achievement was bringing everyone together for the first time, not least because, as NUT president John Gray observed, with all the unions coming together it became easier for the UTU to co-operate with its counterparts in the Republic.[98] It set a precedent, and within six months representatives of the four unions had met again, this time in London, and they were joined by representatives of the NATFHE and the ASTI, the first in what became annual meetings of the British and Irish Group of Teachers' Organisations.[99]

THE TROUBLES

The UTU's attempts to secure a merger with the NUT had taken place just as the Troubles were escalating, which contributed a great deal to the NUT's reluctance to get involved.[100] Internment had been introduced on 9 August 1971, with some 342 people arrested that morning, provoking an upsurge in violence that resulted in 17 people being killed over the next 48 hours, ten of whom were Catholic civilians shot by the British army. The violence was the worst since August 1969, and again, thousands of people, most of them Catholic, were forced to flee to the South. There was a call from left and republican groups in Derry for a rent and rates strike, and on 15 August the SDLP announced it was starting a civil disobedience campaign, which would continue until the last internee was released. The SDLP also withdrew its representatives from a number of public bodies.

On 28 August, the NC held an emergency meeting at which it roundly condemned internment without trial as contrary to civil rights. One of its members, the People's Democracy activist Michael Farrell, had been among those lifted on 9 August and the NC telegrammed prime ministers Heath and Faulkner protesting at Farrell's detention. It also decided to call on the CEC to lodge a formal protest with the International Labour Organisation and the World Confederation of Organisations of the Teaching Profession, which the CEC agreed to do, and decided to call a special conference in October to consider whether the INTO would continue to be represented on public bodies under the circumstances.[101] The result of this was that INTO representatives were asked to withdraw from public bodies, but given freedom of conscience in the matter.[102] The request was subsequently lifted eight months later at an NC meeting at the end of May 1972, when, in light of the suspension of Stormont and the imposition of direct rule from Westminster, INTO representatives were asked to resume attendance, but advised that they had complete freedom of choice in the matter. All members concerned resumed their positions.[103]

The NC also drew up a six-point policy on internees, adopted by the NI Committee of the ICTU, which demanded work protections for internees, while it (the NC) supported the NIC's direction that trade unionists should disregard calls for industrial action coming from any source other than official trade unions.[104] If this call to ignore strike demands outside the trade union movement might have been regarded by some as unduly moderate – and there was pressure from republicans inside and outside the profession that the INTO go much further – it was further than the NAS was prepared to go. Although its members were among those detained, the NAS refused to support the call for the internees' release since the object of the association was representing school-masters in respect of employment and educational issues.[105]

The situation had a deep impact on people inside and outside schools. Children were naturally affected by the unrest, and were often involved in rioting themselves. There were instances in Belfast and Derry of groups of young boys being arrested and interrogated by British forces, which saw the INTO general secretary telegram members of the British and Stormont govern-ments to express the organisation's abhorrence that school children be treated in such a fashion.[106] There had been accusations in Derry that the British army was effectively using school children for cover in its operations, which was condemned by local teachers. The NC outlined its policy in a statement drawn up in January 1972. Expressing its opposition to internment, which was contrary to basic human rights, it noted, 'we have done our utmost to keep the present conflict out of the schools' and appealed to parents to ensure young people still at school did not become involved in community violence. It urged 'the military authorities to end the harassment of children whether in their homes or on the way to and from school. For many years to come the teachers of Northern Ireland will have to cope with the bitterness and hatred that will inevitably follow those ill-advised security policies which have already alienated whole sections of our community.'[107]

In fact, the most overt incursion into school life began six months later, at the end of July 1972. During Operation Motorman, three schools in west Belfast were occupied by the British army, and this continued in two schools, St Peter's Secondary and Blessed Oliver Plunkett, when the schools returned after the holidays.[108] In the case of St Peter's, the INTO demanded that the army withdraw or the school would be closed, but the ministry refused the INTO's demand, even though it was unsafe, and pupil attendance was between eight and 25 per cent. Occasions of friction arose constantly, with teachers and pupils being generally harassed or merely treated with disrespect by the British army, and on one occasion a teacher was assaulted when confirming the identity of a colleague.[109] Eventually, INTO members voted unanimously in favour of an immediate strike after a shot was fired into the school yard during PE, a decision subsequently endorsed by the general secretary and later the CEC.[110] Shortly afterwards, the INTO secured an agreement that the British army would vacate the school by the end of term and the teachers arranged to take classes in temporary facilities until they left. In the case of Blessed Oliver Plunkett School, teachers continued to take classes while the occupation continued until, on 27 September, INTO members voted to go on strike from 3 October, after which the Northern Ireland Office agreed that the army would vacate the school, which it did a few weeks later.[111] As an INTO memo put it at the time, resolute action by the organisation, partly by their representations to the government but mainly by industrial action, had worked, but the INTO had been 'left to fight this dispute on its own'. It complained that school managements had been weak and ineffective and that the NAS, which had members in the schools, had actually hindered the INTO efforts, noting that 'official NAS behaviour in this dispute was pathetic, whether due to confused policies or lack of expertise, and was a matter of serious embarrassment to many NAS members in the area'. The author of the memorandum was scathing about the unreliable NAS, which 'in this dispute, as in other recent issues, the interest of NAS members in Northern Ireland have clearly been sacrificed in order to avoid a reaction from their members in England and Wales'.[112]

Action such as this, however correct, did give the INTO the appearance of being explicitly political, a perception that would have been bolstered by the INTO's campaign during 1972 for the removal of the statutory oath or declaration for teachers 'to render true and faithful allegiance' to the British Crown.[113] As well as seeking advice from senior counsel on the oath's legality – he was unable to give a definitive answer – the NC also tried to secure the support of its sister unions for its repeal. Most of them deferred giving an answer, but while the NAS stated its view that 'teachers should not be subject to political or religious tests of any kind', the UTU bluntly replied that the current requirements presented 'no difficulty' to its members.[114] In the end, change came from London a year after the introduction of direct rule. The government had been reluctant to act, not least because of the opposition to its removal from unionists, but the campaign against the oath had spread from the teachers to other areas of local authorities, including forestry workers. Eventually the oath was abolished by order on 5 April 1973, after which only members of the RUC were required to take it.[115]

In the heightened political and sectarian climate, there was a sense that the INTO's stance on matters such as the oath or the army's occupation of schools made it a target, and, towards the end of 1972, the NC voted to postpone the northern conference, believing that were it to go ahead it might put delegates and their families at risk.[116] As then CEC member Al Mackle recalled, it was a very difficult time to carry out the role and function of union representative and it was especially difficult to travel at night, something which was particularly problematic when INTO representatives had to do their union work after school.[117] Around this time, the NC decided to move the northern congress from Christmas to the first Friday in March and to hold its meetings on Saturdays from October to April and on weekday evenings between May and September.[118]

EDUCATION UNDER DIRECT RULE

On 30 March 1972, the British government prorogued the Stormont parliament and introduced direct rule from Westminster. With the exception of the short-lived power-sharing arrangement under the Sunningdale Agreement between January and May 1974, Northern Ireland affairs would be administered from London for the next 27 years. Overall responsibility for the administration of the North rested with the secretary of state for Northern Ireland and the Northern Ireland Office (NIO). Initially, a British minister of state was given responsibility for health, social services and education, but soon after a Department of Education, Northern Ireland (DENI), was established. In addition to direct rule, the Education and Library Board Order of 1972, based on the 1970 Macrory Report, replaced the eight LEAs with five education and library boards (ELBs), significantly diminishing their role in supervising schools in favour of placing education in the hands of central government.

All this meant that education administration in the North had never been so centralised, even compared to the situation before 1921. Policy and administration came from London, from a minister of state who, as an outsider unfamiliar with the Northern Ireland context, was 'tremendously dependent' on their civil servants' advice.[119] One exception to this was Brian Mawhinney, education minister between January 1986 and December 1990. While he represented an English constituency, he was originally from Northern Ireland and asserted himself accordingly, which, considering his policies, was not entirely welcome.[120] However, Ken Bloomfield, head of the Northern Ireland civil service between 1984 and 1991, once counselled that the shorthand of titles such as 'minister for education' was misleading: 'all the departments [were] under the "direction and control" of the secretary of state' and, in the last resort, that one person 'was minister for everything in Northern Ireland'.[121] When direct rule was first introduced in 1972, the Conservatives were in office under Edward Heath, followed by five years of Labour government, first under Harold Wilson (1974–76), then James Callaghan (1976–79). During this time Peter (Lord) Melchett was the minister of state at the NIO, and Northern Secretary Al Mackle enjoyed a good relationship with him.[122]

There was little in the way of education reform during this time. One issue that was on the educational agenda, but which never quite made it to permanent implementation, was selection for secondary schools. It had been opposed by the INTO since its introduction, and a 1973 report of the Advisory Commission on Education recommended that academic selection be abolished. Between 1975 and 1979, interim moves in this direction were put in place by the Labour government, but while the INTO supported the removal of the 11+, it did not support any efforts to replace it with another form of academic selection and threatened to boycott the procedure.[123] As it was, when the Conservatives returned to office in 1979, the 11+ was reinstated anyway. At first the INTO boycotted talks with DENI on the matter but reversed the decision in 1981, having concluded that 'non-selective education [would] not come tomorrow or during the reign of Mrs Thatcher', and it was better to engage in the talks to make selection as fair as was possible.[124] Selection would remain a divisive issue in the North, however. Split largely along political lines, it would come to the surface again under the devolved government in the 2000s.[125]

The May 1979 election had precipitated 16 years of Conservative government, the first 11 of which were led by Margaret Thatcher. Thatcher, whose time as education secretary (1970–74) had earned her the nickname 'Maggie Thatcher, Milk Snatcher', was a neo-liberal ideologue who sought to introduce market forces to the public sector and diminish the power of the trade union movement. In education, this saw efforts to diminish teachers' autonomy and professional status in place of a culture of managerialism and perpetual testing, although it was not until the late 1980s that these policies manifested themselves.

As well as the change in government in Britain, there were other significant changes of personnel in Belfast around the same time. After 24 years as northern secretary, Gerry Quigley moved to Dublin to become INTO general secretary. In the competition for his replacement, two candidates were interviewed, and Al Mackle, principal of St Mary's School, Maghery, who had represented Armagh on the NC since 1960 and had served on the CEC since 1965, was appointed. He took up his new role on 1 January 1978 and remained in the post until he retired 13 years later, in 1991. Following his appointment, Patricia Grant, who had been personal secretary to Gerry Quigley, was promoted to senior official. She was famed for her encyclopaedic knowledge of national insurance and pension rights.[126] They were joined in 1981 by Teddy Martin. Mackle and Quigley had been close friends and colleagues and they went back a long way; Mackle had assisted Quigley during the general secretary campaign, and they were both of a similar outlook and the same age, so Mackle's appointment did not represent a significant shift in outlook or any sort of generational change. More crucial for the organisation were the external changes that took place around the same time.

Apart from the change in government there was also a change of personnel in the UTU; Brian Toms, with whom Gerry Quigley had worked hard to establish good working relations between the two unions and make sure there were no 'really sharp differences', was replaced by David Allen, described as 'once the right hand man of Bill Craig in the Vanguard Party'.[127] Toms, originally from Wales, but living in the North since 1940, had been rather in advance of his membership when it came to co-operation with the INTO and had shown real leadership on the matter.[128] Once he was gone, the co-operation between the INTO and UTU, which had been in operation from 1973, declined under Allen's leadership, and while the NC agreed that 'every effort should be made to maintain the link' with the UTU, the UTU was less committed. Its 1980 conference decided to withdraw UTU support from the *Northern Teacher* and reduce the cost of its subscription, contrary to a formula it had agreed with the INTO.

Further indication of the gap between the two groups came in 1981 when UTU members voted by more than six to one against affiliating to the ICTU. Only eight years earlier, a similar motion had been defeated by a single vote. The INTO had made no secret of its support for the UTU's affiliation, particularly at a time when the public sector unions were under attack from the Tory government, but the political polarisation that characterised the North around the time of the hunger strikes played a part in the voting, with David Allen also pointing to the 'adverse publicity associated with the left-wing bias of some unions across the water'.[129] By October 1982, the Joint Central Standing Committee of the two unions had agreed that the previous agreement was no longer tenable.[130] Instead, they agreed to hold a joint annual meeting of executives, to release joint statements 'where possible' and to try to co-ordinate their activities before and after each meeting of the Northern Ireland Teachers' Council.[131]

Much of the INTO's concern about maintaining strong relations with the UTU was that it saw it as an ally against the National Association of Schoolmasters/ Union of Women Teachers (NAS/UWT), which had been growing in strength during the 1970s. The INTO's membership was on a rather halting upward trajectory throughout the 1970s, but it was having trouble with retention and recruitment, and had been significantly overtaken by the NAS/UWT, which had 7,700 members in 1980, about 2,100 more than the INTO had around the same time.[132] The INTO and UTU continued to be considerably over-represented in Northern Irish educational bodies, but when it came to pay, the NAS/UWT was represented where it mattered, in London on the Burnham Committee.

There was little that the NC could come up with to broaden its appeal. It was adamant, as it always had been, that it would be dangerous to increase its subscription rates, which was particularly important after the UTU had broken its agreement to keep parity. It also felt that the all-island nature of the INTO was part of its appeal; it had argued in the past that there was strong pressure on teachers to join a British union, and any weakening of the North–South links would encourage further pressures.[133] The NC suggested, among other things, that a greater level of participation by northern members in the organisation as a whole would be beneficial, and that northern members should be fully informed about the work of the entire organisation. It is worth bearing in mind that the two regions were working largely independently of each other by this time, with little or no reference to the other in their respective publications, and any lack of engagement with part of the organisation across the border was not unique to the North. The fact that the general secretary was himself from Belfast made little difference. In fact, perhaps it was because of this that Gerry Quigley, the man who had blocked a merger between the UTU and the NUT a decade earlier, felt able to make a radical suggestion to the NC: that the organisation in the North could introduce a dual membership so that INTO members would simultaneously be members of the NUT, thus giving them a seat at the table for Burnham, but the NC was unanimous in rejecting the idea which, they felt, would not be in the INTO's best interests.[134]

SALARY CAMPAIGN 1985

In a three-person contest, Róisín Carabine was elected INTO vice-president in 1984, and in 1985 became the first northern president in 24 years.[135] The first time both general secretary and president were from the North was a year of agitation on both sides of the border, prompting the accusation, perhaps in jest, that 'belligerent Northerners' had been stirring things.[136] The 1985 disputes saw broadly the same issues at play. In the South, the government had refused to pay an arbitration award, leading to the Teachers United campaign, while in March 1985, the Northern Ireland Negotiating Committee (Schools) talks ended in deadlock after the employers' side refused to respond positively to the teachers' salary claim for the year. There was similar deadlock in England and Wales, where teachers sought to rectify what they felt was a fall in relative pay, but were offered less than half of what they sought. The teachers went to arbitration, but even before there was an award, the secretary of state, Keith Joseph – a close political ally of Margaret Thatcher's – had signalled that he would ignore an arbitration award if it was more than four per cent. The result of this was that the teachers in Britain began what would be their longest and largest national dispute.[137] There was a separate dispute in Northern Ireland, where, following a ballot, the INTO instructed members to follow a 'no cover' order and to refuse to participate in any meetings outside normal school hours. There was co-operation between the INTO, UTU and NAS/UWT on meetings and cover. Afterwards, the industrial action was expanded, with the NAS/UWT and INTO holding a series of strikes during the second half of October 1985. But there was also a show of solidarity with British teachers, with the INTO joining the UTU, NUT and EIS (all members of the British and Irish Group of Teachers' Unions) in London for a lobby of parliament in November 1985.[138]

During the dispute, Keith Joseph chose to flag up a number of issues that were part of the neo-liberal approach to education, such as performance-related pay and securing codified conditions of service, of which dissolving Burnham would be a part,[139] but by the time Joseph retired in 1986, the regime of testing and managerialism he had envisaged had not yet been put in train in Britain, or in the North. His successor, Kenneth Baker, proved most capable of taking up where he left off, however, and it was also towards the end of the 1980s that the direct rule Conservative ministers were for the first time inclined towards significant change.[140]

Baker's Education Reform Act of 1988 has been described as the 'the single most important piece of education legislation for England, Wales and Northern Ireland since the war',[141] and the British reforms were closely followed in the North. These were led by Dr Brian Mawhinney, who had been appointed parliamentary under-secretary of state with responsibility for education in January 1986. Mawhinney was the first northerner to have responsibility under direct rule. His predecessors came in as outsiders and, assured by their Belfast-based civil servants that education reform was unnecessary, they avoided tinkering with the system in the North. Mawhinney, however, felt at home, and when he left the post five years later he was described as having played the 'most radical role of any minister since direct rule'.[142] Not only did he lack his predecessors' reticence, he was deeply convinced of the need for reforms, and with a background as an academic scientist, he was sure he knew what he was talking about. This was a man who described the teacher unions as self-satisfied, belligerent know-alls;[143] many in the teacher unions might have said the same of Mawhinney. Mawhinney introduced a number of policies which were specific to Northern Ireland. His first major change was in the management of Catholic primary and secondary schools, which he agreed with the Catholic bishops in the North in 1987. A new central council, the Council for Catholic Maintained Schools (CCMS), would be responsible for teachers' appointments from September 1988. This was rejected by the Catholic bishops but welcomed by the INTO as an important and significant development.[144] The INTO was less positive when Mawhinney announced a series of reforms modelled on what Baker was introducing in England and Wales. In March 1988, Mawhinney published 'Education in Northern Ireland – Proposals for Reform', a consultative paper based on Baker's 1988 Education Reform Act, which 'introduced a statutory curriculum and new assessment system, provided a basis for greater market competition between schools by enhancing pupil choice using league tables and gave greater administrative and financial autonomy to schools'.[145] The INTO, along with the other teacher unions, roundly attacked the proposals, which, like Baker's bill, showed a fundamental lack of trust in teachers and if implemented would wreak 'untold damage' on the North's education system.[146] In its response to the paper, the INTO noted that it appeared to be 'based on the Market Philosophy', which naively assumed that 'education standards can be raised by introducing a competitive spirit, setting pupil against pupil and school against school in league tables of published results'.[147]

In March 1987, Kenneth Baker's Teachers' Pay and Conditions Act received royal assent. It abolished teachers' negotiating rights, getting rid of the Burnham Committee, and set out new conditions of service, legislating for the number of days teachers were to be available to teach, and introducing the 'Baker Days' for in-service training. This had been effectively imposed on English teachers. In the

North, there was some negotiation on the form the new terms and conditions would take, and this ultimately resulted in the Jordanstown Agreement, reached in May 1987, which would be the framework for teachers' conditions over the next two decades. The agreement represented a major change to teachers' conditions, most notably with the introduction of directed time, which set out maximums of 1,265 hours per year and 195 days annually and the idea of a 'time budget' for each member of staff. While inevitably unpopular, it was somewhat less onerous than English legislation. Brendan Harron, who was northern chairman at the time, recalls how Al Mackle managed to subtly secure changes to the wording that ameliorated it somewhat, including having marking and preparation included in the 1,265 hours.[148] As ever, but especially so in this case, the task of negotiating this kind of agreement was made more difficult by the number of unions involved, and the presence of the British-based unions. As always, implementation was key. The INTO and UTU tried to impress on its own members who were principals that the Jordanstown figures were maximums not minimums and encouraged them to avoid the managerialism that underpinned the agreement, but the existence of a separate association for principals meant that INTO members could find themselves working under a regime operated by members of other associations. In any case, Jordanstown changed for good the way teachers worked in the North, and much of the INTO's time in the years that followed were devoted to holding the line on terms and conditions. The INTO in the North could also find themselves acting as Cassandras, warning their colleagues in the South of the dangers of Thatcherite education policy, no matter how it was dressed up.

1990 TO DATE: FROM PEACE PROCESS TO DEVOLUTION

The 1990s was a period of immense change in Northern Ireland, beginning with an embryonic peace process and ending with a power-sharing devolved government. The path from peace process to devolution was tortuous. The 1994 ceasefires collapsed in 1996, to be revived the following year, with the Good Friday Agreement signed in Easter 1998. But if most paramilitary organisations were on ceasefire, sectarian violence did not suddenly become a thing of the past, while dissident republican groups conducted a bombing campaign in which 29 people were killed and some 300 injured when the Real IRA bombed Omagh town centre on Saturday 15 August 1998. Nor did electoral politics become magically straightforward after the Northern Ireland Assembly was set up. In October 2002 the assembly was suspended and was not reconstituted until May 2007, but during this period the ceasefires held. The 1990s, then, was a time of progress, but it was hard reached and often beset by crises and setbacks. Perhaps unsurprisingly, then, it was relatively calm in the sphere of education policy, particularly in comparison with the late 1980s which had been dominated by a raft of far-reaching educational reforms. Implementation, rather than reform, would be the watchword of the 1990s.

Whatever about any relative calm in policy at the time, the INTO in the North was about to enter particularly stormy seas. In 1991, Al Mackle retired after some 14 years as northern secretary. Six people were called for interviews, conducted by a board of seven, five of whom were INTO representatives (including two from the North), and two externals, while general secretary designate Joe O'Toole was present as a non-voting member. By a majority decision it was recommended that Frank Bunting be appointed to the position, and this was subsequently approved at a meeting of the CEC. This was highly controversial. Several of those interviewed were long-standing activists and/or officials, whereas Bunting was an external candidate. Though he had spent a short time teaching in west Belfast in the mid-1970s, he had been working as education officer in the Northern Ireland ICTU since 1976. Members of the NC felt that it was a mistake to appoint someone without significant experience in teaching or of trade union negotiation, and when they failed to get the CEC to reconsider the matter, the NC resigned en masse, with two exceptions, at the end of June. By the end of the year, most of them had returned, but it was a difficult time. In the 1990s Frank Bunting led on terms and conditions. The 'Enough is Enough' campaign against bureaucracy in schools was launched in November 1992 and the INTO workload campaign after that, both of which tried to fight the impact of the Baker reforms of the late 1980s. In 1997 a general election in the UK saw Labour return to office for the first time in 18 years. For all Tony Blair's electoral mantra of 'education, education, education', the Labour victory did not result in any real change for teachers' lives in the classroom or their pay packets.

A greater political development at that time was the revival of the peace process. Having run aground in the middle of the decade, it moved forward once more with the signing of the Good Friday Agreement in 1998 and, after a succession of missed deadlines, the setting up of a Northern Ireland executive in November 1999. This meant that education policy would be run from Belfast for the first time in about 27 years. In a historic development, a Catholic nationalist came to hold the position of minister for education for the first time in the North's existence. Sinn Féin chose the Education portfolio for itself and nominated Martin McGuinness to the role. McGuinness's position on a number of issues was similar to that of the INTO. Once in office, he abolished the recently introduced school league table and in 2000 he commissioned a report on academic selection. In 2002 he announced that he would abolish the 11+, something the INTO had demanded and campaigned for for over 50 years.[149] The timing was spectacularly unfortunate, however, as McGuinness made his announcement the day before the assembly was suspended. It would be almost five years before devolved government was restored and in the meantime the abolition of the 11+ was stalled. This period also saw a rise in loyalist hostilities centred around a school in an interface area of Belfast during 2001 and 2002. Over several weeks, crowds of loyalists aggressively protested outside Holy Cross, a Catholic primary school for girls, shouting sectarian abuse and throwing objects at the children and their parents and guardians. The parents and teachers in the school received death threats and on one occasion a bomb was thrown. In January 2002, the Red Hand Defenders declared that Catholic teachers were legitimate targets – a serious threat not least because the UDA, for which it was a front, had killed a Catholic postman days earlier.[150] It was a difficult time, during which a number of schools were damaged in arson attacks and the Northern Office in College Gardens was attacked on several occasions.

Following the St Andrews Agreement in 2006, a new northern executive was established in May 2007. Caitríona Ruane became minister for education and held the position until May 2011, when she was succeeded by John O'Dowd. The restoration of devolved government did not mark the beginning of any improvements in education in the North, coming as it did on the eve of the global economic crisis and a period of austerity and cut-backs in the public sector. The next decade would be defined by a fight against cuts in the North. In 2011, Frank Bunting retired as northern secretary following a period of ill-health and was succeeded by Gerry Murphy, a principal teacher and former chairman of the Northern Committee. While his predecessor had held office at a time of relative calm, Gerry Murphy enjoyed no honeymoon period. The INTO and its sister unions faced cut-backs, attacks on pensions, threats to jobs, and disputes over inspections. The United Kingdom's decision to leave the European Union in June 2016 gave cause for more concern. It created uncertainty for everyone in the North, but particularly for teachers along the border region. In the context of greater North–South co-operation during this time, the INTO made some progress on long-standing practical issues for teachers on an all-Ireland basis: teacher mobility, the recognition of teacher qualifications on either side of the border and the transfer of pension entitlements between the North and South. The latter affected both teachers who had moved on retirement and also the many INTO members who lived and worked on different sides of the border. Naturally, the INTO was worried that its hard-won gains, and the movement of people more generally, were threatened by Brexit. The collapse of the power-sharing executive in January 2017 and the failure to form a new executive after the March 2017 election only heightened the sense of instability. Whatever challenges lay ahead, the INTO in the North faced them when the organisation was at its strongest ever, with over 7,000 members, making it the largest teacher union in Northern Ireland, as well as the largest teacher union on the island of Ireland.

CONCLUSION

An early editorial in the *Irish Teachers' Journal* from 1868 observed, 'It is an undoubted fact that the existence of a great many of the grievances of the Teachers of Ireland may be traced to their want of co-operation with each other in demanding their removal. There is no unity amongst them – none of that influence and power which always result from concentrated efforts to attain a legitimate object.'[1]

The grievances at that time were many. Pay was probably of greatest concern to the greatest number, as low as a day labourer's but paid quarterly and handed over from the manager at his doorstep to the teacher, as though the teacher was a supplicant looking for alms. Teachers' insecurity in their positions was the other great concern, since they had no security of tenure and could be fired by their managers for any reason or none, without any recourse to appeal. Then there was the lack of pensions and accommodation and the dilapidated buildings in which they spent their working days, all of which caused very genuine material hardship.

Since the rules under which the teachers were employed prohibited them from being politically active or expressing their grievances publicly, and their paymasters in the Board of Education refused to accept any communication from them, still less enter into dialogue, the teachers found themselves in a particular place in society. Socially influential in their communities, they were materially poor and officially marginalised. As Tom Garvin has noted, 'the teacher experienced a curious mixture of power and powerlessness', which led many towards radicalism, drawing political opinion from the radical, nationalist provincial and Irish-American press.[2] Of course, this was not true of the teachers as a whole, and there were others who were either more politically conservative or more cautious, but radicalism was evident in the anti-clericalism within sections of the INTO during the 1890s. This was something that emerged periodically during the many individual disputes, and was reflected into the 1960s with the Ballina dispute. To put this solely down to anti-authoritarianism would be disingenuous; most teachers had little problem with authority when it rested among themselves. Rather, as the Irish Protestant National Teachers' Union pointed out in the mid-1910s:

> [T]he arrangement that places teachers under the control of clergymen is one that was almost designed to produce friction. There are no two classes of men in existence so much inclined to censoriousness as clergymen and

teachers. The former are so accustomed to oversee their flocks and to notice the irregularities of conduct and of morals, that criticism of conduct and censoriousness become ingrained in their very nature. Similarly teachers have to act in the same way towards their pupils with like results. To place one of these classes under the supervision of the other is to put a premium on friction and to make serious quarrels a matter of course.[3]

Nevertheless, as one writer put it in 1919 (perhaps influenced by the comments by J.P. Mahaffy after the 1916 Rising):

When men and women in such a position are underpaid, insecure and goaded into a position of profound discontent, they are likely to become active agents of revolution, none the less powerful because they cannot act openly. It is impossible to estimate, though it is interesting to guess, how far the present condition of Ireland is due to the influence of National School Teachers.[4]

If some of the teachers' anger manifested itself in nationalism, much of it was channelled into their organisation and its fight for better conditions. Petitioning and lobbying, including the employment of a parliamentary secretary in the House of Commons, were the means used by the INTO in its early years. Notably, however, the INTO went beyond the idea of itself as a professional organisation to develop a trade union consciousness at a relatively early stage. It was 1917 when the INTO first took the decision, in principle, to strike. This was controversial within the organisation, with some members regarding it as below their status as white-collar workers, but if striking was below their status, it was not as insulting to the teachers' sense of professionalism as their pay. Nor was it unheard of. Close to home, the first local teachers' strike in England had taken place in Portsmouth in 1896.

Crucially, however, not only did the INTO decide to consider strike action as a means of redress, it also decided to throw its lot in with the trade union movement, joining what was then the Irish Trade Union Congress (ITUC). This was a whole 50 years before any of its sister unions in the United Kingdom would join the British Trade Union Congress.[5] Affiliating to the ITUC was not uncontroversial among members, but it was less its trade unionism than its perceived links to advanced nationalism and to Bolshevism that caused the greatest controversy. It led to the organisation's only enduring split when a handful of Ulster branches seceded, ultimately resulting in the formation of the Ulster Teachers' Union (UTU). For 50 years until then the INTO had, for the most part, managed to maintain unity against any potential splits on religion or politics. Clashes were inevitable, but they were usually resolved sooner rather than later. The UTU marked an end to that. While the INTO remained an important organisation representing teachers in the North after partition, the existence of a rival union (and others would follow) was one crucial difference between the context in which the INTO operated there and in the South.

In 1920 the INTO won a significant salary increase from the British government. It was a notable but short-lived victory. Within two years Ireland had been divided, and in no time, teachers on both sides of the border found their salaries cut. The cuts in pay hurt teachers materially, North and South, but their impact on morale was somewhat different on either side of the border. Catholic teachers in the North found themselves working in the lower tier of a two-tier school system in maintained schools, but while the political circumstances had changed, their working lives were broadly the same.

In the South, teachers were disillusioned by the new state, of which so much had been hoped. Their financial gains were clawed back by the Free State government, and to add further hardship, it now expected teachers, many of whom had no Irish themselves, to single-handedly revive the Irish language. Instead of an independent Ireland that valued education and the educators, as Thomas Davis or Pearse had envisaged, there were huge classes in run-down schools staffed by ill-paid and often resentful teachers. This resentment built up over the first two decades after independence, culminating in the 1946 teachers' strike, which lasted seven months. While the 1946 strike failed in its immediate goals, teachers were no less belligerent at its end. They played an important part in forming a new political party, Clann na Poblachta, and crucially they helped to make sure that Fianna Fáil did not return to office in the general election that followed a little over a year later. Perhaps that, more than anything, caused politicians to recognise the INTO's strength, although that is not to say that they were treated generously in the following years. Primary teachers in the North were put on a common pay scale with secondary teachers in 1945 and in the years after the 1946 strike, their colleagues in the South sought the same, but it was 1970 before the government in the South conceded this, even if, by the end, the delay was due to opposition from post-primary teachers.

When the INTO celebrated its centenary in 1968, it did so by holding an international conference of teachers in Dublin. But if it was outward looking it was somewhat backward looking too. The salary machinery achieved during the 1950s and the new salary scales were important successes for the INTO, and as they began the 1970s, the organisation's long-time demand of degrees for national teachers finally became a reality. Success meant it had become a little complacent, a 'sleeping giant' in John Horgan's words.

From the late 1970s, following Gerry Quigley's election as general secretary, the organisation began to modernise and professionalise. Women, whose role in the INTO's administration had in no way matched their numbers, played an increasingly active role in the organisation. The INTO also began to take on more paid officials. Local representatives and members of the CEC continued to play an active and important role in running the organisation, though from the 1990s, the numbers of staff increased in head office in Dublin and the northern office in Belfast, and they took on more of the workload representing members, not least in individual cases.

At the same time as this increased professionalism in the organisation, the political and macroeconomic policy of the South began to operate through the social partnership model. The INTO was an important factor in negotiations, due to its size and the role played by the politically astute general secretary Joe O'Toole, and though by no means without its critics within the membership, the organisation managed to avoid any serious fissures over the question of partnership. With salary issues siphoned into the partnership arrangements, more attention could be devoted to the professional aspects of teaching, including professional training and education policy, at a time during the 1990s when education reform appeared never-ending.

From the late 1980s, in the North, 'reform' meant increased bureaucracy, mandatory hours and assessment, introduced by Thatcherite politicians, which the teacher unions in the UK had been unable to resist. There was not quite the same political impetus to introduce neo-liberal education policies in the South, but when attempts were made to move in this direction, the INTO had the political capital to ensure that regimes of constant testing, assessments and league tables were not introduced. During the 1990s and into the 2000s, teachers' salaries increased and with more teachers employed (an increase of one-third between 1996 and 2006) for fewer pupils, class sizes fell.

Much of the gains of this period came under pressure during the economic crisis after 2008, the bank bailout and the arrival of the Troika. Compulsory redundancies were avoided, but teachers, like the rest of the public service, had their salaries cut, taxed and levied, while new entrants were taken on at a lower rate. The issue of equal pay for equal work, once the demand of women members, now came to dominate meetings and congresses once again. If the North's teachers in recent years escaped the levels of cuts meted out in the South, they faced their own austerity. Although devolution meant that education policy now came from Belfast, London still held much of the purse strings.

On 15 August 1868, a couple of dozen men met in a small room at 33 Denmark Street in Dublin to discuss how they would go about setting up a nationwide organisation for national teachers. That small gathering was described at the time as the 'largest meeting of teachers ever in Ireland'. It seems trite to suggest that 150 years later they would not recognise the organisation they brought about, numbering almost 45,000 members across Ireland, but the contrast is remarkable nonetheless.

In face of the opposition of the British educational authorities and the Church, it overcame political and religious divisions that could have sundered it before it had properly established itself and managed to maintain a united front rather than being split by sectionalism. The INTO operated as a professional body and as a trade union. But for many teachers, often working on their own in rural areas, it became a family.

As a 'schoolmaster's daughter' put it in 1948, her father and his contemporaries 'lived for the organisation and were proud of it', and 'the friendship which existed between teachers in those days was no make-believe. Indeed it was not until I was about twelve or thirteen years of age that I realised the host of teachers whom I thought were all uncles and aunts of mine were no relations at all – just teachers from the surrounding district.'[6]

Naturally, there were rivalries and disagreements, as there are in any family, but more than anything there was a strength of purpose, for themselves and for education. There was much to point towards by way of successes along the way – in pay, pensions, tenure, class size, conditions and status – but in many ways the INTO's greatest success was its survival, and one of its greatest achievements was fostering a sense of solidarity, unity and professionalism among the men and women whom the authorities, whether secular or clerical, so keenly wished to keep divided.

ENDNOTES

Chapter 1: Beginnings, 1868–1900

1 *Dublin Evening Mail* 1 January 1869, quoted in Harte, *Irish Teachers' Grievances.*
2 Bartlett, *Ireland: A History* p.273.
3 Akenson, *The Irish Educational Experiment* p.1.
4 In 1852, only 175 out of 4,795 schools were managed on a joint basis. Ó Buachalla, *Education Policy* p.22.
5 Harte, *Irish Teachers' Grievances* pp.19–24.
6 Akenson, *Irish Education Experiment* p.154.
7 *The Nation* 17 November 1848.
8 O'Connell, *100 Years* p.2.
9 Ibid.; *The Nation* 19 November 1849; *ISW* 24 June 1916.
10 *The Nation* 19 November 1849, 23 November 1849; *Freeman's Journal* 21 November 1848.
11 *ISW* 24 June 1916.
12 See Seventeenth Report of the Commissioners (1850–1) p.6.
13 O'Connell, *100 Years* p.3; *The Nation* 27 September 1851; *ISW* 24 June 1916.
14 *ITJ* 8 November 1884.
15 *ITJ* 15 December 1872, quoted in Ward, 'INTO's pre-history'; *ISW* 24 June 1916.
16 W.H. Adair, 'Struggle for Freedom' in *Irish Protestant National Teachers' Union Annual* 1923 p.26.
17 Ward, 'INTO's pre-history'; *AMN* November 1976.
18 O'Connell, *100 Years* p.4.
19 MacNeill, *Vere Foster* p.111.
20 O'Connell, *100 Years.*
21 O'Connell, *100 Years* p.5; *ITJ* 1 June 1868 features a report of a meeting between teachers and one of the journal's editors, Mr Browne. *ITJ* 3 January 1874.
22 *ITJ* 1 June 1868.
23 *ITJ* 1 June 1868.
24 Ibid.
25 *ITJ* September 1868. The description of the room is from Mr Shannon, one of the delegates at the first congress in 1877.
26 *ITJ* January 1869.
27 Moroney, *National Teachers' Salaries* p.26.
28 *ITJ* March, June 1869.
29 *ITJ* May, November 1869.
30 'Evidence of the Irish National Teachers' Associations in Reply to Queries addressed by the Commissioners to Vere Foster esquire, and submitted by him for their consideration' (London, 1869).

31 Harte, *Irish Teachers' Grievances* pp.19–24.

32 *ITJ* 1 January 1869.

33 *ITJ* January 1870.

34 See, for instance, *ITJ* 15 January 1872.

35 Adair, 'Struggle for Freedom' in *Irish Protestant National Teachers' Union Annual* 1923.

36 *ITJ* 1 February 1869.

37 *ITJ* 1 October and 1 November 1869. The reference to serfs was quoting an alleged comparison made by the late head inspector of national schools, Mr Kavanagh.

38 *ITJ* January 1870.

39 Ibid.

40 Ibid.

41 *Irish Times* 2 January 1871.

42 Ibid.

43 *ITJ* January 1872. The journal reported that there had been confusion over the vote, with some delegates protesting that they thought they were voting for the resolution rather than the amendment, but the result stood.

44 See Coolahan, *Irish Education*; Moroney, *National Teachers' Salaries* p.29; Powis Report.

45 Powis Report p.385.

46 Ibid. p.388.

47 *Irish Times* 26 February 1873.

48 See, for example, the letter from John Doyle PP, Philipstown in the *Freeman's Journal* 21 January 1873.

49 Moroney, *National Teachers' Salaries* p.30.

50 A letter referring to the issue in the *ITJ* in March 1874 had met with a unanimous response that it was not to be broached again.

51 *ITJ* 18 April, 25 April, 13 June, 20 June 1874. Charles Henry Meldon (1841–1892) was called to the bar in 1863. He was first elected as MP for Kildare in a by-election in 1874 and held his seat until he stood down at the 1885 election. He lived in what is now 25 Parnell Square, most recently occupied by Coláiste Mhuire. While an MP he also advised the Irish Medical Association about the promotion of their superannuation and redress bills, and the IMA issued a sympathetic note on his death, but it was not greatly remarked on by the INTO at the time.

52 *ITJ* 25 May 1878.

53 *ITJ* 1 June 1878.

54 Quoted in *ITJ* 29 June 1878.

55 INTO Bangor Congress Committee, *A Short Biographical Study of Vere Foster, First President* (1956) p.22.

56 Moroney, *National Teachers' Salaries* p.35.

57 Ibid. p.37.

58 See, for example, letter from A.K. O'Farrell, central secretary, in the *ITJ* 2 August 1879.

59 *ITJ* 2 August 1879. In fact, Meldon's name is largely absent from the INTO's annals, and is never mentioned in O'Connell's *100 Years*.

60 O'Connell, *100 Years* p.273.

61 *ITJ* 20 December 1884.

62 *ITJ* 10 December 1881.

63 Frank Callanan, 'Timothy Michael Healy', *DIB*.

64 Felix M. Larkin, 'Thomas Sexton', *DIB*.

65 *ITJ* 19 January 1884. Four were from Belfast, five outside Belfast, two were from Cork, one from Dublin and two from the midlands.

66 *ITJ* 12 January 1884.

67 See Fergus D'Arcy, 'The Dublin Police Strike of 1882', *Saothar* 23 (1998).

68 *ITJ* 26 January 1884; NLI, Minutes of the Board of National Education, MSS 5560 Vol. 18. The matter was first raised by Chief Justice Morris at the board's meeting on 8 January 1894, when he dissented to a warning being issued to William Cullen in Belfast on the grounds that 'the particular cases now dealt with form but a very small part of a very large subject – viz. the present attitude of the NTs and recent proceedings of their congress'.

69 *ITJ* 12 April 1884; *Weekly Irish Times* 5 April 1884. See Minutes of the Board of National Education.

70 *ITJ* 3 January 1885.

71 Ibid.

72 *Freeman's Journal* 30 April 1886. Some 20 teachers were present on the first day.

73 *Freeman's Journal* 25 October 1886; at the Northern Union's congress in April 1888, the President, D.H. Simmons, regretted that the chief secretary had not afforded them an opportunity of putting their case to him. *Belfast Newsletter* 4 April 1888. See also *Cork Examiner* 5 April 1889.

74 *ITJ* 2 June 1888.

75 *ITJ* 5 January 1889.

76 Quoted in *ITJ* 5 January 1889. See also *Cork Examiner* 5 April 1889.

77 Thomas J. Morrissey, 'William Joseph Walsh', *DIB*.

78 Ó Buachalla, *Education Policy* p.41; *ITJ* 12 January 1889.

79 The original letter from Rev. Edward Rowan was published on 12 January 1889. It and many of the INTO responses were reprinted in *ITJ* 9 March 1889.

80 *ITJ* 23 November 1889.

81 *ITJ* 4 January 1890.

82 *ITJ* 4 June 1892.

83 *ITJ* 16 July 1892.

84 *The National Teacher* 7 April 1893.

85 Aisling Walsh, 'Michael Cardinal Logue 1840–1924: striving for a Catholic education system' Part III, *Seanchas Ardmhacha: Journal of the Armagh Diocesan Historical Society* Vol. 19, No. 2 (2003) 233.

86 *ITJ* 3 September 1892.

87 *Freeman's Journal* 14 October 1892.

88 *ITJ* 22 October 1892.

89 *National Teacher* 7 April and 28 April 1893.

90 The account of the Carey case is based on the report of the sub-committee published in *ITJ* 23 December 1893. See also Ó Buachalla, *Education Policy* p.41; HC Deb 10 August 1894, vol. 28, col. 565.

91 Board of National Education Minutes, 21 February, 7 March, 14 March and 2 May 1893; *National Teacher* 19 May 1893.

92 Reprinted in the *National Teacher* 20 October 1893.

93 Board of National Education Minutes 13 February, 20 February, 10 April, 24 April 1894.

94 Fr Connolly's letter of resignation, dated 21 March 1894, was accepted by the Board of National Education at its meeting on 3 April 1894.

95 Board of National Education Minutes, 20 February, 10 April 1894.

96 *ITJ* 31 March 1894.

97 *ITJ* 12 May 1894.

98 *ITJ* 28 July 1894.

99 Quoted in *ITJ* 8 September 1894.

100 As he told Archbishop Walsh after Simmons' address to the 1894 congress, 'I am sure it has not escaped Your Grace's notice that the teachers are being urged on to their present action by the Parnellites.'

101 *Freeman's Journal* 26 July 1894.

102 *Freeman's Journal* 10 September 1894.

103 *ITJ* 2 February 1895. In fact, the case of the Careys, far from being prominent in the INTO's annals, was largely forgotten, and unlike other subsequent dismissal cases, is not mentioned at all in O'Connell's *100 Years*.

104 See *ITJ* 12 January 1895. There was also a campaign regarding the case of a Mr Gibson, an Ennis teacher who had recently been dismissed. See *ITJ* 1 June 1985.

105 See the *National Teacher* 17 June 1898 and *ITJ* 11 June 1898 for the Sligo case.

106 It is dealt with at length in O'Connell, *100 Years* pp.44–52, on which this section is based.

107 The full memorial is quoted in O'Connell, *100 Years* p.54.

108 *Freeman's Journal* 24 June 1898.

109 *National Teacher* 27 January 1899.

110 *Freeman's Journal* 28 November 1898.

111 *National Teacher* 14 October 1898; *ITJ* 25 June 1898.

112 See, for example, *Freeman's Journal* 10 October 1898.

113 *ITJ* 29 August 1896.

114 *ITJ* 19 November; *Freeman's Journal* 23 November 1898.

115 *National Teacher* 16 December 1898.

116 *ITJ* 14 January 1899.

117 Brown did not seek re-election and, contrary to Miller's claim that the organisation 'solidly voted out the president and vice president' who were responsible for the memorial (*Church, State and Nation* p.33), the elections were ultimately a defeat for the opponents of the memorial.

118 *Freeman's Journal* 6 April 1899.

119 Quoted in *ITJ* 15 April 1899.

120 O'Connell, *100 Years* p.59.

121 *Freeman's Journal* 8 June 1899.

122 *Freeman's Journal* 23 May 1899; *ITJ* 27 May 1899.

123 *ITJ* 5 January 1901.

124 *Cork Examiner* 25 October 1900.

125 Miller, *Church, State and Nation* p.122 (source: *Freeman's Journal*).

126 *Cork Examiner* 29 April, 5 June, 17 June, 3 May 1899. It had briefly deferred action at the beginning on the advice of the bishops of Waterford and Clonfert.

127 O'Connell, *100 Years* p.61.

128 IPNTU, *1911 Annual* p.44, *ITJ* 11 November 1899.

129 O'Connell, *100 Years* p.60.

130 *ITJ* 6 January 1900.

131 *ITJ* 20 April 1901; IPNTU, *1911 Annual*; *ITJ* 19 July 1902.

132 In the words of its president, David Elliott, who, when asked by the Dill Commission if IPNTU members were also members of INTO, responded, 'oh, yes, decidedly' (Dill Report, Appendix 3 p.79).

133 IPNTU, 'Its History, Aims and Objects' from IPNTU *1911 Annual*.

134 Membership was 5,250 in 1899 and approximately 3,661 in 1902. Figures derived from annual reports.

Chapter 2: 'Years of Civil War': The INTO and the Starkie Regime, 1900–1922

1 Maume, *Long Gestation* p.78.

2 Thomas Walsh, *Primary Education* p.12.

3 *AMN* April 1962.

4 Christina O'Doherty, 'William Joseph Myles Starkie' (unpublished PhD thesis) pp.66–70.

5 O'Connell, *100 Years* p.154. Catherine Mahon, statement on behalf of the INTO to the Dill Commission, see Dill, appendix to the third report p.377.

6 *Kerry Weekly Reporter* 3 March 1900; CEC resolution 3 March 1900, statement on behalf of the INTO; Dill, appendix to the third report.

7 The official title was the Commission on Manual and Practical Instruction. See Thomas Walsh, *Primary Education* p.33.

8 Ibid. p.49; O'Doherty, 'William Starkie' p.128, CEC Report 1900–1901 p.20.

9 Dill Report Appendix 3 p.325.

10 Thomas Walsh, *Primary Education* p.55.

11 Moroney, *National Teachers' Salaries* p.55.

12 Dill Report Appendix 3, Catherine Mahon p.325. Under the old system, an average of 35 was sufficient.

13 *ITJ* 21 July 1900.

14 Dill, appendix to the third report p.379.

15 Dill, appendix to the third report p.380.

16 Titley, *Church, State and the Control of Schooling* p.17; O'Doherty, 'William Starkie' p.9.

17 J.J. Hazlett to W.J.M. Starkie, nd (November 1902) TCD MSS 9209 (78).

18 Gaughan, *Thomas O'Donnell* p.19.

19 He had also threatened to establish a breakaway union for assistant teachers some years earlier, accusing the organisation of overlooking their needs. See ibid. The CEC offered its warm congratulations and entertained him at a 'jubilant' dinner, but a testimonial established to cover his expenses and maintain him was slow to attract funds. By the time it was due to close in July 1901, it had attracted a paltry £70. Kept open as a consequence, it amounted to almost £475 by the time the fund closed. *ITJ* 5 April 1902, 2 May 1902.

20 Catherine Mahon evidence, Dill Report Appendix 3 p.333.

21 *ITJ* 11 October 1902.

22 *ISW* 13 August 1904, CEC Report 1903–4 pp.43–4.

23 The event was instigated by a prominent former teacher and was noted by O'Connell in *100 Years* (p.28), who named him as Seumus MacManus. Without acknowledging his role in proceedings, MacManus wrote afterwards that 'this thing of toasting English royalty has been tolerated too long in Ireland and it is the duty of every Irishman to make active protest'; 'The Irish youth who quits school without realizing his duties as a rebel is, or should be, a discredit to his schoolmaster, as well as his country', *Irish Independent* 15 May 1905. MacManus wrote a column called 'Passing Events' in the *ISW* during 1905 under the pen name 'Seumas', which continued after the Sligo incident. O'Connell did not explain this in mentioning MacManus's role in the incident, although he did observe that 'it should be stated that at this period the INTO was not responsible for, and had no control over, the editorial department of the *School Weekly*'.

24 See *Cork Examiner* 28 April 1905; *Irish Independent* 18 May 1905; *Daily Express*, quoted in *Western People* 20 May 1905. HL Deb 5 June 1905, vol. 147, cols 624–8.

25 *Freeman's Journal* 6 June 1905.

26 Circular from the Office of National Education, June 1905 in Dill Report Appendix 3 p.283.

27 *ISW* 22 July 1905.

28 *ISW* 9 September 1905; O'Connell, *100 Years* p.28. Hazlett gave his account of what happened after the congress of 1906, after reading the CEC's version in its annual report, which, he said, had totally misrepresented his actions and its writer having 'gone out of his way to state several falsehoods about me', *ISW* 12 May 1905.

29 Dale Report.

30 Ibid. p.86. See p.12 on management of country schools.

31 Quoted in Thomas Walsh, *Primary Education* p.64.

32 Ibid. p.76.

33 Dale Report p.89 (pp.34–5).

34 Ibid. p.37.

35 CEC Report 1904–5 p.48.

36 *ISW* 18 February 1905.

37 Ní Bhroiméil, 'Rule 127(b)' 36.

38 Salaries ranged from £56 to £139 for men and from £44 to £114 for women.

39 *Irish Independent* 28 February 1905; HC Deb 30 March 1905, vol. 143, col. 1727; *ISW* 4 March 1905; Ní Bhromiéil, 'Rule 127(b)' 38.

40 HC Deb 5 April 1905, vol. 144, cols 465–6; Dill Report Appendix 3 p.382.

41 O'Connell, *100 Years* p.138.

42 *ISW* 18 March 1905

43 Ní Bhroméil, 'Rule 127(b)' 46, 50 n.8.

44 *ISW* 3 February 1906.

45 Chuinneagáin, *Catherine Mahon* p.36.

46 *ISW* 5 May 1906.

47 *Irish Independent* 21 April 1906.

48 Chuinneagáin, p.26.

49 *Irish Independent* 21 April 1906.

50 *ISW* 15 September 1906.

51 Chuinneagáin, p.44

52 Chuinneagáin, p.49.

53 INTO Annual Directory 1908 p.41.

54 Miller, *Church, State and Nation* p.145.

55 Pat Jalland, 'Augustine Birrell (1850–1933)', *Oxford Dictionary of National Biography* (Oxford University Press, 2004; online edn, May 2012).

56 Maume, *Long Gestation* p.82.

57 *ISW* 6 April 1907; CEC Report 1907–8 p.25.

58 O'Connell, *100 Years* p.158.

59 *ISW* 11 July 1908.

60 O'Connell, *100 Years* pp.161–2.

61 CEC Annual Report 1908–9 p.27.

62 *ISW* 19 June 1909.

63 In District 1, for instance, density ranged from an unusually high 92% in Louth to a low of 53.4% in Dublin. In District 7 it ranged from 70% in Tyrone to 46% in Armagh. See *ISW* 4 February 1911.

64 See O'Connell, *100 Years* pp.30–1.

65 *ISW* 26 February 1910.

66 *ISW* 4 March 1911.

67 *ISW* 8 October 1910.

68 CEC Report 1907–8 p.42; O'Connell, *100 Years* p.18.

69 *ISW* 24 September 1910.

70 To the Dill Inquiry, quoted in Chuinneagáin, *Catherine Mahon* p.111.

71 Chuinneagáin, *Catherine Mahon* p.104

72 O'Doherty, 'Starkie' p.349.

73 See Coolahan with O'Donovan, *Ireland's Inspectorate*; O'Doherty, 'Starkie' p.347.

74 O'Doherty, 'Starkie' p.355.

75 Ibid. p.356.

76 See *ISW* 19 October 1912.

77 *ISW* 26 October 1912; *Freeman's Journal* 28 October 1912.

78 *Limerick Leader* 18 October 1912; O'Connell, *100 Years* p.410.

79 Dill Third Report Appendix pp.405–6.

80 See for example the cuttings published in *Irish Independent* 4 November 1912.

81 *ISW* 26 October, 9 November 1912; HC Deb vol. 42 cols 2357–8, 24 October 1912; *Irish Independent* 1 and 2 November 1912.

82 *Irish Independent* 1 November 1912.

83 *ISW* 9 November 1912.

84 Birrell to Starkie, 8 November 1912 TCD MSS 9209.

85 Quoted in O'Doherty, 'Starkie' p.364.

86 O'Doherty, 'Starkie' p.367. The other members of the Commission were Most Rev. Denis Kelly, bishop of Ross; Sir Hiram Shaw Wilkinson, a former diplomat and retired imperial judge; Henry E.B. Harrison, an English former school inspector; Walter McMurrough Kavanagh, a former IPP MP; and T.M. Kettle, professor of national economics in the NUI and former MP. See *Weekly Irish Times* 8 February 1913. John Coffey died in an accident at his home shortly afterwards, in March 1914.

87 *Weekly Irish Times* 22 February 1913.

88 Evidence to Dill, appendix to third report, appendix LII p.30.

89 Dill, appendix to the third report p.307

90 Coolahan with O'Donovan, *Ireland's Inspectorate* p.74.

91 *ISW* 6 November 1913.

92 Annie Connolly to Starkie, 4 December 1913 TCD MSS 9209 (80).

93 Moroney, *National Teachers' Salaries* p.69.

94 Ibid. p.69.

95 See for instance *ISW* 25 July 1914.

96 HC Deb 1 August 1918, vol. 109 col. 594.

97 Robert Donovan to Starkie 8 October 1915 TCD MSS 9209 (166).

98 *ISW* 13 November 1915.

99 HC Deb 1 August 1918, vol. 109, col. 594.

100 Noel Ward, 'INTO – 1916 Rising', *InTouch* December 2015.

101 Maurice Day, bishop of Clogher, to Starkie 9 October 1915 TCD MSS 9209 (112).

102 Chunneagáin, *Catherine Mahon* p.149.

103 *ISW* 8 January 1916.

104 *ISW* 8 January 1916.

105 For more on O'Connell, see Cunningham and Puirséil, 'T.J. O'Connell'.

106 O'Connell, *100 Years* p.279.

107 *ISW* 22 January, 12 February 1916.

108 *ISW* 20 May 1916.

109 *Western People* 1 April 1916.

110 *ISW* 1 and 8 January 1944.

111 See Puirséil, 'The INTO and 1916'.

112 *Freeman's Journal* 19 June 1916.

113 See the Eighty-Second Report of the Commissioners of National Education p.7 and minutes.

114 *Irish Times* 26 June 1916.

115 See O'Connell, *100 Years* pp.286–7; INTO, 'INTO Facts and correspondence in connection with the dismissal of Mrs Flanagan, Kilkeel Association' (March 1917).

116 See Ó hEithir, *Begrudger's Guide* pp.28–38; Queally, *Fanore School Case*; O'Connell, *100 Years* pp.62–70.

117 See Queally, *Fanore School Case* p.8; O'Connell, *100 Years* p.63.

118 Proceedings of 1917 congress p.136.

119 See INTO Congress 1917 p.248.

120 'That in order to secure uniformity of procedure under the Maynooth Resolution of June 1898, the bishops will interpret the said resolution in the sense suggested by the teachers, namely that the teacher shall be afforded the opportunity of being heard in his own defence before he is either summarily dismissed or served with notice of dismissal.' See O'Connell, *100 Years* p.69.

121 INTO Congress 1917 p.136.

122 *ISW* 21 July 1917; CEC Annual Report for 1917–18 p.42.

123 Chuinneagáin, *Catherine Mahon* p.155.

124 Ibid. p.168.

125 Ibid. p.175.

126 *ISW* 30 December 1916, 7 April 1917.

127 *ISW* 2 December 1916.

128 See *ISW* 12 October 1918; INTO Congress Programme 1919 p.40; O'Connell, *100 Years* p.14.

129 O'Connell, *100 Years* p.172.

130 *ISW* 10 November 1917.

131 *ISW* 8 December 1917.

132 *ISW* 6 April 1918. See Seifert, *Teacher Militancy* pp.1–2.

133 *Irish Independent* 1 November 1917.

134 O'Connell, *100 Years* p.175.

135 O'Doherty, 'Starkie' p.395.

136 O'Connell, *100 Years* p.180; *ISW* 16 March 1918.

137 *ISW* 6 April 1918.

138 Starkie to Solicitor General 8 April 1918 TCD MSS 9209/484.

139 O'Connell, *100 Years* p.184.

140 O'Connell, *100 Years* p.187; Moroney, *National Teachers' Salaries* p.78.

141 *ISW* 27 April 1918.

142 PRONI IPNTU minute book, Executive Council meeting 27 April 1918.

143 BMH, witness statement by Mícheál Ó Droighneáin (WS 178) pp. 17–23.

144 O'Connell, *100 Years* pp.457–8.

145 PRONI D3944/A1 UTU, 'Reasons for the formation of the union', ILP&TUC pp.8–19

146 Mitchell, *Labour in Irish Politics* p.91; ILP&TUC, 'Report of a Special Conference' 1 and 2 November 1918.

147 *Belfast Newsletter* 19 June, 28 November 1918; *ISW* 16 November 1918.

148 *ISW* 7 December 1918, 4 January 1919.

149 INTO CEC Report 1918–19 p.35.

150 Report of the INTO Congress 22–24 April 1919 (Dublin) p.26.

151 INTO CEC Report 1918–19 p.35.

152 Ibid. p.72

153 Ibid. A meeting of the CEC later decided against contributing to the Limerick strike fund, but eight local associations collected over £30. The largest single contribution by far from a teachers' association was £10 from Gweedore and Rosses Teachers' Association. Perhaps coincidentally, its county secretary a year earlier had been a young Peadar O'Donnell, but he had left teaching in the summer of 1918 to become a full-time official of the ITGWU.

154 PRONI D517/1 IPNTU Minute Book, Meeting of EC 10 May 1919; Report of Eighteenth Annual Conference 21 June 1919.

155 Mapstone, 'Ulster Teachers' Union' p.38.

156 *ISW* 22 January 1921.

157 Moroney, *National Teachers' Salaries* p.79; *Irish Independent* 27 February 1919; Viceregal Committee of Enquiry into Primary Education (Ireland) 1918 Report, Vols 1 and 2 (London, 1919).

158 Headlam to Starkie, 30 March 1919 TCD MSS 9209/282.

159 *Irish Independent* 15 August 1919.

160 Titley, *Church, State and the Control of Schooling* p.60.

161 Starkie to Macpherson 28 November 1919 TCD MSS 90209/412

162 INTO CEC Report 1919–20 p.32.

163 *Freeman's Journal* 1 December 1919.

164 *Freeman's Journal* 29 November 1919; O'Connell, *100 Years* p.293.

165 ILP&TUC Annual Report 1920 p.32.

166 Miller, *Church and State* p.437; *Freeman's Journal* 10 December 1920. See Titley, *Church, State and the Control of Schooling* pp.62–3.

167 O'Connell, *100 Years* pp.302–3 (the date given by O'Connell is incorrect); *Skibbereen Eagle* 17 January 1920.

168 Miller, *Church and State* p.238; *Irish Times* 22 December 1919

169 INTO CEC Report 1919–20 p.31–5.

170 *Irish Independent* 20 January 1920; Chuinneagáin, *Catherine Mahon* p.206; O'Connell, *100 Years* p.312.

171 O'Connell, *100 Years*; Chuinneagáin, *Catherine Mahon* p.212.

172 O'Connell, *100 Years* pp.322–3.

173 *Irish Independent* 28, 29 January 1920.

174 HC Deb 24 February 1920 vol. 125 cols 1504–5.

175 Ó Fiaich Archive, Patrick Cardinal O'Donnell Papers, Macpherson's Irish Education Bill. Circular to the bishops from Cardinal Logue, 27 February 1920, also printed in the *Irish Independent* on 5 March 1920.

176 Starkie to Macpherson 28 November 1919 TCD MSS 9209/412.

177 O'Connell, *100 Years* p.320.

178 Minutes of the INTO Easter Congress 1920 p.13; O'Connell, *100 Years* p.327.

179 *ISW* 17 April 1920.

180 Minutes of the INTO Easter Congress 1920 p.13; O'Connell, *100 Years* p.326.

181 G.A. Waters, 'Macpherson, (James) Ian, first Baron Strathcarron (1880–1937)', rev. Marc Brodie, *Oxford Dictionary of National Biography* (Oxford University Press, 2004; online edn, January 2008).

182 *ISW* 24 April 1920.

183 Ó Fiaich Library, Nunan to O'Donnell 8 May 1920.

184 Titley, *Church, State and the Control of Irish Schooling* p.68.

185 Starkie to Macpherson 28 November 1919 TCD MSS 9209/412.

186 *ISW* 13 November 1920; Moroney, *National Teachers' Salaries* pp.82–7.

187 *ISW* 26 February 1921.

188 CEC Report 1921–22 p.35; *ISW* 2 July 1921; *Freeman's Journal* 27 June 1921.

189 Minutes of the 1922 Annual Congress p.47; O'Connell, *100 Years* p.23.

190 Minutes of the 1922 Annual Congress p.47.

191 INTO Annual Directory and Year Book for 1923.

192 Thomas Walsh, *Primary Education in Ireland, 1897-1990* p.132

193 See O'Connell, *100 Years*, pp.343–51; Hyland and Milne (eds), *Irish Educational Documents* Vol. II, p.86; Coolahan, *Irish Education* p.38.

Chapter 3: The INTO in Independent Ireland, 1922–1946

1 *ISW* 28 January 1922.

2 *ISW* 11 February 1922.

3 *ISW* 22 April 1922.

4 *ISW* 20 May 1922.

5 Report of CEC meeting 6 May 1922 in *ISW* 13 May 1922. Two CEC members voted against the grant. 'Jottings' on 27 May features a letter from Tom Johnson, who writes that he appreciates the reasons why the INTO has not nominated anyone directly. See also *ISW* 6 June 1922.

6 See *ISW* 10 June 1922 and 1 July 1922 for O'Connell's account of his nomination. He did not refer to the CEC's refusal to nominate a candidate directly, or his circuitous route to the Dáil, in *100 Years*.

7 *ISW* 8–15, 22 July, 5 August 1922.

8 *ISW* 23 September 1922.

9 See *ISW* 27 January 1923 for regulations governing national school teachers who joined the National Army.

10 *ISW* 6 March 1925.

11 *ISW* 28 February 1925.

12 See Desmond and Callan, *Irish Labour Lives* pp.170–1. The account in *100 Years* merely states that 'at the last minute he failed to take his seat' (p.145). Cummins, a teacher based

in Kildare, was a close friend of T.J. O'Connell and an active member of the Labour Party. He retained the seat in subsequent Senate and Seanad elections (*Irish Labour Lives* p.64), but failed to win a seat in the Dáil, despite a number of attempts.

13 *ISW* 18 November 1922.

14 One figure for attendance was 12,000. *ISW* 8 and 15 July 1922.

15 Akenson, *A Mirror to Kathleen's Face* p.51.

16 Report of Kerry County Committee meeting, 24 June 1922 in *ISW* 22 July 1922.

17 *ISW* 29 July 1922; see Report of the Ballyhaunis Branch meeting 14 October for complaints about observance of boycott, *ISW* 11 November 1922.

18 'Report on the State of the Organisation for 1922' in INTO Year Book 1923 p.93.

19 The 1922 figure is from the 1923 Year Book. The final figure for 1921 is not available and is based on an estimate derived from the Preliminary Congress Report 1921.

20 Year Book 1923 p.93.

21 *ISW* 15 September 1923.

22 See Ward, *Teachers' Club.*

23 Ibid. p.17.

24 Titley, *Church, State and Control of Schooling* p.85.

25 See Farrell, 'Drafting of the Free State Constitution'. See also Akenson and Fallin 'The Irish Civil War and the Drafting of the Free State Constitution'.

26 DD 25 September 1922, vol. 1, col. 696.

27 DD 25 September 1922, vol. 1, cols 697–8.

28 DD 25 September 1922, vol. 1, col. 699.

29 DD 25 September 1922, vol. 1, col. 701; see also T.J. O'Connell, 'Education and the constitution', *ISW* 7 October 1922, which examined the constitutions of the German Republic (1919); the Kingdom of the Serbs, Croats and Slovenes (1921); the Polish Republic (1921); the Estonian Republic (1920); the Czechoslovak Republic (1920); the United States of Mexico (1917); and the Russian Socialist Federal Soviet Republic (1918).

30 Quoted in Titley, *Church, State and Control of Schooling* p.86.

31 *ISW* 28 October 1922.

32 Ibid.

33 *ISW* 25 November 1922. The branch's letter was discussed at the CEC meeting on 9 December and 'a suitable reply was ordered to be sent in answer thereto' (*ISW* 16 December 1922).

34 *ISW* 18 November 1922.

35 Labour Party and Trade Union Congress, 'Labour's Policy on Education' (Dublin, 1925), NLI MS 17,213.

36 Seán Broshanan in SD 8 February 1967, vol. 62 col. 1054.

37 *ISW* 28 February 1925.

38 See Linehan, 'A programme of Catholic action'.

39 'Labour's Policy on Education' pp.18–19.

40 John A. Murphy, 'Alfred O'Rahilly'. Then professor of mathematical physics and UCC registrar, O'Rahilly was a polymath who had been constitutional adviser to the Irish delegation at the Treaty negotiations in 1921 and was subsequently brought on to the

committee who were drafting the Free State Constitution. O'Rahilly, a Catholic Actionist, had differed fundamentally with his secular-minded colleagues; where they endeavoured to write a purely legal, non-sectarian document, O'Rahilly had sought to create a constitution based on Catholic social teaching that was much more prescriptive in its rights, and in this context had sought in vain to include a detailed section on education into the document. Subsequently, he expounded on this idea at the congress. Farrell, 'Drafting of the Free State Constitution', part 2.

41 DD 18 October 1922, vol. 1, cols 1699–1700.

42 DD 17 November 1922, vol. 1, col. 2244; see also *Irish Times* 18 November 1922, *ISW* 25 November 1922.

43 DD 17 November 1922, vol. 1, cols 2255–6.

44 John Ryan, quoted in Titley, *Church, State and Control* p.91; see also p.93.

45 Undated manuscript of speech on education, UCDA LA1/F/277.

46 The training colleges were St Patrick's Drumcondra and De La Salle in Waterford for Catholic men, and Mary Immaculate and Our Lady of Mercy, Carysfort for Catholic women. Protestant teachers, male and female, went to the Church of Ireland Training College. The Marlborough Street Training College that was part of the Model School closed around this time.

47 See for instance *ISW* 9 August 1924.

48 *ISW* 27 January, 10 February 1923.

49 See Valerie Jones, 'The Preparatory College System of recruitment to primary teaching', *Irish Educational Studies* vol. 12 no. 19 (1993).

50 The only exception to this was the Protestant preparatory college, Coláiste Moibhí in Glasnevin, which was kept open. See Jones, *A Gaelic Experiment.*

51 Report of the 1937 Congress.

52 Report of the 1935 Congress.

53 Report of the Department of Education 1930–31 p.5.

54 A resolution on this subject passed at the 1934 congress in Derry was criticised by the Blueshirt newspaper *United Ireland* (*ISW* 21 April 1934), which accused teachers of wanting their children to follow in their professional footsteps.

55 See Duffy, *The Lay Teacher* p.32.

56 DD 4 June 1926, vol. 16, col. 399.

57 DDA, Byrne Papers, J.M. O'Sullivan to Bishop O'Doherty 9 January 1929.

58 DDA, Byrne Papers, Padraic Ó Brolchain to Archbishop Byrne, 21 December 1933.

59 DDA, Byrne Papers, Dignam to Byrne 29 September 1934.

60 DDA, Byrne Papers, joint meeting of bishops and managers, 24 July 1934. They were split 11–9 on the question of funding buildings.

61 DD 2 November 1923, vol. 5, col. 671. See O'Connell, *100 Years* pp.199–200.

62 Quoted in *ISW* 17 November 1923.

63 *ISW* 17 November 1923 featured two pages of extracts from local and national newspapers.

64 See for instance Dublin City Branch Minutes 23 October 1923 INTOA; see also resolution passed by Roscommon teachers in *Irish Times* 7 November 1923.

65 *ISW* 1 December 1923.

66 O'Connell, *100 Years* pp.201–2. He was also secretary of the Dublin City branch. Leyden was later elected president of the organisation (1939–40).

67 O'Connell, *100 Years* p.200.

68 *ISW* 17 May 1924; the accusations of the CEC's efforts at 'muzzling Congress' were referred to by O'Connell in his 'Jottings' column, *ISW* 25 April 1925.

69 O'Connell, *100 Years* pp.200–1.

70 Ibid. pp.201–2; Moroney, *National Teachers' Salaries* p.103; DD 25 March 1926, vol. 14, cols 1705–8.

71 Moroney, *National Teachers' Salaries* p.107.

72 See ibid. pp.37–8 on the establishment of the scheme. See also *ISW* 26 October 1929.

73 O'Connell, *100 Years* p.264; Moroney, *National Teachers' Salaries* pp.110–11.

74 Blythe to O'Connell, 5 December 1931 in minutes of CEC special meeting 5 December 1931.

75 O'Connell *100 Years* p.265.

76 See Puirséil, *Irish Labour Party* pp.36–7.

77 *ISW* 5 March 1932.

78 O'Connell, *100 Years* p.467.

79 Congress Minutes Wednesday 30 March 1932, private session.

80 Boland to Secretary of the Executive Council 8 February 1926, NAI D/T S 3 925.

81 Memorandum on the Eligibility of National School Teachers for Membership of the Oireachtas, 11 November 1925 NAI D/T S 3925.

82 Memorandum on National Teachers who become TDs or Senators 15 March 1932 D/T S 3925.

83 Memorandum for the EC by the Minister for Finance on the question of Membership of the Oireachtas by National School Teachers, 23 September 1932 D/T S 3925.

84 Congress Minutes; *ISW* 9 April 1932.

85 Congress Minutes Wednesday 30 March 1932. The debate took place in private session. Kelleher, who was strongly identified with the 'anti-cut' side was elected Assistants' Representative by a margin of 2:1.

86 O'Connell, *100 Years* p.266

87 Ibid. p.266. Of those who voted the figure was 226 for the government's proposals and 2,809 against. Only one branch, Cloghan and Banagher, unanimously approved of the government offer while Rosguill and Doe was evenly divided. See CEC Minutes 26 July 1932.

88 CEC Minutes 26 July 1932; Moroney, *National Teachers' Salaries* p.114.

89 *ISW* 28 January 1932.

90 *ISW* 8 April 1933. The election saw the return of the three Fianna Fáil teacher deputies who had been first elected the previous year.

91 *Irish Times* 18 April 1933.

92 NAI D/T Department of Finance memorandum, February 1933.

93 NAI D/T Department of Education memorandum, 27 February 1933.

94 See Moroney, *National Teachers' Salaries* p.115; O'Connell, *100 Years* p.267.

95 *ISW* 8 April 1933; O'Connell, *100 Years* p.267.

96 *Irish Times* 3 April 1933; *ISW* 8 April 1933. A similar proposal calling on members to 'sever their connections' with various groups including the Gaelic League, the GAA and public libraries, and to 'abandon the teaching of the Irish language in schools' was passed at a large meeting of the Tralee branch. *Irish Times* 10 April 1933.

97 *Irish Times* 8 April 1933. The last day's strike had been during the general strike against conscription in 1918.

98 *Irish Times* 10 April 1933.

99 See *ISW* 29 April 1933; congress 1933 verbatim transcript p.81.

100 Proceedings of the 66th congress, 1934, p.51.

101 *Irish Times* 27 April 1933.

102 *ISW* 6 May 1933.

103 *Irish Times* 27 April 1933.

104 1933 Congress Minutes p.68 (Wednesday private session).

105 *Irish Times* 27 April 1933.

106 See SD 18 July 1933 vol. 17 cols 346–65.

107 See Marie Coleman, 'Alasdair Mac Caba ("Alec" McCabe)', *DIB*; Ward, *The Teachers' Club* p.52; O'Connell, *100 Years* pp.482–4.

108 O'Leary, 'Marriage bar' 48; see O'Connell, *100 Years* pp.286–7. As the Northern Committee report for 1932 noted: 'The North Antrim Regional Education Committee was the first public body to decree that women teachers in their employment must resign on marriage. Ballymena Regional Educational Committee followed the example, and subsequently Belfast, Derry, Limavady, and Co. Down. The Northern Executive Committee took every means to prevent such action being taken' (*1932 Annual Directory*, p.39).

109 *ISW* 20 February 1932.

110 Archbishop Byrne to T.J. O'Connell, 7 August 1928 in the minutes of CEC meeting 15 September 1928. Opinions on the question differed radically on a person by person basis, with divisions within the churches rather than between them. See O'Leary, 'Marriage bar' 52 n. 21.

111 O'Leary, 'Marriage bar' 48.

112 Ibid.

113 CEC meeting, 6 February 1932; O'Connell, *100 Years* p.280.

114 *ISW* 4 June 1932; O'Connell, *100 Years* p.281.

115 O'Leary, 'Marriage bar' 51; O'Connell, *100 Years* p.283.

116 *ISW* 10 December 1932.

117 Emphasis added. Quite apart from the supposition of absences, there is no data for the rates of absence by women teachers or how this compares with male rates of absence.

118 O'Connell, *100 Years* p.282.

119 *ISW* 3 December 1932.

120 See *ISW* 3 December 1932; Gerard Hogan, quoted in McCullagh, *The Reluctant Taoiseach* p.128.

121 Coolahan, *Irish Education* p.49.

122 See *ISW* 12 May 1934.

123 See for example *ISW* 1 January 1938. Others put the figure at 600 (*ISW* 5 March 1938).

124 Report of the 1937 Congress pp.26–7.

125 *ISW* 14 August 1937; *Irish Independent* 5, 6 August 1937.

126 DD 24 November 1937, vol. 69, col. 1143.

127 INTO Annual Directory 1939 pp.8–10; O'Connell, *100 Years* p.284; *Irish Times* 16 April 1938.

128 O'Connell, *100 Years* p.284

129 *ISW* 1 October 1938.

130 A letter to *ISW* 29 October 1938 from a woman calling herself 'Disillusioned' put it, 'On this same date that the war was declared on the older women teachers all other teachers were given five per cent increase of salary. Why? To keep them quiet of course, and quiet they all remained.'

131 *ISW* 25 February 1939. This issue became a bone of contention between the Athenry branch and the general secretary for several years.

132 See for example *ISW* 14, 21 May 1938, *ISW* 13 August 1938.

133 Report of CEC meeting, 25 June 1938 in *ISW* 2 July 1938.

134 INTO Annual Directory 1939 pp.8–10; Proceedings of the 1940 Congress, private session. p.21.

135 A delegate from the Longford branch told congresses of 1939 and 1940 that he had legal advice to the contrary but failed to provide it when asked. In 1941, a Longford addendum to a motion on compulsory retirement at 60, calling for the organisation to take a test case on the issue, was heavily defeated.

136 *ISW* 26 November 1938.

137 *ISW* 29 October 1938.

138 *ISW* 5 November.

139 *ISW* 1 October 1938.

140 *ISW* 22 October 1938. The Skibbereen branch report published in *ISW* 5 November 1938 noted a terrible attendance of 13 out of 76 members. There were 40 women teachers in the branch and none of them attended.

141 *ISW* 18 April 1942.

142 Report of the 1935 Congress.

143 Report of the 1941 Annual Congress.

144 *ISW* 18 April 1942.

145 At a function in the Gresham Hotel to honour past presidents, Catherine Mahon spoke with emotion, observing that 'she expected that when she broke the ice the INTO would elect a woman president at intervals. There had been many women presidents in Scotland and England but only one here.'

146 Ward, 'INTO and the Catholic Church' p.8.

147 Ibid.

148 Titley, *Church, State and Control* p.108.

149 See INTO circular regarding a Council for Education 30 September 1933.

150 Titley, *Church, State and Control.*

151 Ibid. pp.108–9.

152 Ibid. pp.109, 129.

153 INTO circular regarding a Council for Education 30 September 1933. The organisations were: ASTI; Irish Technical Education Association; Managers' Association; Headmasters' and Schoolmasters' Association; Trinity College; University College Dublin; University College Galway; University College Cork; Irish Christian Brothers; the training colleges; and the Association of Assistant Mistresses in Secondary Schools. There was no provision for parents' representation.

154 Confidential INTO memorandum on the proposed establishment of an Education Federation (INTO Archive).

155 Some months earlier, McQuaid had been told of the ASTI's proposal to set up an advisory council by Canon James Staunton, then president of St Kieran's College, Kilkenny, who presumed that the bishops would not favour such a scheme. Staunton to McQuaid, 20 May 1933, DDA.

156 Ward, 'INTO and the Catholic Church' p.77.

157 Memorandum on Proposed (Advisory) Council of Education, first and second meetings by John Charles McQuaid (nd) DDA, McQuaid papers AB8/A/vi.

158 Ó Cuiv to O'Connell, 25 November 1933 (INTO archives).

159 DDA notes.

160 McQuaid wrote several drafts of his memorandum on the proposed council, none dated. DDA.

161 Memorandum on Proposed (Advisory) Council of Education, first and second meetings by John Charles McQuaid (nd), DDA, McQuaid papers AB8/A/vi; confidential INTO memorandum (nd), INTO archives.

162 Second memorandum, Education Council (nd); confidential memorandum (by McQuaid) on the proposed non-denominational council or Federation of All Education Bodies: the Remedy Suggested, annual education day in the Catholic Truth Society week (nd, *c.* June 1934) DDA, McQuaid papers.

163 Confidential memorandum (by McQuaid) on the proposed non-denominational council.

164 Second memorandum, Education Council (nd), DDA, McQuaid papers AB8/A/vi.

165 Fr T. O'Donnell to McQuaid, 13 June 1934, DDA, McQuaid papers.

166 Confidential memorandum (by McQuaid) on the proposed non-denominational council.

167 McQuaid to Archbishop Byrne, 1 October 1934, DDA, McQuaid papers.

168 Fr T. O'Donnell to McQuaid, 3 October 1934, DDA, McQuaid papers.

169 Confidential INTO memorandum (nd), INTO archives

170 McQuaid to Byrne in Cunningham, *Unlikely Radicals* p.73; dee also McQuaid's memo on Annual Education day in CTS Week (nd), DDA, McQuaid papers.

171 *Irish Press* 15 January 1935.

172 Ward, 'The INTO and the Catholic Church' p.160.

173 *Irish Press* 26 January 1935.

174 CEC Annual Report 1934–5 pp.35–6.

175 Report of the INTO congress 1935 p.49.

176 Quoted in McGarry, '"Catholics first"' 63. On the INTO and the Workers' Republic see also Puirséil, *Irish Labour Party,* Dermot Keogh, *Education: Church and State: Proceedings of the Second Daniel O'Connell School* (1992) and Whyte, *Church and State.*

177 While it was true that a small number of communists had become active in Labour, the ITGWU split was largely the result of a personality clash and a belief in the ITGWU that it was not being accorded sufficient influence in the party. See Puirséil, *Irish Labour Party.*

178 Report of the 1943 Easter Congress p.202.

179 Ward, 'INTO and the Catholic Church' p.85.

180 Report of the 1944 Congress pp.148–9.

181 CEC Minutes 12 August 1944. On this issue, see also Noel Ward, 'The INTO and the Labour Party' in *Proceedings of the Tenth Annual Drumcondra Educational Conference* (1993).

182 John Horgan, 'T.J. O'Connell', *Dictionary of National Biography.*

183 As O'Connell put it in the *ISW,* 'There were times during Mr Derrig's period of office when the relations between himself and the teachers were not exactly cordial' (9 September 1939).

184 *ISW* 21 October 1939. See O'Connell, *100 Years* pp.205–7

185 *ISW* 2 December 1939.

186 O'Connell, *100 Years* p.207; *ISW* 18 May 1940.

187 Moroney, *National Teachers' Salaries* p.135.

188 See 1941 Congress Report p.26.

189 *Anglo Celt* 6 January 1940.

190 *Irish Press* 1 January 1940.

191 See *Donegal News* 6 January 1940.

192 *ISW* 10 February 1940. Although there is no evidence of lasting ill-feeling over the episode, perhaps it is significant that Leyden did not attend congress that Easter because he was 'unwell'.

193 This inquiry was conducted on the instructions of the 1936 congress.

194 Moroney, *National Teachers' Salaries* p.136.

195 *ISW* 13 January 1940.

196 NAI D/T S 10 236 A Letter from the Minister for Education to the Cabinet 8 August 1942.

197 See for example NAI D/T S10 236 A memorandum to the executive council on salaries of national teachers, 3 November 1937, in which he stressed the unique role played by national teachers in their 'task of national reconstruction' and noting that the refusal to restore the cuts had led to 'a deep sense of grievance which is rankling in their minds and infects the whole body. It is obvious that a body of teachers who are in such a state of mind cannot be expected to pull their full weight either in education or in the revival of the Irish language and Irish culture.'

198 *Quarterly Bulletin* October 1940.

199 Moroney, *National Teachers' Salaries* pp.136–7; *Quarterly Bulletin* April 1943.

200 Moroney, *National Teachers' Salaries* p.137.

201 *Quarterly Bulletin* October 1943.

202 DD 29 November 1944, vol. 95, col. 8. The executive had written to the hierarchy in February 1944 but its usual June meeting had been cancelled, so a response was not forthcoming until October. *Quarterly Bulletin* January 1945. The CEC meeting of 4 November decided that a meeting on the letter should be asked in the Dáil, leading to Halliden's approach.

203 McCormick, 'INTO and the 1946 Teachers' Strike' p.15.

204 NAI D/T 10236 B In an undated memorandum from the minister for education to the minister for finance, Derrig pleads with Aiken to reconsider the amount; but, responding, Aiken argued that Derrig's proposals were based largely on Northern Ireland figures, a comparison which, he argued, was not relevant.

205 The CEC had met the minister on 24 March, only days before congress, and had predicted that the 'deep dissatisfaction which exists throughout the whole body of teachers would find definite express' at congress. Letter from Mícheál Breathnach to Michael Moynihan 27 March 1945, NAI DT S 10236 B.

206 *ISW* 5 and 12 October 1946, Liam Forde, 'Could the strike have been avoided?'.

207 *ISW* 5 and 12 October 1946.

208 *ISW* 21 and 28 April 1945, 5 and 12 October 1946, INTO archive (Kerry papers), T.J. O'Connell to J. Allman, 4 May 1945. O'Connell refers to this in *100 Years of Progress* as follows: 'an *ad hoc* committee, chosen from the delegates, recommended that a Propaganda Committee should be set up to carry on a vigorous campaign in cooperation with the executive' p.211.

209 *ISW* 5 and 12 October 1946, *Quarterly Bulletin* July 1945. Some members had taken the idea of the CPC at face value and they were criticised at congress the following year for their failure to engage in any propaganda.

210 NAI DT S 10236 B notes of interview between CEC deputation, the minister for education and an taoiseach, 19 April 1945.

211 The action had been decided upon at a meeting of the Dublin City Branch committee on 18 May 1945. Craobh Cathrach Atha Cliath committee minutes. See *Irish Times* 27 April 1945. It received scant attention in the *ISW* apart from motions of support for the protest passed at branch meetings. See *ISW* 19 and 26 May, 2 and 9 June 1945.

212 *Irish Times* 27 April 1945.

213 See p. 82 above on the 1933 plan. The plan had been drawn up at a meeting of the CPC on 18 May; see CEC Minutes 1 June 1945.

214 According to the *Quarterly Bulletin* (October 1945), only one small branch, with fewer than 20 members, formally refused to contribute and in that case a number of members sent individual subscriptions.

215 McCormick, 'INTO and the 1946 Teachers' Strike' p.17.

216 The reasons for rejection were listed as follows: 1. Scale of figures was all round too low; 2. Women teachers shamefully treated; 3. 'Highly efficient' retained in more objectionable

form than ever; 4. Fundamental principles in congress scale ignored (with the exception of marriage allowance); 5. Existing anomalies perpetuated; 6. Date of operation indefinite; 7. Nothing for pensioned teachers. *ISW* 19 and 26 October 1946. See minutes of CEC meeting 17 November 1945.

217 DDA, McQuaid papers, O'Connell to Derrig, 10 December 1945.

218 Handwritten memo of events 10–11 December 1945. For O'Connell's account of events see *100 Years* p.214.

219 Minutes of CEC meeting 19 December 1945.

220 DDA, O'Connell to McQuaid 22 December 1945.

221 DDA, McQuaid to O'Connell 24 December 1945.

222 While the war had ended in 1945, the Emergency (or the Emergency Powers Act) did not end until September 1946. On the eve of the special conference the government did make one concession, however, agreeing to an implementation date of 1 September. *ISW* 19 and 26 October 1946.

223 *Irish Press* 11 February 1946. According to the *Press* report, the Dublin amendment was defeated by 216 to 183 or 54 per cent to 46 per cent. O'Connell, *100 Years* p.213.

224 Minutes, CEC meeting 15 and 16 February 1946.

225 Minutes, CEC meeting 9 March 1946.

226 DDA, McQuaid to Derrig, 14 March 1946.

227 *Irish Times* 21 March 1946.

228 *Irish Times* 22, 23 March 1946. It also listed the schools that were still operative.

229 DDA, Derrig to McQuaid 22 March 1946. See *Irish Times* 21 and 22 March 1946 for open schools.

230 DDA, copy of letter from McQuaid to Linehan, 17 March 1946. See *Irish Times* 20 March 1946. The letter was addressed to Linehan (not O'Connell, as he wrote in *100 Years* p.218) because O'Connell had taken ill that week and Linehan was deputising for him. As McQuaid noted in his letter, 'his absence, at this juncture, is indeed unfortunate'.

231 McCormick 'INTO and the 1946 Teachers' Strike', p.23.

232 *Irish Times* 23 March 1946.

233 Noel Ward, 'The INTO and the 1946 Teachers' Strike', *InTouch* March 2006.

234 On the committees see O'Connell, *100 Years* pp.231–2. Officers: Sean O'Grady, Bill Mullarkey and Michael Doherty with Mrs Breen, Mrs Byrne, Misses Skinnider, Bergin, McBride and McGrath and Messrs Finn, Moore, O'Regan, Clandillon, Wright, Roycroft, Ryder, Burke, Lyons, Costello, O'Reilly, Walshe and Coffey, Giles Cooper.

235 *Irish Times* 3 April 1946.

236 *Irish Times* 4 April 1946, 9 April 1946; Ward, 'The INTO and the 1946 Teachers' Strike'.

237 Daithi Ó Seannachain to de Valera, 27 June 1946, Frank McDonnell to de Valera, 10 October 1946 NAI D/T S 10236.

238 Dublin Strike Committee minute book, 18 October 1946.

239 *Quarterly Bulletin* July 1946.

240 *Irish Times* 28 March 1946.

241 *Irish Times* 6 April 1946.

242 *Irish Times* 12 April 1946.

243 DDA, Barton to McQuaid 2 April 1946, McQuaid to Barton 4 April 1946.

244 DDA, McQuaid to O'Connell 5 April 1946, O'Connell to McQuaid 5 April 1946, O'Connell to McQuaid 6 April 1946, McQuaid to O'Connell; Minutes of CEC meeting 6 April 1946.

245 The correspondence was published in the press on 24 April 1946.

246 *Irish Times* 22 March 1946.

247 *Irish Times* 24 April 1946.

248 See for instance *ISW* 27 July and 3 August 1946 on the *Irish Press* and the strike.

249 *Quarterly Bulletin* July 1946.

250 Ward, 'The INTO and the 1946 Teachers' Strike' p.27. The Shakespeare is now better known as the Hop House.

251 *Irish Times* 7 October 1946.

252 *Irish Times* 8 October 1946.

253 CEC Minutes 15 October 1946, *Irish Times* 16 October 1946.

254 O'Connell, *100 Years* p.229.

255 Report of the 1947 Congress (private session, Tuesday 8 April) p.32.

256 CEC Minutes 29 October 1946.

257 DDA, draft letter and press release dated 28 October 1946.

258 CEC Minutes 29 October 1946; Report of the 1947 Congress (private session, Tuesday 9 April) p.46.

259 McCormick, 'The INTO and the 1946 Teachers' Strike' p.44.

260 *Irish Times* 30 October 1946, quoted in ibid. p.42

261 *ISW* 16 and 23 November 1946.

262 *Irish Independent* 31 October 1946.

263 *ISW* 16 and 23 November 1946.

264 Report of the 1947 Congress p.51.

265 DDA, McQuaid to Canon James Sherwin 15 June 1946.

Chapter 4: The Pot Boiled Over, 1946– 1962

1 Farren, *Politics of Irish Education* pp.200–1.

2 Ibid. p.202.

3 Following its completion, the CEC paid honorariums to six people. Of those, John D. Sheridan was paid £40 and Messrs Brosnahan, Ryder and McMahon £25 each; however, this does not seem to reflect the contribution to the final report put in over the time it took to complete it. (Very small sums were paid to two others.)

4 Membership was 10,709 in 1945 and had fallen by almost 20% to 8,638 in 1947.

5 See O'Connell, *100 Years* pp.234–7; *ISW* 8 and 15 January 1947; DD 11 February 1947, vol. 104, cols 679–82.

6 *Quarterly Bulletin* January 1947; CEC Minutes 9 November 1947, 22 November 1947.

7 Report of the 1947 Congress p.136.

8 CEC Minutes 29 October 1946.

9 *ISW* 11 and 18 January 1947.

10 MacDermott, *Clann na Poblachta* pp.36–7.

11 Ibid. p.37.

12 Kelly's election address (see *ISW* 22 February and 1 March 1947) was rather weak and focused on the unfairness of his being 'passed over' as president.

13 Seán Brosnahan was born August 1911 in Killaloe, Co. Clare. He trained in De La Salle in 1931–3, before moving to Dublin. He taught in Dublin until his election as INTO treasurer in 1961. From 1967, he served 11 years as general secretary. A dedicated educationalist, he was awarded a BA, H Dip Ed and MA from UCD, and later obtained a diploma in public administration. He took a special interest in teaching children with special educational needs and was a pioneer in the area. As well as lobbying the government for policy changes, during the 1950s he encouraged the INTO to give funds to UCD to have educational psychology taught in the university. He was later instrumental in setting up the Special Education Course for primary teachers in St Patrick's College, Drumcondra. He was a founder member of the National Association for the Mentally Handicapped in Ireland. Elected to the Senate in 1961, he served there until 1977. He lived in Artane with his wife Sheila and four children. He died in December 1987. A Seán Brosnahan memorial fund was launched in his honour by District 14 to fund special education projects.

14 *ISW* 11 and 18 January 1947.

15 See 'An evolving bill of rights for teachers', an election address from Brosnahan, Sheehan and Griffin in *ISW* 22 and 29 March 1947.

16 Ibid.

17 As Sean Sweeney, standing against Matt Griffin in the Eastern District, put it, 'programmes of reform are irrelevant in this contest where the issue is my action as a member of the CEC in agreeing to terminate the strike', *ISW* 22 and 29 March 1947.

18 *ISW* 3 and 10 May 1947.

19 *ISW* 19 and 26 April 1947.

20 1947 Congress p.132. It failed to reach the required two-thirds majority first time round but was retabled as an emergency motion, where the levy would not be applicable in the North, and passed unanimously.

21 1947 Congress pp.121–4.

22 Chuinneagáin, *Catherine Mahon* p.214.

23 *ISW* 6 and 13 March 1948.

24 CEC Minutes 14 and 15 July 1948.

25 *ISW* 29 May and 5 June 1948.

26 *ISW* 1 and 8 May 1948.

27 *ISW* 12 and 19 June 1948.

28 *ISW* 3 and 10 May 1947.

29 CEC Minutes 3 May 1947.

30 See *ISW* 17 and 24 May 1947 for short profiles of the three.

31 Kelleher died in January 1976 and was survived by his widow Daisy, son Sean and three daughters, Sr Kathleen, Eibhlis and Maire. His grandson, Seán Ó Foghlú, was appointed secretary general of the Department of Education and Skills in 2012. See ANM January 1976.

32 One election address put it, 'I am applying to you as my employer for the past twenty three years to grant me the promotion which the vacancy provides.' *ISW* 14 and 21 June 1947.

33 *ISW* 12 and 19 July 1947; 6 and 13 September 1947. He did, however, declare that he would definitely remain in situ until the Bundoran congress at Easter.

34 *ISW* 24 and 31 January 1948. There was no response at all from the farmers' party, Clann na Talmhan, or from the breakaway National Labour.

35 See John Coolahan, 'Educational Policy for National Schools, 1960–1985' in Mulcahy and O'Sullivan (eds), *Irish Education Policy* p.28; Seán O'Connor, *A Troubled Sky* p.1.

36 John M. Regan, quoted in Ronan Fanning, 'Richard Mulcahy', *DIB*.

37 *ISW* 6 and 13 March 1948.

38 McCullagh, *Makeshift Majority*.

39 Ó Buachalla, *Education Policy* p.68.

40 CEC Minutes 6 March 1948, *ISW* 20 and 27 March 1948. See also O'Connell, *100 Years* pp.241–2.

41 E.g. *ISW* 1 and 8 May 1948.

42 *ISW* 28 and 5 June 1948.

43 See Martin Maguire, 'Civil service trade unionism (part II)' 53.

44 DD 23 October 1946, vol. 103, col. 284.

45 O'Connell, *100 Years* p.241.

46 Conciliation and arbitration machinery was also announced for the civil service. See Maguire, 'Civil service trade unionism' 54.

47 Ibid.

48 See O'Connell, *100 Years* pp.242–4. There was considerable dissatisfaction about the appointment of Canon W. Nesbit Harvey as a representative of the Church of Ireland managers. He had been vocally opposed to the 1946 strike and had kept his school open, but they were unable to have him removed and acceded to the minister's request not to make a public protest on the matter. As it turned out, the INTO representatives felt Canon Harvey had 'proved to be their friend' on the committee. See CEC Minutes 6 January 1949, Kelleher in 1948 congress report pp.35–7.

49 *ISW* 15, 22 and 29 October, 5 November 1949.

50 See Moroney, *National Teachers' Salaries* p.154.

51 CEC Minutes 3 June 1950.

52 Ibid.

53 CEC Minutes 22 July 1950, 9 September 1950; CEC Report 1950 pp.24–5; *Irish Press* 12 October 1950.

54 CEC Minutes 25 November 1950; CEC Report 1950 pp.24–5, Kelleher in Report of the 1951 Congress pp.45–6.

55 Miss Bergin in Report of the 1951 Annual Congress, pp.33–4.

56 *ISW* 9 and 16 June 1951.

57 *ISW* 26 May and 2 June 1951.

58 *ISW* 23 and 30 June 1951.

59 Carroll, *Seán Moylan* p.252.

60 O'Connell, *100 Years* pp.221–2.

61 As the Aknefton column (jointly written by two Labour activists) put it, 'Mr Moylan … is a liberal man and a sympathetic man. It is obvious that Mr Moylan, given a free hand, might do wonders for education in Ireland.' *Irish Times* 11 April 1953.

62 See Moloney, *National Teachers' Salaries* p.156, Minutes of Special CEC Meeting 11 July 1951. They were accepted with one abstention and one vote. *ISW* 21 and 28 July, 10 and 17 November 1951. The Dublin branch passed a motion of no confidence in the CEC at a meeting in November and subsequently opposed the adoption of the CEC report on the award at congress in 1952. The section of the CEC report on the award was only adopted by the 1952 congress on a card vote.

63 Two opinions advised against the action; another had offered it even chances of success. See CEC Report 1951 p.21, Report of the 1952 Congress (Tuesday, private session) p.42.

64 The matter of the INTO lending its support to the action by two men was not on the original agenda and an attempt by the Standing Orders Committee to have it included was rejected by a special meeting of the CEC on the first night (Tuesday). The following evening, the Standing Orders Committee attempted to have a motion supporting the men debated once again, the chairman having informed the president that the committee would resign if it was refused. Once again the CEC deemed the motion out of order and nominated an alternative Standing Orders Committee in the event of the original committee resigning. On Thursday, delegates were informed that the motion was out of order because the action had taken place outside the relevant time period, and finally, because it had not secured the prior permission of the Finance Committee. Eventually, the Finance Committee withdrew for a 'brief session', on its return advising that it had given permission for legal proceedings to take place. See Report of the 1952 Congress p.104.

65 Report of the 1952 Congress (Thursday, private session) p.105. Skinnider subsequently put her objections to the behaviour of the CEC and the Finance Committee on the record in a letter to the CEC and was the only member of the CEC to object to the action. CEC Minutes 10 May 1952.

66 Report of the 1952 Congress (Tuesday).

67 CEC Minutes 26 September 1953.

68 O'Connell, *100 Years* p.242.

69 CEC Report 1953 p.18. Moloney says it was granted from 1 October 1952, and the report says 'Minister announced during the year' (i.e. 1953).

70 CEC Report 1953 p.19.

71 The points in full were: (1) Unity; (2) Importance of primary education; (3) Inherent difficulty of primary teaching; (4) The type of child in post-primary; (5) Size of classes and hours of work in the three services; (6) Qualifications.

72 General secretary's account of the meeting in the Report of the 1954 Congress (Tuesday, private session) p.38.

73 Report of the 1954 Congress p.17.

74 See *Irish Times* 15 May 1954.

75 CEC Minutes 23 October 1954

76 O'Connell, *100 Years* p.250; *Irish School Monthly* November 1955.

77 Coolahan, *ASTI* p.191.

78 Murphy, 'Association to trade union' p.63.

79 Ibid. p.66

80 Report of the 1957 Congress (private session) pp.47, 50.

81 Ibid. p.50. He said, 'A few times they asked me to make a case because I was accustomed to the kind of research and presentation necessary' and because they trusted him. He had been asked to assist again recently and had refused, explaining why.

82 Ibid., p.52.

83 Mulcahy, *Richard Mulcahy* p.229.

84 *AMN* November 1958.

85 See Ruttledge, 'From Miss to Missus'.

86 *Irish School Weekly* 4 and 11 October 1947.

87 NAI D/T S6369A Department of Education Memorandum for the Government on Retirement of Women Teachers on Marriage 14 February 1953.

88 See NAI D/T S6369A, memorandum in response from the Department of Finance 13 October 1952.

89 Ruttledge, 'From Miss to Missus' p.39.

90 DD 15 June 1954, vol. 149 col. 76; CEC Report 1957–8 p.52.

91 Keogh, *Jack Lynch* p.63

92 *AMN* June 1958.

93 Ibid. The general secretary's notes featured an English translation of the minister's remarks, which had been made in Irish.

94 CEC Minutes 1 July 1950.

95 Ó Fiaich Library, D'Alton INTO – Central Executive 1938–57 file, D'Alton to Kelleher 18 October 1952.

96 Kelleher to D'Alton 24 May 1954, in Ward, 'INTO and the Catholic Church'.

97 CEC Minutes 3 May 1958.

98 CEC Minutes 3 May 1958.

99 CEC Minutes 5 February 1966.

100 Very confidential notes of phone conversation between Mrs Eileen Liston and Rev. Fr Martin, Archbishop's House on 2 February 1966. CEC Papers 1966–67.

101 The September–October 1967 issue featured five and a half pages by Mary Purcell on teaching religion. The following issue featured three further pages on the same topic by Purcell and three pages on the Votive Mass.

102 O'Connell, *100 Years* p.99.

103 Ó hEithir, *Begrudger's Guide* p.36.

104 Duffy, *The Lay Teacher* p.87.

105 INTO statement quoted in *Irish Times, Irish Independent* 12 May 1956.

106 O'Connell, *100 Years* p.102.

107 CEC Minutes.

108 Minutes of special CEC meeting on 14 May 1956.

109 Ó Fiaich Library, D'Alton Papers, McQuaid to Cardinal D'Alton 24 April 1956/

110 See CEC Minutes 31 August 1957.

111 Account of meeting with the Bishop of Killaloe on 20 July 1957 in CEC Minutes 26 July 1957.

112 CEC Report 31 August 1957.

113 Ó Fiaich Library, D'Alton Papers, undated memorandum.

114 Ó Fiaich Library, D'Alton Papers, draft submission from the Irish bishops, nd.

115 Frank Cunningham, quoted in the Report of the 1957 Congress (private session) p.66.

116 Report of the 1959 Congress (private session) p.78.

117 See *Irish Times* 19 January 1957; CEC Minutes.

118 Report of the 1960 Congress (private session) p.67; Archbishop McQuaid's correspondence is included in the Report of the 1961 Congress pp.76–7 and the hierarchy's pp.78–9.

119 CEC Minutes 7 March 1959.

120 Minutes of special CEC meeting 5 December 1959; Report of the 1961 Congress p.82.

121 Coolahan, *Irish Education* p.49.

122 Minutes of CEC meeting 4 February 1961.

123 The Fethard on Sea Boycott in 1958.

124 *Northern Teacher* April 1961

125 CEC Minutes 22 July 1961, minutes of special CEC meeting 9 September 1961.

126 *Irish Times* 7 February 1962.

127 *Irish Times* 10 January 1962.

128 Special meeting of the CEC 7 February 1962. See O'Connell, *100 Years* p.119 for the text of the letter.

129 Ó hEithir, *Begrudger's Guide* p.38.

130 Report of the 1961 Congress (Thursday afternoon, private session) p.144.

Chapter 5: The Sleeping Giant? 1962–1978

1 The second programme was abandoned midway through following Ireland's unsuccessful attempt to join the EEC. A third programme was introduced in its stead.

2 Farren, *The Politics of Irish Education* p.237.

3 The survey team comprised two economists (Patrick Lynch, UCD, and Martin O'Donoghue, TCD), a statistician (William Hyland) and the inspector of secondary schools (Padraig Ó Nualláin) with a Department of Education official (Cathal Mac Gabhann) acting as secretary.

4 Teachers' Salaries Committee, Reports and Appendices presented to the Minister for Education (July 1960) p.84; p.87.

5 See CEC Minutes 23 March 1963.

6 *AMN* February 1960.

7 CEC Minutes 18 March 1967.

8 See for instance CEC Minutes 20 June 1964, 18 March 1967, 21 March 1970. The appointment of editor of *AMN* was made in September 1955. Only applications from members in good standing were to be considered. Sean Sweeney BA, a teacher in the Oblates School in Inchicore (later its principal), active member of the Dublin branch, and one-time CEC representative, was unanimously elected editor and began in the position on 1 October, initially on a salary of £25 per issue. (See *AMN* February 1977 for his obituary.) In the summer of 1960, Sweeney sought permission to employ an assistant to help him, at his own expense if need be; when he was given permission to do so, Eamon O'Regan was officially taken on as his assistant at £10 a week. Sweeney indicated his desire to resign as editor in June 1962 but stayed on until December when he was succeeded by O'Regan, who continued to edit the journal until he retired in June 1978. The role was then filled on an interim basis by the executive officer, Charlie Lennon, until the journal was replaced.

9 Brosnahan was the only person to receive enough nominations (133), while three other potential candidates received five between them. CEC Minutes 18 June 1960.

10 *AMN* November 1963.

11 Report of the 1964 Congress p.75.

12 Quoted in Submission to the CEC of the INTO from the Committee of the Dublin City Branch INTO on the Role of the INTO in Education Matters.

13 See *Quarterly Bulletin* April 1964. The resolution was not listed in the official programme for congress and, since it was in private session, did not feature in reports of the congress.

14 Report (amended) of the reorganisation committee, 12 October 1966. CEC Papers 1966.

15 CEC Minutes 2 October 1964.

16 CEC Minutes 29 January 1966; *Irish Times* 31 January 1966.

17 CEC Minutes 2 July 1966.

18 McGahern, *All Will be Well: A Memoir* (2005) p.265.

19 *Irish Times* 6 May 1965.

20 *Irish Times* 2 June 1965.

21 McGahern, *Memoir* p.333.

22 Ibid. Interviewed in Julia Carlson (ed.), *Banned in Ireland: Censorship and the Irish Writer* (Athens, Georgia, 1990) p.56.

23 *Sunday Independent* 6 February 1966: *Irish Times* 7 February 1966.

24 CEC Minutes 8 January 1966.

25 McGahern, *Memoir* p.335. See also Carlson, *op.cit.* p.59; interview with Noel Ward January 1991.

26 *Sunday Independent* 6 February 1966; *Irish Times* 7 February 1966.

27 *Irish Times* 14 April 1966.

28 *Irish Times* 15 April 1966.

29 Carlson, *op.cit.* p.59.

30 Ibid.

31 Noel Ward 'When a teacher was engulfed by "The Dark", and his union failed' *Irish Times* 27 August 2002.

32 The possibility of teachers losing their posts in smaller schools due to falling averages caused by emigration had been considered in the 1950s, when emigration was averaging 40,000 per annum. The INTO proposed lower retention levels as a solution. See CEC Minutes 6 April 1957.

33 Report of the 1965 Congress p.57; Report of the 1966 Congress p.114.

34 See DD 16 June 1965, vol. 216, col. 1968; DD 21 July 1965, vol. 217, col. 1968.

35 John Walsh, *Politics of Expansion* pp.124–5.

36 Quoted in Seán O'Connor, *Troubled Sky* p.101.

37 DD 16 February 1966, vol. 220, col. 1731.

38 Coolahan, 'Educational Policy' p.41.

39 Report of the 1966 Congress p.149.

40 *Irish Times* 15 April 1966, reprinted in *AMN* May 1966.

41 See letter from Richard Morgan, Drogheda in *AMN* June 1966.

42 John Walsh, *Politics of Expansion* p.127.

43 Ibid. p.136.

44 Coolahan, 'Educational Policy' p.43.

45 CEC Minutes 13 October, 11 November 1967; *Irish Press* 15 January, *Evening Herald* 16 January 1968.

46 *Irish Independent* 18 January 1968.

47 *Irish Independent* 22 January 1968.

48 *Irish Press* 22 January 1968.

49 CEC Report 1968–9 p.29.

50 *AMN* May 1968.

51 See Report of the Teachers' Salary Committee, 1960.

52 Ibid. p.42.

53 Ibid. pp.42–3.

54 Ibid. p.43.

55 Ibid., p.28.

56 Ibid. p.122.

57 Ibid. p.136.

58 *Irish Times* 7 March 1961.

59 *Irish Times* 4 May 1964.

60 CEC Report 1964–5 p.16; *Irish Times* 11 May 1964; CEC Minutes 9 May 1964.

61 Cunningham, *Unlikely Radicals* p.132.

62 Ibid. p.128.

63 Minutes of special CEC meeting 13 October 1967.

64 Cunningham, *Unlikely Radicals* p.134

65 Report of the Tribunal on Teachers' Salaries p.5, *Irish Times* 16 December 1967

66 CEC minutes 18 May and 22 June 1968.

67 McCarthy, *The Decade of Upheaval* p.208.

68 Logan, 'The making of a modern union' p.177.

69 See Coolahan, *ASTI* p.277; Cunningham, *Unlikely Radicals* p.137.

70 Cunningham, *Unlikely Radicals* p.135.

71 McCarthy, *The Decade of Upheaval* p.209.

72 Ibid. pp.209–10

73 The result of the INTO ballot on 1 November was 7,607 of 8,389 votes recorded (or 90%) in favour of accepting the offer. CEC Report 1968–9 p.54.

74 Faulkner, *As it Seemed to Me* p.63.

75 See *AMN* October 1969.

76 Transcript of evidence on behalf of the INTO to the Commission on Higher Education, 46th day, Friday 6 April 1962, CEC Papers 1963–4.

77 *Irish Press* 6 May 1969.

78 *Irish Press* 12 December 1970.

79 *Irish Independent* 18 December 1971; Ciaran Sugrue, 'Three Decades of College Life' in Kelly (ed.), *St Patrick's College Drumcondra* p.226; Faulkner, *As it Seemed to Me* p.66.

80 O'Toole, *Looking under Stones* p.107.

81 *Irish Independent* 29 and 30 November; *Irish Press* 29 November 1973. The *Press* reported that the dispute was over academic reasons; the *Independent* said it was because they were 'fed up being treated like children' and had tired of 'petty restrictions', including having to wait days to read 'their loved one's letters'.

82 *Irish Independent* 11 January 1974. Of course, Pat Rabbitte is from Mayo.

83 *Irish Independent* 24 January 1974; *Irish Press* 18 December 1974.

84 *Irish Independent* 18 April, 2 May 1974.

85 John Coolahan, 'Towards a new era for teacher education and the engagement of the teaching profession' in *Irish Teachers' Journal* Vol. 1, No. 1 (November 2013) 13; John Coolahan, 'The Historical Development of Teacher Education in the Republic of Ireland' in Andy Burke (ed.), *Teacher Education in the Republic of Ireland: Retrospect and Prospect* (2004).

86 Thomas Walsh, *Primary Education in Ireland* pp.163–4.

87 Coolahan, *Irish Education* p.43.

88 *A Plan for Education* p.40.

89 Ibid. p.53.

90 *AMN* May 1957.

91 See for instance the letter from Diarmuid Ó Briain, Scoil Iosagáin in *AMN* April 1958.

92 Emphasis added. See Hyland and Milne, *Irish Educational Documents* Vol. II pp.130–1; Seán O'Connor, *Troubled Sky* p.44.

93 See John Walsh, *Politics of Expansion* pp.43–5.

94 Teachers' Study Group, *Report on the Draft Curriculum for Primary Schools* (Dublin, 1969) p.5.

95 Coolahan, 'Educational Policy' p.60.

96 Stephen Collins, *The Cosgrave Legacy* (Dublin, 1996) pp.137, 141.

97 *Irish Times* 19 March 1973.

98 *Education Times* 19 September 1974.

99 Memorandum on Proposals on Shared Management of National Schools by Seán Brosnahan, 8 April 1975, CEC Papers.

100 Coolahan, 'Educational Policy' p.57.
101 *Irish Times* 29 September 1975.
102 CEC Minutes 11 October 1975.
103 *Education Times* 27 March 1975.

Chapter 6: Teachers United, 1978–1990

1 CEC Minutes, 18 December 1976.
2 *Irish Times* 21 April 1977.
3 Interview with Gerry Quigley, October 1991.
4 *Irish Times* 21 April 1977.
5 CEC Minutes 30 April 1977.
6 See *AMN* April 1977 for his election literature.
7 *Irish Times* 4 and 17 May 1977; CEC report 1977–8 p.1.
8 *Irish Times* 30 March 1978.
9 Ibid.
10 See editorial 'Them and Us' in *AMN* December 1977; for the list of candidates for election see *AMN* January 1978.
11 See *AMN* February 1972.
12 *Sunday Independent* 30 March 1975.
13 *Irish Times* 28 April 1976.
14 CEC Report 1975–6 pp.20–1; Kennedy, *Cottage to Crèche* p.114; INTO, *A Decade of Progress: An INTO Handbook on Gender Equality in Primary Education* p.9.
15 CEC Minutes 22 October 1982.
16 *AMN* January 1977.
17 *AMN* February 1977.
18 *AMN* April 1977.
19 CEC Minutes 30 April 1977. Report of *AMN* sub-committee, 19 September 1977. CEC Papers 1976–7.
20 *AMN* October 1978.
21 Fiona Poole, 'STSG – a short history' http://www.into.ie/ROI/InfoforTeachers/ TeacherSpecialInterestGroups/SeparatedTeachersSupportGroup/History/.
22 *Irish Press* 20 March 1978.
23 *Irish Press* 8 March 1978.
24 Emily O'Reilly, *Masterminds of the Right* (Dublin, 1992) p.20.
25 *Irish Times* 11 March 1978; *Irish Press* 10 March 1978,
26 *Irish Times* 24 March 1978.
27 Rita Caball stood for vice-president in 1980, going forward on the basis that since 70 per cent of the membership were women, they should have a greater voice in the running of their affairs (*Tuarascáil* March 1980). The following year Molly O'Duffy contested the election.
28 CEC Minutes 12, 13, 14 October 1978.
29 *AMN* December 1978.
30 Interview with Gerry Quigley, 1991.

31 CEC Minutes 25 November 1978.

32 Standing Committee III Minutes 30 October 1981.

33 Interview with Gerry Quigley, October 1991.

34 See interview with John Joe Connelly Ward, in *The Teachers' Club* pp.162–70.

35 See the judgment of Mr Justice McMahon, *Irish Press* 22 July 1978.

36 CEC Papers, Drimoleague dispute background memo.

37 CEC meeting 1 November 1975; special CEC meeting 15 November 1975.

38 *Irish Press* 22 July 1978. The judgment was reprinted in full in the October issue of *AMN*.

39 CEC/FC Minutes 28 July 1978.

40 CEC Minutes 10 February 1979.

41 CEC Report 1981–2 p.122.

42 Special CEC meeting 22 October 1981.

43 CEC Report 1982–3 pp.174–5; *Irish Press* 8 April 1982.

44 This figure does not include Charles Haughey and Gerard Brady, who held the office temporarily for three weeks and almost seven weeks respectively.

45 *Irish Times* 30 June 1977.

46 Cunningham, *Unlikely Radicals* p.207.

47 See Moroney, *National Teachers' Salaries* pp.206–7.

48 Ibid.; CEC Report 1978–9 pp.5–6.

49 Moroney, *National Teachers' Salaries* p.207

50 Coolahan, *ASTI* p.370; CEC Report 1979–80 p.8; Special CEC meeting 15 September 1979; CEC meeting 1 December 1979; CEC Report 1979–80 p.13.

51 *Irish Times* 9 October 1980.

52 *Irish Times* 11, 14 October 1980.

53 *Irish Times* 24 October 1980. See Moroney, *National Teachers' Salaries* pp.215–16.

54 Special CEC meeting 19 November 1980.

55 Moroney, *National Teachers' Salaries* p.217; CEC Report 1991–2 pp.64–78.

56 Cunningham, *Unlikely Radicals* p.213.

57 See ibid. pp.199–203.

58 CEC meeting 23 June 1981.

59 *Irish Times* 17 December 1981; memo, second draft Proposed Council of Education Unions NB CEC 81/114.

60 *Irish Times* 17 December 1981.

61 See Lawrence White, 'John Boland', *DIB*.

62 Hussey, *Cutting Edge* p.23.

63 *Irish Times* 3 September 1981.

64 Special CEC meeting 26 August 1981; CEC Report 1981–2 p.9. See John Coolahan, 'Who makes the rules for national schools?', *AMN* Autumn 1982 p.9 for the rules concerning age of entry from 1930.

65 Fiona Poole was the only INTO member to come out vocally in favour of changing the age of entry to five years of age.

66 CEC Report 1981–2 pp.10–11.

67 Ibid. p.29

68 *Tuarascáil* February 1982.

69 The first notices were placed in Sunday papers on 3 January 1982 and then again in national dailies on 5 January.

70 *Irish Times* 14 January 1982.

71 See letters to members of the Parliamentary Labour Party, February 1982 CEC 82/27. Frank Cluskey and Michael D. Higgins had taken a position at odds with the rest of the parliamentary Labour Party. The results of the circular were published in *Tuarascáil*, February 1982. Fianna Fáil's pledge to restore the age of entry to four years featured prominently in its campaign and was also featured in a stand-alone leaflet featuring two children and a lollipop sign reading 'stop – children 4 years'.

72 *Irish Times* 9 March 1982.

73 Seán O'Connor, *Troubled Sky* p.25.

74 Mary Daly, 'The Role of Parents in Education', *Éire-Ireland* 44:1 and 2, Spring/Summer 1998 p.201.

75 *Irish School Weekly* 13 December 1931.

76 Maguire and Ó Cinnéide, 'A good beating' p.632.

77 Ibid. p.636.

78 Report of proceedings of the 1943 Congress, p.67.

79 Daly, 'The Role of Parents' p.201.

80 See *Irish Times* 13 July 1968; Maguire and Ó Cinnéide, 'A good beating' p.643.

81 *Irish Times* 22 October 1954, 2 April 1956; Andrée Sheehy Skeffington, *Skeff* pp.169, 172–3, Seán O'Connor, *Troubled Sky* pp.25–6.

82 Kelleher to McQuaid 5 December 1955 DDA Box 12; CEC Report 1954-5 p.130. The motion by the Dublin City branch was as follows: 'That in view of the activities of a so-called School Children's Protection Association, the misguided press campaign, the "smug" attitude of the authorities and the consequent difficult position in which teachers are placed, Congress directs the Executive to consider the desirability of issuing instructions to INTO members to refrain from *all* corporal punishment in schools.' An amendment by the Carlow Co. Committee called for this and the other motion to be withdrawn 'as no useful purpose would be served by a discussion of these motions'.

83 Seán O'Connor, *Troubled Sky* p.29; Daly, 'Role of Parents' p.206.

84 John Joe Connolly told a reporter that he had challenged Deputy Barry Desmond to pass the INTO's picket 'and to our shock he did'. *Irish Times* 4 December 1969.

85 CEC meeting 31 October 1981; *Tuarascáil* November 1981.

86 CEC meeting 30 January 1982. Three weeks later the European Court of Human Rights ruled that beating children *against their parents' wishes* was a violation of the Human Rights Convention but caning was not. It was not until 1987 that corporal punishment was banned in state schools.

87 Cunningham, *Unlikely Radicals* p.214.

88 See Cunningham, *Unlikely Radicals* pp.225–31.

89 *Tuarascáil* February 1984.

90 Fiona Poole, 'STSG – a short history'.

91 By this stage the three unions had printed letterheads with the three unions' details on them.

92 *Irish Times* 27 January 1983.

93 And over 100 per cent of GDP the following year. See Michael Somers, 'The management of Ireland's national debt', *Journal of the Statistical and Social Inquiry Society of Ireland* (1992) p.134.

94 Emmet O'Connor, *Labour History of Ireland* p.240.

95 CEC Report 1984–5 p.7; Moroney, *National Teachers' Salaries* p.253.

96 CEC Report 1985–6 pp.2–3.

97 *Irish Times* 9 August 1985; CEC Report 1985–6 p.2.

98 *Irish Times* 15 and 19 August 1985

99 CEC Report 1985–6; *Irish Times, Irish Independent* 20 August 1985.

100 *Irish Times* 26 November 1985; *Sunday Independent* 9 March 1986; *The Kerryman* 13 December 1985. The speech was also deeply resented by the ICTU. See *Irish Independent* 19 September 1985.

101 Special CEC meeting 28 August 1985.

102 *Irish Times* 13 September 1985.

103 *Evening Herald* 14 September 1985; *Irish Times* 16 September, 16 October 1985.

104 Guidelines for CEC representatives on public service pay dispute (nd (September)), private papers.

105 Teachers United Campaign 1985 pack.

106 See for example district co-ordinator, Ballina to Gerry Quigley (nd) CEC 85/227.

107 *Irish Press* 5 May 1986.

108 Memorandum of the meeting of representatives of the three teacher unions and representatives of the Parliamentary Labour Party, 6 November 1985, private papers.

109 Hussey, *Cutting Edge* p.178.

110 Quoted in Cunningham, *Unlikely Radicals* p.205.

111 *Irish Times* 6 December 1985.

112 Observations on Teachers' Campaign, Cavan 23 October 1985, CEC 85/227.

113 CEC Report 1985–6 p.36; special CEC meeting 25 April 1986.

114 CEC Report 1986–7 p.10.

115 Cunningham, *Unlikely Radicals* p.219; special CEC meeting 9 May 1986.

116 CEC Report 1986–7 pp.12–15; Ruairí Quinn, *Straight Left* p.232.

117 See CEC papers 1986 and transcript of Special Congress 10 and 11 October 1986, private papers.

118 Michael Laver, Peter Mair and Richard Sinnott (eds), *How Ireland Voted: The Irish General Election 1987* (Dublin, 1987) p.15.

119 *Irish Times* 1 April 1987.

120 Brian Girvin, 'The Campaign' in Michael Gallagher and Richard Sinnott (eds), *How Ireland Voted 1989* (Galway, 1990) p.7.

121 Ibid.

122 See Hastings *et al.*, *Saving the Future* p.29 The PDs had taken almost 12 per cent of the national vote in the February 1987 election. On the left, Labour's vote had fallen to less than 6.5 per cent and the Workers' Party, on its left, to under four per cent. This meant that the combined left-wing vote in Ireland in 1987 was barely ten per cent. The prospect of a coalition including the low-tax, small-government, anti-union party was not one relished by the unions.

123 Hastings *et al.*, *Saving the Future* p.38.

124 CEC Report 1987–8 p.1.

125 *Irish Times* 9 October 1987. They had first featured on RTÉ's *Today Tonight* programme.

126 Moroney, *National Teachers' Salaries* p.276.

127 Ibid. p.275; CEC Report 1987–8 p.5.

128 Extract of the PNR in CEC Report 1987–8 p.3.

129 *Irish Press* 31 July 1987; CEC Report 1987–8 p.22.

130 See CEC Report 1987–8 p.28.

131 Ibid. pp.30, 36. There were 21,193 teachers in service on 30 June 1987. *Department of Education Statistical Report 1986–7* p.27; *Tuarascáil* November 1987.

132 *Irish Times* 14 October 1987.

133 O'Rourke, *Just Mary* p.47; CEC Report 1987–8 p.55.

134 *Irish Times* 25 November 1987.

135 Information from Séamus Puirséil, 23 November 2014. See also interview with Tom Gilmore, July 2014.

136 CEC Report 1987–8 pp.61–5; *Irish Times* 23 December 1987.

137 *Tuarascáil* January 1988.

138 *Irish Press* 23 January 1988.

139 Ibid. June 1988.

140 CEC Report 1988–9 p.26.

141 CEC Report 1987–8 p.77.

142 *Irish Press* 28 March 1989.

143 CEC Report 1990–91 pp.33–5.

144 Moroney, *National Teachers' Salaries* p.300.

145 As the Teachers' Action Alliance (with an address in Sallynoggin, Co. Dublin) stated in a pamphlet, it stood (1) For union democracy; (2) For militant action on pay and conditions; (3) Against Church control of education; (4) Against sexism and elitism in education; and (5) For one strong teachers' union.

146 CEC Report 1988–9 p.159.

147 *Irish Press* 5 July 1988.

148 CEC minutes 25–26 March 1988. The INTO's representatives were the general secretary, Gerry Quigley; northern secretary Al Mackle; and incoming president Michael Drew. CEC minutes 16 and 17 June 1988. The Trade Union Act 1975 provided for grants towards expenses incurred in amalgamating unions. The FWUI and the ITGWU were also involved in negotiations to merge around this time, CEC Report 1988–9 p.160.

149 INTO 50 per cent, ASTI 30 per cent, TUI 20 per cent.

150 CEC special meeting 2 March 1990.

151 1989 congress, Tuesday recording.

152 *Sunday Independent* 24 June 1990; *Irish Times* 25 June 1990.

153 *Irish Times* 19 October 1990.

154 INTO, 'A Decade of Progress. An INTO handbook on gender equality in primary education' (1991) p.3.

Chapter 7: Change, Consultation and Crisis, 1990–2018

1 Ferriter, *The Transformation of Ireland* p.752.

2 Quoted in Walshe, *New Partnership* p.5.

3 INTO, *Change in Primary Education: Challenges for Teachers* (2004) p.1.

4 See Moroney, *National Teachers' Salaries* pp.189, 295.

5 Recording of 1992 Congress.

6 CEC minutes 13 and 14 May 1993; *Tuarascáil* June 1993.

7 See Marjorie Murphy, 1991 congress, *Tuarascáil* March 1991.

8 Roddy Day, Dublin North West branch, 1989 congress.

9 Cunningham, *Unlikely Radicals* p.263; CEC report 1994–5 pp.9–19.

10 *Tuarascáil* April–May 1995; *Irish Press* 24 May 1995; *Irish Times* 22 May, 30 May 1995.

11 See Moroney, *National Teachers' Salaries* p.318.

12 *Irish Times* 29 February 1996.

13 Moroney, *National Teachers' Salaries* p.327; CEC 97.4, speaking notes for branch secretaries, 6 January 1997; *Tuarascáil* January/February 1997.

14 See Hastings *et al.*, *Saving the Future* p.81.

15 Ibid. p.82.

16 *Irish Times* 29 January 1997.

17 INTO, *Change in Primary Education* p.9.

18 Walshe, *New Partnership* p.7.

19 DD 22 November 1990, vol. 402, col. 2267.

20 *Irish Times* 22 April 1992.

21 Ibid.

22 Finlay, *Snakes and Ladders* p.155. Its significance was noted at the time, although Catholic education groups said they had no concerns that Labour was holding the portfolio for the first time. See *Irish Times* 13 January 1993.

23 See interview in *Irish Times* 8 March 1993. Taylor says that the story that he was turned down for Education because he is a Jew and the mainly Catholic controllers of schools would have none of it was 'pure fantasy'.

24 Another Labour minister was Brendan Howlin, 'whose roots in the INTO and in local politics' had aided him greatly, according to one profile, with Fianna Fáil's Maire Geoghegan-Quinn the second national teacher in the cabinet. *Irish Times* 13 January 1993.

25 *Irish Times* 13 January 1993.

26 *Irish Independent* 14 April 1993; *Tuarascáil* May 1993.

27 *Irish Press* 17 July 1993; special CEC meeting 17 September 1993.

28 *Irish Times* 24 September 1993.

29 *Tuarascáil* February 1994. See also SD 10 February 1994, vol. 139, col. 339, for Joe O'Toole's contribution to the debate on the National Education Convention Report.

30 SD 2 November 1995, vol. 145, col. 121.

31 *Tuarascáil* September 1995; CEC Report 1995–6 p.76.

32 *Irish Independent* 30 December 1995.

33 CEC Report 1995–6 p.80.

34 *Irish Times* 11 March 1994.

35 See Walshe, *New Partnership* pp.100–16.

36 See *Tuarascáil* September 1994.

37 Walshe, *New Partnership* p.107.

38 Ibid. p.112

39 CEC Report 1996–7 p.121.

40 Ibid.; *Irish Times* 29 November 1996.

41 CEC Report 1996–7 p.122; *Irish Independent* 11 December 1996; *Irish Times* 18 March 1997.

42 *Irish Times* 2 October 1995.

43 The other grounds being disability, race or membership of the Travelling community.

44 In the words of Mr Justice Declan Costello, the appellant, Eileen Flynn, should have known 'from her upbringing as a Catholic, and previous experience as a teacher, the sort of school in which she sought employment and she should have been well aware of the obligations she would undertake by joining the staff'. Quoted in Cunningham, *Unlikely Radicals* p.230.

45 Quoted in INTO, 'The Place of Religious Education in the National School System' p.16.

46 Ibid.

47 Don Thornhill 15 February 1994; NLI, Taylor Papers MS 46,450/3 ß.

48 *Irish Independent* 9 April 1996; Recording of the 1996 annual congress.

49 *Irish Times* 25 June 1996.

50 Walton Empey to Mervyn Taylor 16 December 1996, NLI, Taylor Papers, MS 46,452.

51 Attorney general's memorandum on the legality of section 37, 21 November 1996. NLI, Taylor Papers MS 46,448. The cases referred to were the 1985 Flynn case and *McGrath and O'Ruairc v Maynooth College* (1979). This advice was backed up the following year in the judgment in the *Campaign to Separate Church and State Ltd. v. Minister for Education* (1998).

52 Christopher Robson, co-chair of GLEN, to Mervyn Taylor 22 August 1996, NLI, Taylor Papers MS 46,452.

53 *Irish Times* 10 January 1997, 10 February 1997; *Irish Independent* 7 February 1997. Note of 'Say no to sectarian laws for schools' meeting, organised jointly by Teachers for Pluralism and the Campaign to Separate Church and State, NLI, Taylor Papers MS 46,448/6.

54 Joe O'Toole to staff representatives, 6 December 1996, CEC White Papers 1998 NC-049. The minister held meetings with various representatives, including the ICTU, the ASTI and one with members of the Church of Ireland and Roman Catholic hierarchy, but the INTO, the only organisation he met more than once, had four meetings with him. See Fintan O'Toole in *Irish Times* 1 November 1996.

55 See handwritten note from Proinsias (De Rossa) to Taylor, 22 October 1996 and Taylor to De Rossa, 22 November 1996, NLI Taylor Papers MS 46,448/5.

56 Notes of meeting on the Employment Equality Bill 9 January 1997, NLI, Taylor Papers, MS 46,453/2.

57 Note of meeting with Roman Catholic and Church of Ireland hierarchy 8 November 1996, NLI, Taylor Papers, MS 46,453/2.

58 Letter from Richard Humphreys to Jim McDaid TD 20 February 1997 NLI, MSS 46,452/1.

59 *Tuarascáil* June 1997; *Irish Times* 16 May 1997.

60 See for example *InTouch* January/February 1998.

61 *Irish Times* 14 January 2006.

62 Walshe, *New Partnership* p.190; INTO response to the Education Bill, draft, 11 March 1997.

63 Walshe, *New Partnership* p.192.

64 Ibid., p.193.

65 Ibid., p.196, *Irish Times* 14 April 1997.

66 As usual, the INTO sent questionnaires to each of the political parties seeking their positions on a number of education questions. Labour was the only party that did not complete the questionnaire.

67 *Irish Independent* 5 March, 2 June 1997.

68 *Irish Times* 2 September 1997. The NCCA, established in 1987 as the successor to the interim Curriculum and Examinations Board (1984) had been acting as a consultative body but, according to an internal discussion document produced in 1997, its role in briefing on the curriculum had been seldom exercised in recent years and it wished to take a more active role. See *Irish Times* 6 November 1997.

69 *InTouch* March 1998.

70 *Irish Independent* 10 December 1997.

71 CEC Report 1999–2000 p.8, draft memo on pay negotiations 14 January 2000, CEC White Papers 2000 NC-051.

72 *Tuarascáil* April/May 1999.

73 Ibid.

74 See *Tuarascáil* December 1999; *Irish Times* 20 January 2000.

75 *Irish Times* 26 April 2000.

76 See Cunningham, *Unlikely Radicals* pp.270–1.

77 *Irish Independent* 5 November 1999; *Irish Times* 4 February 2000.

78 *Irish Times* 8 March 2000.

79 *InTouch* April 2003.

80 CEC 169/02 report of discussion workshops, branch and district secretaries and cathoirligh briefing and training.

81 See Catherine Breathnach, 'The relationship between membership participation, organisational learning and strategic change in democratically structured voluntary organisations' (PhD, NCI, 2002).

82 *InTouch* January 2000.

83 In 2007, the INTO was the seventh largest union in the republic and the third largest public sector union after IMPACT and the INO. ICTU Executive Report.

84 See Catherine Breathnach, 'Participation: a view from branch level of the INTO, Autumn 1999' (February 2000), CEC White Papers 2000.

85 *InTouch* March 1999.

86 See *InTouch* December 2000.

87 *The Kerryman* 29 March 2001. Crea Ryder, an opponent of the PPF who was active in the anti-partnership ginger group Teachers United, and worked as a teacher at St Vincent's NS in Dublin, initially put herself forward as an anti-agreement candidate but did not run (*Irish Times* 27 April 2000; *InTouch* December 2000). For each candidate's nominations by branch, see *InTouch* March 2001.

88 See *Irish Times* 29 August 2000, 17 April 2001; *Irish Independent* 2 April 2001.

89 See *InTouch* March 2001.

90 John Carr had 7,547 first preferences and Catherine Byrne 5,257, *Irish Times* 20 April 2001.

91 *InTouch* October 1999. There were some calls for non-co-operation with the new curriculum at the time, prompting Joe O'Toole to use his editorial to emphasise that the curriculum had been drawn up under the guidance of teachers and at the teachers' insistence, and as professionals, the teachers were obliged to implement what was best for the pupils.

92 As Sheelagh Drudy notes, 'during the 1990s, [Ireland] was the fastest growing economy in Europe (European Commission, 2008). However, income inequality remained a feature of the economy and, in fact was exacerbated by the state's own budgetary policy in the 1990s – although the lowest income groups gained slightly in the budgets of 2000–2005', 'Education and the Knowledge Economy: A Challenge for Ireland in Changing Times' in Drudy (ed.) *Education in Ireland*.

93 Nic Craith, 'Policy for primary teacher education' p.101.

94 An Agreed Programme for Government between Fianna Fáil and Progressive Democrats (June 2002) p.23.

95 *Irish Times* 13, 18 November, 3 December 2002.

96 *Irish Times* 4 December 2003; *InTouch* January 2004.

97 Interview with Noel Dempsey 9 July 2015.

98 INTO Education Committee, 'Supporting Special Education in the Mainstream School' (2003) p.3.

99 See Education Committee, 'Supporting Special Education' (2004).

100 *Eolas* 3/4 November 2004.

101 *Irish Times* 22 October 2004.

102 Leahy, *Showtime* p.207; *Irish Times* 30 September 2004.

103 Congress 2004.

104 *Irish Times* 11 April 2007; *Eolas* 1/4 February 2004.

105 CEC Papers 2003.

106 *InTouch* November 2004.

107 Leahy, *Showtime* p.235.

108 *Irish Times* 30 March 2005.

109 *InTouch* December 2006.

110 *Irish Times* 8 March 2011.

111 *Irish Times* 21 May 2010.

Chapter 8: The INTO in Northern Ireland, 1922–1950

1 *ISW* 2 July 1921; *Belfast Newsletter* 27 June 1921.

2 *ISW* 2 July 1921.

3 See Chapter 2 above; Minutes of the 1922 Annual Congress p.47; O'Connell, *100 Years* p.23.

4 Report of the Vigilance Committee of Northern Ireland, CEC Report 1922 p.62.

5 *Belfast Newsletter* 27 June 1921; Vigilance Committee Report 1924–5 in *ISW* 28 February 1925.

6 Eamon Phoenix in *Irish News* 11 May 2004; *Irish Independent* 26 April 1921.

7 James L. Fitts, 'The Rebel Teachers: A Study in Contentious History' (unpublished manuscript).

8 Ibid. p.9; Harris, *Catholic Church* pp.110, 119.

9 O'Connell, *100 Years* p.462.

10 Phoenix, *Irish News* 2004.

11 PRONI ED/13/1/400.

12 Harkness, *Northern Ireland* pp.5–6.

13 Bridget Hourican, 'Steward, Charles Stewart Henry Vane-Tempest', *DIB*.

14 Farren, *The Politics of Irish Education 1920–65* p.38.

15 McGrath, *Catholic Church and Catholic Schools* p.32.

16 Farren, *Irish Education* p.39; Neil C. Flemming 'Lord Londonderry and Education Reform in 1920s Northern Ireland', *History Ireland* (Spring 2001).

17 McGrath, *Catholic Church and Catholic Schools* p.33

18 Akenson, *Education and Enmity* p.52.

19 Vigilance Committee Report 1922; *ISW* 6 January 1923.

20 *ISW* 31 March 1923.

21 Farren, *The Politics of Irish Education*.

22 Ibid. pp.71–78.

23 *ISW* 3 February 1923.

24 *ISW* 9 June 1923.

25 *Derry Journal* 23 April 1924.

26 Minutes of the 1925 Congress in Belfast p.58.

27 Mapstone, 'UTU' p.50.

28 *ISW* 15 December 1923.

29 PRONI D3944/A/1 UTU executive minutes, January 1924.

30 Minutes of the 1925 INTO Congress in Belfast pp.143–7.

31 Minutes of the 1925 INTO Congress in Belfast pp.191–5.

32 The teachers' union movement in England and Wales has generally exhibited an 'unusually high degree of organizational fragmentation' compared to that in many states. Thornton, 'Teacher unionism' 377.

33 PRONI D3944/A/1 UTU executive minutes, April, May 1926.

34 PRONI D3944/A/1 UTU executive minutes, November 1926.

35 *ISW* 18 February 1928; *Belfast Newsletter* 25 January 1928.

36 *ISW* 14 March 1931.

37 *ISW* 28 March 1931; NC Report 1931–2; *Northern Whig* 24 March 1931.

38 Northern Committee report 1932–3; *Belfast Newsletter* 20 April 1932. In the Statutory Rules and Orders issued in 1928 there was the following: 'The attendance of teachers at meetings held for party political purposes or the taking part by them in parliamentary or local government elections, except by voting is forbidden.' This regulation was repealed in 1930 and the following substituted for it: 'While teachers are not forbidden to attend political meetings, they are not at liberty to take an active part in them, and they may not take part in parliament or local government elections except by voting.'

39 *Northern Whig* 19 April 1933.

40 Mapstone, 'UTU' pp.91–2, p.101 n.29.

41 Northern Committee Report, 1933–4.

42 See e.g. *Northern Whig* 23 March 1936; *Belfast Newsletter* 15 October 1938.

43 *Belfast Newsletter* 8 August 1934.

44 *Belfast Newsletter* 25 August 1934.

45 Belfast Branch minutes 1936.

46 Mapstone, 'UTU' pp.88–9.

47 Ibid. p.90.

48 Figures derived from annual reports.

49 Minutes of the 1933 Congress.

50 Minutes of the 1934 Congress.

51 Minutes of the 1937 Congress p.123; Belfast branch minute book 6 January 1937.

52 Belfast branch minute book March 1940.

53 Minutes of the 1940 Congress p.129.

54 King-Carson was appointed in December 1944.

55 Minutes of the Belfast branch 28 June 1947.

56 Minutes of the Belfast branch 4 September, 2 October 1948; *ISW* 16 and 23 October 1948.

57 Armagh Committee minutes 4 June 1948.

58 Minutes of the 1947 Congress p.130; Belfast branch minutes 4 May 1946.

59 Minutes of special meeting of the Belfast branch 28 June 1947.

60 Belfast branch minutes January 1948.

61 *ISW* 24 and 31 January 1948; Minutes of the Belfast branch 10 January 1948.

62 Minutes of the Armagh committee 26 November 1948; Minutes of the Belfast branch 2 October, 6 November 1948, 5 February 1949.

63 INTO, 'Killean dismissal' pp.8–10.

64 Ibid. p.12.

65 Ibid. p.27.

66 Ibid.; *ISW* 22 April 1939.

67 *See Irish Times* 14 April 1939. The phrase was later used as the title of the INTO's booklet on the matter published in 1942.

68 See INTO, 'Killean dismissal' p.35.

69 Ibid. p.30.

70 Ibid. p.59.

71 Ward, 'The INTO and the Catholic Church, 1930–1955' p.167.

72 O'Connell *100 Years* p.42.

73 See 1940 Congress Report p.29; 1941 Congress Report p.43.

74 CEC minutes 4 June 1955; *ISW* September 1955.

75 *ISW* September 1955.

76 Ward, 'The INTO and the Catholic Church, 1930–1955' p.168

77 NC Minutes 17 May 1941.

78 Hyland *et al.*, *Irish Educational Documents* vol. 3 p.242.

79 Ibid.; *ISW* 3, 10 May 1941.

80 *ISW* 24 May 1941.

81 *Northern Whig* 11 April 1943.

82 See Farren, *Politics* p.164.

83 *ISW* 24 February and 3 March 1945.

84 Farren, *Politics* p.170–3.

85 Ibid. p.180; *ISW* 11 and 18 January 1947.

86 *ISW* 17 and 24 April 1948.

87 Report of the 1948 Congress pp.113–21.

88 *ISW* 25 December 1948 and 1 January 1949.

89 *ISW* 2 and 9 April 1949.

90 Interview with Gerry Quigley October 1991.

91 Armagh County Committee minutes, September 1942.

92 Belfast branch minutes, 10 April 1948.

93 CEC minutes, 24 April 1948; *ISW* 1 and 8 May 1948.

94 *ISW* 4 and 11 September 1948.

95 *ISW* 31 May and 7 June 1947.

96 Minutes of the 1949 Congress p.164; annual report of the Northern Committee p.37; *Quarterly Bulletin* April 1949.

97 Minutes of the Belfast branch 11 March 1950.

98 CEC minutes 22 March 1952.

99 Minutes of the 1952 Congress p.106.

100 *Belfast Telegraph* 2 May 1945. The 'step by step' policy had been announced by James Craig back in March 1922.

101 Northern Committee Report 1950 p.36.

102 *Northern Whig* 14 November 1945.

103 *ISW* 1 and 8 December 1945.

104 *ISW* 15 and 22 December 1945.

105 *Belfast Newsletter* 26 November 1945.

106 *ISW* 29 December 1928. Trinity was already the awarding body for Magee teacher training college. The northern government was quite unhappy at the 'anomalous' position where

a university outside the jurisdiction was awarding qualifications to teachers in the North and strongly encouraged Magee (which was under the General Assembly of the Presbyterian Church) to seek recognition from Queen's University, refusing to fund it until it did so. See *Irish Times* 19 June 1929.

107 *Belfast Newsletter* 21 June 1946.

108 *Northern Whig* 16 January 1946.

109 *Belfast Newsletter* 26 March 1948.

110 Lawrence White, 'Henry Cassidy ("Harry") Midgley', *DIB*.

111 In his address to the UTU conference in 1952, he criticised the attitude of voluntary schools, which, he said, were engaged in a 'boycott' of the state sector which was inflicting 'appallingly inadequate' accommodation and segregation on its pupils. *Irish Times* 17 April 1952.

112 Northern Committee Report 1950 p.39.

113 *Northern Whig* 13 January 1950.

114 Belfast Branch Minutes 11 March 1950.

115 Belfast Branch Minutes 11 March, 1 April, 6 May 1950; NC Report for 1950, pp.36–9.

116 Belfast Branch Minutes 3 June 1950.

117 NC Report for 1950, p.42.

118 *Northern Whig* 8 November 1950; *ISW* 25 November and 2 December 1950; Mapstone, 'UTU' pp.93–4; *Northern Whig* 14 November 1950.

119 Belfast Branch Minutes 11 November 1950; Roisin Carabine at 1991 congress.

120 *Northern Whig* 18 December 1950.

121 Belfast Branch Minutes 2 December 1950, 20 January 1951.

122 Belfast Branch Minutes 20 January 1951; NC Report for 1951 pp.42–3.

123 Belfast Branch Minutes 3 February 1951.

Chapter 9: The INTO in Northern Ireland Since 1950

1   CEC Minutes 10 May 1952.

2   CEC Minutes 28 June, 1 November 1952. The sub-committee included the president, vice-president, ex-president, treasurer and general secretary, along with Messrs Carney, McCune Reid and Looney.

3   CEC Minutes 1 November 1952.

4   Interview with Gerry Quigley October 1991.

5   Minutes of special meeting of the CEC 14 February 1953.

6   CEC Minutes 9 May, 20 June 1953.

7   D.W. Bleakley, 'The Northern Ireland trade union movement', *Journal of the Statistical and Social Inquiry Society of Ireland* 20 (1954); interview with Gerry Quigley October 1991.

8   Interview with Róisín Carabine January 2017.

9   CEC Minutes 28 February 1953; meeting in December 1955.

10 *Northern Teacher* Spring 1968.

11 Report of the 1957 Congress p.206.

12 Ibid.

13 Ibid. pp.207–8.

14 Ibid. pp.9–10.

15 Report of the 1957 Congress, pp.88–90.

16 Ibid. pp.99–102.

17 NC Minutes 25 May 1957.

18 *Northern Teacher* July 1960.

19 De Gruchy, *NASUWT* p.334.

20 Report of the 1957 Congress, pp.197–8.

21 'Does the Organisation need a change of name?' in *Northern Teacher* July 1960.

22 *Ulster Herald* 8 January 1955; *Irish Times* 14 April 1955.

23 *Irish Times* 16 April 1955.

24 *ISW* 16 and 23 January 1954.

25 Smith, 'The problem of "Equal Pay for Equal Work"', 654, 652.

26 Perhaps not surprisingly, a minority opinion signed by all three women on the committee dissented from the second opinion, observing that the evidence did not seem to support the majority view.

27 *ISM* April, October, November 1955. Nine years later, at the NC conference in January 1964, the idea of a married man's scale or marriage allowance was rejected by delegates. *Northern Teacher* January 1964.

28 O'Connell, *100 Years* p.286.

29 A case in Portadown in 1924 was raised in parliament, but a resolution on the matter was withdrawn after the minister for finance assured the House that 'a sympathetic attitude would be taken with regard to *existing* married women teachers'. *ISW* 5 April 1924 (emphasis added).

30 Oram, *Women Teachers* p.26.

31 *Belfast Newsletter* 20 April 1932.

32 NC Report for 1929–30.

33 PRONI ED 23/1/1148 Department of Finance letter 8 February 1932.

34 *Northern Whig* 16 January 1931.

35 Ibid.; *Derry Journal* 26 October 1931; *Belfast Newsletter* 31 October 1931; *Northern Whig* 6 May 1932; NC Report for 1931–2 p.39.

36 *Northern Whig* 13 May 1932.

37 *Derry Journal* 25 November 1931; *Belfast Newsletter* 29 February 1932.

38 *Northern Whig* 29 November 1946; *ISW* 14 and 21 December 1946.

39 NC minutes 16 October 1954.

40 Interview with Gerry Quigley October 1991; NC Minutes 14 November 1958.

41 Northern Office Papers, Gerry Quigley (to the Limavady and Dungiven Branch), 8 March 1958.

42 NC Report for 1957–8 p.83.

43 Interview with Gerry Quigley October 1991.

44 NC Annual Report 1958–9 pp.49–63.

45 NC Annual Report 1959–60 pp.41–7.

46 Armagh County Committee Minutes 5 October 1959.

47 See Minutes of Special NC Meeting 25 August 1959.

48 *Irish Times* 22 September 1977.

49 CEC Minutes 31 August 1957; see Chapter 8 (pp.215–17).

50 *Northern Teacher* April 1960.

51 NC Report 1961 p.31.

52 NC Report 1962 pp.24–5. It does not seem as though there was any approach in 1963.

53 NC Report 1964 pp.29–30; NC Report 1965 p.37.

54 De Gruchy, *NASUWT* p.334.

55 NC Paper 24/66 Catholic School Appointments.

56 PRONI ED/13/1/1336.

57 See NC Report 1967 p.34.

58 NC Report 1967, pp.25–33.

59 NC Report 1969 pp.34–5.

60 NC Report for 1967 pp.36–41.

61 *Irish Times* 25 October 1967.

62 *Irish Times* 20, 24 October 1967.

63 *Irish Times* 2 November 1967.

64 NC Report 1967 p.37; NC Report 1968 pp.16–17.

65 NC Report 1968 p.19.

66 *Northern Teacher* Autumn 1969.

67 NC Report 1969 p.44; NC Minutes 7 October 1969.

68 Mapstone, 'UTU' p.115; McGrath, *Catholic Church and Catholic Schools* pp.178, 182. A notable exception was Bernadette Devlin, elected as an MP for Mid Ulster on 17 April 1969, who expressed her opposition to denominational education on socialist grounds.

69 *Irish Times* 15 October 1969; McGrath, *Catholic Church and Catholic Schools* p.182.

70 The following day the *Belfast News Letter* reported that delegates had 'overwhelmingly condemned' the reference to integrated education, and subsequently refused to publish a letter from the NC correcting the inaccuracy. The next issue of the *Northern Teacher* published a clarification.

71 *Northern Teacher* Spring 1970.

72 NC Report 1970 p.27.

73 Ibid. pp.23–5.

74 *Irish Times, Irish Press* 1 January 1971; Aughey and Morrow, *Northern Ireland Politics*.

75 NC Report 1969 pp.46–51.

76 CEC Minutes 2 May 1970.

77 NC Report 1970 pp.47–8.

78 Information from Al Mackle.

79 *InTouch* March 2003.

80 Mapstone, 'UTU' p.120.

81 Ibid.

82 Interview with Gerry Quigley October 1991; CEC Minutes 31 October 1970.

83 CEC Minutes 16–17 October 1970; CEC Report 1971–2 pp.18–27.

84 CEC Minutes 30 October 1970.

85 CEC Report 1971–2 p.19; CEC Minutes 19 December 1970; *Irish Press* 14 January 1971.

86 NC Report 1971 p.26; interview with Gerry Quigley October 1991.

87 CEC Report 1971–2 pp.20–1.

88 Ibid. p.25.

89 Mapstone, 'UTU' p.121.

90 Ibid.

91 Ibid.

92 CEC Report 1971–2 p.25; *Irish Press* 29 December 1971.

93 CEC Minutes 29 January, 12 February 1972.

94 NC Report 1972 p.51.

95 NC Minutes 2 May 1973.

96 NC Report 1973 pp.33–4; *Times Educational Supplement* 3 August 1973.

97 NC Report 1974 p.56.

98 *Irish Times* 30 June 1977.

99 CEC Minutes 21 January 1978.

100 CEC Report 1971–2 p.25.

101 NC Report 1972 p.23; CEC Minutes 4 September 1971.

102 Three members terminated their membership as a result of the decision, and another wrote protesting the decision. NC Minutes 21 December 1971.

103 NC Report 1972 p.47.

104 *Irish Press* 31 August 1971. NC Minutes 2 March 1970: a discussion about having INTO representation on the NIC of ICTU, Michael McKeown suggesting that Gerry Quigley go forward. Quigley said he could only undertake additional work of that kind if an executive officer were appointed to assist him in the office. The NC decided to nominate the northern secretary for election to the NC, ICTU, subject to him being satisfied that there was a reasonable prospect of success.

105 De Gruchy, *NASWUT* p.338.

106 Ó Dochartaigh, *Civil Rights to Armalites* p.242; *Cork Examiner* 10 December 1971; CEC Report 1971–2 p.38.

107 NC Report 1972 p.49.

108 It was not the first time that schools had been occupied, with soldiers having been billeted in St Peter's for a six-month period after August 1969.

109 NC Papers, Statement by Teachers of St Peter's Secondary School, 12 September 1972.

110 NC Report 1972 p.40; CEC Minutes 23 September 1972.

111 NC Report 1972 p.43.

112 NC Papers, 'Army occupation of schools'.

113 This had been one of the demands to Stonham in 1969; it came to the fore again during 1972 when the NC decided to seek senior counsel's advice on the matter.

114 NC Report 1972 p.44; Mapstone, 'UTU' p.117.

115 *Irish Times* 5 January 2004.

116 CEC Minutes 2 December 1972.

117 Interview with Al Mackle February 2012.

118 NC Minutes 17 February 1973, 7 June 1973.

119 Alex McEwen and Matthew Salters, 'Public policy and education in Northern Ireland', *Research Papers in Education* vol. 10 no. 1 (1995) 135.

120 Ibid.136.

121 Kenneth Bloomfield, 'Who runs Northern Ireland?', *Fortnight* November 1991.

122 Interview with Al Mackle February 2012.

123 Gallagher, 'Northern Ireland: An Overview' p.227; *Irish Times* 6 March 1978.

124 *Irish Times* 9 March 1981.

125 Simpson and Daly, 'Politics and education in Northern Ireland' 173.

126 Interview with Al Mackle, February 2012; *InTouch* March 2003.

127 Interview with Gerry Quigley, *Irish Times* 30 June 1977; interview with Gerry Quigley October 1991, *UTU News* Spring 2016.

128 See *Education Times* April 1975.

129 *Irish News* 30 August 1981.

130 NC Minutes 10 June 1980; NC Report 1982 p.70.

131 NC Report 1982 p.70.

132 De Gruchy, *NASUWT* p.334.

133 NC Papers, Proposed changes in INTO rules and constitution, nd (1980).

134 Joint CEC/NC meeting 25 September 1982. In fact, three years later, in 1985, the UTU approached the NUT once again to ask it to consider a merger. Once again, the INTO approached the NUT asking it to reject the approach, which the NUT subsequently did.

135 *Tuarascáil* congress issue 1985. Her immediate predecessor had been P.J. Looney from Tyrone in 1961.

136 Interview with Róisín Carabine January 2017.

137 Ironside and Seifert, *Industrial Relations* p.37.

138 NC Report 1985 pp.8–15.

139 Ironside and Seifert, *Industrial Relations* p.38.

140 Gallagher, 'Northern Ireland' p.270.

141 'The legacy of Blue Ken', *Guardian* 25 March 2008.

142 *The Linen Hall Review* vol. 9, no. 1 (Spring 1992).

143 Mawhinney, *Just a Simple Belfast Boy* (2013).

144 McGrath, *Catholic Church and Catholic Schools* p.196; *Irish Times* 31 July 1987.

145 Gallagher, 'Northern Ireland' p.270.

146 *Irish Times* 31 March 1988; NC Report 1988 p.33.

147 Ibid. p.35.

148 Interview with Brendan Harron 21 February 2017.

149 Samuel McGuinness, 'Education policy in Northern Ireland: a Review' *Italian Journal of Sociology of Education* 1, 2012 p.215.

150 *Belfast Telegraph* 15 January 2002.

Conclusion

1 *Irish Teachers' Journal* 1 March 1868.

2 Garvin, *Nationalist Revolutionaries* p.26.

3 Statement on behalf of the Protestant National Teachers' Union, Ó Fiaich Archive.

4 George A. Birmingham, quoted in Garvin, *Nationalist Revolutionaries* p.27.

5 The NAS affiliated with the TUC in 1968, the NUT did so in 1970 and the EIS in 1978. In contrast, in the USA, the American Teachers' Union was a member of the American Federation of Labor from its foundation in 1916; the National Education Association has not affiliated, although state chapters have associated themselves with it.

6 *Irish School Weekly* 30 October, 6 November 1948.

SELECT BIBLIOGRAPHY

ARCHIVAL MATERIAL

Irish National Teachers' Organisation
— CEC minutes since 1944
— CEC papers since 1957
— Northern Committee minutes and papers since 1941
— Branch minutes, Dublin, Belfast, Armagh, Coleraine
— CEC Annual Reports
— NC Annual Reports
— Reports of Annual Congress from 1917 and audio and video recordings of congress
— NTO Year Books
— *Quarterly Bulletin* (1932–50)
— Dublin Strike Committee Book 1946–47
— Irish Protestant National Teachers' Union annual reports (1911–24)

National Archives of Ireland
— Department of An Taoiseach files

Public Record Office of Northern Ireland
— Ulster Teachers' Union papers
— Irish Protestant National Teachers' Union deposit
— Jack Beattie papers
— INTO material
— Cabinet papers
— Department of Education, Northern Ireland files
— Minutes of the Primary Teachers' Council 1941–53

National Library of Ireland
— Minutes of the Board of National Education
— Mervyn Taylor papers

Dublin Diocesan Archives
— William Walsh papers
— Edward Byrne papers
— John Charles McQuaid papers

Cardinal Ó Fiaich Memorial Library, Armagh
— Michael Logue papers
— John Francis D'Alton papers
— Patrick O'Donnell papers
— Joseph MacRory papers

Trinity College Dublin
— W.J.M. Starkie papers

UCD archives
— Michael Hayes papers
— Eoin MacNeill papers
— Richard Mulcahy papers

Bureau of Military History
— Witness statements

NEWSPAPERS, PERIODICALS AND PAMPHLETS

INTO and teacher publications – reports and pamphlets

— *Evidence of the Irish National Teachers' Associations in reply to queries addressed by the Commissioners to Vere Foster esquire, and submitted by him for their consideration* (London, 1869)
— Harte, John, *The duties and obligations of every system of primary education in Ireland; or, the Irish Teachers' Grievances* (Dublin, 1869)
— *The History of the INTO for the past few years with the true causes of the disturbances therein* (1874)
— INTO, 'Facts and correspondence in connection with the dismissal of Mrs Flanagan, Kilkeel Association' (March 1917)
— ——, 'The Use of Irish as a Teaching Medium' (1941)
— ——, 'The Killean dismissal. A harsh, unwarranted and arbitrary exercise of managerial authority' (1942)
— ——, 'A Plan for Education' (1947)
— ——, 'A Decade of Progress: An INTO Handbook on Gender Equality in Primary Education' (1991)
— ——, 'The Place of Religious Education in the National School System' (1991)
— ——, 'The Role of the Principal Teacher' (1991)
— Teachers' Action Alliance, 'Teacher Unions: The Case for a Merger' (October 1979)
— ——, 'Sexism in Irish Education' (April 1980)

Teachers' periodicals
— *An Múinteoir Náisiúnta* (1956–84)
— *InTouch*
— *Irish School Weekly* (1904–55)
— *Irish Teachers' Journal* (1868–1904)
— *The National Teacher* (1890–99)
— *The Northern Teacher* (1953–83)
— *Printout*
— *Tuarascáil* (1979–97)

Local and national newspapers
— *Belfast Newsletter*
— *Cork Examiner*
— *Daily Independent*
— *Derry Journal*
— *Dublin Evening Mail*
— *Education Times*
— *Evening Herald*
— *Freeman's Journal*
— *Irish Independent*
— *Irish Press*
— *Irish Times*
— *Kerry Weekly Reporter*
— *The Kerryman*
— *Limerick Leader*
— *The Nation*
— *Northern Whig*
— *Southern Star*
— *Western People*

Official reports
— Commissioners of National Education annual reports
— Department of Education (Dublin), annual reports since 1922
— Irish Trade Union Congress annual reports
— Irish Protestant National Teachers' Union reports
— Labour Party and Trade Union Congress, 'Labour's policy on education' (Dublin, 1925)
— Ministry of Education (Belfast), annual reports since 1922
— OECD, *Investment in Education* (1963)
— Report of Mr F.H. Dale, His Majesty's inspector of schools, Board of Education on Primary Education in Ireland (1904)
— Report of the Royal Commission on Nature and Extent of Instruction by

Institutions in Ireland for Elementary or Primary Education and Working of System of National Education (Powis Commission) (1870)
— Teachers' Salaries Committee, Reports and Appendices presented to the Minister for Education (July 1960)
— Vice-Regal Committee of Inquiry into Primary Education (Ireland) (Dill Inquiry) (1913)

— Dáil Éireann and Seanad Éireann debates
— Debates of the Houses of Parliament, Westminster

INTERVIEWS

I have spoken to people both formally and informally in the course of researching this book. I have also had the benefit of listening to interviews conducted by Noel Ward over several years (see below) and the interviews on Seán Delaney's *Inside Education* radio show.

Frank Bunting (2010)
Róisín Carabine (January 2017)
John Carr (May 2015)
John Joe Connolly (August 1988)
John Coolahan (2015)
Tom Gilmore (July 2014)
Brendan Harron (February 2017)
John Horgan (February 2014)
Al Mackle (February 2012)
Michael McKeown (November 2016)
Tom O'Sullivan (August 2015)
Joe O'Toole (March 2015)
Gerry Quigley

SECONDARY SOURCES

— Akenson, D.H., *The Irish Education Experiment: The National School System in the Nineteenth Century* (London, 1970)
— ——, *Education and Enmity: The Control of Schooling in Northern Ireland 1920–1950* (London, 1973)
— ——, *A Mirror to Kathleen's Face: Education in Independent Ireland 1922–1960* (London, 1975)
— —— and J.F. Fallin, 'The Irish civil war and the drafting of the Free State Constitution: "The drafting process"' *Eire-Ireland*, Summer 1970, vol. V, no. 2
— Aughey, Arthur and Duncan Morrow, *Northern Ireland Politics* (Oxford, 1999).
— Bartlett, Thomas, *Ireland: A History* (Cambridge, 2010)
— Blum, Albert A., *Teacher Unions and Associations: A Comparative Study* (Illinois, 1959)
— Carroll, Aideen, *Seán Moylan: Rebel Leader* (Dublin, 2010)

— Chuinneagáin, Síle, *Catherine Mahon: First Woman President of the INTO* (Dublin, 1998)

— Coleman, Marie, *IFUT, a History: The Irish Federation of University Teachers, 1963–1999* (Dublin, 2000)

— Coolahan, John, *Irish Education: History and Structure* (Dublin, 1981)

— ——, *The ASTI and Post-primary Education in Ireland 1909–1984* (Dublin, 1984)

— ——, 'The Historical Development of Teacher Education in the Republic of Ireland' in Andy Burke (ed.), *Teacher Education in the Republic of Ireland: Retrospect and Prospect* (2004)

— ——, with Patrick F. O'Donovan, *A History of Ireland's School Inspectorate* (Dublin, 2009)

— Brady, Conor, *Up with the Times* (Dublin, 2005)

— Cunningham, John, *Unlikely Radicals: Irish Post-Primary teachers and the ASTI 1909–2009* (Cork, 2010)

— Cunningham, John and Niamh Puirséil, 'T.J. O'Connell: Pioneer of the Irish National Teachers' Organisation and Labour Party Leader' in Gerard Moran and Nollaig Ó Muraíle, *Mayo History and Society* (2014)

— Daly, Mary E., 'Women and Trade Unions' in Donal Nevin (ed.), *Trade Union Century* (Dublin, 1994)

— ——, '"The primary and natural educator"? The role of parents in the education of their children in independent Ireland', *Éire-Ireland* 44:1/2 (2009)

— De Gruchy, Nigel, *History of the NASUWT 1919–2002: The Story of a Battling Minority* (Suffolk, 2013)

— Desmond, Barry and Charles Callan, *Irish Labour Lives: A Biographical Dictionary of Irish Labour* (Dublin, 2010)

— Drudy, Sheila (ed.), *Education in Ireland: Challenge and Change* (Dublin, 2009)

— Duffy, Patrick S., *The Lay Teacher: A Study of the Position of the Lay Teacher in an Irish Catholic Environment* (Dublin, 1967)

— Farrell, Brian, 'The drafting of the Irish Free State Constitution' parts 1 and 2, *Irish Jurist*, 5:1, 5:2 (1970) 115–40, 343–56

— Farren, Sean, *The Politics of Irish Education 1920–1965* (Belfast, 1995)

— Farry, Michael J., *Education and the Constitution* (Dublin, 1996)

— Faulkner, Padraig, *As it Seemed to Me: Reviewing over 30 years of Fianna Fáil and Irish Politics* (Dublin, 2005)

— Ferriter, Diarmaid, *The Transformation of Ireland 1900–2000* (London, 2004)

— ——, '"For God's sake, send me a few packets of fags": The College, 1922–45' in James Kelly (ed.), *St Patrick's College Drumcondra, 1875–2000: A History* (Dublin, 2006)

— Finlay, Fergus, *Snakes and Ladders* (Dublin, 1998)

— FitzGerald, Garret, *All in a Life: An Autobiography* (Dublin, 1991)

— Gallagher, Tony, 'Northern Ireland: An Overview' in Colin Brock (ed.), *Education in the United Kingdom* (Bloomsbury, 2015)

— Garvin, Tom, *Nationalist Revolutionaries in Ireland 1858–1928* (Dublin, 2005)

— Gaughan, J.A. *Thomas O'Donnell* (Dublin, 1983)
— Gowran, Sandra, '"See no Evil, Speak no Evil, Hear no Evil?" The Experiences of Lesbian and Gay Teachers in Irish Schools' in Jim Deegan, Dympna Devine and Anne Lodge (eds), *Primary Voices: Equality, Diversity and Childhood in Irish Primary Schools* (IPA, 2004).
— Harkness, David, *Northern Ireland since 1920* (Dublin, 1983)
— Harris, Mary, *The Catholic Church and the Foundation of the Northern Irish State* (Cork, 1993)
— Hastings, Tim, Brian Sheehan and Padraig Yeates, *Saving the Future: How Social Partnership Shaped Ireland's Economic Success* (Dublin, 2007)
— Hussey, Gemma, *At the Cutting Edge: Cabinet Diaries 1982–1987* (Dublin, 1990)
— Hyland, Áine, 'The investment in education report 1965: recollections and reminiscences', *Irish Educational Studies* 33:2 (2014)
— —— and Kenneth Milne, *Irish Educational Documents* vols 1–3
— Ironside, Mike and Roger Seifert, *Industrial Relations in Schools* (London, 1995)
— Jones, Valerie, *A Gaelic Experiment: The Preparatory System 1926–1961 and Coláiste Moibhí* (Dublin, 2006)
— Kelly, James (ed.) *St Patrick's College Drumcondra, 1875–2000: A History* (Dublin, 2006)
— Keogh, Dermot, 'Episcopal decision making in Ireland' in Maurice R. O'Connell, *Education, Church and State* (Kerry, 1991)
— ——, *Jack Lynch: A Biography* (Dublin, 2008)
— Leahy, Pat, *Showtime: The Inside Story of Fianna Fáil in Power* (Dublin, 2009)
— Lee, J.J., *Ireland 1912–1985* (Cambridge, 2009)
— Linehan, M.P., 'A programme of Catholic action', *Irish Monthly* vol. 65, no. 766, April 1937.
— McCarthy, Charles, *The Decade of Upheaval: Irish Trade Unions in the 1960s* (Dublin, 1973).
— McCormick, Eugene, 'The INTO and the 1946 Teachers' Strike' (Dublin, 1996)
— McCullagh, David, *A Makeshift Majority: The First Interparty Government 1948–51* (Dublin, 1998)
— ——, *The Reluctant Taoiseach: A Biography of John A. Costello* (Dublin, 2010)
— MacDermott, Eithne, *Clann na Poblachta* (Cork, 1998)
— McGahern, John, *Memoir* (London, 2009)
— McGarry, Fearghal, '"Catholics first and politicians afterwards": the Labour Party and the Workers' Republic, 1936–39', *Saothar* 25 (2000)
— McGrath, Michael, *The Catholic Church and Catholic Schools in Northern Ireland* (Dublin, 2000)
— McGuinness, Samuel J., 'Education policy in Northern Ireland: a review', *Italian Journal of Sociology of Education* 1 (2012).
— McManus, Antonia, *Irish Education: The Ministerial Legacy, 1919–99* (Dublin, 2014)
— MacNeill, Mary, *Vere Foster* (Alabama, 1971)

— Maguire, Martin, 'Civil service trade unionism in Ireland (part II), 1922–90', *Saothar* 32 (2009).
— Maguire, Moira J. and Séamus Ó Cinneide, '"A good beating never hurt anyone": the punishment and abuse of children in twentieth-century Ireland', *Journal of Social History* 38:3 (2005)
— Male, George A., 'Problems in Research on Teachers' Organizations', *History of Education Journal* 6:4 (1955)
— Mapstone, R.H. 'The Ulster Teachers' Union. A Historical Perspective', University of Ulster, Coleraine (1986)
— Maume, Patrick, *The Long Gestation: Irish Nationalist Life 1891–1918* (Dublin, 1999)
— Mawhinney, Brian, *Just a Simple Belfast Boy* (London, 2013)
— Miller, D.H. *Church, State and Nation* (Pittsburgh, 1973)
— Mitchell, Arthur, *Labour in Irish Politics* (Dublin, 1974)
— Moroney, Michael, *Irish National Teachers' Salaries and Pensions: A Review of the Role of the INTO* (Dublin, 2007)
— Morrissey, Thomas, *William J. Walsh, Archbishop of Dublin, 1841–1921* (Dublin, 2000)
— ———, *Edward Byrne, 1872–1941: The Forgotten Archbishop of Dublin* (Dublin, 2010)
— Mulcahy, D.G. and Denis O'Sullivan (eds), *Irish Educational Policy: Process and Substance* (Dublin, 1989)
— Mulcahy, Risteard, *Richard Mulcahy (1986–1971): A Family Memoir* (Dublin, 1999)
— Murphy, John A., 'Association to trade union: the organising of secondary teachers' (review essay of Coolahan, *ASTI*), *Saothar* 11 (1986)
— Neary, Aoife, 'Unravelling "Ethos" and Section 37 (1): the Experiences of LGBTQ Teachers' (UL, nd)
— Ní Bhroiméil, Úna, '"Sending gossoons to be made ou' mollies of": Rule 127(b) and the feminisation of teaching in Ireland', *Irish Educational Studies* 25:1 (March 2006)
— Ó Buachalla, Séamus, *Education Policy in Twentieth-century Ireland* (Dublin, 1988)
— O'Connell, T.J., *100 Years of Progress: The Story of the Irish National Teachers' Organisation 1868–1968* (Dublin, 1969)
— O'Connor, Emmet, *A Labour History of Ireland 1824–2000* (Dublin, 2011)
— O'Connor, Fionnuala, *Cottage to Crèche* (Dublin, 2001)
— O'Connor, Seán, *A Troubled Sky: Reflections of the Irish Educational Scene 1957–68* (Dublin, 1968)
— Ó Corráin, Daithí, *Rendering to God and Caesar* (Manchester, 2006)
— Ó Dochartaigh, Niall, *From Civil Rights to Armalites: Derry and the Birth of the Irish Troubles* (New York, 2004)
— Ó hEithir, Breandán, *The Begrudger's Guide to Irish Politics* (Dublin, 1986)

— Ó Tuathaigh, Gearóid, 'Cultural visions and the new state: embedding and embalming' in Gabriel Doherty and Dermot Keogh (eds), *De Valera's Irelands* (Cork, 2003)

— O'Leary, Eoin, 'The Irish National Teachers' Organisation and the marriage bar for women national teachers, 1933–1958' *Saothar* 12 (1987)

— Oram, Alison, *Women Teachers and Feminist Politics, 1900–1939* (Manchester, 1996)

— O'Toole, Joe, *Looking under Stones: Roots, Family and a Dingle Childhood* (Dublin, 2003)

— Parkes, Susan M., *A Guide to Sources for the History of Irish Education, 1780–1922* (Dublin, 2010)

— Puirséil, Niamh, *The Irish Labour Party, 1922–73* (Dublin, 2007)

— ———, 'The INTO and 1916', *Saothar* 41 (2016)

— Queally, Joe, *The Fanore School Case* (2004)

— Quinn, John (ed.), *Golden Threads: A Celebration of the Class of '61, St Patrick's College Drumcondra* (Roscrea, 2011)

— Quinn, Ruairí, *Straight Left: A Journey in Politics* (Dublin, 2005)

— Redmond, Jennifer and Judith Harford, '"One man, one job": the marriage ban and the employment of women teachers in Irish primary schools', *Paedagogica Historica* 46:5 (2010)

— Regan, John M., *The Irish Counter-Revolution 1921–1936* (Dublin, 1999)

— Seifert, Roger V., *Teacher Militancy: A Short History of Teacher Strikes, 1896–1987* (Sussex, 1987)

— Simpson, Kirk and Peter Daly, 'Politics and education in Northern Ireland: an analytical history', *Irish Studies Review* 12:2 (2004)

— Smith, Harold, 'The problem of "Equal Pay for Equal Work" in Great Britain during World War II', *Journal of Modern History* 53 (December 1981)

— Thornton, Robert J., 'Teacher unionism and collective bargaining in England and Wales', *Industrial and Labour Relations Review* 35:3 (1982)

— Titley, E. Brian, *Church, State and the Control of Schooling* (Dublin, 1983)

— Walsh, Aisling, 'Michael Cardinal Logue 1840–1924', *Seanchas Ardmhacha: Journal of the Armagh Diocesan Historical Society* (2003)

— Walsh, John, *The Politics of Expansion: The Transformation of Educational Policy in the Republic of Ireland, 1957–72* (Manchester, 2009)

— ———, *Patrick Hillery: The Official Biography* (Dublin, 2009)

— Walsh, Thomas, *Primary Education in Ireland 1897–1990* (Bern, 2012)

— Walshe, John, *A New Partnership in Education: From Consultation to Legislation in the Nineties* (Dublin, 1999)

— ———, *An Education* (Dublin, 2014)

— Walker, Graham, *The Politics of Frustration: Harry Midgley and the Failure of Labour in Northern Ireland* (Manchester, 1985)

— Ward, Noel, 'INTO's pre-history: teacher organisation before our official date of birth'

— ——, *The Teachers' Club: A History 1923–1998* (Dublin, 1999)

— ——, 'The INTO strike of 1946', *InTouch* March 2006

— Whyte, J.H., *Church and State in Modern Ireland 1922–79* (Dublin, 1980)

UNPUBLISHED THESES AND MANUSCRIPTS

— Breathnach, Catherine, 'The relationship between membership participation, organisational learning and strategic change in democratically structured voluntary organisations' (PhD, NCI, 2002).

— Byrne, Catherine, 'Management roles in a teachers' union: the need for training and development' (MEd, Sheffield, 1998)

— Coolahan, John, 'The origins of the payment by results policy in education and the experience of it in the national and intermediate schools of Ireland' (MEd, TCD, 1975)

— Fitts, James L., 'The rebel teachers: a study in contentious history' (nd)

— Howley, Brian, 'The INTO and the remuneration of National Teachers in Ireland 1916 to 1920' (MA, UCD, 1985)

— Nic Craith, Deirbhile, 'Policy for primary teacher education in Ireland: an exploration of a public policy process' (PhD, UCD, 2013)

— O'Doherty, Christina, 'William Joseph Myles Starkie (1860–1920): the last resident commissioner of national education in Ireland' (unpublished PhD, UL, 1997)

— Ruttledge, Elayne, 'From Miss to Missus: the marriage ban' (MA, DCU, 2005)

— Ward, Noel, 'The INTO and the Catholic Church 1930–55' (MA, UCD, 1987)

Appendix 1 ~

INTO OFFICE HOLDERS 1868–2018

YEAR	PRESIDENT	GENERAL SECRETARY	GENERAL TREASURER/ DEPUTY GENERAL SECRETARY
		James Kavanagh	
1868	Vere Foster	John O'Harte	
1869	"	"	
1870	"	"	
1871	"	John Morrin	
1872	"	"	
1873	John Boal	"	
1874	"	"	
1875	John Traynor	"	
1876	"	"	
1877	J. Ferguson	J. W. Henly	
1878	"	A. K. O'Farrell	
1879	"	"	
1880	"	"	
1881	"	"	
1882	W. Cullen	"	
1883	J. Nealon	"	
1884	"	James Thompson	
1885	"	"	
1886	"	"	
1887	"	"	
1888	"	"	
1889	P. Ward	"	
1890	"	"	
1891	"	M. O'Kelly	

YEAR	PRESIDENT	GENERAL SECRETARY	GENERAL TREASURER/ DEPUTY GENERAL SECRETARY
1892	D. A. Simmons	"	
1893	"	"	
1894	"	J. Coffey	
1895	"	"	
1896	"	"	
1897	T. Clarke	"	
1898	P. Brown	T. Clarke	
1899	J. Hegarty	"	
1900	"	"	
1901	"	"	Mr John Moore
1902	"	"	"
1903	"	"	"
1904	J. Nealon	"	"
1905	J. J. Hazlet	"	"
1906-1907	D. C. Maher	"	"
1907	P. Gamble	"	"
1908	D. Elliott	"	"
1909	J. McGowan	"	"
1910	E. Mansfield	Michael Doyle	David Elliott
1911	G. O'Callaghan	"	"
1912	Catherine M. Mahon	"	"
1913	"	Eamonn Mansfield	"
1914	G. O'Callaghan	"	"
1915	"	"	"
1916	G. Ramsay	Thomas J. O'Connell	"
1917	J. Cunningham	"	"
1918	R. Judge	"	"
1919	T. J. Nunan	"	"
1920-1921	D. C. Maher	"	"
1921	J. Harbison	"	"
1922	C. Breathnach	"	"
1923	D. A. Meehan	"	Mairead Ashe
1924	J. McNeelis	"	"
1925	C. P. Murphy	"	"
1926	T. Frisby	"	"
1927	H. O'Donnell	"	M. P. Linehan

YEAR	PRESIDENT	GENERAL SECRETARY	GENERAL TREASURER/ DEPUTY GENERAL SECRETARY
1928	P. J. Quinn	"	"
1929	E. Caraher	"	"
1930	W. P. Ward	"	"
1931	R. Neilly	"	"
1932	M. Kearney	"	"
1933	C. Breathnach	"	"
1934	J. Hurley	"	"
1935	L. McSweeney	"	"
1936	D. F. Courell	"	"
1937	J. F. O'Grady	"	"
1938	T. J. Nunan	"	"
1939	M. Leyden	"	"
1940	H. A. Macaulay	"	"
1941	J. P. Griffith	"	"
1942	M. Coleman	"	"
1943	H. O'Connor	"	"
1944	T. Frisby	"	"
1945	K. M. Clarke	"	"
1946	D. J. Kelleher	"	"
1947	Seán Brosnahan	"	"
1948	Liam Forde	"	"
1949	Joseph Mansfield	D. J. Kelleher	M. P. Linehan
1950	Brighid Bergin	"	"
1951	I. H. McEnaney	"	"
1952	P. Gormley	"	"
1953	H. J. McManus	"	"
1954	M. Griffin	"	"
1955	H. F. McCune Reid	"	"
1956	M. Skinnider	"	"
1957	L. O'Reilly	"	"
1958	G. Hurley	"	"
1959	W. M. Keane	"	"
1960	S. McGlinchey	"	"
1961	P. J. Looney	"	Seán Brosnahan
1962	P. O'Riordan	"	"
1963	D. O'Scanaill	"	"
1964	P. Carney	"	"

YEAR	PRESIDENT	GENERAL SECRETARY	GENERAL TREASURER/ DEPUTY GENERAL SECRETARY
1965	E. Liston	"	"
1966	R. S. Holland	"	"
1967	J. Allman	Seán Brosnahan	M. J. Griffin
1968	A. J. Faulkner	"	"
1969	T. Martin	"	"
1970	T. Warde	"	"
1971	A. Brennan	"	"
1972	S. O'Connor	"	"
1973	S. O'Brien	"	"
1974	S. Carew	"	"
1975	S. Eustace	"	"
1976	B. Gillespie	"	"
1977/78	B. Scannell	"	"
1978/79	F. Poole	Gerry Quigley	Michael Moroney
1979	G. Keane	"	"
1980	M. McSweeney	"	"
1981	F. Cunningham	"	"
1982	T. Waldron	"	"
1983	Morgan O'Connell	"	"
1984	John Joe Connelly	"	"
1985	Roísín Carabine	"	"
1986	Seamus Puirseil	"	"
1987	Tom Honan	"	"
1988	Michael Drew	"	"
1989	Tom Gilmore	"	"
1990	John White	Joe O'Toole	"
1991	Jimmy Collins	"	"
1992	Brendan Gilmore	"	"
1993	Eddie Bruton	"	"
1994	Michael McGarry	"	"
1995	Sally Sheils	"	"
1996	Liam McCloskey	"	"
1997	Tony Bates	"	John Carr
1998	Brian Hynes	"	"
1999	Des Rainey	"	"
2000	Donal O'Loingsigh	John Carr	"
2001	Joan Ward	"	"

YEAR	PRESIDENT	GENERAL SECRETARY	GENERAL TREASURER/ DEPUTY GENERAL SECRETARY
2002	Gerry Malone	"	Catherine Byrne
2003	Sean Rowley	"	"
2004	Austin Corcoran	"	"
2005	Sheila Nunan	"	"
2006	Denis Bohane	"	Sheila Nunan
2007	Angela Dunne	"	"
2008	Declan Kelleher	"	"
2009	Máire Ní Chuinneagáin	Sheila Nunan	"
2010	Jim Higgins	"	Noel Ward
2011	Noreen Flynn	"	"
2012	Anne Fay	"	"
2013	Brendan O'Sullivan	"	"
2014	Sean McMahon	"	"
2015	Emma Dineen	"	"
2016	Rosena Jordan	"	"
2017	John Boyle	"	"

INTO NORTHERN SECRETARIES

— Joseph Boyce 1921–1934
— Jack Beattie 1934–1956
— E.G. (Gerry) Quigley 1956–1978
— Al Mackle 1978–1991
— Frank Bunting 1991–2011
— Gerry Murphy 2011+

Appendix 2 ~

INTO STAFF 2017–2018

INTO HEAD OFFICE

— **General Secretary:** Sheila Nunan
— **Deputy General Secretary and General Treasurer:** Noel Ward
— **Assistant General Secretaries:** Anne McElduff, Peter Mullan, Deirbhile Nic Craith, Deirdre O'Connor
— **Senior Officials:** Gráinne Cleary, Alison Gilliland, John O'Brien, David O'Sullivan
— **Officials:** Eimear Allen, Zita Bolton, Niamh Cooper, Síne Friel, Lori Kealy, Elizabeth-Ann Kirwan, Maeve McCafferty

Administrative Staff
— Réiltín Bowes, Val Cleary, Audrey Cullen, Elaine Daly, Claire Garvey, Fidelma Heston, Ashling Lynch, Eileen O'Donnell, Ruth Warren; Mary Bird Smyth, Merrilyn Campbell, Selina Campbell, Jane Dowdall, Mandy Drury, Georgina Glackin, Kim Lally, Joanna O'Byrne; Terri Boland, Deirdre Branagan, Collete Cassidy, Carmel Cunningham, Maxine Cros, Laura Crowley, Karen Francis, Aida González Alonso, Michelle Goode, Linda Johnston, Sharon Kane, Yvonne Kenny, Cara Kirwan, Gráinne Lynch, Patricia McCarthy, Ann McConnell, Erin McGann
— **Caretaker:** Michael Toner
— **Housekeepers:** Helen Byrne, Samjhana Dhakal, Karen O'Brien
— **Interns:** (secondment from teaching 2017–18), Michael McConigley, Aoife Mullen, Ciara Sotscheck
— **Buildings Maintenance:** Christy Kilcoyne

INTO NORTHEN OFFICE

— **Northern Secretary:** Gerry Murphy
— **Assistant Northern Secretary:** Mark McTaggart
— **Senior Officials:** Tommy McGlone, Nuala O'Donnell
— **Official:** Paul Groogan

Administrative Staff
— Paul Donnelly, Trevor Leonard, Marian McAuley, Christine McDonnell, Clare Martin, Helen Mawhinney

Appendix 3 ∾

INTO CENTRAL EXECUTIVE COMMITTEE 2017–2018

— John Boyle, President
— Joe Killeen, Vice President
— Rosena Jordan, Ex-President
— Seamus Hanna, District I
— Dorothy McGinley, District II
— Michael Weed, District III
— Vincent Duffy, District IV
— Catherine Flanagan, District V
— Tommy Greally, District VI
— Carmel Browne, District VII
— Gerry Brown, District VIII
— Carmel Hume, District IX
— Joe McKeown, District X
— Brendan Horan, District XI
— John Driscoll, District XII
— Anne Horan, District XIII
— Pat Crowe, District XIV
— Shane Loftus, District XV
— Mary Magner, District XVI
— Sheila Nunan, General Secretary
— Noel Ward, Deputy General Secretary & General Treasurer
— Gerry Murphy, Northern Secretary

INDEX